The Vienna School Reader

Politics and Art Historical Method in the 1930s

Edited by Christopher S. Wood

ZONE BOOKS · NEW YORK

2003

Published with the assistance of the Getty Grant Program.

ZONE BOOKS
40 White Street, 5th Floor
New York, NY 10013

First Paperback Edition

Printed in the United States of America.

Distributed by The MIT Press,
Cambridge, Massachusetts, and London, England

Library of Congress Cataloging-in-Publication Data

The Vienna School reader : politics and art historical method in the 1930s / edited by Christopher S. Wood.
    p.   cm.
  Includes bibliographical references.
  ISBN 1-890951-15-3 (pbk.)
  1. Art – Historiography. 2. Art – Research – Austria – Vienna. 3. Riegl, Alois, 1858–1905 – Influence.
  I. Wood, Christopher S.
N7480.V54 2000
707'.22–dc21   99-11460
                       CIP

Contents

Acknowledgments

I am indebted to Jonathan Crary for supporting this project, to Meighan Gale and Amy Griffin at Zone Books for producing it, and to the translators Tawney Becker, Mia Fineman, Brian Fuchs, Amy C. Smith, Jacqueline E. Jung, Frederic J. Schwartz, and Kimberly Smith. For critical conversation and comments I am especially grateful to Jonathan Alexander, but also to Hans Belting, Benjamin Binstock, Walter Cahn, T. J. Clark, Whitney Davis, Mia Fineman, Romy Golan, Sir Ernst Gombrich, Gabriele Hammel, Karsten Harries, Michael Holly, Martin Jay, Thomas Da Costa Kaufmann, Wolfgang Kemp, Joseph Koerner, Thomas Y. Levin, Sergiusz Michalski, Elly Miller, Alexander Nagel, Friedrich Polleross, Artur Rosenauer, Willibald Sauerländer, Frederic J. Schwartz, Martina Sitt, Kimberly Smith, and Henri Zerner.

Introduction

by Christopher S. Wood

This anthology introduces the so-called New Vienna School of art history to an English-speaking audience. The school coalesced in the late 1920s and early 1930s around two young university instructors, Hans Sedlmayr (1896–1984) and Otto Pächt (1902–1988). Sedlmayr and Pächt were radical formalists who insisted on the independence of the figuring imagination, the untranslatability of the work of art, and the pointlessness of any empiricist reconstruction of the art-making process. At the same time, they argued that a single work of art, if read properly, would reveal the deep structure of the world that produced it.

They found their model in the formalist art history of the Viennese museum curator and university professor Alois Riegl (1858–1905). In his treatises on late Roman art and the Dutch group portrait, Riegl had introduced a method of close formal analysis and an evolutionary schema of world art that together promised to upgrade the study of art history into a general science of culture. Riegl's terms and oppositions — coordination, participation, attention, surface and depth, internal and external unity, the tactile and the optical gaze — seemed to reconnect the beholder of the painting or the building with an initial perceptual event and ultimately with an entire worldview. The work of art in

Riegl's analyses was stripped of its pretensions to universal truth or value and recast as the material trace of a historical subject's experience of space, time, and matter.

Sedlmayr and Pächt were too young to have studied with Riegl himself. But they believed that Riegl's dry, measured exegeses could liberate art history from both the paralyzing injunctions of empiricism and the cul-de-sac of *l'art pour l'art* aestheticism. In 1929, Sedlmayr prefaced a collection of Riegl's shorter writings with an essay titled "The Quintessence of Riegl's Teachings."[1] Here Sedlmayr used the term *Struktur* (structure) to designate the fundamental unit of art historical research. Structure was meant to replace Riegl's ambiguous concept *Kunstwollen* (artistic will). *Kunstwollen* was Riegl's loose way of designating the aesthetic impulse within culture, the aesthetic principles of an individual artist, or the aesthetic dimension of a given artifact. In fact, the word *Kunstwollen* in Riegl can almost always be replaced by the word "style." But Riegl was trying to get at something deeper than style. Sedlmayr's *Struktur*, accordingly, was a kind of design principle that informed the entire work of art, even to the most insignificant details. *Struktur* was a schema or diagram that had to be extracted from the work; to apprehend it, the beholder would have to ignore representational and symbolic content, to "see through" form in the conventional sense — the disposition of lines and colors on a surface — and finally to suspend all judgments of value.[2] In Pächt's terms, "the true object of art history is not identical with the physical presence of the work of art: it is something to be extracted from the material substrate through an act of seeing that is also a re-creation."[3] Structure for Sedlmayr and Pächt was the diagram of the artist's perception of the world understood in the broadest sense: not the mere physiological workings, but the entire event of perception with all its "interest," tendencies, and predilections; perception as a socially and ideologically embedded activity. Sedlmayr and Pächt's triangulation between artifact and worldview came to be called *Strukturanalyse* (structure analysis) or *Strukturforschung* (structure research).

Sedlmayr and Pächt found a platform for their ideas in the art historical review journal *Kritische Berichte zur kunstgeschichtlichen Literatur*, edited by their friend Bruno Fürst (1891–1965), who had written a dissertation at Munich on medieval Austrian sculpture. *Kritische Berichte*, according to Wilhelm Pinder's preface to the first number, offered itself as the successor to *Kunstgeschichtliche Anzeigen*, the Viennese review journal founded by Franz Wickhoff in 1904 and continued by Max Dvořák until 1913. *Kritische Berichte* ran from 1927 to 1937 under the editorship of Fürst and Friedrich Antal and published all the younger, theoretically oriented art historians of the day, including Sedlmayr, Pächt, Erwin Panofsky, Meyer Schapiro, Ernst Gombrich, Nikolaus Pevsner, Rudolf Wittkower, Ludwig Heydenreich, and Herbert von Einem. In an editorial statement in the final volume — which included articles by Hugo Buchtal, Otto Demus, Paul Frankl, Gombrich, Pächt, and Fritz Novotny — Fürst referred gloomily to the new anti-intellectual climate.[4]

Meanwhile, Sedlmayr and Pächt launched their own journal, *Kunstwissenschaftliche Forschungen*. It appeared only twice, in 1931 and 1933. Sedlmayr published his manifesto "Toward a Rigorous Study of Art" in the first volume of *Kunstwissenschaftliche Forschungen*. Here he identified two "levels" of art history. The first level comprises all those empirical inquiries that supposedly take no account of the artifact as an aesthetic construction (*Kunstgebilde*): attribution and dating, but also iconography, patronage, the social history of art, and the chronicling of stylistic change. The second level is art history that manages to adopt an attitude or point of view (*Einstellung*) toward the work of art that reveals its aesthetic nature, its *Struktur*, and ultimately its relationship to the world and the culture that produced it. The historical studies published in the two volumes of *Kunstwissenschaftliche Forschungen* were meant to exemplify "rigorous" work on this second level. Not all the contributors followed Sedlmayr's instructions to the letter. Nevertheless, the tension maintained in these essays between formalist restraint and cultural-historical explanation makes for some of the most ingenious and dramatic art historical writing of the century.

Too ingenious for some: the reception of this body of work in the English-speaking world has been almost uniformly cool. The formal analyses of the New Vienna School have seemed mannered, the pretensions to methodological rigor hollow, the cultural-historical conclusions abstract and portentous. Few have been seduced by the sharp formulations and urgent, doctrinaire tone of Sedlmayr's writings. Meyer Schapiro (1904–1996) delivered a negative judgment in a long review of the second volume of *Kunstwissenschaftliche Forschungen* published in the *Art Bulletin* in 1936 ("The New Viennese School"). Here Schapiro conceded that the periodical was "perhaps the most advanced organ of European academic writing on art history today." But he went on to deplore the grandiose contextualizing ambitions of the group and their taste for meaningless aprioristic entities such as "race" and "spirit." He found their scholarship "relatively poor in positive historical conclusions, and rich in ingenious, but unverified insights and in vague assertions" (p. 457). Schapiro's misgivings about the "mythical, racial-psychological constants" animating New Vienna School art history were borne out by Sedlmayr's increasingly public sympathy for National Socialism in the late 1930s and the 1940s. For example, in a congratulatory letter prefacing his essay in the 1938 Festschrift for Wilhelm Pinder — who had helped launch *Kritische Berichte* — Sedlmayr wrote with enthusiasm about Hitler's annexation of Austria. He explained that this "elemental event" had prevented him from properly completing his essay and closed the letter with the words "Heil Hitler!" The prefatory letter was omitted from the postwar edition of Sedlmayr's collected writings.[5] Sedlmayr's anti-Semitism and extreme conservatism quickly poisoned his art history. By the time of the Pinder Festschrift, the New Vienna School had already disintegrated: Pächt, a Jew, was forced to emigrate to England in 1938. Sedlmayr had already in 1936 succeeded his teacher Julius von Schlosser as chair of the art historical institute at Vienna.[6]

In 1945 Sedlmayr lost his university post but stayed in public view by writing an ingenious, neo-Spenglerian polemic against modern art, *Verlust der Mitte* (1948), a huge popular success eventually translated into English as *Art in Crisis: The Lost Center* (1957),[7] Spanish (1959), Japanese (1965), and Italian (1967). But many German art historians had lost all sympathy for Sedlmayr, and his reappointment at the University of Munich in 1951 was fiercely contested.[8]

Leading voices in postwar German art history — for instance Werner Hofmann, Willibald Sauerländer, Max Imdahl, Martin Warnke, and Hans Belting — have again and again deprecated Sedlmayr's irrationalism, spiritualism, interpretative hubris, and inattention to historical fact.[9] Ernst Gombrich, a younger contemporary of Sedlmayr's and Pächt's at Vienna who also moved to England, knew the group well and has always given them a wide berth intellectually. He repudiated *Strukturanalyse* in an outraged review of a Festschrift for Sedlmayr (1964), where he denounced Sedlmayr's pupils as "enemies of reason," and again in a lecture at the International Congress of the History of Art in Vienna (1983).[10] There was not much interest in Riegl, either, in the decades after the war.[11] Until 1982 not a single complete text of Riegl's was translated into English. In the postwar *rappel à l'ordre* and empiricist consensus, there was little sympathy for the New

Vienna School's strained, anti-commonsensical formalism. Anthony Blunt in his monograph on the architect Francesco Borromini — the subject of one of Sedlmayr's major books — disparaged the "alembicated" Viennese mode of art history.[12]

But in recent years the taste within the discipline for the alchemy of formalism seems to have returned. Confidence in the close and creative reading of images has grown. Riegl's work has become more accessible in the last fifteen years through translations and book-length expositions. He is now widely admired for his willingness to ground his historical interpretations in the present-tense reception of the image; for his attentiveness to unclassical styles and periods of supposed decline; for his sensitivity to prosaic and insignificant detail; and for his shifting of emphasis away from masterpieces and major artists and onto undistinguished, even unattributed artifacts. More and more neo-formalist and New Historicist art historians invoke Riegl; many claim him as a forebear.[13] The philosopher of science Paul Feyerabend even took Riegl's value-free art history as a model for his own demonstration of the relativity of scientific progress.[14]

We are also starting to see that Riegl's writings had a robust afterlife in Weimar Germany. According to Sedlmayr, at least, many of Spengler's ideas were drawn from Riegl.[15] The architects Walter Gropius and Peter Behrens repeatedly invoked Riegl's thinking on ornament.[16] Georg Lukács in 1922 named Riegl, alongside Wilhelm Dilthey and Max Dvořák, one of the "really important historians of the nineteenth century" who recognized that the essence of history lies in the changes in "those *structural forms* which are the focal points of man's interaction with the environment at any given moment and which determine the objective nature of both his inner and his outer life."[17] The literary critic Hermann Bahr in his book *Expressionism* (1920) praised Riegl's *Late Roman Art Industry* (1901) as a book "more exciting than any other since Goethe's *Farbenlehre*."[18] Bahr found in Riegl not only an antidote to "Hellenism" in taste, but also a doctrine of the "expressive" relationship of art to culture. Walter Benjamin counted *Late Roman Art Industry* among the crucial touchstones of his intellectual life.[19] Mikhail Bakhtin contrasted the pure formalism of the Russian literary theorist Viktor Shklovsky to the properly ideological "European formalism" of Riegl and Konrad Fiedler.[20]

But interest in Riegl's disciples has been growing more slowly. Postwar German art history is highly aware of, even somewhat obsessed with, the "case" of Sedlmayr. The devolution of his imaginative and aggressive attack on scholarly convention into reactionary, antimodern irrationalism is repeatedly invoked as a cautionary tale about the perils of ungrounded interpretation. The postwar critique of Sedlmayr addresses not only the antimodernist tirade *Verlust der Mitte*, an easy target, but also the art historical writing. Still, no one has undertaken a full-scale study of Sedlmayr's work and significance or of the New Vienna School in general.[21] The New Vienna School is rarely referred to by British or American art historians.[22] There have been no English translations of the early writings of Sedlmayr, Pächt, and Guido Kaschnitz von Weinberg. And because the German and the American art historical academies live by such different myths and points of reference, Sedlmayr is never compared directly to Panofsky, the contemporary scholar who most effectively contested his reading of Riegl. In fact, the profound dependence of the early writings of Panofsky on Riegl has been recognized in this country only relatively recently.[23]

Admittedly, Riegl is easier to love than his posthumous disciples. His world-historical scheme of archaic tactility gradually giving way to modern opticality is grounded in liberal optimism about the capacity of the freethinking subject concretized in aesthetic experience — the subject that democratic institutions are built on — to overcome obscurantism and prejudice. His tone is consistently reasonable and expository. Sedlmayr's writing, by contrast, can be bombastic, hectoring, even devious. His nostalgia for the Austro-Hungarian empire and ultimately for medieval theocracy put a probably unbridgeable distance between him and us. Sedlmayr's monstrous dimension would be unmistakable even if he had not embraced National Socialism.

Nevertheless, the art history of Sedlmayr, Pächt, and Kaschnitz von Weinberg claimed to be the authentic extension of the methodological project initiated by Riegl. If Riegl's project is felt in some sense to be still active, then *Strukturanalyse* needs to be reevaluated. The problem of the New Vienna School was in fact posed by Walter Benjamin (1892–1940) in 1933 in a review of *Kunstwissenschaftliche Forschungen* in which he endorsed the new art historical experiments ("On the First Volume of *Kunstwissenschaftliche Forschungen*"). From Benjamin's vantage point outside the discipline, the work of the younger Viennese art historians was admirably philological and materialist. In their attentiveness to the insignificant detail, they confronted "the concrete bedrock of past historical existence." Here Benjamin, projecting his own methodological ambitions onto what he was reading, slightly overrated the philological dimension of the new work.[24] But he did recognize the threat that Sedlmayr's group represented to empiricist complacency and to the overwhelming bias within the humanistic disciplines in favor of classicism. Most important, he saw that the concept of structure, in managing to bypass both content and style, sometimes achieved an original and unexpected recasting of the basic visual encounter between beholder and image. The new art history took its place, Benjamin felt, "in the movement that — ranging from Konrad Burdach's work in German studies to the investigations of the history of religion being done at the Warburg Library — is filling the margins of the study of history with new life" (p. 451).

Benjamin's remarks suggest that the foundation for the objection to Sedlmayr and Pächt's formalism has to be rethought. In the last two decades the confidence in empirical method, inferential reasoning, and the testimony of fact shared by Schapiro, Gombrich, Blunt, and Sauerländer has been corroded. Many art historians today would accept Sedlmayr's propositions that causal models offer incomplete accounts of the relationship between works of art and the societies that produce them; that theories of representation built on the idea of adequation to nature will not account for the ambitions of most works of art; and that in some art historical subfields the basic cataloging and fact gathering can start to give way to more mature interpretation of the works. Many would agree with Sedlmayr that interpretation begins already at the level of perception. In fact, Sedlmayr argued that the "second," interpretative level of art historical inquiry would feed back and contribute to the "first," empirical level, assisting in the tasks of attribution, dating, and iconographic decoding.[25] Many would accept his principle that a close analysis of the rhetoric and structure of the individual work of art can in principle unfold into an analysis of culture or ideology and that the interpretation of a society or a political institution is not a different kind of activity than the interpretation of a work of art. Many would agree with him, finally, against Gombrich, that reason, too, has its history.[26] One would have to concede, for example, that Sedlmayr's critique of the neo-Kantian faith in the unity and immutability of human nature and reason, as expressed for example by Panofsky in "Perspective as 'Symbolic Form'", was right on the mark.[27]

It would seem that we have arrived at an ideal moment to reread the marooned texts of Riegl's disciples. *Strukturanalyse* clearly has a part within the larger methodological drama of the century, that is, the effort to write a critical, contextual history of figuration, the effort that Gombrich finally dismissed as the "search for cultural history."[28] It ought to be possible to compare the extension of Riegl's project in the 1930s with Panofsky's contextualist art history and ultimately with the neo-formalist art history of our own time. This comparison pivots on the relationship between Sedlmayr's methodological program and his reactionary and indeed Fascist ideas about modernity, spirituality, the body, health and disease. The proximate context and even provocation for this examination is the debate in America and France, now two decades old, on the political dimensions of the work of Martin Heidegger and Paul de Man, a debate that has forced the humanities to reflect on the implications of the philosophical uprooting of the concepts "man" and "reason."

The anthology begins with two pieces by Alois Riegl. Riegl is increasingly available in translation. The major works *Spätrömische Kunstindustrie* and *Stilfragen* were translated into English in 1985 and 1992; a translation of *Das holländische Gruppenporträt* (*The Dutch Group Portrait*) is expected soon. Book-length English-language studies of Riegl's art history were published in 1992 and 1993.[29]

Nevertheless it seems useful to begin *The Vienna School Reader* with a pair of texts that recapitulate the basic principles of his art history. I have included the conclusion to *Late Roman Art Industry* (1901, reprinted 1927), the most influential of his writings, because it concisely lays bare the contextualizing ambitions of his patient, methodical formal analyses ("The Main Characteristics of the Late Roman *Kunstwollen*"). I have also included an essay by Riegl on a famous pair of Mycenaean or Minoan gold cups, written in 1900, first published in 1906, and reprinted in 1929 ("The Place of the Vapheio Cups in the History of Art"). Riegl interprets the agitated scenes of bulls and captors on these cups, which date from the middle of the second millennium B.C., as expressions of revolutionary new concepts of nature, causality, and freedom.[30] He explains the conventionalized formal devices of the reliefs — the ground line, the gazes, the backgrounds — not as a struggle with recalcitrant material or as a stage in a technical development, but as indexes of a newly optical and subjective perception of reality that fundamentally broke with the ancient Near East and foreshadowed classical Greek art.

The other eight pieces in the *Reader* all date from the 1930s. I have chosen two texts by Sedlmayr and two by Pächt to illustrate the theoretical underpinnings of the school. Sedlmayr's "Toward a Rigorous Study of Art" (1931), from the first volume of *Kunstwissenschaftliche Forschungen*, assumes the peremptory tone of a manifesto. As explained above, Sedlmayr distinguishes here between a "first" art history that collects and arranges data, a necessary foundation but on its own nothing more than the study of art corpses (*Kunstleichen*), and a "second" art history of imaginative acts of interpretation of aesthetic constructions (*Kunstgebilde*). With insight akin to the artist's, the scholar grasps that inner lawfulness and necessity of the work that enmeshes it with culture in general. Ideally the scholar will arrive at an understanding (*Verstehen*) of the whole work rather than dismember it with a merely analytic comprehension (*Begreifen*). Sedlmayr's preference for the organic over the loosely articulated or paratactic derives generally from a hermeneutic or anti-philosophical tradition and more immediately from Gestalt psychologists like Kurt Koffka and Kurt Lewin.

Pächt's "The End of the Image Theory," originally published in *Kritische Berichte* in 1930/1931, is a critique of a mode of writing about art that pretends to translate aesthetic qualities into prose. This is the most pointed statement of the Vienna School's aestheticist protectiveness toward the work of art. Following Benedetto Croce, Pächt derides self-indulgent critics who project subjective states of the soul onto works of art.[31] This polemic must be understood against a background of German literary writing about art stretching back to Winckelmann. Pächt was unwilling, however, to look for the antidote to belletristic subjectivism in the empiricist compilation of historical facts. Like Sedlmayr, he had learned from Gestalt theory that perception was never innocent and would yield different results depending on orientation or attitude (*Einstellung*). Nor was Pächt ready to forsake the work of art. The key to a historicism that would at the same time preserve the aesthetic character of the object was the hopeful idea that it was precisely in the "art-ness" of the object that its historical situation got concretized.

Four pieces in this anthology exemplify Vienna School art history in practice. Guido Kaschnitz von Weinberg's "Remarks on the Structure of Egyptian Sculpture," first published in the second volume of *Kunstwissenschaftliche Forschungen* in 1933, is a highly abstract analysis of the ancient Egyptian understanding of mass, gravity, movement, and time. Kaschnitz (1890–1958) saw ideas about gravity or about the repetitiveness of movements in time enshrined in the formal principles of Egyptian sculpture. He argues that Egyptian sculpture broke with ancient Near Eastern sculpture by abandoning the real experience of mass as an artistic content. Although still materially embodied in blocks of carved stone, the three dimensions of space were now understood as idealized metaphors of nature. This detachment of the *idea* of matter from actual matter liberated the surface of the stone as a screen for pure appearance, in other words, naturalism.

Pächt's "Design Principles of Fifteenth-Century Northern Painting," which also appeared in *Kunstwissenschaftliche Forschungen* in 1933, differentiates Flemish, Dutch, and French painting on the basis of figure-ground relationships, treatment of space, and framing devices. The basic thesis of the article is that the concern for two-dimensional pattern — the aesthetic effect of the projection of space onto a plane — was a permanent, constitutive factor in the development of painterly perspective systems in the Renaissance. Pächt argues that picture making was a matter of nuanced calibrations of the relationship between figure and ground and between illusions of real objects and the patterns formed by their projected forms in the plane. Pächt's essay is still the most powerful corrective to the crude assumption that Renaissance painting was fundamentally driven by the quest for ever more accurate renderings of space.

Sedlmayr's "Bruegel's *Macchia*" is an analysis of several works by Pieter Bruegel the Elder, principally his painting *Netherlandish Proverbs* (Berlin, Gemäldegalerie, 1559). Sedlmayr begins with Croce's use of the word *macchia* ("stain" or "color patch") to denote a vague, general impression of a distant object. To perceive the *macchia* of a painting is to grasp all at once its fundamental formal principles. In Sedlmayr's pictorial analyses, confusingly, the term *macchia* shifts meanings and comes to signify the particular pictorial device used by Bruegel to describe human bodies. Sedlmayr argues that Bruegel deliberately abandoned the achievements of Renaissance painting — perspective, color harmony, atmosphere, compositional balance, narrative unity — and instead remade the world as a chaotic aggregation of colored patches: an entire Flemish village, for instance, mechanically and absurdly acting out the metaphors of a hundred vernacular proverbs. Bruegel renders his moral distance from the modern world in the form of the blur, the perceptual *macchia*. Several of his encyclopedic or panoramic paintings share this structure: *Children's Games*, *The Battle Between Carnival and Lent*, *Christ on the Road to Calvary*. What Sedlmayr sees in these multicolored Rorschach blots is a profoundly pessimistic vision of an unarticulated, despiritualized, indeed modern, society. Sedlmayr describes the fragments of "crippled or contorted" humanity with chilling, sinister relish and contrasts them to the "dynamic and organic continuum" of Bruegel's natural world, where even bare trees blend into space (pp. 342, 337). In a footnote, Sedlmayr compares Bruegel's deadpan compositions to the montages of the surrealists and cites Jean Cocteau on De Chirico's ability to make the familiar strange.

Finally, I have selected two long passages from Fritz Novotny's remarkable monograph *Cézanne und das Ende der wissenschaftlichen Perspektive* (*Cézanne and the End of Scientific Perspective*; 1938), an endlessly patient and subtle reading of the structural properties of Cézanne's landscapes.[32] Novotny (1902–1983) did not publish in *Kunstwissenschaftliche Forschungen* and in some ways did not belong to the core group. Still, his book on Cézanne is one of the purest, most rigorous, and, from our point of view, least alien examples of the method. Novotny's readings of the minute departures from correct linear perspective in Cézanne's landscapes are closely related to Sedlmayr's and Pächt's analyses of pictorial space in the two preceding essays. The book describes a whole repertoire of highly nuanced adjustments that Cézanne made to his compositions and the effect of inaccessibility and expressionlessness they generate. For Novotny, the force and meaning of Cézanne's achievement emerge out of the sensitive, almost pedantic registration of these adjustments.

The volume closes with the two divergent contemporary responses already mentioned: Walter Benjamin's review of the first volume of *Kunstwissenschaftliche Forschungen* in the *Frankfurter Allgemeine Zeitung* (1933, originally written in 1931) and Meyer Schapiro's review of the second volume in the *Art Bulletin* (1936).

All these texts need to be read within a history of the discipline of art history. It is fair to say that academic art history was never more sure of itself and never more methodologically ambitious than in Germany and Austria between the wars. Many younger art historians wrote explicitly about the history and theoretical foundations of the discipline: Hans Tietze (1880–1954), Ernst Heidrich (1880–1914), Erwin Panofsky (1892–1968), Joseph Gantner (1896–1962), Edgar Wind (1900–1971).[33] Wilhelm Waetzoldt (1880–1945) wrote a two-volume history of German art history from the seventeenth through the nineteenth century.[34] New university chairs were established, libraries and institutes, journals, publishing projects, and reference works initiated. Art history saw itself as a powerful new *Kulturwissenschaft*, a synthetic, explanatory discipline uniquely positioned to mediate among the history of religion, anthropology, folkloric studies, intellectual history, social history, and the history of political institutions.

The new self-regard of the discipline was not just a matter of more professorships and deeper card catalogs. Art history's cultural-historical pretensions were rooted in a sense of the special eloquence and explanatory power of its objects. Images and other artifacts seemed different from ordinary historical documents. They were material relics that promised unmediated sensory access to the minds and experiences of historical subjects. The historian who could grasp the principles of artistic figuration could circumvent the thickets of distant and alien symbolic systems and arrive at the foundations of culture.

The theories of figuration most routinely invoked by art historians in the early decades of the century were derived from neo-Kantian philosophy. In the German academy it had become practically a commonplace that the world had no reality outside the *Vorstellung* (idea) imposed on it by the mind.[35] Matter, time, nature, and man were all constructs of the dynamically perceiving mind. Many art historians were influenced by the writings of the philosopher and critic Konrad Fiedler (1841–1895), who in a famous essay of 1881 had dismissed the theory of painterly naturalism on neo-Kantian grounds.[36] Fiedler had credited the true artist or poet not with reproducing the world but with creating a world. And virtually everybody at the time read the idealist treatise on relief sculpture by the artist and critic Adolf von Hildebrand, *The Problem of Form in the Visual Arts* (1893), which defined artistic vision as the apprehension of an idea of form (*Formvorstellung*) abstracted from the contingent, shifting phenomena perceived by the eyes.[37] Hildebrand (1847–1921), a close friend of Fiedler, attacked the positivists who conceived of representation as the mechanical reproduction of the results of perception. The work of art, he argued, offers the "form of existence" (*Daseinsform*) as a pure visual effect.

All of this left the historian little room to maneuver. For to call something a work of art is precisely a way of calling attention to properties of self-containment, formal coherence, detachment from instrumental application, even radical self-reflexivity. The discontinuity of the work of art with conventional symbol systems would seem to limit its usefulness as a historical document. Fiedler, Hildebrand, and the Italian idealist philosopher Benedetto Croce (1866–1952) all stressed not the intelligibility of the work of art but its opacity and untranslatability. In their writings, the work of art fails to provide straightforward accounts about the world outside its boundaries. Fiedler's thought had explicitly challenged the theory of painterly naturalism. His ideas about the illegibility of the work of art implicitly discourage any sort of historiographical "naturalism" that might try to domesticate the process of figuration by explaining it.

Thus if there was a growing consensus at the beginning of the century about the peculiarity of the figured artifact, there was no agreement on how to build an art history on it. The new documentary apparatus with its scientific pretensions collided with the elusive and inexplicably eloquent aesthetic object. There is a sense in which everyone suddenly became aware of the insufficiency of the documentary apparatus at the very moment it was installed. In fact, awareness of the poverty of empiricism was much more widespread in these decades than is often realized. Turn-of-the-century art historians under the spell of Fiedler and Hildebrand, in other words, found themselves at an impasse.

In retrospect, the most original strategy for historicizing the hermeneutically recalcitrant image was the symbology of Aby Warburg (1866–1929). Warburg proceeded from a vitalistic conception of the symbol as a form that concretized the energies of a culture. His ideas developed unsystematically in a series of essays on marginal episodes in the history of religion and culture. But he was not well known or creatively understood in his own time.[38]

Institutionally more successful was the elegant, rarefied project of the Swiss art historian and follower of Jakob Burckhardt, Heinrich Wölfflin (1864–1945). In his dissertation "Prolegomena to a Psychology of Architecture" (1881) and his later handbook *Principles of Art History* (1915), Wölfflin proposed to use the work of art as the basis for a history of vision.[39] Ultimately, in neo-Kantian fashion, the history of vision was meant to give way to a history of cognition. But Wölfflin in practice, at once exercising Burckhardtian restraint and succumbing to fatigue, never took the project that far. Moreover, despite his famous extrapolation of the entire mentality of the high medieval world from the pointed Gothic shoe, and despite his promise in *Principles of Art History* to shift the focus from "quality" to the "mode of representation as such," Wölfflin in fact wrote only about major works of art.[40] His preference for the most complex and irreducible images, the most radically abstracted from ordinary habits of perception, was typical of neo-Kantian formalist art history.[41] Walter Benjamin expressed his disappointment with Wölfflin in the first paragraph of his review of *Kunstwissenschaftliche Forschungen* (p. 439).[42]

The Viennese art historian Alois Riegl faced the problem of the autonomy and incommensurability of the aesthetic object with greater determination. Like Fiedler and Wölfflin, he had little use for materialist or naturalist theories of representation. But Riegl was dissatisfied with Fiedler's self-reflexive aesthetic artifact, which threatened never to reconnect with the world.[43] As the basic unit of art history Riegl proposed not the work of art, but the drive to make art, the ineradicable impulse to design and figuration that he named the *Kunstwollen*. He left the work of art behind by burrowing deeper into it, below the technologies of illusionism, below the level of content, below style to this fundamental level of figuration where the maker had carried out some primal negotiation with space-time and the material conditions of existence (p. 95).

Riegl had no strong theory about the motor behind the *Kunstwollen*. He considered the plastic imagination an irreducible mystery and preferred to leave it unpsychologized and unexplained, in effect to bracket it out of the historiographical equation.[44] The *Kunstwollen* became a mere taxonomic tool, a neutral designation of a set of formal properties. This bracketing operation is similar to the bracketing of vision performed today by the concept of visuality. Visuality and the *Kunstwollen* are both ways of suspending inquiry into the physiological and psychological workings of vision in order to emphasize the dependence of figuration on convention and history.

Riegl tended to associate the formal sets designated by the term *Kunstwollen* not only with individual artists or historical epochs, but also with nations or "races." Wölfflin had done the same with his *Sehformen* (forms of seeing). Nationalism was traditionally a more imminent and virulent threat in literary studies, where the primary material was inescapably partitioned according to national languages, than in art history.[45] Riegl was nevertheless, from our point of view, mired in Orientalist clichés. For example, after contrasting the "objectivist," additive approach of the ancient Near Eastern sculptor to the "subjectivist," impressionistic approach of the early Greeks, he remarks that "the influence of the Near Eastern peoples, ultimately always a retarding element, was at the proper moment useful to Westerners. Yet true progress, and therefore the upper hand in politics and culture finally fell for all time to the Indo-Germanic people" ("The Place of the Vapheio Cups," p. 117). One cannot but wonder whether formalist taxonomies actively encourage the hypostatization of concepts such as nation and race.[46] On the one hand, there is a theoretical void behind the *Kunstwollen*, just as there is behind Wölfflin's forms of seeing. One could therefore argue that the conventional but profound Eurocentrism of Riegl and Wölfflin has no theoretical teeth and is not *more* pernicious for being coupled with a formalist schema. It is certainly not very effectively masked by that schema. Moreover, the nationalist and racist generalizations in Wölfflin and Riegl tend to fall in behind the taxonomic stylistic terms in a somewhat random, ill-considered fashion. On the other hand, it is possible that the abstraction from historical detail and contingency achieved by formalist analysis, and the reluctance to take into account the physiology of perception, make formalist art history especially vulnerable to ideological muddle.[47]

Riegl brought to his prosaic chronicles of stylistic change an aestheticist notion of how works of art worked. He devised a way of reading the artifact that would exploit it as a historical document and at the same time do justice to it as a complex whole greater than the sum of its parts, even as an open-ended text whose meaning was not intrinsic to it but only concretized in a succession of historical, subjective readings. To take an example: Riegl saw the peculiarly Dutch convention of the group portrait, which emerged in the fifteenth century and culminated in Rembrandt, as the expression of a national propensity toward communitarian structures and egalitarian respect for the individual rooted in respect for privacy and the interior life. He showed how picture surfaces were knit together not merely by shapes and lines but also by represented gazes, the visible vectors of mutual psychological involvement. The group portraits in Riegl's analysis are revealed simultaneously as literal representations of democratic social structures and, on the level of pure form, as metaphors for those structures.

If Riegl grounded his art history in aestheticist principles, this was not to defend the idea of the work of art, which hardly needed defending around 1900, but rather to force upon historical science a more complex model of pictorial representation. Riegl took no interest in *value.* He recognized no hierarchies among the images and artifacts of the past. Any shaped object—even a scrap of paper—was subject to formal analysis.[48] Today it is easy to sympathize with this evenhanded approach to material evidence. Riegl sought to disengage art history from the art market, from collecting, from the public's appetite for masterpieces. But it is important to see that he arrived at this position not by repudiating art, but by imposing the idea of art on ordinary objects, indeed on the entirety of the shaped environment. The idea of the coextension of work and world, under the sign of what we might call "aesthetic textuality," does permanent damage to the frame around the work of art and indeed to the very institution of the work of art. We might think of Riegl's radical formalism as *aestheticism without judgment.*

Riegl died in 1905 at the age of forty-seven. His legacy in Vienna was kept alive for a short time by his colleague and contemporary Franz Wickhoff (1853–1909), a scrupulous scholar influenced by the connoisseurial principles of Giovanni Morelli and the author of a pioneering monograph on the Vienna Genesis, which, like Riegl's work on Roman art, had radically overturned received judgments about late antique art. Already by this time, it seems, there was a sense of what "Vienna School" art history might be.[49] Riegl and Wickhoff were generally uninterested in iconographic studies, which tended to reduce art history to an auxiliary to theology or political history; they professed inordinate respect for primary documents and at the same time held a dim view of their ultimate explanatory power; they took some interest in the psychology of perception and reception; they observed in their choice of subjects no classicizing or idealizing hierarchy of styles; they insisted on the independence of academic art history from the museum and the art market; they used Morellian connoisseurship as a diagnostic and taxonomic tool, not as a means of endorsing aesthetic value systems.

After Wickhoff's death in 1909 there was a struggle over his and Riegl's intellectual legacy, resulting in the creation of a second chair at Vienna. This was given to the maverick Josef Strzygowski, a scholar of eastern European and Near Eastern architecture who had a strong effect on students (including Fritz Novotny and Otto Demus) but for decades remained institutionally isolated.[50] The main chair went to a protégé of Riegl and Wickhoff, Max Dvořák (1874–1921).[51] Dvořák's imaginative essays on the origins of the style of the van Eycks, the rise of naturalism in Gothic art, El Greco, and other topics were collected posthumously under the title *Kunstgeschichte als Geistesgeschichte* (Art history as the history of the spirit).[52] Dvořák's writing came to rely heavily on intuitive and unsystematic analogies between works of art and broader cultural patterns. This sort of art history is sometimes characterized as "expressionist" in part because it originates in the willfulness and creativity of the interpreter, in part because it understands art to be the expression of culture in some quasi-poetic fashion.[53] In early-twentieth-century German art history, this mode of writing usually verged on the popular, the sensational, and the grandiose, for example in Wilhelm Worringer (1881–1965), a follower of Riegl and the author of the hugely successful tract *Abstraction and Empathy*[54]; in Fritz Burger (1877–1916), who was trained as an artist and in some ways was the most thorough exponent of Fiedler's ideas[55]; and in Wilhelm Pinder (1878–1947), whose smoldering tributes to medieval German art were widely read in the Nazi period.[56] Burger's explosive writings on modern, primitive, and German late medieval and Renaissance art celebrated the independence and transcendental authority of the work of art. For Burger, art does not passively reproduce nature but sets its own creations against nature; art concretizes the forms and categories of human thought; art is the liberation of man from both history and material nature. His *Introduction to Modern Art* (*Einführung in die moderne Kunst*) (1917), in the series Handbuch der Kunstwissenschaft that he himself founded, sold 23 thousand copies in the first year. "Expressionist" art history was too smoothly blended with German nationalist sentiment and with *völkisch* and anti-Semitic hostility to theory and abstraction. Burger, for example, insisted on the peculiarity of the *Strukturformen* of national mentalities. In a text published a year after his death at Verdun, he argued that the world war had revealed the bankruptcy of internationalism.[57] Pinder, for his part, expressed the hope in 1939 that the removal of Jews from academe would purge art history of excessively "conceptual" thinking (*allzu begrifflichen Denken*).[58]

But two decades earlier Pinder himself had been widely regarded as the most progressive thinker in the discipline.[59] On Dvořák's death in 1921 a group of students at Vienna, among them Hans Sedlmayr, convinced the administration to offer Dvořák's chair to Pinder.[60] But Pinder declined and remained at Leipzig. Instead the chair went to Julius von Schlosser (1866–1938), an aloof, patrician figure and a prolific and creative historian of medieval and postmedieval art.[61] Schlosser edited a series of textual sources of medieval art; he compiled a massive handbook to the "literature of art" from the early Middle Ages through the eighteenth century; he wrote on unorthodox subjects from the social history of art like wax portraits, carved ivory saddles, musical instruments, the model books of medieval wandering artists, and the late Renaissance *Kunst- und Wunderkammer*. He maintained a close friendship with Benedetto Croce. It was not indifference to art but the fastidious conviction that nothing pertinent could be said about art — that art could never be used as a document — that steered Schlosser away from the interpretation of the individual work of art and onto the unorthodox topics. Schlosser supervised the dissertations of Sedlmayr, Pächt, Ernst Kris, Karl Tolnai, Karl Oettinger, Otto Kurz, Ernst Gombrich, and many others.[62] He won over many of those who had preferred Pinder in 1921, like Sedlmayr. The younger generation was impressed by Schlosser's methodological austerity and respect for fact and was inspired to purge art historical discourse of belletristic nonsense and subjectivist preening. The younger scholars in Vienna in the mid- and late 1920s professed a fierce, iconoclastic rationalism. Even Gombrich — Schlosser's last doctoral student — admits to having been swept into the mood.[63]

This was the generation that began to reread Riegl. The young Hamburg scholar Erwin Panofsky published an analysis of Riegl's term *Kunstwollen* in 1920 in which he tried to rescue the improbable project of an intellectual and cultural history grounded in the analysis of autonomous works of art with a renewed and newly rigorous neo-Kantianism. Panofsky sketched out an art history that would begin with a priori, transcendental categories of "aesthetic volition" and culminate in the elucidation of "the sense of historical meaning as an ideal unity."[64] In his long essay "Perspective as 'Symbolic Form'" of 1924, Panofsky interpreted the various perspectival systems implemented throughout the history of Western art not as a sequence of steadily improving technologies of illusionism but as registrations of shifting worldviews. This was a philosophically fortified specimen of how Riegl's project might be extended.[65]

But Panofsky's Viennese contemporaries quickly reclaimed Riegl's legacy. Sedlmayr, four years younger than Panofsky, sketched out an alternative Riegl in his introduction to Riegl's *Collected Essays* (1929). He argued that Panofsky's version of the *Kunstwollen* was too far abstracted from any real, psychological sources and therefore would never grasp the inner dynamic of history, and that it depended on a universal, unchanging model of human reason. Sedlmayr countered with an interpretation of the *Kunstwollen* as a set of "structure principles," rooted in the mind, that determined the outward appearance of the artifact.[66] From our point of view, it must be admitted, the distinction between Panofsky's immanent, a priori categories and Sedlmayr's structure principles has lost some of its urgency.

Sedlmayr had already introduced the term *Struktur* in his essay "Gestaltetes Sehen" (1925), a concise analysis of the interior of Borromini's San Carlo alle Quattro Fontane.[67] Here Sedlmayr argued that to apprehend this pulsating space in terms of underlying architectonic principles or intersecting volumes was to miss the point of the building. The key to San Carlino's *Gestalt,* or artistic structure, is an undulating, tripartite segment of wall that occurs four times in the ground plan. Structure is found paradoxically in a surface element without structural function. The correctness of the observation is confirmed by the echoing of the tripartite motif not only in the facade, but also in the low balustrades in front of the altars. In other words, structure may reveal itself most clearly in apparently marginal or meaningless features.

"Gestaltetes Sehen," which translates roughly as "shaped vision," is an idea drafted from Gestalt psychology. Sedlmayr cites here, and again in "Bruegel's *Macchia*" and "Toward a Rigorous Study of Art," the psychologists Kurt Koffka, Kurt Lewin, Ernst Kretschmer, Eugen Bleuler, and Max Wertheimer.[68] Sedlmayr's point is simply that one must understand something of the aesthetic principles animating the entire building before one can begin to see it at all. He draws an analogy with music, observing that raw, "unshaped" listening will hardly suffice to grasp the meaning and aims of modern (presumably twelve-tone) music. To perceive the structure is to reorganize one's perception of the work so as to "see through" function, architectonic structure, period style, or, in the case of representational works, content. Structure is not an objective feature of the work but a quality that is generated by a description made from a carefully chosen point of view.

"Shaped" vision is an active, creative vision that springs conventional categories. The analogy with Borromini's own vision is unmistakable. The deliberate, paradoxical reversal of the structure-surface hierarchy characteristic of baroque or rococo architecture became in effect the fundamental maneuver of *Struktur-analyse*. And the key historical figure in Sedlmayr's entire oeuvre, a kind of hero interfering with the shift to the value-free analysis of single works, was Johann Bernhard Fischer von Erlach, the brilliantly inventive eighteenth-century Austrian architect and spiritual successor to Borromini.[69]

Clearly Sedlmayr's claims of rigor and rationalism were specious. The "rococo" readings of the New Vienna School were nothing if not intuitive. Sedlmayr in "Bruegel's *Macchia*" and Pächt in "Design Principles of Fifteenth-Century Northern Painting" do not arrive at the historical meanings of the paintings by argumentation; they simply apprehend them, in a flash. *Strukturanalyse* rests on the intuitive, nondiscursive, holistic apprehension of meaning. At the moment of interpretation — like the *anagnorisis* that the plot of classical drama turns on — the art historian simply recognizes the world concretized in the work. In the shapeless bodies, masklike faces, and jerky actions of Bruegel's peasants, Sedlmayr saw a post-Renaissance crisis of confidence in the transcendental grounding of human nature. In the rhomboid surface patterns of the Limburg brothers or Jean Fouquet, Pächt saw the French predilection for social organization, judicial assemblies, festive ceremonies, "life encompassed by social conventions" (p. 53). These recognitions were purely eidetic insights unobtainable by ordinary analytic procedures.

Instantaneous, unanalyzable acts of recognition are also the basis of connoisseurship, or the intuitive identification and taxonomy of works of art. With its roots in Gestalt theory, *Strukturanalyse* could well have provided a foundation for an advanced theory of connoisseurship. But since connoisseurs are almost constitutionally allergic to theory, and since no one understands connoisseurship except connoisseurs themselves, this avenue has never been explored.[70]

The intuitive foundations of the structure-analytical method, masked behind scholarly conventions, were both its promise and its undoing. Sedlmayr and Pächt and their colleagues had at first protected themselves from the charge of intuitionism by using Max Dvořák as a foil. Supposedly they had rejected Dvořák's loosely knit cultural-historical schemes. They dismissed his writing as unscholarly and too detached from close observation and instead turned back to Riegl. Kaschnitz von Weinberg in his review of *Late Roman Art Industry* in 1929 placed Riegl in a tradition of "autonomous" art history, following Winckelmann, Karl Schnaase, and Jakob Burckhardt; he accused Dvořák, by contrast, of reducing art history's object to a mere "expression" of *Weltan-schauung*.[71] But it is important to remember that Dvořák, like the popularizer Worringer, had his roots in Riegl. Riegl, too, had permitted himself wild and basically meaningless analogies between form and world. An example in the essay on the Vapheio cups is this remark about the two bulls at the center of the composition of the second cup: "The Mycenaean artist seems already to have felt that a single point as the dominant motif was too rigid a restraint. Who does not recall here that classical Greek composition would also prefer a double to a single motif...? One may perhaps forgive the imagination if one is reminded of the dual monarchies or dual consulates of certain ancient states" (p. 109).

Intuitionism is either the magic of Riegl's art history or the beginning of its unraveling into mysticism, lyricism, and ahistoricism. Riegl's intuitionism flashes rarely; but it may turn out that any cultural analysis grounded in formal analysis will have to rely at some point, with more or less explicitness, on intuitive links between form and world. Whether this kind of writing actually gets disparaged as expressionist may simply depend, in the end, on rhetoric, tone, and the degree of belletristic or demagogic ambitions.

After repudiating Dvořák, Sedlmayr and his colleagues went on to make the same sorts of interpretative leaps. Meyer Schapiro noted this disapprovingly when he called Kaschnitz's essay on Egyptian sculpture "expressionistic" (p. 464). But this is perhaps not quite on the mark, since the stated ambition of the New Vienna School was to find a way to write about fundamentally subjective and irrational phenomena in rigorously objective terms. In this respect they were the true children of Riegl, or for that matter of Freud, as Wolfgang Kemp pointed out.[72] The New Vienna School indulged a secret taste for paradox and the unexpected, but they framed it all in a rhetoric of objectivity. Better than the comparison with expressionism is Artur Rosenauer's comparison of Viennese *Strukturanalyse* to Neue Sachlichkeit painting.[73]

This tremendous, unmaintainable tension between scholarly convention and intuitionist insight in Sedlmayr and Pächt was what caught the attention of Benjamin and Schapiro. The two reviewers made similar observations but drew opposite conclusions. Benjamin thought he had seen the future of art history. Schapiro's admonitory tone proved more prescient. Admittedly he was writing in 1936, three years after Benjamin. He may have known that Sedlmayr, like Pinder, had joined the Nazi Party for a year in 1932–1933.[74] He almost surely had learned of the personal break between Sedlmayr and Pächt after Hitler's accession to power.[75] Still, he could not have foreseen the full extent to which the potential for nonsense in Riegl's syntheticism would return in the later Sedlmayr's sweeping, virulent theses on modern art and culture.

In 1938, in the context of a scholarly Festschrift, Sedlmayr saluted the *Anschluss* of Austria to the German *Reich*. His teacher Schlosser, we now know, shared his satisfaction with the turn of events.[76] In an article of 1939–1940 on the future of Vienna, Sedlmayr discussed the advantages of a proposed second city center, the "new city" or *Hitlerstadt*, to be constructed on the site of the "former Jewish quarter."[77] Sedlmayr was no revolutionary, however. He seems to have been driven by bourgeois and Catholic nostalgia for the Old Europe, the Habsburg *Mitteleuropa*, that he had known as a child.[78] Habsburg restorationism and Romantic-Catholic hostility to the Enlightenment made an imperfect but comfortable match with National Socialism.

After he lost his university chair in 1945, Sedlmayr recoiled into an indignant, high-strung ultraconservatism. In 1948 he published his neo-Spenglerian, pessimistic, anti-intellectual assault on modern art, *Verlust der Mitte* (Loss of the center; trans. *Art in Crisis: The Lost Center*). The book appealed to the defensiveness and conservatism of many postwar readers, and not only in Germany.[79] Sedlmayr argued in a demagogic, vulgar-Nietzschean mode that modern art was a disease of the spirit bent on distorting and corrupting the analogy between God and man. He has been compared to Lukács, who also held up an ideal image of "whole" man — Marxist, not Christian — against modern art.[80] Sedlmayr singled out as the precursors of modern chaos Bosch, Bruegel, and Goya, artists who were increasingly popular with the middle-class picture-book-buying and museum-going public. But Sedlmayr had also caught the tune of modernism, especially in contrast to other academic art historians, whose remarks on contemporary art were nearly always obtuse. Sedlmayr's book was the natural extension of the Nazis' exhibition *Degenerate Art* in 1937, which was meant to deride and undermine cubism, surrealism, and expressionism but which in the event amounted to the most spectacular and widely viewed showcase that modern art had ever had.[81] Sedlmayr's second book on modern art, *Die Revolution der modernen Kunst* (1955), sold 100 thousand copies in the first two years.[82]

The scholarly counterpart to *Verlust der Mitte* was Sedlmayr's magnum opus, his treatise on Gothic architecture, *Die Entstehung der Kathedrale* (The origins of the cathedral; 1950), still untranslated into English.[83] Here he argued that the cathedral could not be understood as an expression of architectonic function or as a visible text of theological ideas, but rather only as a literal embodiment — an image (*Abbild*), not a conventional representation — of the Heavenly Jerusalem described in the Apocalypse. From our point of view the book amounts to a critique of the rather narrow understanding of representation that prevails in the humanistic disciplines and the projection of that understanding onto historical periods. At the same time it is easy to read it as an expression of utopian nostalgia for a premodern theocratic, organic society, not so far in spirit from the neo-medieval fantasies of German and English romanticism.[84]

In 1951, the year after the publication of *Die Entstehung der Kathedrale*, Sedlmayr was professionally rehabilitated and offered a chair at Munich. Some students protested the appointment, unsuccessfully.[85] In the 1950s he published three interpretations of individual works that represented a final unfolding of the structure-analytical method into a kind of neo-Scholastic exegesis.[86] At the end of his essay on Bruegel's *Blind Leading the Blind*, Sedlmayr actually reprinted the letter by Dante to Can Grande Scaliger on polysemy and the four levels of interpretation. Sedlmayr taught at Munich until 1963, and then at Salzburg until 1974. He was never re-embraced by the art historical community. Moreover, the defensiveness of some of his old pupils from Vienna and Munich, like Frodl-Kraft and Friedrich Piel, has complicated and emotionally polarized the critical assessment of his career and work in Germany and Austria. Frodl-Kraft, for example, in a recent memoir of Sedlmayr, compared the 1951 protest to the intervention of the Viennese students in favor of Wilhelm Pinder over Julius von Schlosser in 1921, implying that Sedlmayr, like his teacher Schlosser, had barely avoided an unjust rejection at the hands of the short-sighted students. Frodl-Kraft mentions Sedlmayr's National Socialist engagement in a footnote.[87]

By the mid–1930s, as noted, Sedlmayr and Pächt were no longer on friendly terms. Pächt got a teaching post at Heidelberg in 1933 but was prevented by Nazi law from ever occupying it. He visited England in 1935 and again in 1936–1937 and was finally forced to seek refuge there in 1938. Eventually he took a position at Oxford.[88]

Pächt's two main areas of expertise were medieval manuscript illumination and fifteenth-century northern panel painting. In 1929 he had written a pioneering book on fifteenth-century Austrian painting.[89] To submit these ugly panels to long, intense formal analyses was as perverse as Riegl's decision to write on colonial Roman brooches or Constantinian relief sculptures. In his refusal to define ugliness as the opposite of a transcendentally sanctioned beauty, Pächt, like Riegl, proved himself truly godless.[90] Sedlmayr, too, clearly perceived the alternative that modernism offered between a primordial and revolutionary ugliness — what we would call the *informe* — and the old morally laden ugliness associated with evil and disease; he simply made a different choice than Riegl and Pächt. In 1931 Pächt had published his most remarkable essay, on the concept of history embodied in the complex scenic altarpieces of the late-fifteenth-century Tyrolean painter and sculptor Michael Pacher.[91]

In England, Pächt worked mostly on medieval manuscripts. Apart from an article on Riegl in *Burlington Magazine*, he wrote little about his methodological principles.[92] Only fragments of Pächt's extremely original thinking on early panel painting found their way into English, for example in a well-known essay on the French painter Jean Fouquet, which grew out of the piece translated for the present anthology, and in a long critique of Panofsky's *Early Netherlandish Painting*, which became a touchstone for the post–1960s rebellion against iconology.[93] With his indifference to the Romantic cult of artistic genius, his skepticism toward the explanatory claims made by empiricist social history, his distaste for poeticizing expressionist writing on art, and his disaffection with text-based iconographic studies, Pächt may be the most intellectually living and congenial thinker of the whole New Vienna School. With its consistent application of a few basic formal-analytical tools — figure and ground, spatial illusion and planar pattern, frame and format — Pächt's art history provides something approaching a practical model for the study of premodern painting. One glimpses the outlines of the method, arguably, in Millard Meiss's classic essay on fifteenth-century Crucifixion compositions, "'Highlands' in the Lowlands."[94]

Pächt was never intellectually at home in England; he was never on good terms with Gombrich or Panofsky; and in 1963 he returned to Vienna. His university lectures on the principles of art history were published by his students in 1977 and have recently been translated into English.[95] His Viennese lectures on Netherlandish painting have also been posthumously edited and in some cases translated.[96]

Besides Pächt, the original member of the group who remained most committed to Riegl and to the concept of structure analysis was the classical archaeologist Guido Kaschnitz von Weinberg. Both Kaschnitz and the German archaeologist Friedrich Matz (1890–1974) — who had no direct connection with Vienna — published doctrinaire statements of the method as late as the 1960s.[97] It is as if the remoteness of the ancient cultures made it easier to achieve the puristic exclusion of nonformal aspects of the work of art demanded by the method. The symbolic and cultic functions of a Near Eastern relief or an Etruscan object were so inscrutable that the art historians could bracket them out of the analysis almost with relief. Today the writings of Matz and Kaschnitz are hardly read by classical archaeologists. They are considered too detached from primary research and indeed from archaeology. Admittedly, one is struck by the extent of Kaschnitz's reliance on standard examples illustrated in handbooks like Ludwig Curtius's *Antike Kunst*. Kaschnitz's wife remembers how he wrote his essay "The Structure of Greek Sculpture" sitting on the French Riviera, without any books.[98] On the other hand, many art historians who work on post-Renaissance art routinely interpret important paintings as if they were coherent, philologically "chastised" texts; here they imitate the great majority of literary scholars. There is no intrinsic reason why historians of ancient art should not do the same if they wish.

Kaschnitz von Weinberg, an Austrian like Riegl, Sedlmayr, Pächt, and Novotny, completed a dissertation in classical archaeology in Vienna in 1913. He spent the 1920s in Rome, where he intensively read Riegl. He published his major experiments in *Strukturanalyse* in the 1930s while teaching in distant Königsberg. In Kaschnitz's writings the history of art is played out, almost unrecognizably, on a purely philosophical field: the morphology of style is transposed into conflicts of will and matter, expressions of "life force" and cosmic energies.[99] Kaschnitz completely disregarded technique, symbolic content, and in general all contingent historical detail, including the historical functions of art. He also maintained that judgments of taste and value interfered with the analysis of structure. In this respect he, alongside Pächt, was the truest disciple of Riegl.[100]

Structure analysis in the field of archaeology had a deeply conservative dimension, more complacently so than in Sedlmayr. This is concealed, perhaps not so effectively, under Kaschnitz's metaphysics. It was more directly expressed in 1938 by Bernhard Schweitzer in an article for a journal with National Socialist ties, *Neue Jahrbücher für antike und deutsche Bildung*. Schweitzer argued that the roots of the new method lay in the Romantic reaction to the Enlightenment and that therefore "*Strukturforschung* could be characterized as a specifically German branch (*Sonderzweig*) of art historical scholarship."[101] Certainly the nationalist and racist generalizations that animate Kaschnitz's historical schemata are hard to stomach.

Fritz Novotny wrote a dissertation under Josef Strzygowski on Romanesque architectural sculpture in Austria (1929/1930). He later wrote principally on nineteenth-century painting. From

1961 he was director of the Österreichische Galerie in Vienna. Novotny is best known to English-speaking readers for his volume on nineteenth-century art for the *Pelican History of Art* (1960). His difficult book on Cézanne (1938) remains in many ways the most disciplined extended exercise in the formal-analytic method. Meyer Schapiro in his book on Cézanne cited Novotny and Roger Fry as the two authors who had given him the "greatest stimulus."[102] Another Viennese scholar who put the method into practice but never saw himself as a theorist was Karl Oettinger (1906–1979). Oettinger, who together with Novotny worked as an assistant professor under Sedlmayr in the late 1930s, wrote one of the most remarkable pieces in the mode, "Laube, Garten und Wald" (Bower, garden, and forest), an imaginative new taxonomy of German Renaissance art based on the existential encounters between man and nature framed by the grove, the garden, and the forest.[103]

By no means were all young Viennese art historians in the 1920s and 1930s dedicated to Sedlmayr's program.[104] Those who were a bit older than Pächt and Sedlmayr and in some cases had completed their dissertations under Dvořák — including Ludwig von Baldass, Fritz Saxl, Friedrich Antal, Johannes Wilde, and Ernst Garger — maintained a clear methodological distance, no doubt for varying reasons. Others, like Otto Benesch, were more loyal to the legacy of Dvořák. Ernst Kris, Otto Kurz, and Ernst Gombrich pursued an interest in psychology and psychoanalysis far more intense than Sedlmayr's. Some of the most imaginative scholars who wrote for *Kunstwissenschaftliche Forschungen* or *Kritische Berichte* ended up following their own methodological paths entirely: Carl Linfert; the Russian Mikhail Alpatov; Dagobert Frey, a theoretician whose rather windy, idealistic reflections lack the negativity of *Strukturanalyse*.[105]

Julius von Schlosser in his 1934 history of the Vienna School did briefly mention the *Strukturforscher*. He described Sedlmayr as "one of my most original pupils" and credited him with forging, with "somewhat youthful boisterousness," a link to Gestalt psychology. But he also pointed out that Sedlmayr, this time "one of my most gifted students," had lost sight of the real Riegl behind the methodological "system."[106]

What are we to make of this tradition? *Strukturanalyse* sometimes looks like a structuralism, especially in Kaschnitz von Weinberg but also in Pächt and Novotny.[107] Structuralism is the study of the meanings generated by the interrelationship of signs within larger symbolic systems or fields. Kaschnitz von Weinberg is a structuralist when he shows how Egyptian sculpture managed to represent infinity by manipulating a system of sculptural values established by earlier Near Eastern art. But as we have seen, Viennese *Strukturanalyse* often relied on intuition and strong, creative interpretation to generate its cultural-historical insights. This is especially true of Sedlmayr, despite his boasts of methodological rigor and consistency. The unsystematic, performative aspect of *Strukturanalyse* distinguishes it from true structuralisms, which mistrust the subjective, volatile encounter between an individual interpreter and a complex sign like a work of art.

The interpretative freedom that the structure-analytical method insisted on in practice follows from its conception of its proper object, the work of art. In *Strukturanalyse* the work of art does not signify anything by manipulating a symbolic code. The premise of *Strukturanalyse* is that the work of art has violently refigured reality and offers not an image of but an alternative to the world, what Sedlmayr called a *kleine Welt*, a microcosm ("Toward a Rigorous Study of Art," p. 155). The historical world is concretized in that *kleine Welt*. This virtual, fictional presence of the world in the work is in fact what is designated by the term "structure." Structure is not an objective property of the material artifact but a projection onto it by the interpreter, supposedly symmetrical to the projection performed by the original maker of the artifact. Structure is "a *simulacrum* of the object, but a directed, *interested* simulacrum, since the imitated object makes something appear which remained invisible or, if one prefers, unintelligible in the natural object. Structural man takes the real, decomposes it, then recomposes it.... The simulacrum is intellect added to object."[108] The interpreter sees stories and tensions, for example, in the planar pattern of the painting or in the ground plan of the building. Interpretation is a perceptual imposition on the data not unlike the procedure that Richard Wollheim calls "seeing-in" and places at the very origin of the figuring activity.[109] The structure analyst thus reactivates the aesthetic artifact's initial relationship to the historical world by emulating the creative seeing of the artist. *Strukturanalyse* is more like making than reading.

Sedlmayr's early invocations of Gestalt psychology are misleading. Gestalt psychology implies an ideal reconstruction of a "whole" work that would govern the interpretation of the component parts. But it turns out that to impose structure on a work of art is not to pull it together, but rather to turn the work inside out and display its joints and ligatures. The work flattened out in the art historian's text suffers the breakdown of its representational devices and the foiling of its references and symbolic notations. *Strukturanalyse* ends up abrogating the work's autonomy and self-sufficiency and undoing any "making whole" or reconciliation the work might aspire to. In *Strukturanalyse*, the dynamism of the interpretative procedure and the fictional integrity of the work are on a collision course. Just as in modernism, the adherence to the idea of the work of art and the impulse to dismantle that idea are complementary. The similarity between this methodological project and the revocation of picture-making conventions undertaken by avant-garde painting in the first decades of the twentieth century is obvious.

The notion of an eidetic recognition of history in its material relics, meanwhile, recalls the project of Walter Benjamin. Benjamin wanted to represent the past in his own writings through paratactic constellations of "ideal symbols." This entailed extracting objects and images from a linear, developmental history and reconstructing them philosophically into an "Ur-history" that would reveal the origins of the present.[110] Benjamin got the idea of the unmediated eloquence of the isolated image from a number of sources: the late Renaissance concept of allegory; Goethe's biological *Urform* as explicated by the philosopher Georg Simmel; Riegl's art history. In insignificant and accidental details Benjamin saw allegories of an underlying and otherwise inscrutable historical truth (see "On the First Volume of *Kunstwissenschaftliche Forschungen*," p. 442). No concept could be more familiar to us today, since so much recent imaginative work in cultural history, perhaps especially in the Early Modern European field, is animated by Benjamin's example and by confidence in the explanatory power of the single, striking emblematic image or a historiographical montage of such images. It is true that recent neo-formalist or New Historicist cultural histories routinely distance themselves from the concept of eidetic intuition by claiming a semiotic rather than phenomenological philosophical provenance. But the actual practical workings of such histories very often amount to a quasi-mystical allegoresis. Any historical method that tries to keep faith with the density and singularity of the image will have to resort to allegory when it gets around to doing history.

Eidetic apprehension as a historiographical tool, whether used by the *Strukturforscher* or by Benjamin, is of course extremely vulnerable to an empiricist, materialist critique. Theodor Adorno chastised Benjamin for hinging his critical history on the effect of

a "shock-like montage."[111] For Schapiro and Gombrich, the intuitive recognition of the world in the work of art was no way to do
history. But empiricist strictures are difficult to live by. A lot of
the most creative art history and cultural history of the last hundred years will fall short of the strictest standards of empiricist
responsibility. Therefore the critique of the New Vienna School
cannot simply be grounded in rationalist fear of ideological mysti-
fication. For if one loses patience with emblematic, allegorical, or
"poetic" cultural history, then one has to be prepared to give up a
lot more than Sedlmayr.[112] By the same token, if the examples of
Benjamin and the rest suggest that there is no *intrinsic* peril in the
allegorical method, no preprogrammed bias toward spiritualism,
nationalism, or cultural nostalgia, then the New Vienna School
would have to be normalized.

A normalization of Sedlmayr would entail a painful, even obscene "reading through" of his Nazism. A normalized Sedlmayr
would come to look more like other progressive art historians
of the 1920s and early 1930s. Both Panofsky and Sedlmayr, for
instance, aimed at a totalizing comprehension of historical phenomena.[113] Both rejected the choice implied by the conventional
dichotomies of connoisseurship and history, form and content.[114]
Both took the risk of extending Riegl's project and trying to make
the individual work of art do more historiographical work than it
was capable of. Both trusted in the fundamental, deep-structural
affinity between works of art and the world at large, what Charles
Rosen calls the "unified stylistic field-theory."[115] One could argue
that the links that Panofsky posited between work and world
under the quasi-philosophical rubric "symbolic forms" were as
irrational and unprovable as any of Sedlmayr's.[116] Peter Betthausen gave the example of the juxtaposition of Neoplatonic ideas
and Michelangelo's drawings in the article "The Neoplatonic
Movement and Michelangelo" (1939).[117] Many aspects of the

"Viennese" Panofsky survived the emigration to America and his turn to plain English and common sense. Indeed none of Panofsky's eidetic intuitions was more creative, and more difficult to prove, than the extended analogy between the Gothic cathedral and the Scholastic encyclopedia in *Gothic Architecture and Scholasticism* (1951).[118] This is not such a different kind of book from the treatise on the cathedral written the year before by his methodological "evil twin" Sedlmayr.[119] Only a decade later the comparison between the two methods was explicitly drawn by George Kubler when — in order to dismiss them both as wishful thinking, basically — he described iconology and *Strukturanalyse* ("configurational analysis") as two modes of inquiry into "adherent meaning," with *Strukturanalyse* slightly preferable for being more "perplexed" about discontinuities in the cultures under study.[120]

In the end, it is impossible to normalize Sedlmayr. The totalitarian vision is intrinsic to his art history. Joseph Koerner showed this in a reading of Sedlmayr's essay "Bruegel's *Macchia*."[121] Sedlmayr, in his formal analysis of the atomized blobs of subhumanity on Bruegel's picture surfaces, recapitulated the pitiless vertical pitch of Bruegel's own society and the inhumanity of his original aristocratic patrons and admirers. In this sense Sedlmayr was truly re-creating the work of the historical artist, just as he had promised to do in "Toward a Rigorous Study of Art " (pp. 147–48). His Bruegel essay is a chilling, anachronistic reanimation of a lost ideological world. Interpretative violence, which we prize in Riegl, Warburg, or Pächt, here converges with ideological violence.

But it is important to realize that the objection is not to Sedlmayr's historical interpretation of Bruegel as such, but to the role that he forces Bruegel to play within his own grandiose, bitter critique of modernity. Sedlmayr's historical reading of Bruegel's paintings is powerful and not so easy to overturn.[122] And that reading is the direct product of the insight into the meaning of the color patch in the encyclopedic paintings. Empirical research on its own could never have arrived at the link between the color patch and the worldview. Empiricism is supposed to provide a methodological guarantee against subjective, "interested" interpretations and pernicious ideological mystifications. Many today doubt that empiricism can actually do this. But even if it could, it is not clear that it would be worth sacrificing the historical insights yielded by the anti-empiricist, allegorical method. One might well decide to take one's chances with allegory.

Even more disquieting than this comparison of art historical methodologies is the comparison between the attitudes of Sedlmayr, on the one hand, and of the liberal émigré art historians, on the other, toward modern art. What is striking is Sedlmayr's extreme sensitivity, to the point of inflammation, to modernity and to modern art. Whereas Panofsky and Gombrich, as has often been noted, made no serious effort to understand the art of their time or the function of art in modern life, Sedlmayr hated modern art and wrote quite a lot about it. Not only that, but in his excoriating commentary on modern painting, sculpture, and architecture he managed to hit almost all the right targets. Sedlmayr derided the eighteenth-century French architects Ledoux, Boullée and Lequeu for detaching their utopian buildings from their natural base on the earth.[123] He chose a Duchamp ready-made, the *Porte-Bouteilles* (1914), as the first illustration in his book *Die Revolution der modernen Kunst*. He saw how Walt Disney's cartoons transformed the oneiric, crossbred fantasies of Grandville — sickly, unlawful, and terrifying to Baudelaire — into "an idiom of innocence, a fairy idiom of pure fun."[124] The anti-heroes of *Art in Crisis: The Lost Center* are Bosch, Bruegel, Goya, Ledoux, Friedrich, Cézanne. Sedlmayr's vilification of modern art was even more perspicacious than the National Socialists' *Degenerate Art* exhibition eleven years earlier.

Sedlmayr lamented the tumult of postwar European society but refused to acknowledge how it had all come about. Insolently he compared the images of the European cities reduced to rubble by total war to the "de-compositions" of surrealism, as if all nations somehow shared the responsibility for the war, as they surely did share the blame for surrealism.[125] For modernism was, of course, a European disease: a cosmopolitan and urban condition. Sedlmayr did not even look to German culture as a source of aesthetic salvation, except possibly in architecture.[126] In fact for Sedlmayr the trouble had begun in the age of the ascendant nation-state. The solution was to be found, if anywhere, in the feudal, Christian Middle Ages.[127]

It is hard for us today to understand the impact Sedlmayr's book had in 1948.[128] At the time, he was the only German art historian of premodern art writing about the function and meaning of modern art and was recognized as such even by his enemies. There was no German equivalent to Meyer Schapiro. Sedlmayr's theses were publicly debated at the Second Conference of German Art Historians in 1949.[129] In 1950 he was one of two featured speakers, alongside the Bauhaus artist and teacher Johannes Itten, on the first evening of the Darmstädter Gespräch, a major conference of artists, art historians, philosophers, theologians, sociologists, and scientists.[130] The topic of the conference was "The Image of Man in Our Time." Sedlmayr's lecture was interrupted by whistling, stamping, heckling, including the cry "Heil Hitler!," but also applause. Sedlmayr's surprising ally at the conference turned out to be none other than Adorno, who had returned from the United States only the year before. It has been suggested that Sedlmayr was perhaps one of the few participants who had any clear idea of who Adorno was.[131] In his lecture Sedlmayr cited Adorno on Schoenberg. Later, in 1955 and 1976, he would again quote Adorno in his writings.[132] At the Darmstädter Gespräch, Adorno sided with

Sedlmayr against Franz Roh and others who spoke of the reconcil-
iatory function of art: "As much as I object to the cultural pessimism
Sedlmayr brings to bear, he does on this point quite correctly
define something otherwise neglected by a too unbroken and
naïve belief in progress. Speaking dialectically, I would say that
the harmony of an artwork consists in its bringing the riven, itself
unreconciled, to unmisplaced expression, and that it withstand the
riven."[133] Adorno conceded in 1958–1959 that some of his writing
on modern music ran "parallel to the work of Sedlmayr."[134] Werner
Hofmann has pointed out that Sedlmayr's entire polemic was a
partly understandable response to the ubiquitous postwar apolo-
getics for autonomous art, which wanted to insulate art and exempt
it from any "interrogation" whatsoever.[135] Many artists were sym-
pathetic. Georg Grosz, for example, saluted Sedlmayr in a letter
in 1955.[136] Even Gerhard Richter has commented ruefully on the
"loss of the center" in modern art, with deliberately perverse reference to Sedlmayr but without irony.[137] It has to be admitted that
with his instinct for distortion, degradation, catastrophe, chaos,
deadpan evacuations of meaning, and Nietzschean mismatches
between subject and object, and his fascination with the ruin, the
fragment, and the spectacle, Sedlmayr never lost sight of "art."

The contrast with Panofsky is sharp. After reading Sedlmayr,
one starts to wish that Panofsky's neat analogies between modernist painting and the early twentieth-century "worldview" had
been somehow more anguished. Panofsky the cultural historian
simply absorbed Picasso into the "unified stylistic field" by comparing cubism to Einstein's theory of relativity.[138] In 1933 Panofsky (with his co-author Fritz Saxl) expressed the naive confidence
that artistic and cultural crisis could be "overcome" by the "recourse" to classicism, as it always had been; here too he invoked
Picasso.[139] It is as if Panofsky and Sedlmayr were recognizing the
same crisis, but that one of them considered Picasso part of the

solution and the other considered him part of the problem. Gombrich for his part has affected blasé or supercilious indifference to the art of his own time.[140] His standard model of "making vs. matching" — conformity to schemata vs. direct imitation of nature — leaves little room for a transfiguring artistic vision.[141] Panofsky and Gombrich's discreet response to modern art's promulgation of the abject, the entropic, and the anarchic was to ignore it. Sedlmayr, by contrast, did not repress his panic but rather let it spill out into tasteless, gothic demagoguery.

Strukturanalyse managed to coordinate historical and contemporary art more successfully than other art historical methods because it converted every work, in effect, into a modernist work.[142] *Strukturanalyse* drained works of art not only of mimetic reference but also of meaning in general, almost automatically, and left the works looking more malign, refractory, or prodigal than ever. Panofsky and Gombrich, by contrast, tried to quell the instability they found in past works of art by injecting them whenever possible with redeeming universal or humanist content. *Strukturanalyse*, by liberating itself from any empiricist superintendence, encouraged aggressive, "interested" responses to older art, perhaps the only appropriate kind of response. *Strukturanalyse* became a vehement interpretative gesture that dislocated the historical work and disbelieved the work's own proposed relationships to matter, ideas, and power. *Strukturanalyse* repealed the coding operations and disassembled the illusionistic devices that made ordinary pictorial signification possible. In doing so, the method generated projections of works of art that no longer had any form, neither ideal form with its analogy to a transcendental content nor its scandalous opposite. The brutality of interpretation obliterated or "insulted" the logical distinction between form and content, declassified and abased its objects, "sacrificed" them; but it could not be said to neglect them (Georges Bataille).[143]

Sedlmayr and Novotny — more than Pächt or Kaschnitz, who were interested in art but not what had become of it — used *Strukturanalyse* literally to explain the origins of the modern in art and architecture. They showed how Bruegel and Cézanne neutralized aura — the apparent distance of the near, in Benjamin's terms — by converting it into estrangement — *Entfremdung*, the artificial, "aesthetic" unfamiliarity of the familiar.[144] Their own prose mimetically reproduces the process of disenchantment registered in the works of art. The visual rhymes and citations in Bruegel have their counterpart in the wild analogies and the mannered, agitated overuse of quotation marks in Sedlmayr's own texts; while Cézanne's deadpan transcriptions of perspectival grids in the fields before him, with orthogonals that bend at the crucial moment and thus empty the landscape of all its customary meaning and pathos, almost meet their match in Novotny's relentless, suspenseful formal analyses. And just as formal rhymes, citation, and surface pattern permitted Bruegel to overcome the High Renaissance and Cézanne to overcome impressionism, the shift from the *Kunstwollen* to *Struktur* allowed the followers of Riegl to treat the image not as the notation of a perception but as a metaphor for perception, and thus to banish all lingering nineteenth-century anthropomorphism from the formalist method. *Strukturanalyse* was thus not only a permanent diagnosis of modernism: it was itself a modernist way of seeing. Sedlmayr thought that *Struktur* could only be detected by an aesthetic sensibility; mere historical form, by contrast, was visible even to the *Kunstblinde*, those blind to art.[145] Rosenauer's comparison of *Strukturanalyse* to Neue Sachlichkeit painting has already been mentioned. Sauerländer compared Sedlmayr's vision of the Gothic cathedral to the utopian glass architecture of the 1910s.[146] Meyer Schapiro had seen all this already in 1936: "When we observe the broad abstractions and unverifiable subtleties," he wrote,

the straining to create insights, the conceits of formal observation
that often crop up in such writings, we are reminded of the practices
of contemporary art and art criticism in which the inventive sensibility creates its own formalized objects, delights in its own "laws," and
enjoys its absolutely private fantasy, justifying this activity as an
experimental system of artistic deduction or as an intuitive perception of essences and wholes. (pp. 461–62)

It is as if Sedlmayr in his interpretative attack on the past were
simply emulating the contemporary artist. With his historical
fables about art, Sedlmayr was trying to "save the appearances," to
rescue art, which all at once seemed to him to have been abandoned by God. He takes a vernacular-Catholic approach to the
problem of the destiny of art; his aesthetic eschatology is the true
reverse and complement of the Marxist theory of art. Panofsky,
a "Lutheran" in this respect, had little sympathy for enthralling
fables or allegories that would knit the history of art back together again. Panofsky stood by the classical reading strategies —
postmedieval and pre-Romantic — and thus preserved the insu-
lation of scholarship from art; and by the end he was perhaps
prepared to let art die for lack of any vehement response to it.
Sedlmayr, by contrast, leaves an impression of terrible inquietude
and aggrievance. Sedlmayr the Fascist constantly defined margin-
ality, distortion, and degradation against an ideal of balance and
perfection. But in the event, he never stopped writing about Pieter
Bruegel; about the phantasmagoric spaces of Justinian's basilica or
the Gothic cathedral, grotesquely outsized technological marvels;
about the irreverent negative volumes of Borromini and Fischer
von Erlach or the ludic nihilism of rococo ornament. The ideal is
nowhere to be found.

Notes

1. Sedlmayr, "Die Quintessenz der Lehren Riegls," in Riegl, *Gesammelte Aufsätze*, pp. 11–34; reprinted as "Kunstgeschichte als Stilgeschichte," in Sedlmayr, *Kunst und Wahrheit*, pp. 32–48.

2. Although Sedlmayr derived the concept from Riegl, the term "structure" never figured in Riegl's own writings, any more than it had in the *Cours de linguistique générale* of his contemporary Ferdinand de Saussure.

3. Pächt, *Methodisches zur kunsthistorischen Praxis*, p. 232, translated as *The Practice of Art History: Reflections on Method* (London: Harvey Miller, 1999), pp. 67–68.

4. The entire run of the journal has been reprinted: *Kritische Berichte zur kunstgeschichtlichen Literatur (1927–1937)* (Hildesheim and New York: Olms, 1972). See also Dilly, *Deutsche Kunsthistoriker 1933–1945*, pp. 17–22.

5. Sedlmayr, "Vermutungen und Fragen zur Bestimmung der altfranzösischen Kunst," *Festschrift Wilhelm Pinder* (Leipzig: Seemann, 1938), pp. 9–27. Cf. Sedlmayr, *Epochen und Werke* (Vienna and Munich: Herold, 1960), vol. 2, pp. 322–41.

6. On art historians under National Socialism, see most recently Dilly, *Deutsche Kunsthistoriker 1933–1945*; and Halbertsma, *Wilhelm Pinder und die deutsche Kunstgeschichte*, pp. 129–66.

7. Sedlmayr, *Art in Crisis: The Lost Center* (London: Hollis and Carter, 1957; Chicago: Regnery, 1958).

8. Sauerländer, "Zersplitterte Erinnerung," in Sitt (ed.), *Kunsthistoriker in eigener Sache*, p. 311. Sybille Dürr, *Zur Geschichte des Faches Kunstgeschichte an der Universität München* (Munich: Tuduv, 1993), pp. 74 and 78.

9. For Hofmann, see "Zu einer Theorie der Kunstgeschichte," *Zeitschrift für Kunstgeschichte* 14 (1951), pp. 118–23 (Hofmann's first publication); and "Fragen der Strukturanalyse," pp. 143–69; both reprinted in Hofmann, *Bruchlinien*, pp. 11–18 and 70–89; and finally a response to Belting that amounts to a partial defense of the Vienna School tradition, "Was bleibt von der Wiener Schule?" pp. 4–7.

For Sauerländer, see "Hans Sedlmayrs 'Verlust der Mitte,'" pp. 536–42.

Imdahl compares his own interpretative approach to Sedlmayr's in "Bis an die Grenze des Aussagbaren," in Sitt (ed.), *Kunsthistoriker in eigener Sache*, pp. 250 and 259–60. See also his many remarks on Sedlmayr's Cézanne interpretation, in Imdahl, *Gesammelte Schriften* (Frankfurt: Suhrkamp, 1996), vol. 3, passim (see index).

For Warnke, see "Apologet der Mitte" (1966), reprinted in Warnke, *Künstler, Kunsthistoriker, Museen: Beiträge zu einer kritischen Kunstgeschichte* (Luzern and Frankfurt: Bucher, 1979), pp. 74–76.

For Belting, see *The End of the History of Art?* (Chicago: University of Chicago Press, 1987), pp. 20–21.

10. Ernst Gombrich, review of *Kunstgeschichte und Kunsttheorie im 19. Jahrhundert, Art Bulletin* 46 (1964), pp. 418–20; see the response by the volume's authors and Gombrich's reply, *Art Bulletin* 47 (1965), pp. 307–09; and Gombrich, "Kunstwissenschaft und Psychologie vor fünfzig Jahren," pp. 99–104. See Bakoš, "The Vienna School's Hundred and Sixty-eighth Graduate." But see also Gombrich's close engagement with Sedlmayr's early writings in his dissertation, "Zum Werke Giulio Romanos," *Jahrbuch der Kunsthistorischen Sammlungen*, n. s., 9 (1935), esp. pp. 137–45.

11. Gombrich's discussion of Riegl in *The Sense of Order: A Study in the Psychology of Decorative Art* (Ithaca, NY: Cornell University Press, 1979), pp. 195–204, for example, is balanced but suggests the limits of Riegl's thought rather than its vitality.

12. Anthony Blunt, *Borromini* (London: Allen Lane, 1979), p. 224.

13. Wolfgang Kemp, *Der Anteil des Betrachters: Rezeptionsästhetische Studien zur Malerei des 19. Jahrhunderts* (Munich: Mäander, 1983), pp. 20–24; see also Kemp (ed.), *Der Betrachter ist im Bild: Kunstwissenschaft und Rezeptionsästhetik* (1985; 2nd ed., Berlin: Reimer, 1992), pp. 17–20. Leo Steinberg compared Riegl's revaluation of pre-Rembrandt group portraits to Picasso's admiration for Iberian and tribal art in "The Philosophical Brothel" (1972), reprinted in *October* 44 (1988), pp. 13–14. Hubert Damisch, *Théorie du /nuage/* (Paris: Seuil, 1972), pp. 20–23. Yve-Alain Bois, *Painting as Model* (Cambridge, MA: MIT Press, 1991), for example, p. 259 n.1. Jean-Louis Schefer invokes both Riegl

and Pächt in *Question de style* (Paris: L'Harmattan, 1995), pp. 15–16.

14. Paul Feyerabend, "Science as Art: A Discussion of Riegl's Theory of Art and an Attempt to Apply It to the Sciences," *Art + Text* 12–13 (1984), pp. 16–46; German version in *Wissenschaft als Kunst* (Frankfurt: Suhrkamp, 1984), pp. 15–84.

15. Sedlmayr, "Die Quintessenz der Lehren Riegls," pp. xxx-xxxi. Spengler (1926 ed.) mentions Riegl with respect to the development of the acanthus motif.

16. Frederic J. Schwartz, *The Werkbund: Design Theory and Mass Culture Before the First World War* (New Haven, CT: Yale University Press, 1996), pp. 21–24.

17. Lukács, *History and Class Consciousness* (1922; reprint, Cambridge, MA: MIT Press, 1971), p. 153.

18. Hermann Bahr, *Expressionismus* (Munich: Delphin, 1920), pp. 68–75; *Expressionism* (London: Frank Henderson, 1925), pp. 51–56 ("Who Is Riegl?"), esp. p. 55. Some of Bahr's remarks on Riegl are excerpted in Rose-Carol Washton Long (ed.), *German Expressionism: Documents from the End of the Wilhelmine Empire to the Rise of National Socialism* (New York: G. K. Hall, 1993), pp. 88–91, esp. p. 90.

19. Benjamin's admiration for Riegl was first noted by Kemp, "Walter Benjamin und die Kunstwissenschaft, Teil 1." See also Charles Rosen, "The Ruins of Walter Benjamin" (1977), reprinted in Gary Smith (ed.), *On Walter Benjamin: Critical Essays and Reflections* (Cambridge, MA: MIT Press, 1988), pp. 134–35; and Levin, "Walter Benjamin and the Theory of Art History," pp. 78–80.

20. Cited in Bois, *Painting as Model*, p. xviii. On Riegl and Bakhtin, see also Olin, *Forms of Representation in Alois Riegl's Theory of Art*, p. 181. On Riegl and Russian formalism, see Clausberg, "Wiener Schule — Russischer Formalismus — Prager Strukturalismus." For Riegl's reception by Karl Mannheim and Ernst Bloch, see Olin, *Forms of Representation*, p. 190 n.10. For the reception of Riegl by Italian critics and art historians, see Sandro Scarrocchia, *Studi su Alois Riegl* (n.p.: Nuova Alfa, 1986).

21. The most complete expositions of Sedlmayr's career and writings are

Schneider, "Hans Sedlmayr (1896–1984)"; and Frodl-Kraft, "Hans Sedlmayr (1896–1984)," the latter unfortunately lacking any critical edge.

The best overall treatment of the New Vienna School is Rosenauer, "Zur neuen Wiener Schule der Kunstgeschichte." The most intensive theoretical analysis is Dittmann, *Stil, Symbol, Struktur.* For further discussions and assessments of *Strukturanalyse*, see the bibliography in this volume.

22. See, however, Nodelman, "Structural Analysis in Art and Anthropology." Some briefer references: George Kubler, *The Shape of Time* (New Haven, CT: Yale University Press, 1962), p. 27; Jules Prown, "Mind in Matter: An Introduction to Material Culture Theory and Method," *Winterthur Portfolio* 17 (1972), p. 9 n.15; Paul Crossley, "In Search of an Iconography of Medieval Architecture," in *Symbolae Historiae Artium,* Festschrift Lech Kalinowski (Warsaw: Państwowe Wydawnictwo Naukowe, 1986), pp. 55–66; Crossley, "Medieval Architecture and Meaning: The Limits of Iconography," *Burlington Magazine* 130 (1988), pp. 118–19; Thomas Da Costa Kaufmann, response to "Questionnaire on Visual Culture," *October* 77 (1996), pp. 47–48. Svetlana Alpers invoked both Riegl and Pächt in her campaign to liberate the historiography of northern art from the norms established in the Italian Renaissance in *The Art of Describing: Dutch Art in the Seventeenth Century* (Chicago: University of Chicago Press, 1983), p. xx.

23. See Panofsky, "The Concept of Artistic Volition" (1920), trans. Kenneth J. Northcott and Joel Snyder, *Critical Inquiry* 8 (1981), pp. 17–34; Michael Ann Holly, *Panofsky and the Foundations of Art History* (Ithaca, NY: Cornell University Press, 1984), pp. 69–96, also pp. 101–02 on Sedlmayr; and Christopher S. Wood, introduction to Panofsky, *Perspective as Symbolic Form* (New York: Zone Books, 1991), pp. 7–24.

24. Wolfgang Kemp makes this point in "Walter Benjamin und die Kunstwissenschaft," p. 47.

25. Schapiro seems to have misunderstood this. He also saw it as ultimately a false dichotomy but argued for a colonization in the opposite direction: the second, interpretative stage ought to be carried out on the principles of the first, namely, reason and inference (p. 456).

26. Gombrich in the review of the Sedlmayr Festschrift, *Art Bulletin* 46 (1964), p. 419.

27. Sedlmayr, "Die Quintessenz der Lehren Riegls," p. xxxi.

28. Gombrich, *In Search of Cultural History* (Oxford: Oxford University Press, 1969).

29. Riegl, *Late Roman Art Industry*; *Problems of Style: Foundations for a History of Ornament*; Olin, *Forms of Representation*; Iversen, *Alois Riegl*.

30. The reliefs on the Vapheio cups are no longer considered genre scenes. For recent scholarship, see Ellen N. Davis, "The Vapheio Cups: One Minoan and One Mycenean?" *Art Bulletin* 56 (1974), pp. 473–87; and Castriota in his annotations to Riegl, *Problems of Style*, p. 340 n.v.

31. Kaschnitz von Weinberg cites Konrad Fiedler to the same effect in his essay "Bemerkungen zur Struktur der altitalischen Plastik" (1933), reprinted in Kaschnitz, *Kleine Schriften zur Struktur*, p. 40.

32. A number of passages from this book, including some duplicated in this *Reader* (pp. 379–82, 393), were translated in Judith Wechsler (ed.), *Cézanne in Perspective* (Englewood Cliffs, NJ: Prentice Hall, 1975), pp. 96–107.

33. For Tietze, see *Die Methode der Kunstgeschichte* (Leipzig: Seemann, 1913), dedicated to Wickhoff and Riegl. For Heidrich, see *Zur Geschichte und Methode der Kunstgeschichte* (Basel: Schwabe, 1917). Panofsky's key theoretical essays are collected in *Aufsätze zu Grundfragen der Kunstwissenschaft* (Berlin: Spiess, 1985). For Gantner, see *Revision der Kunstgeschichte* (Vienna: Schroll, 1932). For Wind, see "Der ästhetische und kunstwissenschaftliche Gegenstand" (Ph. D. diss., Hamburg, 1922); and "Zur Systematik der künstlerischen Probleme," *Zeitschrift für Ästhetik und allgemeine Kunstwissenschaft* 18 (1924), pp. 438–86. See also the 1,044-page treatise on methodology published by Paul Frankl (1878–1962), *Das System der Kunstwissenschaft* (Brno and Leipzig: Rohrer, 1938).

34. Waetzoldt, *Deutsche Kunsthistoriker*, 2 vols. (Leipzig: Seemann, 1921–1924).

35. On the vigorous empiricist-realist opposition to neo-Kantianism, especially in Austria, see Olin, *Forms of Representation*, pp. 103–104.

36. Konrad Fiedler, "Moderner Naturalismus und künstlerische Wahrheit" (1881); "Observations on the Nature and History of Architecture" (1878), in Harry Francis Mallgrave and Eleftherios Ikonomou, eds., *Empathy, Form, and Space: Problems in German Aesthetics, 1873–1893* (Santa Monica, CA: Getty Center, 1994), pp. 125–46. Fiedler, *Schriften zur Kunst*, 2 vols., reprint of 1913/1914 edition with additional material and bibliography by Gottfried Böhm (Munich: Fink, 1971); and *Schriften über Kunst* (Cologne: DuMont, 1977). On the neo-Kantian and formalist traditions in German art history, see Podro, *The Critical Historians of Art*; and the introduction by Mallgrave and Ikonomou to *Empathy, Form, and Space*, pp. 1–85.

37. Adolf von Hildebrand, "The Problem of Form in the Fine Arts" (1893), in Mallgrave and Ikonomou, *Empathy, Form, and Space*, pp. 227–79. On Fiedler and Hildebrand, see Michael Podro, *The Manifold in Perception: Theories of Art from Kant to Hildebrand* (Oxford: Oxford University Press, 1972), pp. 111–20 and 82–87.

38. Benjamin did notice and admire his work: see Kemp, "Walter Benjamin und die Kunstwissenschaft, Teil 2," *Kritische Berichte* 3 (1975), pp. 5–25; see also Edgar Wind, "Warburgs Begriff der Kulturwissenschaft und seine Bedeutung für die Ästhetik," *Zeitschrift für Ästhetik und allgemeine Kunstwissenschaft*, 4. Kongress für Ästhetik und allgemeine Kunstwissenschaft, supplement, 25 (1931), pp. 163–79. On Warburg, see fundamentally Ernst Gombrich, *Aby Warburg: An Intellectual Biography* (London: Warburg Institute, 1970); Aby Warburg, *Ausgewählte Schriften und Würdigungen*, ed. Dieter Wuttke (Baden-Baden: Koerner, 1980); Werner Hofmann, ed., *Die Menschenrechte des Auges: Über Aby Warburg* (Frankfurt: Europäische Verlagsanstalt, 1980); Podro, *Critical Historians of Art*, pp. 158–77; Silvia Ferretti, *Cassirer, Panofsky, and Warburg: Symbol, Art, and History* (New Haven, CT: Yale University Press, 1989); and Horst Bredekamp et al., *Aby Warburg*, Akten des internationalen Symposions Hamburg 1990 (Weinheim: VCH, Acta Humaniora, 1991).

39. Heinrich Wölfflin, "Prolegomena to a Psychology of Architecture," in Mallgrave and Ikonomou, *Empathy, Form, and Space*, pp. 149–90; *Principles of Art History* (London: Bell, 1932). On Wölfflin, see esp. Podro, *Critical Historians of*

Art, pp. 98–151; Joan Hart, "Reinterpreting Wölfflin: Neo-Kantianism and Hermeneutics," *Art Journal* 42 (1982), pp. 292–300; Martin Warnke, "On Heinrich Wölfflin," *Representations* 27 (1989), pp. 172–87; the essays by Hart, Warnke, and Roland Recht in Jacques Thuillier (ed.), *Relire Wölfflin* (Paris: Musée du Louvre, 1995); Michael Ann Holly, *Past Looking: Historical Imagination and the Rhetoric of the Image* (Ithaca, NY: Cornell University Press, 1996), pp. 91–111; and Frederic J. Schwartz, "Cathedrals and Shoes: Concepts of Style in Wölfflin and Adorno," *New German Critique* 76 (1999), pp. 3–48.

40. On the pointed Gothic shoe, see Wölfflin, "Prolegomena to a Psychology of Architecture," p. 183. On the shift from "quality" to the mode of representation, see Wölfflin, *Principles of Art History*, p. 11.

41. On the neo-idealism of Croce and the literary scholar Karl Vossler, and their influence on Schlosser, see Michael Podro, "Against Formalism: Schlosser on *Stilgeschichte*," in *Wien und die Entwicklung der kunsthistorischen Methode*, pp. 37–43.

42. See Levin, "Walter Benjamin and the Theory of Art History," pp 79–80, on Benjamin's attitude toward Wölfflin.

43. Olin, *Forms of Representation*, pp. 109–10.

44. On his interest in perceptual psychology, however, especially Helmholtz's ideas about the role of touch, see Olin, *Forms of Representation*, pp. 132–37. *Strukturanalyse* extended this practical exclusion of the psychological even further. Kaschnitz in his 1929 review of *Late Roman Art Industry* questioned the role in Riegl's art history of the subjective beholder, reconstructible only through positivist theories of perception; see Kaschnitz, *Kleine Schriften zur Struktur*, pp. 4–7.

45. Hernand, *Literaturwissenschaft und Kunstwissenschaft*, pp. 8–11 and 12.

46. Cf. the rereading of the early twentieth-century art historians proposed by Claire Farago, "'Vision Itself Has Its History': 'Race,' Nation, and Renaissance Art History," in Farago (ed.), *Reframing the Renaissance: Visual Culture in Europe and Latin America, 1450–1650* (New Haven, CT: Yale University Press, 1995), pp. 67–88. See also Keith Moxey, *The Practice of Theory* (Ithaca, NY: Cornell University Press, 1994), pp. 68–70, on the connection between Riegl and nationalist elements in Panofsky.

47. Cf. Warnke's analysis of Wölfflin's political silences, "On Heinrich Wölfflin."

48. See Riegl, "The Modern Cult of Monuments," p. 22.

49. On Wickhoff, see Ioli Kalavrezou, "Franz Wickhoff: Kunstgeschichte als Wissenschaft," in *Wien und die Entwicklung der kunsthistorischen Methode*, pp. 17–22. For the early history of the Vienna School of art history, see the monograph by Schlosser, "Die Wiener Schule der Kunstgeschichte," pp. 145–228.

50. Schlosser barely mentioned him in his history of the Vienna School, "Die Wiener Schule der Kunstgeschichte," p. 194. Pupils of Strzygowski like Demus and Novotny are omitted from the list of students. See Eva Frodl-Kraft, "Eine Aporie und der Versuch ihrer Deutung: Josef Strzygowski — Julius von Schlosser," *Wiener Jahrbuch für Kunstgeschichte* 42 (1989), pp. 7–52.

51. See the entry by Edwin Lachnit in *The Dictionary of Art* (London: Macmillan, 1996), vol. 9, pp. 472–73.

52. Dvořák, *Kunstgeschichte als Geistesgeschichte* (Munich: Piper, 1924); translated as *The History of Art as the History of Ideas*, trans. John Hardy (London and Boston: Routledge, 1984).

53. See Kultermann, *Geschichte der Kunstgeschichte*, pp. 350–73 (pp. 199–210 of the English translation, *History of Art History*), on "expressionist" art history. Max J. Friedländer, on reading an obituary of Dvořák by Otto Benesch, lamented the "megalomania" and the "sorry results" of Viennese art history; see *Reminiscences and Reflections* (Greenwich, CT: New York Graphic Society, 1969), p. 50.

54. Worringer, *Abstraktion und Einfühlung* (1908), translated as *Abstraction and Empathy* (New York: International Universities Press, 1953). See Bushart, *Der Geist der Gotik und die expressionistische Kunst;* and Neil H. Donahue, ed., *Invisible Cathedrals: The Expressionist Art History of Wilhelm Worringer* (University Park, PA: Pennsylvania State University Press, 1995).

55. See esp. Burger, *Cézanne und Hodler: Einführung in die Probleme der Malerei der Gegenwart* (Munich: Delphin, 1913), and *Einführung in die moderne Kunst*, Handbuch der Kunstwissenschaft (Berlin: Athenaion, 1917). On Burger, see Udo Kultermann, *Geschichte der Kunstgeschichte*, pp. 362–66; *History of*

Art History, pp. 204–07; and Bushart, *Der Geist der Gotik*, pp. 107–20.

56. See Halbertsma, *Wilhelm Pinder und die deutsche Kunstgeschichte*; and Robert Suckale, "Wilhelm Pinder und die deutsche Kunstwissenschaft nach 1945," *Kritische Berichte* 14, no.4 (1986), pp. 5–17, a kind of apology for Pinder; cf. the response by Klaus-Heinrich Meyer in *Kritische Berichte* 15, no.1 (1987), pp. 41–48. Note that Wolfgang Kemp included a short essay by Pinder in his anthology of reception-oriented art history, *Der Betrachter ist im Bild*, 2nd ed., pp. 51–59.

57. Burger, *Einführung in die moderne Kunst*, p. 37.

58. Pinder, "Deutsche Kunstgeschichte," *Deutsche Wissenschaft, Arbeit und Aufgabe* (Leipzig: Hirzel, 1939), p. 13. See also the essay "Kunstwissenschaft" by Alfred Stange in the same volume, pp. 9–10.

59. Two other highly creative formalist art historians admired by the Viennese, but without connections to Vienna, were Theodor Hetzer (1890–1946) and Hans Jantzen (1881–1967).

60. Frodl-Kraft, "Hans Sedlmayr," p. 11.

61. See Schlosser's own memoir, "Die Wiener Schule der Kunstgeschichte," pp. 201–10; Podro, "Against Formalism: Schlosser on *Stilgeschichte*," pp. 37–43; and the issue of *Kritische Berichte* 16, no.4 (1988) devoted to Schlosser.

62. See the list of Viennese dissertations in Schlosser, "Die Wiener Schule der Kunstgeschichte," pp. 213–26.

63. Gombrich, "'Wenn's euch Ernst ist, was zu sagen...' — Wandlungen in der Kunstgeschichtsbetrachtung," in Sitt (ed.), *Kunsthistoriker in eigener Sache*, p. 84. See also *Meditations on a Hobby Horse* (London: Phaidon, 1963), p. 112, where Gombrich says his sympathies were then divided but that he came to side with the "mellow skepticism" of Schlosser.

64. Panofsky, "Der Begriff des Kunstwollens" (1920), translated as "The Concept of Artistic Volition," *Critical Inquiry* 8 (1981), pp. 17–34; quote from p. 30.

65. Panofsky, *Perspective as Symbolic Form*. On Riegl and Panofsky, see also Iversen, *Alois Riegl*, pp. 149–66.

66. Sedlmayr, "Die Quintessenz der Lehren Riegls," pp. xviii–xx. Note that

Sedlmayr does not even mention Riegl in his manifesto "Toward a Rigorous Study of Art."

67. Sedlmayr, "Gestaltetes Sehen," *Belvedere* 8 (1925), pp. 65–73. See also the analysis in Sedlmayr, *Die Architektur Borrominis* (Berlin: Frankfurter Verlagsanstalt, 1930), pp. 24–36. See the account of Sedlmayr's analysis in Leo Steinberg, *Borromini's San Carlo alle Quattro Fontane* (Ph.D. diss, New York University, 1959; New York: Garland, 1977), pp. 119, 187, 346–50.

68. The significance of Gestalt theory for *Strukturanalyse* is sometimes overrated. Sedlmayr seems to have borrowed the concept of Gestalt as a metaphor for artistic structure but without any deep commitment to the discipline of psychology. In his essay on Riegl he also cites the sociologist Alfred Vierkandt.

69. Sedlmayr wrote his dissertation (1925), many subsequent articles, and a magisterial monograph (1956) on Fischer. On Sedlmayr's position within the literature on Fischer, and in particular on Sedlmayr's politically charged notion of a *Reichsstil*, see Friedrich Pollerross, "Johann Bernhard Fischer von Erlach und das österreichische 'Entweder-und-oder' in der Architektur"; and Hellmut Lorenz, "Dichtung und Wahrheit — das Bild Johann Bernhard Fischers von Erlach in der Kunstgeschichte," in Pollerross (ed.), *Fischer von Erlach und die Wiener Barocktradition* (Vienna: Böhlau, 1995), esp. pp. 20–30 and 130–31; cf. my reading of the "rococo" Sedlmayr to Holly's analysis of Wölfflin's writing on the Baroque in *Past Looking*, pp. 91–111.

70. See, however, the remarks on "unspecifiable skills" by Michael Polanyi, *Personal Knowledge: Towards a Post-Critical Philosophy* (Chicago: University of Chicago Press, 1958), pp. 49–65, esp. pp. 54–55 on Gestalt theory and connoisseurship.

71. Kaschnitz von Weinberg, review article in *Gnomon*, reprinted in *Kleine Schriften zur Struktur*, pp. 10–12.

72. Kemp, "Alois Riegl (1858–1905)," p. 47. Kemp remarks that Riegl, like Freud, did not want to contribute to the "crisis of positivism."

73. Rosenauer, "Zur neuen Wiener Schule der Kunstgeschichte," pp. 75–76.

74. Frodl-Kraft, "Hans Sedlmayr," p. 27 n.89.

75. On the correspondence between Pächt and Schapiro, which began in

1934 but does not survive in full, and their disagreement about the intellectual legitimacy of national stylistic constants, see the memoir by Alexander, "Otto Pächt, 1902–1988," pp. 456–57.

76. Thomas Lersch, "Schlosser schreibt an Vossler: Notizen zu einer Gelehrtenfreundschaft (Fortsetzung)," *Kritische Berichte* 15, no.1 (1989), p. 47. See also Gombrich, "Einige Erinnerungen an Julius von Schlosser als Lehrer," *Kritische Berichte* 16, no. 4 (1988), p. 9.

77. Sedlmayr, "Wien — Stadtgestaltung und Denkmalschutz (1)," *Deutsche Kunst und Denkmalpflege* (1939/1940), p. 159.

78. See his memoir, written at the eastern front in 1942 but only published posthumously, *Das goldene Zeitalter: Eine Kindheit* (Munich: Piper, 1986). Cf Gombrich's somewhat alarming contention that, because he grew up in Vienna when the suburbs were still rural, he understands Beethoven's *Pastoral* Symphony better than we do. This implies that there is also a "good" version of cultural nostalgia; see *In Search of Cultural History*, p. 45.

79. See Schneider, "Revolutionskritik und Kritik der Moderne bei Hans Sedlmayr"; and the scintillating analysis by Beat Wyss, *Trauer der Vollendung: Von der Asthetik des deutschen Idealismus zur Kulturkritik an der Moderne*, 2nd ed. (Munich: Matthes & Seitz, 1989), pp. 283–96.

80. Lukács, "Greatness and Decline of Expressionism" (1934). See the remarks of Karsten Harries, *The Meaning of Modern Art* (Evanston, IL: Northwestern University Press, 1968), pp. 146–49; and Beat Wyss, *Trauer der Vollendung*.

81. Peter-Klaus Schuster, ed., *Die "Künstlerstadt" München 1937: Nationalsozialismus und "Entartete Kunst"* (Munich: Prestel, 1987).

82. Sedlmayr, *Die Revolution der modernen Kunst* (Hamburg: Rowohlt, 1955; Cologne: DuMont, 1985). Dürr, *Zur Geschichte des Faches Kunstgeschichte an der Universität München*, p. 79.

83. Sedlmayr, *Die Entstehung der Kathedrale* (Zurich: Atlantis, 1950).

84. Sedlmayr was especially impressed by the writings of the Romantic Catholic mystic Franz von Baader. See Schneider, "Revolutionskritik und Kritik der Moderne bei Hans Sedlmayr."

85. Sauerländer, "Zersplitterte Erinnerung," in Sitt (ed.), *Kunsthistoriker in eigener Sache*, p. 311; and Dürr, *Zur Geschichte des Faches Kunstgeschichte an der Universität München*, pp. 74–81, on Sedlmayr in Munich.

86. "Jan Vermeer: Der Ruhm der Malkunst" (1951), reprinted in *Kunst und Wahrheit*, pp. 134–43; "Johann Bernhard Fischer von Erlach: Die Schauseite der Karlskirche in Wien" (1956), reprinted in *Kunst und Wahrheit*, pp. 143–52; "Pieter Bruegel: Der Sturz der Blinden" (1957), reprinted in *Epochen und Werke* (Vienna and Munich: Herold, 1959), vol. 1, pp. 319–57.

87. Frodl-Kraft also praises Sedlmayr for having "predicted" in *Verlust der Mitte* (1948) the horror of modern technological warfare as we experienced it in the Gulf War of 1991; see "Hans Sedlmayr," pp. 37, 27 n.89 and 31. Piel in his obituary in *Pantheon* 42 (1984), p. 402, and his afterword to the new edition of Sedlmayr's *Revolution der modernen Kunst* (1985) does not raise the issue of politics.

88. See the memoir by Alexander; and Sitt, "Otto Pächt: Am Anfang war das Auge."

89. Pächt, *Österreichische Tafelmalerei der Gotik* (Augsburg: Filser, 1929).

90. See the remarks on negative beauty in Hofmann, "Fragen der Strukturanalyse," pp. 146–48.

91. Pächt, "Die historische Aufgabe Michael Pachers," *Kunstwissenschaftliche Forschungen* 1 (1931), pp. 95–132; reprinted in Pächt, *Methodisches zur kunsthistorischen Praxis*, pp. 59–106. The piece is too long to have been included in this *Reader*. See the complex response to this essay by Bernhard Decker, "Zur geschichtlichen Dimension in Michael Pachers Altären von Gries und St. Wolfgang," *Städel-Jahrbuch*, n.s., 6 (1977), pp. 293–318.

92. Pächt, "Art Historians and Art Critics — VI: Alois Riegl."

93. Pächt, "Jean Fouquet: A Study of His Style," *Journal of the Warburg and Courtauld Institutes* 4 (1940/1941), pp. 85–102; review articles, *Burlington Magazine* 98 (1956), pp. 110–16 and 267–79. See also *The Master of Mary of Burgundy* (London: Faber and Faber, [1948]). Cf. Podro's somewhat cursory defense of Panofsky against Pächt and Lorenz Dittmann, in *Critical Historians of Art*, pp. 195 and 198–99.

94. Meiss, "'Highlands' in the Lowlands," *Gazette des Beaux-Arts*, 6th ser., 57 (1961), pp. 273–314.

95. These lectures were edited as the long piece "Methodisches zur kunsthistorischen Praxis" in the volume *Methodisches zur kunsthistorischen Praxis*, pp. 187–300, translated as *The Practice of Art History*.

96. Pächt, *Buchmalerei des Mittelalters* (Munich: Prestel, 1984), translated as *Book Illumination in the Middle Ages* (London: Harvey Miller, 1986); *Van Eyck: Die Begründer der altniederländischen Malerei* (Munich: Prestel, 1989), translated as *Van Eyck and the Founders of Early Netherlandish Painting* (London: Harvey Miller, 1994); *Rembrandt* (Munich: Prestel, 1991); *Altniederländische Malerei von Rogier van der Weyden bis Gerard David* (Munich: Prestel, 1994).

97. Matz, "Strukturforschung und Archäologie"; and introduction to *Geschichte der griechischen Kunst*. Kaschnitz von Weinberg, "Struktur."

98. "Biographie des Verfassers," by Marie Luise Kaschnitz (the novelist and poet), in *Kleine Schriften zur Struktur*, p. 232.

99. Roß, *Künstlerische Struktur und Strukturontologie*, esp. pp. 30–42, on the essay on Egyptian sculpture.

100. Kaschnitz also quoted Konrad Fiedler to this effect in "Bemerkungen zur Struktur der altitalischen Plastik," *Studi etruschi* 7 (1933), pp. 135ff., reprinted in *Kleine Schriften zur Struktur*, esp. p. 40. In 1937, Kaschnitz responded in the journal *Critica d'arte* to the charge by the art historian and archaeologist Ranuccio Bianchi-Bandinelli that he had left no room for judgments of value — for a transhistorical ideal of art — in his art history. See Scarrocchia, *Studi su Alois Riegl*, pp. 145–49.

101. Schweitzer, "Strukturforschung in Archäologie und Vorgeschichte," p. 163. Friedrich Matz also published an article in the first number of this journal.

102. Meyer Schapiro, *Cézanne* (New York: Abrams, 1952). See the accounts of Novotny's writings on Cézanne by Judith Wechsler, *The Interpretation of Cézanne* (Ph. D. diss., University of Chicago, 1972; Ann Arbor: UMI Research Press, 1981), pp. 50–53; and by Joseph Rishel in the exhibition catalog *Paul Cézanne* (New York: Abrams in association with the Philadelphia Museum of Art, 1996), pp. 59–62. A sample of Novotny's thinking on Cézanne's landscapes

in English is his essay in the exhibition catalog *Cézanne: The Late Work* (New York: Museum of Modern Art, 1977), pp. 107–11.

103. Karl Oettinger, "Laube, Garten und Wald. Zu einer Theorie der süddeutschen Sakralkunst 1470–1520," in *Festschrift Hans Sedlmayr* (Munich: Beck, 1962), pp. 210–28.

104. An analogous but apparently independent trend was the "north German" structuralism of Carl von Lorck and Willi Drost. See Lorck, *Grundstrukturen des Kunstwerks* (Wildpark-Potsdam: Athenaion, 1926); and Drost, *Danziger Malerei vom Mittelalter bis zum Ende des Barock* (Berlin: Verlag für Kunstwissenschaft, 1938). Lorck and Drost focused intensely on the "work structure" rather than on the psychology of creation or on cultural context; see Michalski, "Zur methodischen Stellung der Wiener Schule in den zwanziger und dreißiger Jahren," p. 89. Evidently the New Vienna School had some resonance in eastern Europe: see Mariusz Bryl, "New Art History: Nauka, Polityka, Obyczaj" (with English summary), *Artium Quaestiones* 7 (1995), pp. 185–218, who recommends *Strukturanalyse* as a solution to the "impasse" of recent Anglo-American art history.

105. Frey, "Der Realitätscharacter des Kunstwerkes" (1934) in Frey, *Kunstwissenschaftliche Grundfragen* (Vienna: Rohrer, 1946), pp. 107–49. See also Frey, "Bemerkungen zur Wiener Schule der Kunstwissenschaft," in Hans Tintelnot (ed.), *Dagobert Frey 1883–1962: Eine Erinnerungsschrift* (Kiel: Kunsthistorisches Institut der Universität Kiel, 1962), pp. 4–15.

106. Schlosser, "Die Wiener Schule der Kunstgeschichte," pp. 201 and 190.

107. Nodelman, "Structural Analysis in Art and Anthropology," compares Kaschnitz von Weinberg to Lévi-Strauss. The comparison between the New Vienna School and Russian and Czech literary formalism has been made by Clausberg, "Wiener Schule — Russischer Formalismus — Prager Strukturalismus"; and Bakoš, "Der tschechoslowakische Strukturalismus und die Kunstgeschichtsschreibung." See also Hofmann's discussion of *Strukturanalyse* and classic linguistic and anthropological structuralism, "Fragen der Strukturanalyse," pp. 159–64.

108. Roland Barthes, "The Structuralist Activity," *Critical Essays* (Evanston, IL: Northwestern University Press, 1977), pp. 214–15.

109. Wollheim, *Painting as an Art* (Princeton, NJ: Princeton University Press, 1987), pp. 46–59.

110. See Susan Buck-Morss, *The Dialectics of Seeing: Walter Benjamin and the Arcades Project* (Cambridge, MA: MIT Press, 1989), pp. 71–74 and 217–27.

111. For Adorno's critique of Benjamin's montage, see Buck-Morss, *Dialectics of Seeing*, p. 73.

112. As is Kaufmann, who compares Sedlmayr to Svetlana Alpers and Michael Baxandall and appears ready to give them all up in his response to "Questionnaire on Visual Culture."

113. Hofmann, "Fragen der Strukturanalyse," pp. 150–51.

114. Dilly, *Deutsche Kunsthistoriker*, p. 15.

115. Rosen, "The Ruins of Walter Benjamin," p. 161.

116. See Wood, introduction to Panofsky, *Perspective as Symbolic Form*.

117. Betthausen, "Erklärung oder Deutung." See Panofsky, "The Neoplatonic Movement and Michelangelo," in *Studies in Iconology: Humanistic Themes in the Art of the Renaissance* (Oxford: Oxford University Press, 1939), pp. 171–230.

118. Panofsky, *Gothic Architecture and Scholasticism* (Latrobe, PA: Archabbey Press, 1951).

119. Neither book has been especially endorsed or amplified by subsequent scholarship on Gothic architecture. However, see the afterword by Pierre Bourdieu to his translation of Panofsky, *Architecture gothique et pensée scolastique* (Paris: Minuit, 1967), pp. 136–67, also translated as "Der Habitus als Vermittlung zwischen Struktur und Praxis," in Bourdieu, *Zur Soziologie der symbolischen Formen* (Frankfurt: Suhrkamp, 1974), pp. 125–58. Bourdieu's argument, not as flattering to Panofsky as he would like it to be, is that the book is a structuralist, even Chomskyan demonstration of the total unity and coherence of Gothic culture.

120. Kubler, *The Shape of Time*, pp. 27–28. Holly compares Panofsky to Kaschnitz von Weinberg, *Panofsky and the Foundations of Art History*, pp. 102–03. See the perceptive comparison of Sedlmayr and Panofsky by Sauerländer, "'Barbari ad portas': Panofsky in den fünfziger Jahren," in Bruno Reudenbach (ed.), *Erwin Panofsky*, Beiträge des Symposions Hamburg 1992 (Berlin: Akademie,

1994), pp. 123–37.

121. Koerner, "Albrecht Dürer's *Pleasures of the World* and the Limits of Festival," in Walter Haug and Rainer Warning (eds.), *Das Fest*, Poetik und Hermeneutik 14 (Munich: Fink, 1989), pp. 194–97. Koerner also discusses Pächt's reading of Jean Fouquet.

122. The counterargument was provided, however, by Svetlana Alpers, "Bruegel's Festive Peasants," *Simiolus* 6 (1972–1973), pp. 163–76, and "Realism as a Comic Mode," *Simiolus* 8 (1975–1976), pp. 115–44. Alpers uses, in part, structural analysis to generate her Bakhtinian, celebratory Bruegel, whereas the pessimistic Sedlmayr-type reading was upheld with purely empirical and contextual evidence by Hans Miedema, "Realism and the Comic Mode: The Peasant," *Simiolus* 9 (1977), pp. 205–19; see, finally, Alpers's response, "Taking Pictures Seriously," *Simiolus* 10 (1978–1979), pp. 46–50.

123. Here following Emil Kaufmann, "Die Stadt des Architekten Ledoux," *Kunstwissenschaftliche Forschungen* 2 (1933), pp. 131–60. It is interesting that Werner Hofmann in his early review of *Verlust der Mitte*, "Zu einer Theorie der Kunstgeschichte," p. 118, criticized Sedlmayr for focusing on eccentric, unrepresentative episodes of modern art like Ledoux.

124. Sedlmayr, *Art in Crisis*, p. 129.

125. Sedlmayr, *Die Revolution der modernen Kunst*, p. 111. Cf. *Art in Crisis*, p. 166. Cf. the claims by cubist and futurist artists that their works registered the violence and chaos of modern war; e.g., Kenneth Silver, *Esprit de Corps: The Art of the Parisian Avant-Garde and the First World War, 1914–1925* (Princeton, NJ: Princeton University Press, 1989), pp. 77–79. Adorno echoes both the avant-garde artists and Sedlmayr in his *Aesthetic Theory* (1970; reprint, Minneapolis: University of Minnesota Press, 1997), p. 301, when he praises cubism for *anticipating* the images of destroyed cities of World War II.

126. He admired the grounded and "anthropomorphic" (!) National Socialist style; "Die Kugel als Gebäude, oder: Das Bodenlose," *Das Werk des Künstlers* 1 (1939), p. 309. Cf. Lorenz, "Dichtung und Wahrheit — das Bild Johann Bernhard Fischers von Erlach in der Kunstgeschichte," p. 131, who defends Sedlmayr, oddly, by pointing out that *even* in his most intensive Nazi phase he never denied

the significance of Rome for Fischer von Erlach.

127. Actually the fissures (*Spaltungen*) between abstract and naturalistic form — between intellect and feeling — that led to the calamity of modernity opened already in the middle of the thirteenth century; *Die Entstehung der Kathedrale*, p. 512. See Umberto Eco's derisive commentary on the paranoid, sensationalizing, fuzzy-minded aspects of *The Lost Center*, "Cogito Interruptus" (1967), in *Faith in Fakes* (London: Secker and Warburg, 1986), pp. 221–27.

128. On Sedlmayr and generally on postwar German art history, see Willibald Sauerländer, "Von den 'Sonderleistungen Deutscher Kunst' zur 'Ars Sacra': Kunstgeschichte in Deutschland 1945–1950," in Walter H. Pehle and Peter Sillem (eds.), *Wissenschaft im geteilten Deutschland: Restauration oder Neubeginn nach 1945?* (Frankfurt: Fischer, 1992), pp. 177–90.

129. On this event, see Dilly, *Deutsche Kunsthistoriker*, pp. 83–84; also Dürr, *Zur Geschichte des Faches Kunstgeschichte an der Universität München*, pp. 78–79. The debate was summarized in *Kunstchronik* 2 (1949), pp. 227–33.

130. Sedlmayr, "Über die Gefahren der modernen Kunst," in Hans Gerhard Evers (ed.), *Das Menschenbild in unserer Zeit* (Darmstadt: Neue Darmstädter Verlagsanstalt, 1950) pp. 48–62, also the many discussions, esp. 97–98, 127, 193–95, 206, 215–16. See also the report on the Darmstädter Gespräch in *Kunstchronik* 3 (1950), pp. 166–69. Jutta Held, "Adorno und die kunsthistorische Diskussion der Avantgarde vor 1968," in Andreas Berndt et al. (eds.), *Frankfurter Schule und Kunstgeschichte* (Berlin: Reimer, 1992), pp. 41–45.

131. Held, "Adorno und die kunsthistorische Diskussion," p. 45.

132. Sedlmayr, *Revolution der modernen Kunst*, pp. 56–57; "Kunst, Nichtkunst, Antikunst" (1976), reprinted in Sedlmayr, *Kunst und Wahrheit*, pp. 220 and 225.

133. See the commentary, and the translations of the key passages (from which these sentences are drawn), by Yule Heibel, *Reconstructing the Subject: Modernist Painting in Western Germany, 1945–1950* (Princeton, NJ: Princeton University Press, 1995), pp. 25, 31, 155 n.58, 154 n.44.

134. Adorno, "Reconciliation under Duress" (1958/1959), in Ronald Tay-

lor (ed.), *Aesthetics and Politics* (London: NLB, 1977), p. 167.

135. Hofmann, "Produktive Konflikte," in Sitt (ed.), *Kunsthistoriker in eigener Sache*, pp. 105–06. For an echo of the Darmstädter Gespräch, see the polemic by Donald Kuspit against Michael Fried, with explicit invocation of Sedlmayr, "Authoritarian Aesthetics and the Elusive Alternative," *Journal of Aesthetics and Art Criticism* 41 (1983), pp. 271–88, esp. pp. 283–87.

136. Frodl-Kraft, "Hans Sedlmayr," p. 30.

137. Gerhard Richter, interview with Benjamin H. D. Buchloh (1986), in Gerhard Richter, *The Daily Practice of Painting: Writings and Interviews, 1962–1993*, ed. Hans-Ulrich Obrist (Cambridge, MA: MIT Press, 1993), p. 149.

138. Panofsky, *Perspective as Symbolic Form*, p. 71, and *Early Netherlandish Painting* (Cambridge, MA: Harvard University Press, 1953), p. 5 and n.1.

139. Panofsky and Saxl, "Classical Mythology in Medieval Art," *Metropolitan Museum Studies* 4 (1932–1933), p. 278. See the remarks of Konrad Hoffmann, "Panofskys 'Renaissance,'" in Reudenbach (ed.), *Erwin Panofsky*, p. 143.

140. See, for example, Gombrich, "The Vogue of Abstract Art" (1958), in *Meditations on a Hobby Horse*, pp. 143–50.

141. Gombrich, *Art and Illusion* (Princeton, NJ: Princeton University Press, 1960). Perhaps the schema of "making vs. matching" was only conceivable after modern art had voted decisively in favor of making.

142. See Hofmann, "Fragen der Strukturanalyse" and "Was bleibt von der Wiener Schule?"; and Bogner, "Bemerkungen zum Verhältnis der Wiener Strukturforschung zu Kunsttheorien der zwanziger Jahre." Cf. Günter Bandmann's suggestion that *Strukturanalyse*, because it is so sensitive to the aesthetic, may also be uniquely capable of making contact with the religious essence of the historical work in *Mittelalterliche Architektur als Bedeutungsträger* (Berlin: Mann, 1951), p. 44. Generally on the attitudes toward modern art of early-twentieth-century art historians, see Roland Recht, "L'Écriture de l'histoire de l'art devant les modernes," *Les Cahiers du Musée National d'Art Moderne* 48 (1994), pp. 5–23.

143. See Yve-Alain Bois, "To Introduce a User's Guide [to the *informe*]," *October* 78 (1996), pp. 25 and 29.

144. Cf. Sedlmayr's own comments on expressionism and surrealism, with

a quotation from Cocteau, in "Bruegel's *Macchia*" (p. 335 and n.32). On Novotny, see Wood, "Une perspective oblique." For Sedlmayr's dependence on Novotny's Cézanne interpretation, see *Art in Crisis*, pp. 129–34.

145. Sedlmayr, "Toward a Rigorous Study of Art" (p. 135).

146. Sauerländer, "Abwegige Gedanken über frühgotische Architektur und 'The Renaissance of the Twelfth Century,'" in *Festschrift Louis Grodecki* (Paris: Ophrys, 1981), p. 176. See also Sauerländer's review of *Die Entstehung der kathedrale* in *Die Neue Zeitung* 116 (May 19, 1951), p. 9. Crossley, "Medieval Architecture and Meaning," p. 119, draws the comparison to Frederick Kiesler.

Bibliography

The major works by Alois Riegl are:

Stilfragen (Berlin: Siemens, 1893).

Die spätrömische Kunstindustrie nach den Funden in Österreich-Ungarn, I. Teil (Vienna: K. K. Hof- und Staatsdruckerei, 1901). Reprinted as *Spätrömische Kunstindustrie* (Vienna: Österreichische Staatsdruckerei, 1927).

"Das holländische Gruppenporträt," *Jahrbuch des allerhöchsten Kaiserhauses* 23 (1902), pp. 71–278. Reprinted as *Das holländische Gruppenporträt*, ed. Karl Maria Swoboda, 2 vols. (Vienna: Österreichische Staatsdruckerei, 1931).

Burda, Arthur, and Max Dvořák, eds., *Die Entstehung der Barockkunst in Rom* (Vienna: Schroll, 1907; reprinted 1923). Based on lecture notes.

Swoboda, Karl Maria ed., *Gesammelte Aufsätze* (Augsburg and Vienna: Filser, 1929). Reprinted with afterword by Wolfgang Kemp (Berlin: Mann, 1995).

Swoboda, Karl Maria, and Otto Pächt, eds., *Historische Grammatik der bildenden Künste* (Graz: Böhlau, 1966). Based on lecture notes.

For a more complete bibliography, see Karl Maria Swoboda, ed., *Gesammelte Aufsätze* (Augsburg and Vienna: Filser, 1929), xxxv-xxxix.

In the last years two books and several essays and excerpts from books by Riegl have appeared in English translation:

"Geertgen tot Sint Jans' 'Legend of the Relics of St. John the Baptist,'" in W. Eugene Kleinbauer (ed.), *Modern Perspectives in Western Art History* (New York: Holt, Rinehart and Winston, 1971), pp. 126–38; an excerpt from *Das holländische Gruppenporträt.*

"The Modern Cult of Monuments: Its Character and Its Origin," *Oppositions* 25 (1982), pp. 21–51; originally published in 1903.

Late Roman Art Industry, trans. Rolf Winkes (Rome: Bretschneider, 1985).

"Late Roman or Oriental?" trans. Peter Wortsman, in Gert Schiff (ed.), *German Essays on Art History* (New York: Continuum, 1988), pp. 173–90.

Problems of Style: Foundations for a History of Ornament, trans. Evelyn Kain, annotations and introduction by David Castriota, preface by Henri Zerner (Princeton, NJ: Princeton University Press, 1992).

"Excerpts from *The Dutch Group Portrait*," trans. Benjamin Binstock, *October* 74 (1995), pp. 3–35.

A complete translation of *Das holländische Gruppenporträt* is expected from the Getty Center Publication Program.

The most important post-WW II literature on Riegl is:

Arasse, Daniel, "Note sur Alois Riegl et la notion de volonté d'art," *Scolies* 2 (1972), pp. 123–32.

Binstock, Benjamin, "Postscript: Alois Riegl in the Presence of *The Nightwatch*," *October* 74 (1995), pp. 36–44.

Forster, Kurt, "Monument/Memory and the Mortality of Architecture," *Oppositions* 25 (1982), pp. 2–19.

Harlow, Barbara, "Realignment: Alois Riegl's Image of Late Roman Art Industry," *Glyph* 3 (1978), pp. 118–36.

Iversen, Margaret, *Alois Riegl: Art History and Theory* (Cambridge, MA: MIT Press, 1993).

Kemp, Wolfgang, "Alois Riegl (1858–1905)," in Heinrich Dilly (ed.), *Altmeister moderner Kunstgeschichte* (Berlin: Reimer, 1990), pp. 37–62.

———, "Walter Benjamin und die Kunstwissenschaft, Teil 1," *Kritische Berichte* 1 (1973), pp. 30–50.

Oberhaidacher, Jörg, "Riegls Idee einer theoretischen Einheit von Gegenstand und Betrachter und ihre Folgen für die Kunstgeschichte," *Wiener Jahrbuch für Kunstgeschichte* 38 (1985), pp. 199–218.

Olin, Margaret R., *Forms of Representation in Alois Riegl's Theory of Art* (University Park: Pennsylvania State University Press, 1992).

Pächt, Otto, "Art Historians and Art Critics — VI: Alois Riegl," *Burlington Magazine* 105 (1963), pp. 188–193. Reprinted in Otto Pächt, *Methodisches zur Kunsthistorischen Praxis* (Munich: Prestel, 1977), pp. 141–52.

Podro, Michael, *The Critical Historians of Art* (New Haven, CT: Yale University Press, 1982), pp. 71–97.

Rosenauer, Artur, "Zur Wechselbeziehung von Methode und Forschungsgegenstand am Beispiel einiger Schriften Alois Riegls," in *Problemi di metodo: Condizioni di esistenza di una storia dell'arte*, Atti del XXIV Congresso Internazionale di Storia dell'Arte, Bologna, 1979, vol. 10 (Bologna: CIHA, 1982), pp. 55–62.

Sauerländer, Willibald, "Alois Riegl und die Entstehung der autonomen Kunstgeschichte am Fin de Siècle," in Roger Bauer (ed.), *Fin de Siècle: Zur Literatur und Kunst der Jahrhundertwende* (Frankfurt: Klostermann, 1977), pp. 125–39.

Woodfield, Richard, ed., *Framing Formalism: Riegl and the History of Art* (The Netherlands: G+B Arts International, 1999).

Zerner, Henri, "Alois Riegl: Art, Value, and Historicism," *Daedalus* 105 (1976), pp. 177–88.

Generally on the discipline of art history in Germany and Austria in the first half of the twentieth century, see:

Bushart, Magdalena, *Der Geist der Gotik und die expressionistische Kunst: Kunstgeschichte und Kunsttheorie 1911–1925* (Munich: Silke Schreiber, 1990).

Dilly, Heinrich, *Deutsche Kunsthistoriker 1933–1945* (Munich: Deutscher Kunstverlag, 1988).

———, *Kunstgeschichte als Institution: Studien zur Geschichte einer Disziplin* (Frankfurt: Suhrkamp, 1979).

Dittmann, Lorenz, ed., *Kategorien und Methoden der deutschen Kunstgeschichte, 1900–1930* (Stuttgart: Steiner, 1985).

Halbertsma, Marlite, *Wilhelm Pinder und die deutsche Kunstgeschichte* (Worms: Werner, 1992).

Hernand, Jost, *Literaturwissenschaft und Kunstwissenschaft: Methodische Wechselbeziehungen seit 1900* (Stuttgart: Metzler, 1971).

Kultermann, Udo, *Geschichte der Kunstgeschichte* (Frankfurt: Ullstein, 1981). Translated as *History of Art History* (N.p.: Abaris, 1993).

Podro, Michael, *The Critical Historians of Art* (New Haven, CT: Yale University Press, 1982).

On the Vienna School of art history in particular, see:

Marosi, Ernö, "Die ungarische Kunstgeschichtsschreibung in den 20-er Jahren und die Wiener Schule." in *Die ungarische Kunstgeschichte und die Wiener Schule 1846–1930*, exhibition catalogue (Vienna: Collegium Hungaricum, 1983), pp. 84–87.

Rosenauer, Artur, "L'Ecole de Vienne: L'autonomie de l'histoire de l'art," in Edouard Pommier (ed.), *XVIIIe et XIXe Siècles*, vol. 2 of *Histoire de l'histoire de l'art* (Paris: Klincksieck, 1997), pp. 415–41.

Schlosser, Julius von, "Die Wiener Schule der Kunstgeschichte," *Mitteilungen des Österreichischen Instituts für Geschichtsforschung* 13.2 (1934).

Wien und die Entwicklung der kunsthistorischen Methode, Akten des XXV. Internationalen Kongresses für Kunstgeschichte, Vienna, 1983, vol. 1 (Vienna: Böhlaus, 1984).

For Hans Sedlmayr, see the complete bibliography, including obituary notices, compiled by Friedrich Piel, *Hans Sedlmayr: 1896–1984. Verzeichnis seiner Schrif-*

ten (Munich: Falkenberg, 1996). The best biographical accounts are Norbert Schneider, "Hans Sedlmayr (1896–1984)," in Heinrich Dilly (ed.), *Altmeister moderner Kunstgeschichte* (Berlin: Reimer, 1990), pp. 267–88; and Eva Frodl-Kraft, "Hans Sedlmayr (1896–1984)," *Wiener Jahrbuch für Kunstgeschichte* 44 (1991), pp. 7–46. Sedlmayr's most important theoretical statements, including "Toward a Rigorous Study of Art," were collected in *Kunst und Wahrheit: Zur Theorie und Methode der Kunstgeschichte* (1958; reprint Mittenwald: Mäander, 1978). See also "Zum Begriff der 'Strukturanalyse,'" *Kritische Berichte* 3/4 (1930–1932), pp. 146–60.

For Otto Pächt, see the memoir by Jonathan Alexander, "Otto Pächt 1902–1988," *Proceedings of the British Academy* 80 (1991): 453–72; the autobiographical remarks edited by Martina Sitt, "Otto Pächt: Am Anfang war das Auge," in Martina Sitt (ed.), *Kunsthistoriker in eigener Sache* (Berlin: Reimer, 1990), pp. 25–61; the entry by Sitt in the *Neue Deutsche Biographie*, vol. 19, pp. 752–54; and the entry in Ulrike Wendland (ed.), *Biographisches Handbuch deutschsprachiger Kunsthistoriker in Exil*, 2 vols. (Munich: Saur, 1999), vol. 1, pp. 470–79. See also the Festschrift *Kunsthistorische Forschungen*, ed. Artur Rosenauer and Gerold Weber (Salzburg: Residenz, 1972), with a preface by Bruno Fürst and an incomplete bibliography. Memorial essays by Rudolf Preimesberger, Artur Rosenauer, Gerold Weber, John Mitchell, Dieter Bogner, and Martina Sitt were published in *Kunsthistoriker: Mitteilungen des Österreichischen Kunsthistorikerverbandes* 5 (1988). Pächt's own most important methodological statement, in addition to "The End of the Image Theory," is the long title essay in Pächt, *Methodisches zur Kunsthistorischen Praxis* (Munich: Prestel, 1977), pp. 187–300, translated by David Britt as *The Practice of Art History: Reflections on Method*, introduction by Christopher S. Wood (London: Harvey Miller, 1999), with complete bibliography.

For Guido Kaschnitz von Weinberg, see the bibliography in the posthumous collection of his theoretical writings, *Kleine Schriften zur Struktur*, vol. 1 of *Ausgewählte Schriften* (Berlin: Mann, 1965), with a biographical sketch by Marie Luise Kaschnitz. Kaschnitz's own most important key theoretical statements are the review of the reprint of Riegl's *Late Roman Art Industry*, *Gnomon* 5 (1929), pp. 195ff.; and "Struktur," *Enciclopedia dell'Arte Antica Classica e Orientale*, vol. 7 (1965), both reprinted in Kaschnitz von Weinberg, *Kleine Schriften zur Struktur*, pp. 1–14 and 198–202.

There is little written about Fritz Novotny, who had no role as a theorist of *Strukturanalyse*. But see the volume of his collected essays, *Über das 'Elementare' in der Kunstgeschichte* (Vienna: Rosenbaum, 1968), with two articles on Cézanne; and the entry in *Metzler Kunsthistoriker Lexikon* (Stuttgart and Weimar: Metzler, 1999), pp. 285–87.

Two further programmatic statements of the structure-analytical method are Friedrich Matz, *Geschichte der griechischen Kunst*, vol. 1 (Frankfurt: Klostermann, 1950), pp. 1–36; and Matz, "Strukturforschung und Archäologie," *Studium Generale* 17 (1964), pp. 203–19. See also Matz's review of Riegl in *Gnomon* 10 (1934), pp. 449–54.

Finally, the secondary literature that directly addresses either the institutional history of the "New Vienna School" or the art historical method of *Strukturanalyse*. This list does not include all the many responses to Sedlmayr's polemic against modern art, *Verlust der Mitte* (1948).

Bakoš, Ján, "Der tschechoslowakische Strukturalismus und die Kunstgeschichtsschreibung." *Zeitschrift für Ästhetik und allgemeine Kunstwissenschaft* 36 (1991), pp. 53–101.

————, "The Vienna School's Hundred and sixty-eighth Graduate: The Vienna School's Ideas Revised by E. H. Gombrich," in Richard Woodfield (ed.), *Gombrich on Art and Psychology* (Manchester and New York: Manchester University Press, 1996, pp. 234–57.

Bätschmann, Oskar, *Einführung in die kunstgeschichtliche Hermeneutik* (Darmstadt: Wissenschaftliche Buchgesellschaft, 1984), pp. 27–30, 73–76.

Bauer, Hermann, "Form, Struktur, Stil: Die formanalytischen und formgeschichtlichen Methoden," in Hans Belting et al. (eds.), *Kunstgeschichte: Eine Einführung* (Berlin: Reimer, 1986), pp. 154–58.

————, *Kunsthistorik* (Munich: Beck, 1976), pp. 90–93.

Betthausen, Peter, "Erklärung oder Deutung: Deutsche Kunstwissenschaft um

1930," in *L'art et les révolutions*, Actes du XXVIIe congrès international d'histoire de l'art, Strasbourg, 1989, vol. 5 (Strasbourg: Société Alsacienne pour le Développement de l'Histoire de l'Art, 1992), pp. 103–109.

Bogner, Dieter, "Bemerkungen zum Verhältnis der Wiener Strukturforschung zu Kunsttheorien der zwanziger Jahre," in *Tagesbericht. Erste Österreichische Kunsthistorikertagung* (Graz, 1981), pp. 63–68

Busse, H.B., *Kunst und Wissenschaft. Untersuchungen zur Ästhetik und Methodik der Kunstgeschichtswissenschaft bei Riegl, Wölfflin, und Dvořák* (Mittenwald: Mäander, 1981).

Clausberg, Karl, "Wiener Schule — Russischer Formalismus — Prager Strukturalismus: Ein komparatistisches Kapitel Kunstwissenschaft," *Idea: Jahrbuch der Hamburger Kunsthalle* 2 (1983), pp. 151–80.

————, "Zwei Antipoden der Kunstwissenschaft und einer versunkener Kontinent: Zum methodischen von Pächt, Panofsky und Wygotski," *Kritische Berichte* 6. 3 (1978), pp. 5–12.

Dittmann, Lorenz, "Der Begriff des Kunstwerks in der deutschen Kunstgeschichte," in Dittmann (ed.), *Kategorien und Methoden der deutschen Kunstgeschichte, 1900–1930* (Stuttgart: Steiner, 1985), pp. 51–88.

————, *Stil, Symbol, Struktur: Studien zu Kategorien der Kunstgeschichte* (Munich: Fink, 1967), pp. 140–216.

Einem, Herbert von, "Der Strukturbegriff in der Kunstwissenschaft," in *Der Strukturbegriff in den Geisteswissenschaften*, Abhandlungen der Akademie der Wissenschaften und der Literatur, Mainz, Geistes- und Sozialwissenschaftliche Klasse, no. 2. (1973), pp. 3–16.

Gombrich, Ernst, "Kunstwissenschaft und Psychologie vor fünfzig Jahren," in *Wien und die Entwicklung der kunsthistorischen Methode*, Akten des XXV. Internationalen Kongresses für Kunstgeschichte, Vienna, 1983, vol. 1 (Vienna: Böhlaus, 1984), pp. 99–104.

————, review of *Kunstgeschichte und Kunsttheorie im 19. Jahrhundert, Art Bulletin* 46 (1964), pp. 418–20; response by the volume's authors and Gombrich's reply, *Art Bulletin* 47 (1965), pp. 307–309.

Hofmann, Werner, "Fragen der Strukturanalyse," *Zeitschrift für Ästhetik und all-*

gemeine Kunstwissenschaft 17 (1972), pp. 143–69. Reprinted in Hofmann, *Bruchlinien* (Munich: Prestel, 1979), pp. 70–89.

———, "Was bleibt von der Wiener Schule?" *Kunsthistoriker* 4 (1984/85), pp. 4–7. Expanded version in *Jahrbuch des Zentralinstituts* 2 (1986), pp. 273–90.

Kemp, Wolfgang, "Walter Benjamin und die Kunstwissenschaft, Teil 1," *Kritische Berichte* 1 (1973), pp. 30–50.

Lachnit, Edwin, "Ansätze methodischer Evolution in der Wiener Schule der Kunstgeschichte," in *L'art et les révolutions*, Actes du XXVIIe congrès international d'histoire de l'art, Strasbourg, 1989, vol. 5 (Strasbourg: Société Alsacienne pour le Développement de l'Histoire de l'Art, 1992), pp. 43–52.

Levin, Thomas Y., "Walter Benjamin and the Theory of Art History: An Introduction to 'Rigorous Study of Art,'" *October* 47 (1988), pp. 77–83.

Michalski, Sergiusz, "Strukturanalyse, Gestaltismus und die Kublersche Theorie. Einige Bemerkungen zu ihrer Geschichte und Abgrenzung," in *Problemi di metodo: Condizioni di esistenza di una storia dell'arte*, Atti del XXIV Congresso Internazionale di Storia dell'Arte, Bologna, 1979, vol. 10 (Bologna: CIHA, 1982), pp. 69–75.

———, "Zur methodischen Stellung der Wiener Schule in den zwanziger und dreißiger Jahren," in *Wien und die Entwicklung der kunsthistorischen Methode*, Akten des XXV. Internationalen Kongresses für Kunstgeschichte, Vienna, 1983, vol. 1 (Vienna: Böhlau, 1984), pp. 83–90.

Nodelman, Sheldon, "Structural Analysis in Art and Anthropology," *Yale French Studies* 36/37 (1966), pp. 89–103. Reprinted in Jacques Ehrmann (ed.), *Structuralism* (Garden City, NY: Anchor/Doubleday, 1970).

Rosenauer, Artur, "Zur neuen Wiener Schule der Kunstgeschichte," in *L'art et les révolutions*, Actes du XXVIIe congrès international d'histoire de l'art, Strasbourg, 1989, vol. 5 (Strasbourg: Société Alsacienne pour le Développement de l'Histoire de l'Art, 1992), pp. 73–83.

Roß, Martin Michael, *Künstlerische Struktur und Strukturontologie: Guido Kaschnitz-Weinberg und sein Beitrag zu einer strukturorientierten Kunstwissenschaft* (Munich: Pfeil, 1990).

Sauerländer, Willibald, "Hans Sedlmayr's 'Verlust der Mitte,'" *Merkur: Deutsche Zeitschrift für europäisches Denken*, 47. 531 (1993), pp. 536–542.

Schneider, Norbert, "Revolutionskritik und Kritik der Moderne bei Hans Sedlmayr," in *L'art et les révolutions*, Actes du XXVIIe congrès international d'histoire de l'art, Strasbourg, 1989, vol. 5 (Strasbourg: Société Alsacienne pour le Développement de l'Histoire de l'Art, 1992), pp. 85–91.

Schweitzer, Bernhard, "Strukturforschung in der Archäologie und Vorgeschichte," *Neue Jahrbücher für antike und deutsche Bildung* 1 (1938), pp. 162–79. Reprinted in Bernhard Schweitzer, *Zur Kunstgeschichte des Altertums: Ausgewählte Schriften* (Tübingen: Wasmuth, 1965), vol. 1, pp. 179–97.

"Strukturforschung," *Lexikon der Kunst* (Munich: Deutscher Taschenbuch Verlag, 1996), pp. 101–103.

Wood, Christopher, "Une perspective oblique: Hubert Damisch, la grammaire du tableau et la Strukturanalyse viennoise," *Cahiers du Musée National d'Art Moderne* 55 (1996), pp. 107–29.

PART ONE

Methodological Foundations: Alois Riegl

Alois Riegl, "The Main Characteristics of the Late Roman Kunst-wollen" (1901)

Alois Riegl (1858–1905) was curator of textiles at the Austrian Museum for Art and Industry and, from 1897, professor of art history at the University of Vienna. Late Roman Art Industry *(Spätrömische Kunstindustrie, 1901) grew out of a report he wrote on recent excavations of early-medieval artifacts in the Austro-Hungarian empire. The book is an overview of Roman architecture, sculpture, painting, and decorative arts of the fourth through sixth centuries. The little-known second part, focusing more closely on post-Constantinian and pre-Carolingian decorative arts, was assembled from Riegl's notes and published in 1923. In Riegl's abstract, value-free formal analysis, the belt buckles and brooches from the Austrian provinces are given equal treatment with the Arch of Constantine and the mosaics at San Vitale in Ravenna. All of these forms, according to Riegl, were generated by the "artistic will," or* Kunstwollen, *of late antique culture, a dynamic drive rooted in the basic experience of space and time. Late Roman art was customarily scorned as a debased and sterile descendant of classical Greek and Roman art. Riegl argued instead that the development of an "optical" mode of representation in the late Roman period — manifested, for example, in the play of light and shadows in the deeply cut sarcophagus reliefs — actually prepared the ground for highly spiritualized Christian painting and ultimately for the idealizing and subjective art of modern Europe. One stage in the refinement of the modern mode was the topic of Riegl's last book,* The Dutch Group Portrait *(Das holländische Gruppenporträt, 1902).*

The following passage from Late Roman Art Industry *is the conclusion of the 1901 volume. Here Riegl tries to corroborate his findings with a reading of the literary evidence. He argues that late Roman art and Saint Augustine's thinking on aesthetics are expres-*

sions of the same underlying drive, or *Wollen*. *It is the most explicit statement Riegl ever made of his contextualizing, or cultural-historical, ambitions.*

(Source: Alois Riegl, Late Roman Art Industry, *trans. Rolf Winkes [Rome: Bretschneider, 1985], pp. 223–34; originally published as "Die spätrömische Kunstindustrie nach den Funden in Österreich-Ungarn, I. Teil" [Vienna: K. K. Hof- und Staatsdruckerei, 1901]; reprinted as* Spätrömische Kunstindustrie *[Vienna: Österreichische Staatsdruckerei, 1927].)*

Chapter One

The Main Characteristics of the Late Roman *Kunstwollen* (1901)

Alois Riegl

The late Roman *Kunstwollen*, like the *Kunstwollen* of earlier antiquity, was oriented toward the pure apprehension of the isolated individual form through the immediately evident material phenomenon. Modern art, by contrast, is concerned not so much to distinguish individual phenomena as to associate them into collective phenomena, or indeed even to demonstrate the lack of independence of the supposed individuals. The fundamental artistic means employed by late Roman art to fulfill this aesthetic goal — again in accord with earlier antiquity — was *rhythm*. Rhythm, that is, the sequential repetition of similar phenomena, clarified for the beholder the association of parts into a unified totality. And whenever several such totalities were found together, again it was rhythm that managed to forge a higher unity. But rhythm, if the beholder was to perceive it clearly, was necessarily restricted to the plane. There is a rhythm of elements beside one another and on top of one another, but not behind one another: in the latter case, the individual forms and formal components would overlap one another and thus escape the direct sensory perception of the beholder. An art that wants to present units in a rhythmic composition will be compelled to compose in the plane and avoid the representation of depth. Late Roman art, like all antique art, thus strove for the presentation of individual forms by means of rhythmic composition.

The late Roman *Kunstwollen*, however, *differs* from that of earlier periods — and differs ever more sharply with increasing temporal distance — in that it was no longer content to see the individual form presented in two-dimensional extension. Rather, it wanted to see three-dimensional, fully spatial, and self-contained form. This entailed a liberation of the individual form from the universal optical plane (the ground) and an isolation of the form from this ground plane and from other individual forms. This liberated not only the forms, but also the intervals of ground between them, which until then had been attached to the common ground plane (optical plane). The complete isolation of the individual form led to the simultaneous emancipation of the interval, indeed to the elevation of the hitherto neutral and formless ground to a self-contained aesthetic and formal potency. The means, as we have already established, was rhythm. The intervals, too, had to be organized rhythmically.

Once the intervals, like the individual forms, were contained by three-dimensional space, they started to generate an area of open space of a particular depth. As long as it was not too deep, this open space did not disturb the effect of rhythm in the plane. It sufficed to fill such intervals basically with dark shadows. This, together, with the bright, forward-springing individual forms between them, generated a coloristic rhythm of light and shadow, black and white. Coloristic rhythm was a property especially of works from the earlier imperial period, but also of works of the fourth century (sarcophagi from Rome, for example). In architecture and the applied arts color-rhythm remained standard for a long time. Coloristic rhythm then retreated in the true late Roman figurative reliefs (sarcophagi from Ravenna), which tended back toward tactility in order to restore *linear* rhythm to unchallenged dominance. One encounters throughout the process, however, even in the very late Roman period, figurative reliefs that in the early imperial fashion respect both linear and coloristic rhythm.

In those cases where the aim was to bring out an individual form with full effectiveness, this levelling of ground and individual form led to "mass composition," a phenomenon unheard of until then in antique art, and at the same time clearly the prelude to the modern conception of the collective character of the apparent individual forms.

This isolation of the individual form also had an effect on the modes of expression of rhythm. Rhythm now had to look no longer to articulation and variation, which always have an associative effect, but to simplification and massing. If classical rhythm was a rhythm of *contrast* (*contrapposto*, triangle composition), the late Roman rhythm was one of uniform arrangement (quadratic composition). Since the individual forms have abandoned their connections one to another, their objective appearance — as much as possible detached from momentary connections to other individual forms — must be reproduced. This explains the tendency toward objectivity of appearance in late Roman art, as well as its stereotypical and anonymous character, always associated with an anti-individualistic artistic practice.

In trying to understand these main features of late Roman art we have only been investigating monuments from the four major categories of art. But there is a way of testing our results. We might introduce as comparative evidence the literary expressions of the late Romans on the character of their *Kunstwollen* and artistic practice.

I would like to direct the attention of scholars toward a source of art historical understanding that until now has been neglected to the same degree that literary sources offering information about localization and chronology have been the object of the greatest appreciation and the most diligent study. To be sure, a generation that preferred to see the work of art as the mechanical product of raw materials, technique, and unmediated external functionality was incapable of thinking of the pronouncements of writers on the *Kunstwollen* of their time as anything other than speculative fantasies. In the eyes of the aesthetic materialists there can be no conscious *Kunstwollen*, and whatever was said about it in earlier times could only be, at best, worthless self-deception, if not deliberate deceit. Once one recognizes that mankind wants to see sensory phenomena presented in outline and in color in the plane or in space in different ways in different times, then one will embrace the idea that statements by thoughtful and well-informed individuals about what is to be expected from the work of art in their own time deserve the full consideration of art historians. For what beckons us is a way of convincing ourselves that our views about the prevailing artistic intentions in a given period — based on subjective observation — are in fact also the views of those who lived in that period. In other words, whether in fact people expected from the visual arts that which, on the basis of research into the monuments, we imagined the "willed" to have been. This correspondence would clearly be the only true and reliable proof of the results of our research.

The material available from the third to the fifth centuries is extraordinarily rich and ought to permit the most thorough proofs. Among the later pagan authors it is chiefly the Neoplatonists, above all Plotinus, that come under consideration. An examination of the Christian authors ought to be hardly less fruitful. At this point let us sketch out Saint Augustine's doctrine of beauty in its relationship to late Roman art, not to circumscribe the topic, let alone exhaust it, but simply to demonstrate the practicability of the postulated future art historical research project.[1]

In Augustine's view, the purely beautiful is only to be found in God. On the other hand, there is nothing in creation that does not contain traces (*vestigia*) of the beautiful. Even ugly things are not excluded.[2] It is the task of the visual arts to bring those traces of the beautiful, through the imitation (*imitatio*) of objects in nature, to heightened expression.[3] Everything thus leads to the question of what Augustine understood by these ubiquitous traces of the beautiful. They are — to spell it out right away — the primary aims of all artistic production in antiquity: unity (isolation of the individual form) and rhythm.

For Augustine as for all his predecessors, individual containment of form is the precondition of all being as well as the locus and the form of expression of the beautiful in all created things.[4] The only thing that distinguishes his views from those of the ancient Near Easterns and the early Greeks is his dualism, whereby in everything a spiritual formal unity — of superior value — coexists with a material. This dualism, as is well known, can be traced back to the pre-Alexandrine Greeks.[5] Augustine concludes that the task of the artist consists in nothing other than the effort to bring forth through imitation, to the greatest extent possible, everything in the natural object that makes its individual formal containment evident. Indeed, what is even more valuable to us is that Augustine manages to tell us explicitly how he sees unity and the expressive form of beauty in specific types of art. He does this, for example, in a conversation with an architect where he agrees that the architect in his buildings strives for nothing other than unity and that he tries to achieve this mainly through the symmetrical and proportional combination of the individual components of the building.[6]

Symmetry and proportion are, however, only special phenomenal forms of a higher, universal means of the visual arts: rhythm. For the means by which the work of art expresses the unity — that is, the individual containment of form — of the natural object is for Augustine, too, rhythm (*numerus*).[7] Augustine emphasizes and highlights rhythm to such an extent that Berthaud even wanted to install it as Augustine's true principle of beauty, with unity as the mere form of expression of rhythm, whereas the relationship can only be the other way around. All further marks of the beautiful in works of plastic art (in addition to symmetry and proportion, already mentioned, is *order*) are only special forms of expression of rhythm. Here, too, there is no lack of references to specific works af art in Augustine. For example, he insists that the windows of a building either be identical to one another (a rhythm of uniform arrangement) or, if not identical, be handled in such a way that middle-sized windows are larger than small windows in the same proportion that large windows bear to middle-sized.[8] Clearly, to such a rising sequence there is a corresponding diminishing sequence in the same plane, creating a rhythm of contrast, as in the windows in the semicircular lunettes of the great early imperial buildings (Baths of Diocletian, Basilica of Maxentius).

The selection of this example leads to two further remarks. First, it is striking that Augustine chooses his examples from architecture. The figurative arts, sculpture and painting, are not neglected, but in this respect they bring up the rear. Augustine's reserve vis-à-vis the figurative arts takes on a deeper meaning when one recalls that the subsequent centuries did not favor the figurative arts. The semitic East had permanently abolished them; the Greek East at least for a century threatened them with extinction; and even in the West the pathbreaking achievements at least until the twelfth century were not in sculpture or painting but in architecture (and the applied arts).

Second, I would like to call attention to the way that the decision to have windows that break through architectural form (*perforatis*) mirrors the entire evolution of late antique art. Aristotle would have chosen as an example columns or some other material and positive form. Augustine, by contrast, uses an immaterial perforation. This leads to the question of the extent to which the characteristics of specifically late antique art (early and late imperial Roman), alongside those general features of antique art, get expressed in Augustine's doctrine of beauty.

The distinction between the generally antique and the specifically late antique, as we have seen in the monuments themselves, has to do with the treatment of unity and rhythm. The generally antique tendency to comprehend the individual form still prevails; but now, as a consequence of the heightened spatiality of the individual form, it is clear that this, too, requires an interval. This leads to an emancipation of the interval, of the ground, of space.[9] Moreover, rhythm with its linear composition in the plane dominates just as before. This distinguishes late antique art sharply both from classical antiquity and from modern art: space has emancipated itself (in contrast to the fundamental hostility to space of classical antiquity), but it is formed into rhythmic intervals (in contrast to the formlessness of modern art, which basically stresses the infinity of space stretching into depth).

The emancipation of the interval is thus one of the fundamental principles of Augustine's ethics and aesthetics, recurring in countless passages[10] and proving of great use especially in his struggle against the Manicheans. It is here that he demonstrated, among other things, the right to existence, indeed the necessity, of the ugly and the formless. Evil is merely a *privatio* of the good, the ugly merely the "interval" of the beautiful. They are as necessary as the interval between the words in speech and between the tones in music. We tend to look at the evil and the ugly at close range, and they naturally appear to us evil and ugly. If one looks at it all from a distance, however, one has to concede that there would be no beauty without its complement, the ugly, and that only the two of them together guarantee a complete and harmonious image.[11]

Out of the numerous relevant passages let us single out one that escaped Berthaud, but which for us has special significance. It is one of the few in which Augustine borrows a concrete example from the figurative arts, in this case from painting: Sicut pictura cum colore nigro, loco suo posita, ita universitas rerum, si quis possit intueri, etiam cum peccatoribus pulchra est, quamvis per se ipsos consideratos sua deformitas turpet.[12]

According to this passage, black plays the same role in the painted image as evil within the entirety of mankind. Individual forms appearing in their clear materiality, that is, in light colors, are beautiful. The color black, by contrast, represents shadows, the unintelligible, the immaterial, the formless, the empty, the non-existent. But if black is placed properly within the image, then together with the light-colored material forms it creates, when seen from a distance, an effect of beauty. This displacement to the proper position is carried out according to Augustine's doctrine of *ordo*, which in line with what was previously said is nothing other than a form of expression of rhythm. It follows that Augustine's aesthetic aim, in painting as well as in architecture, was the rhythmic distribution of the black and the luminous, shadow and light. Augustine thus demands from painting exactly that *coloristic* treatment that we have already encountered as a crucial feature of late antique art.[13]

Whether we grasp the essence of late antique — early imperial and late Roman — art on the basis of observation of the monuments or on the basis of the surviving textual evidence, the premise remains the same: in every period there is only *one* orientation of the *Kunstwollen* governing all four types of plastic art in the same measure, turning to its own ends every conceivable practical purpose and raw material, and always and of its own accord selecting the most appropriate technique for the intended work of art. Our conviction of the correctness of the image of late antique art gained in this way is only strengthened when we realize that the *Kunstwollen* of antiquity and in particular of its closing phase is completely identical with the other main forms of expression of the human will in the same period.

All human will is directed toward a satisfactory shaping of man's relationship to the world, in the most comprehensive sense of this word, within and beyond the individual. The plastic *Kunstwollen* regulates man's relationship to the sensorily perceptible appearance of things. Art expresses the way man wants to see things shaped or colored, just as the poetic *Kunstwollen* expresses the way man wants to imagine them. Man is not only a passive, sensorily recipient being, but also a desiring, active being who wishes to interpret the world in such a way (varying from one people, region, or epoch to another) that it most clearly and obligingly meets his desires. The character of this will is contained in that which we call the worldview (again, in the broadest sense): in religion, philosophy, science, even statecraft and law; as a rule, one of those forms will predominate in any period.

There is clearly an inner connection between the will that aims, by means of the plastic arts, to present things in the most pleasing way possible to the eyes, and the will that aims to interpret things in a way corresponding to its desire. Even in the history of antiquity this connection can be tracked step by step. This relationship can be suggested here only in its most general principles. Still, this ought to be sufficient to reveal the wider foundation for our investigations into the meaning of late Roman art within the universal history of culture.

The antique worldview evolved through three clearly differentiated periods running parallel to the three main periods of antique art. What art and worldview have in common, again, is the notion that the world is composed of tangible (plastic) self-contained individual forms. The earliest period held the view that the existence and the vital expressions of forms were determined by arbitrarily ruling forces. The worldview therefore had to be religious, that is, focused on the personal and amicable winning over of those forces. Only the second period, which runs parallel with classical Greek art, aimed — as religion gradually gave way to philosophy and science — to establish a necessary, lawful connection among the individual phenomena. In this postulated connection we immediately recognize the tendency toward that association of individual forms that the plastic arts of the classical period were so devoted to.

Because the ancient only saw closed self-contained forms in the world, he could only conceive of the relationship between them as mechanical (pressure or thrust); in this respect the idealist and materialist (atomistic) systems of antiquity agree. This leads directly to the notion that this relationship, always connecting one individual to its neighbor, can only be a serial, chain-like one. This corresponds exactly to the rhythmic composition of the individual forms in the contemporary plastic arts. It was the task of the arts to extract a certain quantity of individual forms out of the infinite chaos of phenomena and, by arranging them in the plane, binding those forms into a new, clearly contained unity. In the same way, natural science in antiquity tried to untangle the confused skein of phenomena and arrange the forms in a coherent sequence based on their lawful causal sequence.

In the third period of antiquity, the special object of our attention, the (classical) attempt to establish a mechanical, causal connection between phenomena was again devalued; indeed, things had gone so far that individual forms were again put into mutual external isolation from one another. This was no return to primitive disconnectedness. Rather, the merely mechanical connection between forms was no longer satisfying. A different kind of connection was put in its place: the magical. This was true throughout the late pagan and early Christian world, in Neoplatonism and in the syncretic cults as well as in the ideas of the early Christian church. The inner affinity of this process with the isolation of the individual form within the optical plane in the contemporary plastic arts is obvious; and here, too, we must ask whether this is to be seen as progress or as decline.

The answer is once again that the late antique worldview was a necessary transitional phase of the human mind. The mind was moving from the conception of a purely mechanical (in the narrow sense) and sequential association among things, as if projected in the plane, to the conception of a universally distributed chemical association, as if traversing space in all directions.[14] To see decline in that late antique transformation is to presume to dictate the path that the human mind ought to have taken in order to arrive at the modern view of nature. Admittedly, the late antique turn to magic was a detour. But today the necessity of this detour is completely clear, once it is realized that it involved not the invention of any particular natural-scientific theory, but the overcoming of a conception of a world made up of mechanically self-contained individual forms, a conception thousands of years old and common to the whole ancient world. The indispensable precondition for this shift was not only the unsettling of the belief in the purely mechanical association, but also the emergence of a new, positive belief in an extra-mechanical association that nevertheless proceeded from the forms themselves: namely, a magical association. Only when this new belief had borne its indestructible fruits was the mechanical association — never quite forgotten in western Europe — again properly considered, in the plastic arts as well as in the worldview. Now the danger of falling back into the conception of the exclusively mechanistic association of a world made up of inalterable individual forms was set aside once and for all. The idea of the existence of an extramechanical association of all the things of creation — alongside the mechanical — had in the meantime established itself in the western mind as irrevocably as the conceptions of mass composition (instead of the material individual form) and deep space (instead of serial arrangement in the plane) had established themselves in the plastic arts. The development of a culturally dominant European society owes both concepts to the late Roman period.[15]

NOTES

1. In light of the skepticism that usually greets investigations of this sort, it seems to me appropriate to stress from the start that Augustine does not, in the manner of modern philosophers of aesthetics, limit himself to a list of abstract and general theses. Rather, he speaks of individual works of art or particular aspects of the visual arts — not exactly frequently but often enough. Thus we can be confident that Augustine himself felt that his general propositions found clear and specific expression in individual works of art.

In his youth, while still a pagan, Augustine wrote by his own admission several volumes under the title *De pulchro et apto* (On the beautiful and the fitting). In the title we recognize that distinction between artistic purpose and external purpose (whether practical or imaginative) abrogated by the mechanistic approach of the second half of the nineteenth century. Today, in view of the impossibility of explaining mechanistically the pleasure taken in the work of art, that distinction is once again recognized. This early work of Augustine's was already lost in his own lifetime; we regret this more vividly than he himself did. This is because in this work he sought the beautiful less in God than in sensory phenomena: the visual arts, dance, music, poetry. As a Christian he wrote a six-volume work *De musica*, mostly on the problem of meter. Much more important are the numerous remarks on beauty and the fine arts strewn among his other works. Aug. Berthaud in his book *Sancti Augustini doctrina de pulchro ingenuisque artibus e variis illius operibus excerpta* (Poitiers, 1891) attempted a compilation of these passages. This work is so far from comprehensive that even statements of the most basic significance and relevance are missing. Moreover, Berthaud in many cases badly misunderstood Augustine's views. This can be explained largely by Berthaud's unfamiliarity with works of art of Augustine's time. But for reasons of time I was unable to undertake a systematic survey of Augustine's writings and thus have made extensive use of Berthaud's anthology of citations.

2. Augustine is thus one of the first to recognize the relativity of beauty and ugliness. The distinction between his views on this matter and those of earlier antiquity will emerge below. He defines the ugly still in the antique sense, as the formless (*deforme*), that is, as that which is not contained as an individual form.

3. The fact that all works of art without exception have these naturalistic and idealistic aspects could not be more concisely asserted than in this definition. Claiming "naturalism" for one style or another can therefore only lead to misunderstandings. The ancient Egyptians, who tried to reproduce things in their rigorously objective appearance, surely thought they were proceeding as "naturalistically" as possible. The Greek artist, in turn, would have thought of his own works as "naturalistic" only in comparison to those of the Egyptians. And would not the master of the portrait of Constantine see himself as a greater "naturalist" than, for example, the master of the portrait of Pericles? All three, however, would have felt that what we today call "naturalism" was simply unnatural. Every style strives for a true reproduction of nature and nothing else. But each has its own conception of nature, and each has a quite specific phenomenal form of nature in mind (tactile or optical; close view, normal view, or distant view). It is entirely unscientific — although customary — to connect "naturalism" to some characteristic of the motif itself. This betrays an apparently ineradicable tendency to confuse the history of the visual arts with iconography. Art has to do not with the "what" but with the "how" of the phenomenon; it gets the "what" handed to it by poetry or religion. Iconography reveals to us not so much the history of the artistic will as the history of the poetic or religious will. It was already briefly stated earlier [in the original publication — TRANS.] that there is a bridge between the two, and that deeper knowledge of this connection would be important. But in order to make use of this connection between art history and iconography, it is first necessary to differentiate clearly between them. I see this differentiation as a precondition of any progress in art historical research in the immediate future.

4. "omnis pulchritudinis forma unitas" (*Epistolae* 17, *Augustinus Coelestino* II.85).

5. Thus the tree is a unity through its self-contained individual form (*De ordine* 3.18, [vol. 1, col. 1017]) and through its no less individual *anima vegetativa*, to which it owes its development and movement (growth). In the eyes of the modern observer, by contrast, the tree is a collective entity composed of thousands of independent organisms, and in its actions it follows not a single driving

cause, but thousands of causes working on it in thousands of ways. If the ancient artist wanted to produce unity as the essence and beauty of every object, then the modern artist fulfills exactly the same goal in bringing the collective character of natural entities to heightened expression.

6. *De vera religione* 30. For another conversation on the same topic with an *artifex*, (see also 32 [col. 148]). It is characteristic that in both cases the artists hesitate when confronted with Augustine's question about the nature of the beauty that they strive for in their works. Evidently Augustine wants to suggest that artists of his time were generally confused by questions of this sort. That is entirely understandable in an age when artistic production moved in secure, stereotypical paths. In the modern age of hyperindividualism, every artist believes he has to write a book about his own *Kunstwollen*, out of the well-grounded fear that his artistic purpose will not be understood by the public on the basis of his works alone.

7. "Et (ratio) terram coelumque collustrans, sensit nihil aliud quam pulchritudinem sibi placere, et in pulchritudine figuras, in figuris dimensiones, in dimensionibus numeros" (*De ordine* 2.15 [col. 1014]). By *figurae* he means the individual forms, by *dimensiones* he means the dimensions in the plane (height and width). On the identity of *numerus* and rhythm, see *De ordine* 2.14. [col. 1014].

8. *De vera religione* 30 [vol. 3, cols. 146, 147].

9. This process, too, begins already in pre-Constantinian times. Characteristic of the antique view is the statement by Cicero about rhythm "quem in cadentibus guttis quae intervallis distinguuntur, notare possumus, in amni praecipitante non possumus" (*De oratore* 3.48). Cf. the modern *Kunstwollen*, which takes pleasure precisely in the tumbling stream.

10. A list is given in Berthaud, *Sancti Augustini doctrina de pulchro*, pp. 44ff.

11. On the relativity of beauty and ugliness, see *De musica* 6.13 [vol. 1, cols. 1183– 1184]. Harsh light and impenetrable shadows displease us human beings, but please other living creatures.

12. *De civitate dei* 11.23 (Migne, *Patrologia Latina*, 41, p. 336).

13. In this light we can make sense of analogous statements, as in *De civitate*

dei 11.18: "Contrariorum oppositione saeculi pulchritudo componitur"; or when the *ordo saeculorum* is characterized as *pulcherrimum carmen ex quibusdam quasi antithetis.* Or in *Epistolae, Nebridio Augustinus* [vol. 2, col. 65]: "Quid est corporis pulchritudo? Congruentia partium [the rhythm of line] cum quadam coloris suavitate [the rhythm of bright and dark coloring]." The postulate of the distant view follows from the proposition: "quod horremus in parte si cum toto consideramus, plurimum placet." This Augustine immediately demonstrates with a concrete example from architecture: "nec in aedificio iudicando unum tantum angulum considerare debemus" (*De vera religione* 40). This latter would have been possible in a Greek temple, where every column is a self-contained form, but admittedly not in an early Christian basilica.

14. Alchemy, which was as much magic as chemistry, represents a direct connection between the late Roman idea of a magical association of all things and the modern idea of a chemical association. But also the modern idea of continuous forces independent of the individuality of things, for example electricity, and the theory of cells and tissues, rests on the post-antique dissolving of the individual form into a mass composition, and on the notion that something could be influenced by thousands upon thousands of other things, even remote things, in the same instant.

15. The plan and character of this work does not permit further parallels between the visual arts and the worldview of antiquity, extended to all realms of expression. I wish to call attention to just one, for which many points of contact can be found in the chapter on sculpture. This aforementioned parallelism is especially striking in the simultaneous emergence of dualism in Greek thought and a consideration of the physical in the Greek figurative arts. In the starkest contrast to this stands the ancient Near Eastern and archaic Greek period with its materialistic monism (the soul as a more refined matter) and its objective presentation of material individual forms. In the closing phase of antiquity we see the elements of the primitive stage apparently recurring: monism and aesthetic objectivity. In fact, the two epochs are at opposed extremes. The monism is now spiritual (the body as a coarser soul) and the objectivity is directed toward the appearance of the psychic (emphasis on the eye as the mirror of the

soul, figures turning straight out toward the beholder). As for bodies themselves, the goal is now objectivity of the three-dimensional phenomenon, and in order to achieve this perception of space into depth, mental consciousness has to be enlisted. This is contrasted to the two-dimensional phenomenon to which ancient Egyptian objectivity was oriented. The first and last phases have in common the irresistible desire for an absolute norm and the maximum possible exclusion of the subjective. Thus the art of the first and last phases of antiquity was objective and anonymous and closely bound up with the religious cult; the contemporary worldviews were strictly religious or, more exactly expressed, cultic. Only in the intervening, classical period do we encounter subjectivism and personality in art, and philosophy and science (which are always subjective and personal) in the worldview.

The history of the plastic arts since Charlemagne offers a close parallel to all this, at least in its first two phases. The middle ages aimed at the isolation of objects (in this case in space instead of in the plane as in antiquity), at an objective norm for the (three-dimensional) appearance of those objects, and at the closest connection with the religious cult (which is nothing other than the individual's subjective need for religion brought under an objective, collectively binding, lawful norm). Modernity, by contrast, aims at the association of objects one to another (in space, whether by means of line as in the sixteenth century, or by means of light as in the seventeenth century, or by means of individual coloring as in modern art), at the reproduction of the subjective appearance of objects, and at the emancipation from cult, which is where philosophy and science — the disciplines that proclaim the natural connectedness of one thing to another — come in.

Translated by Christopher S. Wood.

*Alois Riegl, "The Place of the Vapheio Cups in the History of Art"
(1900)*

*This essay was only published posthumously, first in a periodical in
1906 and then in Riegl's* Collected Essays *of 1929. It was the first
chapter of a book he planned to write on anachronisms in the
history of art. The Vapheio cups are a pair of gold vessels, Mycenaean
or Minoan, dating from the middle of the second millennium* B.C.
*They were discovered in 1888 near Sparta and are preserved in the
National Museum in Athens. The reliefs on both cups represent men
trying to capture bulls. Riegl assumes — mistakenly, it now appears —
that they are naturalistic proto-genre scenes. He analyzes the pictorial conventions used to represent landscape space and the sudden, violent actions of the bulls. He argues that the artist of the Vapheio
cups, by introducing subjective perception as a criterion of representation, overcame the inertia of ancient Near Eastern and Egyptian figuration and pointed forward to classical Greek art, indeed ultimately to
Roman and Christian art. The essay amounts to a concise, self-contained demonstration of Riegl's method of formal analysis. With its
focus on figure-ground relationships, conventions of spatial representation, and the compositional function of represented gazes, the piece
anticipates his own analyses in* The Dutch Group Portrait *and especially the work of his follower Otto Pächt.*

(Source: Alois Riegl, "Die kunsthistorische Stellung der Becher von Vafio" [1900],
Jahreshefte des Österreichischen Archäologischen Instituts 9 [1906], pp. 1–19;
reprinted in Alois Riegl, Gesammelte Aufsätze [Augsburg and Vienna: Filser,
1929], pp. 71–90.)

Chapter Two

The Place of the Vapheio Cups in the History of Art (1900)

Alois Riegl

It is not my intention here to add one more to the number of existing studies of these artifacts, so frequently discussed from the standpoint of classical archaeology. To this end the author feels no inclination. His intention is rather to describe and formulate the significance of the Vapheio cups, from a general art historical viewpoint, more precisely than has been done in the previous literature.

In every work of art in which things of nature are re-created, one must distinguish between the idea that led to the selection of relevant models in nature and the manner in which these models were rendered by the artist's hand. The artistically decisive factor is unconditionally the latter. Indeed, the question could be posed whether the idea, the given conceptual purpose, should not, like the purposes of use and decoration, be dismissed as external and be strictly separated from the artistic purpose as such. For now, however, we will let this question rest and give our doubts formal expression by discussing the ideas behind the Vapheio reliefs only at the very end.

We turn, therefore, immediately to the second of the main points just mentioned: the manner in which the given ideas are embodied. Here we are essentially talking about two aspects:

composition and the relationship between form and flat surface. The artistic will (*Kunstwollen*) is successfully expressed in both of these; yet for the Vapheio cups the natural hindrances that raw materials and technique pose to an early, struggling art form appear to be overcome to such a degree that we can leave them aside as subordinate factors in the stylistic development.

Composition is the combination of parts into a unified whole, for example limbs into a figure or several figures into a group. The ancient Near Eastern artist, namely the Egyptian, virtually never achieved composition in this sense. It has long been noted that although the component surfaces of Egyptian figures were carefully observed and arranged in as crystalline a fashion as possible, that is, clearly outlined and symmetrically ordered, the compelling connections between them are nevertheless lacking, as is — at least for the modern viewer — the convincing impression of the necessary coherence of the limbs as a whole, upon which depends their capacity to achieve the imagined functions of movement. The same holds true for Egyptian group composition: the figures are of the same height and arranged equidistantly from each other; lacking is the dominant feature that would unify the group in a single glance. The inventors of composition, therefore, are not the Egyptians but the Greeks or — more cautiously expressed — their probable Indo-Germanic predecessors in pre-Homeric times. In respect to composition, the warrior vase from Mycenae, with its one-sided arrangement, does not appear to be superior to the Egyptian approach (although in other respects it is indeed fundamentally superior), whereas the Vapheio cups already provide a backward glimpse on an immeasurable development. That this fact with all its implications has not yet been properly recognized seems to me to have been largely the result of Heinrich Brunn's observations on these artifacts in his *Griechische Kunstgeschichte* (pp. 47ff.), which are always intelligent but not completely free of prejudice. For Brunn, the origin of the development of Greek composition was the rigid crystalline grouping with a dominant center, as it first emerges on Dipylon vases. The Mycenaean composition of the Vapheio cups appeared to him in comparison to represent a more raw and undisciplined early stage. Our task is first to test this conclusion by analyzing the reliefs on the two cups (figures 2.1, 2.2).

At the center of one of the cups, directly across from the handle, a single bull in a net is rolled into a half-spherical form. On each side, to the right and left, is a bull that has successfully escaped the trap; one turns and flees in a great leap, throwing his hind legs high in the air and setting his forelegs down; the other has broken through the net and leaps upward — the hind legs below, the forelegs above — trampling two of his would-be captors. Here we have not only a clear division between center and flanks but also, alongside the ideal, an unmistakable physical correspondence between the two adjacent sides: a bull dives down, a bull rages upward; one throws its head up, in contrast to the overall downward-directed movement of its body, the other lowers its head in the same contrast to its overall movement. Even the movement of their tails, as inconspicuously natural as it appears, is determined by the same law for each bull. This is composition not simply in the sense of unity; it also deliberately works with contrasts. In a word, it is *contrapposto* composition, which was not achieved again in Greek art until the classical period. And yet how finely concealed is the intent and its translation into the self-evident! When looking at the bull on the left, our entire attention is diverted from the latent design by the two male figures. On the right, the tree in the foreground serves the same purpose. Further, even the form of the bull caught in the net at the center is in *contrapposto*: the forelegs at the left, the hind legs at the right; and this unusual contortion of the body does not appear overly con-

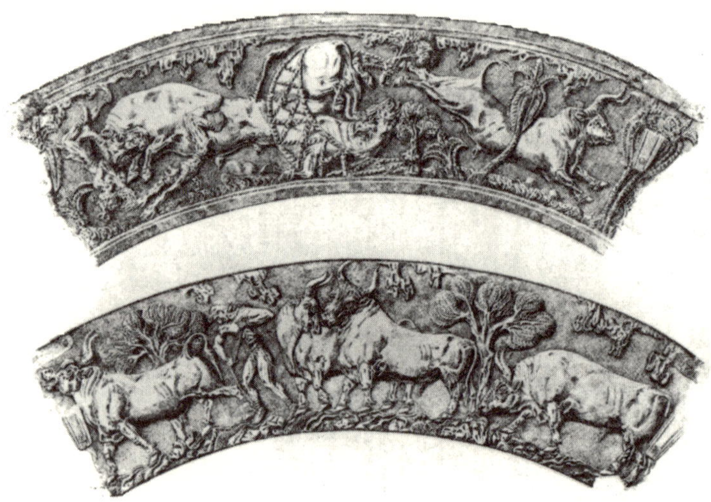

Figures 2.1 & 2.2. Reliefs on Vapheio cups, National Museum of Athens, from Sir Arthur Evans, *The Palace of Minos*, vol. 3 (London: Macmillan, 1930).

spicuous or purposefully affected. It is explained well enough by the momentary situation of the animal that has fallen into the snare.

It is a gift of fate not to be underestimated that, in addition to the cup just discussed, a second cup was found with which one can test past (and future) statements about the first and in this way approach certainty. Most striking is the contrast between the two cups in overall comportment: in one the greatest energy is expressed in violent movements, in the other contemplative standing or quiet measured steps. This cannot be an accident. Let us turn our attention to the details of the composition of the second cup. Once again, the center and the sides are clearly distinguished from each other. Whereas in the first cup a single bull dominates the center area, though in close connection to a second object — the net slung around two trees — in the second cup two bulls occupy the center. The Mycenaean artist seems already to have felt that a single point as the dominant motif was too rigid a restraint. Who does not recall here that classical Greek composition would also prefer a double to a single motif (to name one of the most famous examples, in the *Aldobrandini Wedding*)? One may perhaps forgive the imagination if one is reminded of the dual monarchies or dual consulates of certain ancient states. On each side of the second cup we once again encounter a single bull, the movements of each in *contrapposto* relationship to those of the other: the bull at the right grazes, lowering its head toward the ground; the bull at the left bellows, lifting its head high in the air, its bellowing motivated by the man hobbling one of its hind legs. The distribution of the trees also helps to obscure the impression of intentionality in the composition. We of the modern age are wonderfully touched by these reliefs, for we also wish to see all traces of deliberateness strictly avoided in modern works of art.

The central group of the two bulls on the second cup gives rise to some further observations to which we wish to turn at this point. Only the front portion of the one bull is visible; the remainder of its body is nearly fully covered by the bull in the foreground. The Egyptians as a rule avoided such overlaps, although sometimes the object at hand rendered them necessary: for example, from a team of four, only the horse in the foreground would be drawn in its entirety. Of the remaining three, only the contours would be visible. Our Mycenaean artist handles this situation very differently: he not only reveals the full front half of the rear animal's body but also includes individual, isolated parts of the rest of the body, such as the hind legs and some of the tail, which he deliberately depicts raised above the back of the bull in the foreground. The restlessness apparent in this movement of the tail seems motivated by the parallel restlessness of the position of the head, which we will soon discuss. If one compares it to the quiet stance of the bull in the foreground, it is not difficult to recognize that within this central group a contrast is once again intended. A full appreciation of this divergence from the Egyptian custom of painstakingly avoiding any overlap will emerge later.

The art historian must be especially struck by the so to speak spiritual relationship that appears to unite the two bulls at the center. The rear bull turns its head back, seemingly affectionately, toward the one in front, which, for its part, looks out from the picture plane toward the viewer. At a later point, we will consider the truly epochal significance of this last-mentioned turn of the head in the history of relief sculpture; here it must only be noted that in all of ancient Near Eastern sculpture not a single example can be adduced in which animals that are not directly related to each other, such as a mother and her young, appear in such cozy (*sit venia verbo*) association. Sexual coupling, as depicted commonly in Egyptian murals for all the well-known reasons, represents a material, not an ethical, relationship. Even with human figures, the Egyptian depicts ethical relationships only seldom, and then only with much hesitation, whereas the Mycenaean artist did not shy away from a primitive expression of such relationships even with animals. Is one to be criticized if one feels tempted to see here the Indo-Germanic participation in nature instead of the ancient Near Eastern tendency toward practical exploitation?

Let us return to the more concrete aspects of our examination. Our conclusions up to this point can now be summarized: the composition of the reliefs of the Vapheio cups does not signify, as Brunn claimed, a rudimentary, preliminary stage to the Dipylon composition. Rather it leaves all that is Dipylon-like tremendously far behind. The goal of the Dipylon style was to consolidate a scene with many figures into an ordered, unified whole under a single dominant feature. The Vapheio cups have completely broken free of this. Therefore, the question can only be which solution we value as the more artful: the simple, rigid symmetrical repetition to the right and left of a central axis, or the ingenious resolution of contrasting lines and movements in a balance of masses. Classical art, which has made the latter its compositional goal, gives the answer, and we can be content with that.

But this is not enough: the composition of the Vapheio cups surpasses classical, and indeed ancient, composition altogether in several respects. The strictly classical, pre-Lysippic art never achieved an actual *landscape*. If the object of representation required something that we associate with landscape — trees, shrubs, houses, animals, and such — to be brought into the image, it would be integrated exactly like the human figure in its objective, isolated existence. By contrast, in the Vapheio cups we encounter a true landscape, almost in the modern sense, a thousand years before the analogous Alexandrian efforts. All of the human and animal figures move on shared ground in which all of the trees (with one notable exception) are fixed. This ground does not represent a sculptural division, a breaking into objective, isolated individual objects (stones, clumps of earth, cliffs). Still less is it a simple mathematical line, as seen among the Egyptians and in the Dipylon style. Rather, this ground imitates exactly the amorphous mass as it usually appears in nature to the fleeting glance. On the first cup, with its tumultuous figural content, we recognize grass, the blades bending to one side, sketched onto the ground. On the second cup, the grass growing between the stony clumps of earth is indicated by only a few small dots (the precursor to the late ancient drill technique). As for the trees and shrubs, they do not jut upward as half-geometric forms; they boldly deviate from the normal vertical, just as they occur through the countless accidents of nature. Take for example the palm tree that the fleeing bull hurries behind: the bent line of its wrinkled trunk is completely ephemeral, accidental nature — the deliberate opposite of all archaic-crystalline art. Yet this nature fulfills the most deeply considered artistic purpose in that in a pleasing manner it divides into two halves the unusually elongated body of the bull as it speeds by. At the same time, the broken line effectively echoes the movement of the bull. However, I do not wish to attribute any more definitive meaning to this covering of a main subject (the bull) by a minor subject (the tree) — no matter how unusual and unclassical it is — since I was able to observe a similar overlap (a fleeing bull in shrubbery) in a relief of the temple of Ramses III at Madinat Habu, admittedly a completely artless composition.

This Mycenaean landscape lacks only one aspect of what we moderns might require of it. Of the two trees to which the net is tied, only the one toward the front rests firmly on the ground. The one in the background floats freely in the air. It appears the artist faced two conflicting goals of equal value: on the one hand, he had to preserve the optical unity of the landscape; on the other, he had to depict the event as clearly as possible. Because he could not achieve both together, he chose the latter. A modern artist would not hesitate for a moment to do what the Vapheio artist avoided: he would partially cover the more distant tree. Even in the latest Roman period, the ancients could never bring themselves to sacrifice outright the clarity of optical unity, the objective existence of things, to the subjective appearance on the retina of the human eye. In this respect, Mycenaean art, no matter how much it trampled the restrictions of objectivism in general, shows its allegiance to the unshakable tenet of all ancient art, the tenet that guided the ancient Near East from the very beginning, that was adopted very early on — as the Vapheio cups teach us — from the predecessors of the Greeks, and that was never completely disavowed by fully developed antique civilization even to the very end.

One is inclined to rate the achievement of the Vapheio cups even higher when one sees how far the artist surpasses all ancient art in another respect: the odd stalactite-like forms that hang down from the upper edge in the background of the relief. The artistic purpose they serve is clear: to fill in the empty background. It is the same tendency that we encounter in funerary stele from Mycenae, in contrast to ancient Near Eastern art, which approached this problem very differently.[1] On these, the *horror vacui*, which the Egyptians never knew, appears to be alleviated by regularly composed spiral lines, that is, quasi-crystalline elements. But what do the clustered, amorphous masses on the Vapheio cups signify? They are not ornamentation, since they lack orderly composition. They must be imitations of naturally occurring forms, and of these only two seem possible: either a chain of mountains that ring the horizon or clouds that hang from the heavens. Whichever one settles on, they are both equally unheard of in classical art, even in the latest period. Even after Lysippus, when antiquity had made significant concessions to a subjective sense of space, the eye of the ancient artist never penetrated into depth so far that it would have observed and recorded a horizon or a zenith. And yet to explain these masses we are left no alternative but to choose one of the above-mentioned elements. It can hardly be doubted which way the decision will fall, since only clouds, and not mountains, can explain the openings and the multiple breaks in the hanging masses as they appear on the second cup. Furthermore, if they were mountains, they would appear to be turned upside down, even though the artist, as previously noted, always tried to give the correct optical impression. Nor is this false impression required by the standard of clarity as it was in the case of the more distant of the two trees holding the net.

Our second conclusion about the composition can be summarized thus: the Vapheio cups display a landscape that encompasses a section of the earth's surface intended for subjective momentary viewing, a concept that was completely foreign to ancient Near Eastern art and was attained for the first time in Greek art in Hellenistic times, after Lysippus. In addition, this landscape takes into account the appearance of a cloudy sky above the earth, which never again occurred in ancient art, though it can be observed in late medieval art.

The second purely artistic element of this work is the *relationship between form and surface* it exhibits. Indeed, all things in nature are shaped and at the same time defined by surfaces. However, this does not mean that this relationship is simply copied from the originals onto sculptural reproductions. It is in just this relationship that the change of the times and the people, the succession of styles, is especially perceptible. In what form do we encounter it in the Vapheio cups?

Here, too, we should look back to prior developments. The ancient Near Eastern relief is a shallow relief, in other words, the figures are sharply bounded in height and width but only tentatively and modestly bounded in depth. This is explained by a basic tendency rooted in the worldview of the ancient Near Eastern peoples, which interests us here only in its influence on the plastic arts. Egyptian art seeks to reproduce things objectively, free from the confusing and blurring contingencies of visual perception. The Egyptian artist examines things exactly and at close range, checks his perceptions by the sense of touch, and then models carefully, piece by piece. However, he can only achieve complete clarity, be it of the whole or of the parts, within the confines of height and width. Depth always remains unclear to the eye, but it is nevertheless present, a necessary evil, and must therefore be taken into account, though it should be reduced to its smallest possible, that is, least disturbing, measure. This tendency is found in various types of Egyptian art: the freestanding figure, with its planar frontal view; the flat relief; and, probably most strikingly, painting, with its silhouette-like contour drawing without modeling. Everywhere shadow, the indicator of form, is avoided as much as possible, because it has no body and is therefore apt to create unclarity. The ancient Near Eastern artist with his characteristic sense for objective, material reality builds the work of art piece by piece, comprehending it through close scrutiny, checking it by touch. Yet he never succeeds from his subjective viewpoint in capturing the whole figure (and, even less, a whole group of figures) in a single moment as an optical unity. For this reason, all ancient Near Eastern art is objectivist — without space or time: in painting, the silhouette; in the modeled form, flat undulations with shadows as faint and as broad as possible.

Even the oldest artifacts that have been found on what was later Greek soil demonstrate a very different character. One looks in vain at all of ancient Near Eastern art for representations such as the linearly engraved figures of deer on the surface of Trojan spindle whorls (figure 2.3). Not only is the dimension of depth suppressed; everything is reduced to a single dimension — length.

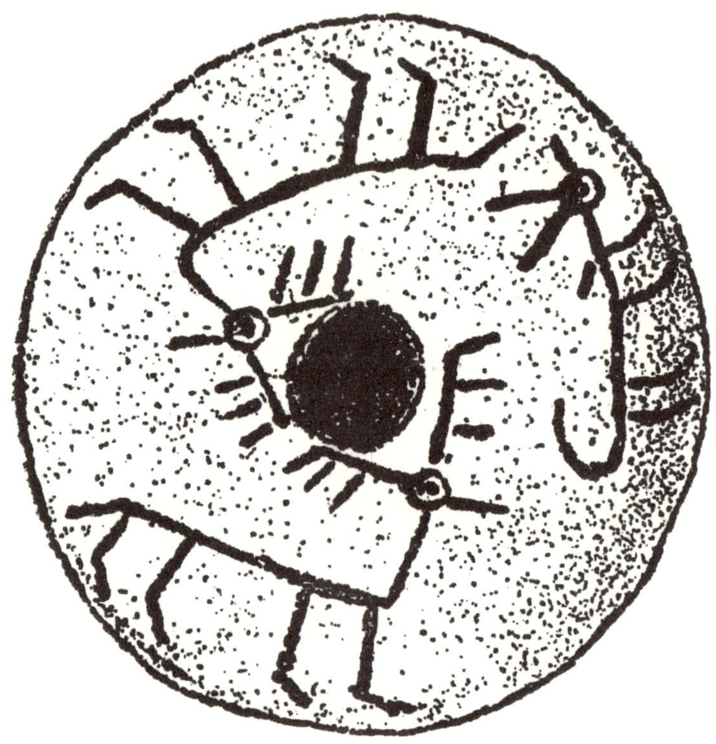

Figure 2.3. Trojan spindle whorl from Alois Riegl, *Gesammelte Aufsätze* (Augsburg and Vienna: Filser, 1929).

The engraved lines are not the boundaries of a body that expands in two dimensions between them; they themselves stand for the body. Certainly these deer are not images derived from close examination, checked by the sense of touch; they are images created from memory, based on purely optical, distant perception. These are fantastic and obscure forms that from the outset relinquish all tactile qualities. These Greek — if we may call them such — artists proceeded in a manner exactly opposite to that of the ancient Near Eastern artists: whereas these latter focused on the parts and created a whole out of them, the predecessors of the Greeks saw primarily the whole, which even today we immediately recognize as such. Yet the parts remain devoid of all meaning. Whereas the Egyptian proceeded objectivistically and attempted to render things as they are experienced in their tactile reality, beyond the contingencies of optical appearance, the Indo-Germanic artist approached his work subjectivistically in that he portrayed only the main features of a momentary optical *impression*. It is clear that such a fantastic, disembodied art as that on the Trojan spindle whorls could have never attained a higher level of perfection. It was a blessing for this culture that it was introduced to objectivist ancient Near Eastern art. It is, however, no less clear that objectivistic art soon had to encounter (and, as Egyptian art proves, did in fact encounter) insurmountable limitations from all sides, which only a subjectivist-fantastic art could overcome. We see here all at once the contrast between ancient Near Eastern-Semitic and Indo-Germanic cultures that has largely dominated all subsequent human development. The influence of the Near Eastern peoples, ultimately always a retarding element, was at the proper moment useful to Westerners. Yet true progress, and therefore the upper hand in politics and culture, finally fell for all time to the Indo-Germanic people.

If the spread of Near Eastern influence was necessary for the emergence of later Greek art, then surely we see this precondition of further progress fulfilled in so-called Mycenaean art. Here the Eastern influence is just as well established as the non-Eastern component. We will focus for now solely on the relief. In Mycenae, we encounter it first as the flat relief on funerary stelae. It is most likely Egyptian (the spiral ornamentation offers secondary proof of this) and even appears at first glance to be an exact copy of the Egyptian flat relief. However, on closer examination an interesting difference emerges: Mycenaean works show no trace of three-dimensional modeling. The Egyptian did not believe he could completely suppress the modeling, since it had been objectively present in the things themselves and could not be missed by the viewer when observed closely. Yet the Mycenaean artist rejected the rather flat, undulating Egyptian modeling: his figures exhibit an absolutely even surface, resembling the deceptive, purely optical appearance of things viewed from a distance. From the single dimensions of the Trojan spindle whorl, the Indo-Germanic artist, under the influence of Egyptian art, has indeed crossed over to two dimensions. However, he still disregards the third because he is accustomed to the subjectivist optical mode of observation.

One must bear in mind this apparently primitive stage in development, in reality a stage deeply integrated in the basic sensibility of a large family of peoples, if one wishes to understand how the relief on the Vapheio cups initially represents an absolutely puzzling anachronism. After having met with only the flattest relief in Egyptian and Mycenaean works, we suddenly and directly stumble upon the most pronounced high relief. Indeed, it is high relief not merely in the absolute height differential of the whole but also in the modeling of the tactile surface. No trace of hesitation vis-à-vis the dimension of depth or any fearful avoidance of shadow; rather, a deliberate accumulation of powerful rises and falls, creases and bumps, purposeful opposition of light and shadow. The manner in which the heads and legs of the animals and the torsos of the human figures are modeled can only be described as distinctly painterly. Instead of the painstaking clarity of the broad and flat elements, a stormy confusion of bodiless light and shadow! Instead of flat undulating transitions in half shadow, passages (like the ribs of the bulls on the second cup) of nearly linear engraving like that found in the fundamentally distance-oriented latest classical art! When next in the history of art can such a relief be found? All of early Greek art from Homeric times onward knows only the flat relief in the Egyptian sense. Where an early high relief crops up, as in Selinunte, it is so only in the absolute depth of its relief from the ground, not in the treatment of the surface, which is smooth and where all modeling is assiduously avoided. In classical times, to be sure, the high relief underwent a fundamental development; but such an untactile, predominantly optical-painterly conception of surface like that of the Vapheio cups is not to be found in the same extreme measure in Alexandrian art and not even in the latest classical art. The conditions required for such a reckless breakthrough of the optical are found only in more recent art.

In this context, we may return to the previously mentioned detail of the two bulls' turning their heads to face outward from the plane of the relief toward the viewer. Ancient Near Eastern art as a rule avoided this in the relief. This avoidance was rooted above all in an objectivism that did not concern itself with the viewer, but also in the tendency to avoid depth or, what is the same, foreshortening. Here difficulties in constructing the nose (the "protrusion of the face") may have been decisive. Exceptions to this rule in ancient Near Eastern art are extremely infrequent; in Egyptian art, they occur only in painting, never in relief. Can one consider it a coincidence that the frontal positioning of the head occurs repeatedly on these two cups?[2] Not until the transitional period to classical art did the problem of foreshortening find new reception. In Mycenaean art, it appears to be already mastered and carefree — and the resulting lack of clarity solved. Only one feature must be emphasized here as characteristic, because it occurs, apparently not accidentally, on other Mycenaean artifacts: the heads of the two bulls are indeed foreshortened vertically in relation to the plane; however, they move not on the normal vertical but on the horizontal. This can only be explained by the artist's desire to avoid having the bull look directly at the viewer. This betrays the influence of objectivism, which classical art adopted in a similar manner after it officially accepted foreshortening. Hence we find foreshortened heads peering out from the image in classical art but, as a rule, in three-quarter, not frontal, profile. It was Christian art that first firmly established the rule of direct dialogue between the head and the viewer.

Having more precisely located the Vapheio cups within the development of composition and relief, it remains for us to consider the *idea* that they embody. In the oldest recorded historical times, when images of religious belief dominated all conceptions of nature and all conditions of life, and art and religion were essentially identical, the idea behind a work of art has the least to contribute to a purely artistically critical evaluation, because the artist had little or no latitude for individual design. Thus, for example, in Egyptian art, the idea deeply interests only the Egyptologist, not the art historian. We would therefore expect to see traces of deities and religion throughout Mycenaean artifacts. Is this the case in the Vapheio bull-capturing scene? Indeed it cannot be altogether excluded; and yet it is extremely difficult to be sure of this. The pleasure with which the various adventures in all their incidental and ephemeral details are depicted awakens the greatest doubts that this scene is about religious ideas. When one considers the majority of other Mycenaean artifacts, however, one finds that in general the religious character present is surprisingly secondary.

One need only cite features of Egyptian art for comparison to become fully convinced of this. Egyptian art not only borrows its most significant decorative motifs (for example, the lotus, papyrus, scarab, uraeus) from the cult. The apparent genre scenes in Egyptian tombs, which exhibit to a certain extent a thematic relationship to our cup reliefs, are also related to well-known Egyptian religious images of death. Only the images of battle from the ramesside period are an exception; however, because they, like the Assyrian war reliefs, are related to the deeds of a king, in principle they also serve to exalt the deeds of the local deity. Thus Mycenaean art differs fundamentally from the ancient Near Eastern creative arts in that it utilizes material created for religious purposes for purely decorative functions. This is generally acknowledged for vegetal ornament types (the lotus); why shouldn't the same interpretation — completely disregarding religious connotation — also be valid for figural representations like our bull-trapping scene? These would be out-and-out genre pictures in the modern sense. Art history teaches us, however, that genre pictures were created only in those periods in which the purpose of art was directed essentially toward optical unity and which did not seek adequate expression for religious content in the fine arts at all or only as a secondary function. How well the first requirement applies to our cups has already been examined here; but the second appears to be confirmed, at least indirectly, by the readily apparent, emphatically diminished religious character of Mycenaean artifacts. In all probability, we have recognizable genre pictures in the reliefs on the Vapheio cups, signifying an early attempt in a direction that did not become possible again until the Hellenistic period, after the collapse of the polytheistic belief system that had developed in the Homeric-Hesiodic age. I admit, however, that I have never come across an ancient genre picture as powerful in its momentary depiction of a lively everyday event. In this respect, the conception of the Vapheio reliefs is most closely analogous to more recent art produced by the Germanic people — primarily the Dutch of the seventeenth century — and the kinship between the two is most strongly expressed in the intimate response to animal nature. Here we come to another noteworthy point regarding the special character of our two cups.

The emotional relationship between the two animals at the center of the second cup has already been discussed. A first glance at the two cups reveals that the bulls and not the people are the main subject. The second cup in particular, with its calmer subject matter, depicts an animal scene quite in the sense of the old Dutch painters. Man is represented here, but he is subordinated to the bulls in two respects.

First of all, in size: the bulls are far larger than the people (and the trees). To our eyes, that — along with the tree floating in the air — is an appreciable fault, the only fault that we can find in these works of art from a modern standpoint.[3] Once more, the tendency toward clarity of all ancient art is expressed here: the main subject can not be clouded by attributes; it must emerge clearly at first glance. Or is the opinion rather that the artist was not aware of this deficiency from the standpoint of a unified, optically distant interpretation of momentary action? How would he then have been in the position to render the bulls (but also the people and the plants) so masterfully as individuals in isolated completeness and above all in such lightning-quick movements, which the ancient Near Eastern artists never attained and which the Greeks achieved only much later?

The second, but no less important, sense in which man is subordinate to the animals is to be found in the content of the representation itself, especially on the first cup. The whole order of the ancient world rests on the rights of the strong: the victor not only was always right, he also was always favored. In the earthly realm, the human being is strongest: all other creation is subordinate to him and must serve his purposes. In the depictions on our two cups, the human does finally prove himself the stronger: in the one instance, the bull is caught through human cleverness; in the second instance, it is led away hobbled with ropes. Indeed, it almost appears as though the final triumph of human wit over the physical superiority of the animal world had been the artist's over-riding theme. Furthermore, doesn't it appear to be equal justice when the artist favorably portrays the wild and elemental power of the animal, which bounds over a hill in a leap equivalent to two men? Here, once again, we touch on a feature characteristic of the Indo-Germanic people in contrast to Near Eastern cultures. Indeed, it is that much more characteristic, the more they remained untouched by Near Eastern influences. The Semitic and Germanic peoples form the extremes; the Romans stand in the middle.

We may now summarize the results of our investigation. If we have come to expect among the earliest Greek artifacts singular forerunners of later national developments, and signs of the in-fluence of a far superior Near Eastern art, then on the Vapheio cups we have found the decisive factors — composition, treatment of the relief, concept — not only vastly different from all ancient Near Eastern art but also far more advanced than the post-Home-ric, early stages of Greek art. To a certain extent, they surpass even the classical and Hellenistic artistic character. We will seek the explanation for this perhaps baffling conclusion along the fol-lowing lines of thought.

Greek art developed not as a simple continuation but through an opposition to ancient Near Eastern art that it maintained from the very beginning. This difference is most clearly evident in the treatment of the relationship between form and surface: in Near Eastern works, the objective close-up grasp of elements in their tangible flatness and their mechanical conjunction; in Greek works, a subjective optical grasp of the whole as viewed from a distance, first as an image from memory. The difference also was latent from the very outset in the composition: in Near Eastern works, the inclination toward a purely material order of parts by means of the most crystalline possible parallelism of lines and surfaces; in Greek works, a loosening of the inorganic, lifeless crystallization in keeping with the observance of organic movement — first physical movement, which the Egyptians continually regarded as a necessary evil, then intellectual movement, which the Egyptians fundamentally excluded from the fine arts. On the level of the idea, finally, the opposition is no less striking: in the ancient Near East, the identity of all art with religion, that is, the identification of all appearances and all events with the workings of an objective personal deity; among the Greeks, a subjective interest in the relationships and causal connections of objects, either with the viewer or among each other. Already the Mycenaean period heralds that people who would later invent philosophy and the natural sciences and who would create the notion that man is the measure of all things.

We observed the earliest modest expressions of non-Oriental perception in the Trojan spindle whorl. This primitive art, which art historians categorize as Indo-Germanic through analogies with Celtic and Germanic works, also took account of Near Eastern art and made use of what had been learned. Now for the first time it brings out its own properties at a higher, more monumental level: the Vapheio cups give testimony that this is what occurred in Mycenaean art. As far as the optical material appearance of things is concerned, this art is, at least in relief, lacking only a few ingredients. As has already been noted, even the modern sculptor does not have much to add here. The key is to determine what was lacking in this art — in spite of its completeness in this one respect — such that it could never itself give rise to classical art. Above all it is the embodiment of moral ideas through the vehicle of the human figure, which could scarcely have been possible within the Mycenaean artistic character. Such an embodiment requires perception at close range, perception not so much of landscape and animals but of man and his physiognomy.[4] Here lies the point in which the ancient Near Eastern one-sided, close viewed development of the human figure became decisively important for the Indo-Germanic peoples. Ancient Near Eastern art had excluded all spirituality from the figures; however, it had created a type of human physical appearance in the crystalline tranquillity of objective being. The Greeks had to take this, not a more or less fantastic image from memory, as their point of departure in order fully to reproduce corporeal and spiritual beauty and, as a further consequence, intellectual movement.

This explains how Mycenaean art, so puzzling, interesting, and in one sense highly refined, could disappear in order to make way for the Dipylon style. That said, I can see in the Dipylon style — at least as far as the figural is concerned — essentially a mere regression into the ancient Near Eastern, as much as I am aware that this regression formed a necessary transitional stage in the development of classical art. Where the arms on the marching warriors in the background on the warrior vase from Mycenae had been hidden, because this corresponded to the optical appearance, the arms of the human figures in the Dipylon style were brought into view alongside the frontally composed torso. This corresponds to the objective nature of man and is therefore a rule seldom broken in Egyptian art. Where the contours of thigh and calf muscles of the bull leapers from Tiryns had been delineated, thus introducing the element of modeling — which the Egyptians in their horror of depth never and post-Homeric art only centuries later depicted — the Dipylon figures are once again pure silhouettes after the Egyptian model. Again, the composition approaches the rigid order of Egyptian art, and the content of the Dipylon painting, with its religious funeral scenes, approximates Egyptian imagery more closely than do the Vapheio cups. Of course, the Dipylon style is not lacking in elements that we may describe as specifically Greek, and the most essential among them is probably the condition that the center of the composition no longer be sacrificed. However, what dominates the outward impression are symptoms of regression as well as a return to the Near Eastern school.

In conclusion, a few words about the further development of the opposition in ancient art we have been describing. The second phase, too, of the receptivity to Near Eastern achievements at the height of the Attic period, in that glorious and unique balance of contrasts in composition, form and surface, and the idea, returned to a specifically Indo-Germanic conception. When, in the further course of history, an Indo-Germanic strain that was less affected by Near Eastern influences than the Greeks — the Italic peoples — creatively entered into ancient art production, it was only natural that specifically Indo-Germanic elements — perspective, painterly composition, representations of phenomena not purely for the sake of religious meaning — won the upper hand. If one wants to contrast this Roman art in principle not only with the ancient Near Eastern but also with Greek art, one must remember that it is not the Greeks as such who appear in opposition to the Italic people (an opposition, moreover, of a more gradual than habitual nature) but rather the Greeks in that Orientalizing mode that they experienced time and again and used to their advantage. What the Italic people achieved in the first century of the Roman Empire was executed in a still more radical way by the Greeks, in principle already thousands of years earlier and under completely different conditions, as the Vapheio cups demonstrate. If proof is still needed that the one-sided Indo-Germanic direction, in spite of its singularly inherent ability to continue, in the long run cannot forgo rejuvenation through Orientalizing, art history delivers that proof at the end of antiquity: from the time of the Antonines, a new Orientalism proliferates in politics and law, culture and art, that encompasses not only the Greeks, long since half-Oriental-ized, but also the Italic peoples. It would be a thousand years before one would again encounter the artistic level achieved in the Vapheio cups, although substantially surpassing it. The role of the stormers, the progressives, falls this time to the Germanic peoples; compared to them, the Romans now represent Oriental-ism, as before the Greeks did in comparison to the Italic peoples, and the Egyptians and Near Eastern people did in comparison to them.

NOTES

1. The rigid objectivism seen in ancient Near Eastern works must necessarily develop the tendency to remove whenever possible anything connoting space and time. This holds true also for the background (of reliefs as well as of paintings), recognition of which, as the Egyptians well understood, would in the end mean the emancipation of space. Hence the deliberate disregard, the disavowal, of ground in Egyptian art as it is expressed in relief *en creux* and in the intentional incongruity of ground and figure. In contrast, the filling in of empty ground with ornament is the first element introduced by Mycenaean relief sculptors. This was not necessary on the warrior vase, because the many protruding points already established a satisfactory relationship between ground and pattern. All of this clearly shows that the figure-ground relationship had to bring this art quickly to a recognition of space.

2. The heads of the human figures on the cups are represented in two cases in pure profile, whereas in the gored figure something more than this is depicted. Unfortunately, the galvanoplastic cast that was available to me does not reveal the formation of the facial features of this man clearly, for which the artist is primarily to blame in his obsession with a painterly impression of the heads. The absolute profile of the torso of the man who falls from the back of the bull headfirst is that much more important in view of the Egyptian imperative for a clear frontal representation of the torso and both arms. This motif of movement alone, in which the figure of the human body is literally set on its head, is vastly different from anything ancient Near Eastern. The precondition for the success of such a figure was its optical presentation as a whole. We do not encounter such remarkable confidence in a rendering of violent movements until after the rehabilitation of optical reception in Greek art in the Hellenistic period. In general, the baroque forms of this period relate extensively in outward appearance to the reliefs from Vapheio. This apparently lies in the mutual intensification of movement in the motif and in the design.

3. Brunn's identification of deficiencies in the forelegs of the fleeing bull and in the projection of the one caught in the net is completely unjustified [*Griechische Kunstgeschichte* (Munich: Verlagsanstalt für Kunst und Wissenschaft,

1893–1897)]. The second reproach was most likely incited by a view from a photograph, for the galvanoplastic cast shows a completely correct dorsal line from the head to the tail. But as regards the first point, one would like to ask whether Brunn has ever observed a bull at full gallop.

4. Viewed in this light, it seems characteristic that Mycenaean art left no large figural representations like those so numerous in Egyptian art, which would have required close observations and the imitation of objects. Even recent art history teaches that predominantly optical problems are always solved most successfully with small figures.

Translated by Tawney Becker.

PART TWO

Structure Analysis: Theory

Hans Sedlmayr, "Toward a Rigorous Study of Art " (1931)

Hans Sedlmayr (1896–1984) studied first architecture and then art history in Vienna. He wrote a dissertation under Julius von Schlosser on the Austrian baroque architect Johann Bernhard Fischer von Erlach in 1925. In the same year, he published an essay on Borromini, "Gestaltetes Sehen" (Shaped vision), in which he showed how a radically abstracting formalist analysis of a building could be the basis for a new historical reading. In 1929, Sedlmayr wrote the introduction to Alois Riegl's Collected Essays. *Sedlmayr and Otto Pächt developed a method that came to be called* Strukturforschung *(structure research) or* Strukturanalyse *(structure analysis). The essay translated here, "Toward a Rigorous Study of Art," served as a kind of manifesto of the new group. It was published in* Kunstwissenschaftliche Forschungen, *a journal founded by Sedlmayr and Pächt that appeared only twice, in 1931 and 1933. Here Sedlmayr calls on the discipline to move beyond mere empirical research. He sketches out a "second," interpretative art history that would do justice to the aesthetic nature of its objects. The historical studies published in the two volumes of* Kunstwissenschaftliche Forschungen, *including essays by Pächt and Guido Kaschnitz von Weinberg translated in this reader, were meant to exemplify the new art history.*

(Source: Hans Sedlmayr, "Zu einer strengen Kunstwissenschaft," Kunstwissenschaft-liche Forschungen 1 [1931]; *reprinted as "Kunstgeschichte als Kunstgeschichte," in Hans Sedlmayr,* Kunst und Wahrheit [Mittenwald: Mäander, 1978], pp. 49–80.)

Chapter Three

Toward a Rigorous Study of Art (1931)

Hans Sedlmayr

Anyone presently working in the field of art history begins his particular task having already taken a position on a whole set of problems — even if he is not aware of it, even if his position consists only in having overlooked the problems or having taken his own solution as self-evident. It is in this dark, half consciously traversed zone before the "real" and valued work that the significance of his efforts for the evolving field of study is determined, and even whether his endeavor qualifies as the study of art at all. The typical "schools of thought" within the current field of art history may be distinguished according to their success or failure in resolving certain fundamental problems; if a school of thought wanted to describe its scholarly ambitions as precisely as possible, it could do no better than to indicate where it stands on the fundamental questions that no study of art can avoid addressing.

The following essay will therefore address these fundamental problems. The antitheoretical scholar who views the consideration of these problems as fruitless "theorizing" overlooks the fact that he too theorizes implicitly and, moreover, that his material "results" depend on his unarticulated theory.[1]

Two Histories of Art

Wherever the study of art has gone beyond the primitive, prescientific stage — the stage at which logical and conceptual activity diffusely merges with other sorts of interests — two different histories of art develop alongside and through each other. I would immediately add that the notion of two histories or studies of art is theoretically incorrect and admissible only as a hypothetical construct. In reality, there are two isolable components of one ideal discipline of art history. In the practice of research as well, the two are not sharply separated but blend into each other. Nevertheless, it is useful to consider them in hypothetical isolation; in this way, the extremely muddled situation can be greatly clarified.

The "First" Study of Art

We will begin by describing the "first" study of art. And we will formulate it by considering the following questions: What would a study of art look like that did not understand its primary objects, the works of art? Which problems could it see and resolve? Which could it not? In which areas would it achieve a degree of rigor? Which epistemological desires could it satisfy? It would be worthwhile to think thoroughly through all of these questions; for our purposes, however, a few preliminary suggestions will suffice.

For instance, this hypothetical study of art that precedes an understanding of the work of art as such could use documentary evidence to establish the date and location of works of art, to attribute authorship to historical personages, to reconstruct the objective form of the works, and so on. And it could develop refined and rigorous methods for all of these tasks. Its conclusions, however, would be completely dependent on the accidental existence of documentation (in the broadest sense) and would therefore be thoroughly fragmentary.

Over and above such conclusions — merely assigning dates to

things — it could draw conclusions about the properties of artistic products at a *second* level: it could compare and classify these products on the basis of their properties, it could infer genetic connections (connections to a common ancestor or original source) from similar properties, and it could observe the transformations in works from one historical time and place to another. It could do all of this, but with an essential restriction: it could only make statements and draw conclusions about properties *that can be ascertained without understanding the product as an artistic product.* Later we will demonstrate precisely what this "understanding" is and on what it depends.

Which properties meet these conditions? I will list several of these unsystematically and in no particular order. Elements that can be understood without understanding the work of art as such include, for example, pictorial themes — naively put, "what a picture represents." Even if one were incapable of gleaning a specific "artistic" approach from pictorial works, it would still be possible (within certain limits) to determine what a particular picture represents or signifies or that its theme is similar to or derived from other themes. An "external" iconography is possible. I say "external" because this type of contemplation can only seize hold of pictorial meanings that *do not change* when they are detached from the particular artistic manifestation of this theme.[7]

The same is true (with similar restrictions) of research into formal "themes" or "forms" and the "formal opportunities" (*Formgelegenheiten*) (Wilhelm Pinder). Even those blind to art can see that the form of the basilica emerged at a particular historical time and place. They will manifest their incompetence, however, when it turns out that only an understanding of the artistic properties of this form can explain why it occurred precisely then and there — in other words, when it depends not on absolute form but on form as the vehicle for artistic properties, on form as *motive*, when it depends not on an abstracted, empty schema but on a clear and concrete "gestalt" that serves as the basis of a work of art.

But "parts" of a work of art and the properties of these parts are not the only things one can grasp without having understood anything about its artistic form, sense, and construction; even the object as a whole and the properties of the whole can be seen in this way. For example, one could determine that Hagia Sophia, in its overall formal appearance, is closer to San Vitale than to a Gothic building — even if the artistic sense of this work was not understood. The overall properties of the type suggested in our example are called the "style" of the work, but here again — just as in iconography — we must distinguish the "external style" from the "internal style," which can only be grasped through an understanding of the work. Works with a very similar "external style" may be fundamentally different when considered according to their "internal style." It would certainly be better not to call such different things by the same name; many errors and false problems have arisen from the fact that the term "style" must encompass so many different entities.

The results of this second stage of the "first study of art" can be used in the service of various research goals. First, they can be used to resolve problems from the first stage — determining date, locale, and attribution — in the absence of documents. The property of "style," for example, can be used in the service of attribution — this is the well-known method of "stylistic criticism." The goal of these investigations will have been reached when all these primary tasks have been resolved — and this is the point at which the genuine study of art begins. Second, one could take an interest in these results themselves, but then one would be conducting not the study of *art* but the study of forms, the study of (external) style, and so on — that is, the study of objects that first come into being after the dissolution of the work of art. These disciplines remain mere auxiliary reflections of a genuine study of art.

Third, one could also use these conclusions as the foundation for a genuine study of art, albeit with the awareness that one would *not* have direct access to the facts essential to the domain of "art." (Early studies of "primitive" peoples, for example, were in a similar position.) One would then be forced to rely on a speculative method to determine and interpret "external" facts retrospectively. This method of study would undoubtedly find itself in an extremely difficult situation, since it would run the risk of formulating a science of the "living" and of "life" based on the examination of "dead" organisms — a dangerous, although not necessarily fruitless, endeavor.

For, at least in certain cases, this "first" study of art could arrive at results that also appear in the realm of the "second" study of art — that is, an art history that has a direct understanding of its objects. If we take "external similarities" to mean those similarities between objects that can be ascertained without an understanding of the objects, then the "first" study of art will arrive at accurate and tenable conclusions in cases in which an external similarity corresponds to an internal similarity (this terminology requires no further explanation). And it will err when this is not the case, for then it will group together artistic products that do not belong to the same natural class (as well as the other way around); based on this, it will posit an evolutionary progression among products that, in fact, have no genetic connection: its dating and attribution will be incorrect; it will falsely assess the processes of transformation and develop an inaccurate account of the structure and sequence of events that gave rise to the products. And it will do all of this without the ability to distinguish its true conclusions from its false ones. For in order to determine whether an external similarity corresponds to an internal similarity, one must be able to ascertain the "internal" properties of an object, which such an art history, by definition, cannot do. If it could, its methods would be rigorous, astute, and subtle in and of themselves.

If there were *no one* who had direct access to the realm of "art" (the truths of which reside in the experience of its own inherent realities), then this sham study of art, which speculates about art by studying "art corpses," would be the best of all possible methods of studying art. Indeed, there have been and perhaps still are areas in which this fictional state is approached.

The situation would be different if there were, in fact, people who had experiences of this sort, but — for whatever reason — no scholars could be counted among this group of aesthetically "gifted" individuals (for example, if logical and aesthetic abilities were mutually exclusive, which is not the case). Then this study of art would only be intellectually satisfying to those people who have no direct access to "art." For all others, it would be a great disappointment. "You come from some robust, lively thing that has affected you, look up the existing scholarship about it, you read and read (or begin the type of research that has long been customary), and afterward you have the distinct feeling that you have accumulated a great deal, yet it all amounts to nothing. Somehow that which had seemed most important and most essential — the heart of the matter — has gotten lost in the process." At that point, it is useless to tack onto the barren, lifeless, inessential facts a pretty phrase "like creative fantasy, intuition, talent, and so forth, about which you may imagine the most beautiful things, but which, if you wish to grasp the beauty of rigorous scholarly work, usually turn out to be mere designations of a problem with no objective indication of the decisive issues and no deeper penetration. Scholars now have a whole set of such concepts, which have also become fashionable among intellectuals and which happily allow for the most beautiful thoughts, such as personality, essence, contemplation, intuition, and other lovely things. But when you want to penetrate deeper, such things almost entirely fail to bring about concrete results."[3] One might understandably hold the field of study itself responsible for this situation, and this would result in a wholesale rejection of the "dead" field of study, although it is really only a constitutive flaw of the "first" study of art. I leave it to the individual to determine to what extent the fictional situation described here corresponds to aspects of the existing field of art history.

The "Second" Study of Art

In contrast to this "first" study of art, we will consider another study of art, which has the capacity to understand artistic products. In order to emphasize its singularity, we will also assume that it is presented with *nothing* but the products itself — with no data that can be brought into relation to the works of art, either directly or indirectly.

In principle, this hypothetical art history can investigate the properties of works and their internal organization and structure; it can accurately classify works according to their natural groups and establish genetic connections among works on the basis of their properties; it can arrive at an understanding of the historical events whose products it is studying and of the forces at work behind these events.

But it can also accomplish tasks that the first study of art handles in a different way: it can "date" a work, not in the narrow sense of assigning a chronological number (date of origin) to the object but rather in a "topological" sense, by determining its position (earlier or later) in a genetic series; it can locate and attribute — again, not by assigning empirical historical individuals (as creators) to particular things but by establishing natural groups and "aesthetic personages" in Benedetto Croce's sense; it can reconstruct, not because it *knows* from reports or concludes from physical markings that a part looking a certain way is missing from this object and needs to be replaced but rather because it understands the inner organization of a work and immediately *sees* the need for the replacement of a specific missing part. For example, Pinder successfully used this method of "seeing" to replace the missing parts of the Nördlingen Altar; his additions were confirmed by the later discovery of the missing parts. This is a typical achievement of the emerging "second" history of art and one of its greatest.

While many achievements of one art history may be replaced by the achievements of the other, each one also possesses certain knowledge that remains inaccessible to the other. If the second study of art does not enlist the results of the first study of art, it is working in a vacuum, so to speak. (This fictional situation would come into being if, for example, a museum acquired a collection of works whose origins and dates were unknown.) *It is clear that a complete science of art cannot restrict itself to one of these two components but must connect and combine both.* Nevertheless, we can safely say that for this ideal art history, the second component is more "essential" and more "valuable" than the first; if forced to choose between them, one would have to take the second. Although its connections to coarser realities may be artificially suspended, the second offers a true study of *art*, while the first, even in its highest achievements, is not really an empirical study of art but only *approaches* an ever elusive knowledge of artistic phenomena through a problematic series of detours (that is, through the investigation of nonartistic facts about the work of art combined with speculations about art).

On the other hand, it remains to be seen whether this second art history is scientific in the same rigorous sense that the first art history is, and whether it fulfills the single constitutive requirement of a rigorous science: the ability decisively to evaluate contesting claims. There is no doubt that the first art history fulfilled this requirement. Naturally, the possibilities for rigorous decidability rapidly diminish as one progresses from the tasks of the first stage to those of more advanced stages, but that is primarily a matter of the degrees and limits of rigorous knowledge, the accessibility of which remains basically unproblematic in broad areas. The basic question here is whether the subjective certainty that one has correctly understood a work can be objectively verified and universally generalized or whether all "knowledge" in these fields is valid only for those whose experiences of the evidence are essentially compatible. For if only the latter were true, the study of art as a whole would splinter into various studies of art, each based on communally held beliefs and each incapable of rationally refuting the others.

So now the crucial question is this: Can criteria for rigorous decidability be established from within the second study of art? For if that were not possible, then the second study of art would not be viable. At the very least, we can now say that the necessary criteria are available in principle, even if they may not be sufficient to support a decision in individual cases. We have the beginnings of a rigorous study of art, but only the beginnings.

The Two Studies of Art and the Current State of the Field
In the field of art history as it exists today, the components that we have artificially separated actually overlap with no clear boundaries between them. Complete understanding and complete misunderstanding are extreme, borderline cases — in reality, a median level of understanding prevails — though the latter is approached much more frequently than the former. Statistically, however, the first study of art dominates today, both in the number of scholarly works produced and in the number of active scholars.

These hypothetical components of the present study of art are unequal not only in a quantitative sense but in a qualitative sense as well; that is, they exist at different stages of development. The first study of art has already worked through enormous parts of its "given" material; the blank areas on the map of its knowledge are growing ever smaller — it can claim conclusive results and definitive achievements, which, although they may be corrected on minor points, remain essentially valid. This stability and conclusiveness are the results of stable and generally recognized principles and methods of research. The first study of art operates according to the principle of rigorous decidability and with the criteria that support a rigorous decision; it has — if only in its preliminary stages — teachable methods, differentiated techniques, and stable scholarly approaches. It has a precise notion of its tasks, a vivid conception of what has already been achieved and what remains to be done, and the clear sense that it is "shaping" an objectively existing work (a field of study) through its collective efforts. The first study of art immediately loses this sense of certainty, however, when it aspires to answer questions that cannot be precisely formulated without an understanding of objects. The first study of art is thus characteristically quite "solid," on the one hand, yet quite "nebulous," on the other.

In the second study of art, everything is in a state of flux. It does not yet have a clear conception of what really needs to be done; it has no recognized criteria for objectively deciding between true and false; it is only beginning to develop concrete methods; it has no differentiated "organs." Its results are meager and, with a few exceptions, inconclusive; even the problems themselves are just now being formulated. Every scholar works "for himself." And the worst of it is this: ad hoc theories concerning our understanding of art declare the situation immutable. It is said, for example: "Yes, your understanding of scholarship necessarily holds true, but only for the allegedly exact 'first' study of art. There is, however, another area — the 'second' study of art — which must establish its methods in contrast to the 'first' one, and in this second study of art, we must renounce certain things that may be desirable in themselves, such as decidability, the urgent and rigorous pursuit of progress, and exact and objective clarification. And in the strongest and best representatives of the 'second' study of art, this position manifests itself as a truly grandiose resignation" (Paraphrase of Max Wertheimer's essays on the natural sciences and humanities).

As long as this situation persists, anything more than a merely mechanical and fragmentary integration of the two heterogeneous components is inconceivable. As soon as one proceeds beyond the domain of the first history of art, the investigation is in danger of veering away from science and toward literature, away from concepts and toward emotions. Procedures are rigorous and verifiable as long as they concern the completion of a work according to reports, dating it according to documents, assigning it to an artistic movement according to stylistic analysis, differentiating its forms genetically; but then, tacked on at the end, there appear a few loosely connected aperçus about the work's structure and meaning, which are often arbitrary, imprecise, and emotionally colored and which must be accepted as perfectly self-evident. But on the other hand, the conclusions of the second study of art often fail to stand up to verification by the results of the first study of art. So, for example, some of the attributions made by the greatest representatives of the second art history are contradicted by documentary evidence. The significance of this depends on whether one takes this to be a definitive objection or merely an indication that this field of study is not yet sufficiently developed.

We believe that in light of the current situation our most

urgent task is to build up the "second" study of art. A general critique of the existing field could limit itself to this second component of the ideal art history, for the incompleteness of the first component is of a different type and magnitude.[4] Such a critique would be useless if one could not demonstrate that the perceived problems could be rectified and that they are in no way characteristic of the area or objects of investigation.

Toward the Establishment and Organization of the "Second" Study of Art

A New Concept of the Work of Art

Of the various objects of investigation available to the second history of art, individual works of art occupy a special position because they can be directly examined, while events, for example, can only be inferred on the basis of the works themselves. For this reason, we shall designate individual works of art as our primary objects of investigation.

But then the second study of art is faced with a very peculiar situation. Its primary objects of investigation only exist if we take a particular approach toward things that common sense identifies as works of art. They must be re-created each time through real processes of reproduction out of the "external" data of the artifact that stands before us. *This thing only possesses artistic properties when it is approached with an "artistic" attitude, and it only possesses specific artistic properties when it is seen in accordance with a specific attitude.* If one alters one's attitude or approach, the properties of the work of art are altered as well, even though the object itself remains unchanged; thus we construct the same object as a different work of art.

The definition and investigation of such an "attitude" are themselves tasks proper to the study of art conceived in this way. The intentionally colorless delineation of this provisional notion is offered merely as an indication of the problem at hand.

We will say this much, however: such an "attitude" is not merely a way of "seeing," nor is it an intellectual process entirely cut off from physical processes; rather, it involves one's entire subjective being at all levels — psychophysical *and* intellectual, as Heinz Werner's experiments have demonstrated.[5] For a provisional account of the factors that determine a particular attitude, see the experiments of G. J. von Allesch.[6] Although they are concerned with extremely simple aesthetic objects, they are most certainly applicable to aesthetic creations as complex as works of art.

However, it would be a mistake to conclude from all of this that aesthetic products are entirely "subjective" entities. On the contrary: just as works of art are repeatedly re-created and formed anew by viewing subjects, each work of art is itself, in its totality, an objective reality, a separate object world that can be examined and accepted like any other concrete reality and that can be penetrated through contemplation or conceptualization.[7] (For once the "attitude" is firmly in place, the work that results is determined exclusively by the properties of the artifact itself.) When viewers with different attitudes look at the same object, each sees a different, but nevertheless *objective*, entity, which is entirely distinct from the truly "subjective" private reactions that the work may elicit in the viewer but that it does not *demand*.

The realization that objects of inquiry must first be re-created out of the formal data of a given artifact is in itself not new; in theory, it is almost universally accepted.[8] What is new, however, is its formulation. The earlier view erroneously shifted the necessary re-creation of the object out of the sphere of immediate perception (or imagination) and into the sphere of the intellectual processing of perception. It seemed to proponents of this view that different viewers examining the same artifact would have the same perceptual experience (given the same objective conditions — the same vantage point or series of vantage points, the same lighting, and so on) and that only later, in the "intellectual" processes — to which, as a result of philosophical prejudice, they granted a greater dignity than they granted to "mere" perception — would differing "interpretations" and "understandings" arise. The new view, in contrast, supports the empirically well founded and demonstrably more fruitful idea that in the case described above individual viewers may perceive entirely different works that are thoroughly distinct from each other and not merely seen with greater or lesser clarity.

But what is new, above all, is that through this understanding we have come to recognize the fundamental problem of the study of art. Whether or not our efforts will develop into a genuine study of art depends on how effectively these ideas are incorporated into our concrete practice.

The present field is still dominated by the naive view that the work of art is routinely accessible — for the external artifact does appear to stand clearly before us. Since different people today have very different attitudes toward external objects classified as " works of art," this uncontrolled area opens the way for a flood of contradictions. This then leads to skepticism about the possibility of rigorous decidability, since the material results of research now appear inexplicably incompatible. For example, the "boundary" of a particular space will change (to a certain extent) when seen, with a "geometrical" attitude, as a stereometric form and will change again when seen with an adequate "artistic" attitude.[9] Even the notion of a spatial boundary itself takes on a different meaning each time, making it impossible to come to any sort of agreement.

The "Correct" Attitude

The idea that we must first have artistic products present at hand in order to examine them will remain hypothetical unless we can establish criteria to determine whether, in a given case, the work that one *intends* to examine is really present at hand. If it were a matter of examining artistic products in general (as is the case in the general study of art), this would amount to deciding whether or not the attitude toward the given artifact was an "artistic" one. However, if *particular* works of art were to be examined, as is the case in specialized fields (whose findings form the basis of art history), then it would be necessary to establish that the attitude adopted was adequate to this *specific* work. (The first question can only be addressed by way of the second question.)

Such criteria would also be important for those who do not want to investigate a particular work (or draw conclusions about it based on investigation) but who want to behold or admire it — for anyone not satisfied with experiencing whatever aesthetic product happened to result from the accidental encounter between an artifact and the viewer's current attitude. In general, however, the non-scholarly viewer shows little interest in finding a clear resolution of this problem. In choosing among various attitudes, he picks not the correct one but the one that (in his view) yields the most appropriate results. What matters to him is not whether the work that he is examining is as similar as possible to the work he *intended* to examine but that the experiential value of the work be as high as possible. The shaping and reshaping of his attitudes toward works of art are guided by factors other than the desire for knowledge. This hedonistic approach is deeply pervasive in the current field of art history.

In a genuine study of art, it is impossible to proceed with one's daily work without first addressing this question. For it is only through the clean resolution of this problem that a genuine art history *comes to possess its primary objects of investigation.* The greatest objection to the current practice of art history is that it has not recognized the importance of this problem and has not pursued its solution energetically enough.

We cannot take it upon ourselves here to conjure up a solution out of thin air; we need only point toward a new approach that understands this problem to be unavoidable and works toward its solution from various directions. To a large extent, this depends on the conscious and precise deployment of methods that have been used previously but "casually" and without conscious reflection. We can only suggest the direction in which these preliminary solutions are moving.

The simplest case for determining the "correct" attitude is that of determining the "original" attitude — that is, the attitude under whose influence a particular, concrete artifact was formed in this way and no other. The more correct view of a work would be the one that construed previously unexplained aspects of the permanent, objective condition of the work as comprehensible, necessary, and significant.[10] In a strict theoretical sense, this criterion is contestable due to the possibility of false interpretations. However, as long as one cannot point to the existence of another view that explains each separate part and each relationship in the work in a different but no less meaningful way, this criterion remains valuable.

If this does not lead to a decision, it can be supplemented by another criterion: preference would go to the view of a work that elucidated aspects of the greater whole in which the work is imbricated that were incomprehensible as long as the work was viewed with a different attitude. One such "greater whole" might be the course of events that gave rise to the work. If a view of the individual work makes sense out of aspects of this course of events that another view passed over as insignificant or coincidental, this would indicate the correct attitude. The view of the individual work proves itself through its understanding of the structure and sequence of a course of events.[11]

While it is true that this criterion presupposes some knowledge of the course of events, this does not constitute an objection — it is a typical transitional stage in a field of study on its way to completion. No "part" of a unit of scholarship can be completed in isolation: the complete knowledge of the individual work and the complete knowledge of the sum of events to which it belongs are mutually dependent and must be achieved in tandem.

Similarly, the "culture" that gave rise to the work in question can also be viewed as a "greater whole." This rests on the idea that a culture, like a sum of events, is a unified organic whole with a determinable structure and organization. The correct attitude toward a work not only must "fit into" this structure but also must serve a specific function within the overall organization of this whole. (A specifically European attitude toward an African sculpture is spurious and incorrect because it is incompatible with other established knowledge about the primitive mentality.) In this case, one must step outside the realm of artistic phenomena in order to determine whether an attitude is correct: this is *one* good reason for the slogan "art history as the history of the spirit" ("Kunstwissenschaft als Geisteswissenschaft").

This does not exhaust all of the possible deciding factors.[12] If they do not presently accomplish what they should — if the decision in a particular case cannot always be pronounced with the requisite degree of certainty — it is because our ideas about the structure of highly complex constructs, such as a historical course of events or a "culture," are generally far too imprecise, because our conceptions of the organization of such constructs are often too simplistic, and because, in concrete cases, we still know far too little about the things in question. But even those who completely reject these criteria cannot get around the need to replace them with other criteria. Above all, the major task of the evolving second study of art is to seek out evidence that leads to definite decisions in concrete cases.

The naive view takes this extremely complicated state of affairs into account only insofar as it demands that scholars of art possess an "aesthetic sense." However, we are not told how one might recognize such a faculty.

A New View of Understanding
The recognition that the primary objects of investigation in the study of art are only present when one adopts a particular attitude toward artifacts might cripple the entire scholarly endeavor if it did not go hand in hand with a new view of investigation and understanding. For just when one has truly grasped the peculiar nature of this basic situation, another sort of skepticism arises: Is scholarly investigation of such works possible? Wouldn't a scholarly attitude cancel out the very attitude that could make these works available to us? Isn't there an irreconcilable contradiction between artistic contemplation and scholarly observation and understanding? And didn't what we have characterized as the "first" study of art develop precisely out of the desire for a scholarly understanding of works of art? The "life" flowed out of these delicate organisms because the only soil in which they could develop was removed — and scholarly observation was left with only their bare skeletons. These doubts are not ours alone, for they appear among the most sensitive observers of these organisms, particularly in their fear that phenomena will be replaced by their concepts in the process of scholarly investigation. So then they reject the "concept" altogether and content themselves with analogical descriptions and intimations of the "observed phenomena." Works of art are discussed in the same way theology discusses the properties of God.

These doubts, although they are extremely well founded, can be overcome. First of all, the contradiction between observation and understanding that has been accepted on the basis of outdated theories of knowledge does not exist.

What then is the nature of this advance in, for example, the investigation of the individual work? Here (as in scholarship generally) it consists in elucidating features and properties of the work that were formerly accepted without explanation and in developing concepts and interpretations that ascertain as much as possible as efficiently as possible in order to arrive at a better understanding of the work.[13] However, this understanding is not restricted to the realm of the intellect but includes the zone of perception as well. If my understanding of a work is better, then I see it differently — that is, I can better discern its structure and formal organization — so that the phenomenon itself becomes "better." For example, previously I might have seen a piece of architecture as a chaotic, confused mass of different forms; but insofar as I comprehend the function and organization of the parts, each part will appear to have a meaningful and necessary connection to the whole. "Thus to comprehend something means working it through to the last detail, and this means, on the one hand, that all confusion disappears and, on the other hand, that no two parts appear unconnected. Even if I have understood a particular detail to be 'foolish decoration,' I have still done a better job of working through the whole than if I had included the same detail with the whole but in a purely additive manner." (From this point on, this section loosely paraphrases the theories of Kurt Koffka.[14])

It is true that through this process the original construct was replaced by a different one; I was presented with a different phenomenon before and after understanding it. However, the phenomenon that replaced the original construct was not arbitrary but was more adequate and better organized. This is tantamount to saying that the transformation to which we subject phenomena when we investigate them as scholars is not foreign in essence to the phenomena themselves. When we say that phenomena are *better* organized, we mean that we bring certain essential but latent properties to fruition, but that we do nothing against their nature. If a scholar attributes a new property to a work of art, this does not mean that anyone who looks at the same artifact will now see this property; if things were this simple, it would be impossible to understand why it had not been noticed earlier. We are only claiming that if one observes this work with a particular attitude, distancing oneself as much as possible from the usual sort of observation, then it will possess this property. (Furthermore, this may lead even more significantly to explanations of previously unexplained matters.) Thus if someone perceives and comprehends this property for the first time, he will say: "I have never seen this before, and yet what I saw until now was not adequately described by the old concepts; there was something there (which I now see) that definitely pointed in the direction of this new property. Seeing this property has made my phenomenon of this work 'better.'" In this case, we are seeing works not as they are as but transformed in such a way that, to some extent, they approach their own ideal.

However, there is another sort of observation and understanding that does not produce a better organized whole but, on the contrary, allows it to fall to pieces. Here, too, the phenomenon is transformed, but in the opposite way: it is broken down into an additive accumulation of parts. This sort of understanding (which is falsely taken to be the only possibility for a rigorous science) is challenged by the skepticism described at the beginning of this section — and only here is this skepticism justified.

An additional remark: there may be reasons to look not at entire phenomena but only at their constitutive parts. In that case, the analysis itself is, in a broad sense, a process of formation. For when we separate the parts from the whole, they become endowed with their own gestalt. As long as we take this into account, an investigation of the "parts" of works of art is both possible and meaningful. Such a process is undesirable only if it fails to consider this state of affairs, if it believes that it is examining the actual parts of works of art when what it is really examining are the artificial by-products of the analytical process. The distance from the object typical of so much of the current field of art history can be explained, to a large extent, by the careless and destructive practice of analysis. However, analysis is neither the only process nor the highest organizational principle in our field of study.

It is true here too: one may reject the proffered solution, but one cannot evade the problem.

Relevant Objects of Investigation
Above all, it is the stage of development of a given area of investigation that determines which objects are to be given precedence. Before proceeding, however, one must make sure that no investigative task is unilaterally emphasized at the expense of others.

It is thus impossible to regard the investigation of artistic *events* as the sole task of the study of art. This would go without saying were it not for the fact that many people continue to conflate the study of art (*Kunstwissenschaft*) with art *history* (*Kunstgeschichte*) — and this view has left its mark on the study of art as it is carried out in the universities. This view is understandable from a historical perspective, since rigorous methods of scholarly investigation first emerged within the framework of a universal history; it is understandable objectively as well, for, as we have already pointed out, one must often presuppose knowledge of the artistic course of events in order to constitute individual works as well-defined objects. Nevertheless, we cannot consider the investigation of other objects (individual works, types of composition, artistic forms) merely as a stage to be passed through, as a means for constructing a history. The opposite approach, which places historical knowledge in the service of a study of works in themselves, is similarly justifiable. The study of works, alongside the study of events, is an *autonomous discipline* within the "whole" study of art — even though the two can never be completely separated.

The question of whether there are other autonomous "parts" (disciplines) within the study of art cannot be pursued here.

We may determine which research tasks should be pursued in the *present stage* of the second study of art by taking an overview of the parts that have developed until now. The first and most lasting achievement of this study of art was the development of scholarship concerning historically variable forms of representation (period style, generational style, regional style, and so on) and their transformations. In this area, the general goal — to achieve an understanding of the objects of investigation that will elucidate as efficiently as possible the particularities of a "style" — has been successfully approached in many cases. *Nevertheless, the study of stylistic transformations cannot be equated with art history*; nor is it sufficient to consider the individual work solely as the manifestation of a particular style. Rather, *all* of the other tasks, insofar as they are recognized today, must be tackled with the same level of rigor that distinguishes this well-served area of investigation.

To sum up: thus far, the aims of the second study of art have been too much those of art *history*, and its practice has become too much the history of *style*. It is on this basis that we offer the following suggestions:

a. The currently evolving phase in the study of art will have to emphasize, more than ever before, the *investigation of individual works*. Nothing is more important at the present stage than an improved knowledge of the individual work of art, and it is in just this task, above all, that the current field manifests its incompetence.[15] Without a thorough investigation of individual works, we cannot adequately resolve other problems. We can only make conclusive statements about the similarities and dissimilarities of works if we have gone deep enough in our understanding of the individual work. On the basis of observations about similarities and dissimilarities, we can deduce the genetic relationships between works (relationships of derivation), and these observations may then form the basis for the reconstruction of events. An improved knowledge of the individual work thus leads to increased knowledge in *all* areas of the study of art.

The fact that the *individual* work of art is now temporarily in the forefront of research does not mean that this work should be artificially removed from the historical situation that gave rise to it. This error is avoided in that, according to the new view, a work of art *only exists through a particular attitude in which virtually the entire historical situation is concentrated.* Furthermore, this attitude determines what may be regarded as a complete individual work.

In addition, submerged historical conditions can be raised to the level of immediate experience more completely and in greater concentration by adopting the appropriate attitude than would ever be possible through the cultural-historical method of drawing parallels between artistic phenomena and corresponding evidence from other areas (Carl Linfert).

Once the individual work of art is perceived as a still unmastered task specific to the study of art, it appears powerfully new and close. Formerly a mere means to knowledge, a trace of something else that was to be disclosed through it, the work of art now appears as a self-contained *small world* or microcosm of its own particular sort. This is something like the transition from a conception of the "whole world" as a field of action and expression for its creator — a world in which only his *direct* manifestations are of interest — to a conception of the world itself as the object of examination and investigation. The primary consequence of this transition is a tremendous increase in qualitative richness, next to which the old descriptions and the old way of seeing appear pale, schematic, and abstract.

b. The investigation of historically variable types of formal organization (styles) has hitherto been subordinated to the *investigation of relatively invariant types*, which remains within the limits of non-scholarly experience when it speaks of "architecture," "painting," and so on. A comprehensive study of art is faced with the task of verifying the legitimacy of these non-scholarly classifications.

The same is true for the typological concept that delimits our field of study but whose precise meaning is as yet unknown: the concept of "art." In any case, it is now clear that this term — whose application is circumscribed, for the time being, by non-scholarly linguistic usage — describes a wide variety of facts and objects that must be thoroughly understood in order to discover the *natural limits* of the concept.[16]

c. The deferral of genuinely art historical work at the present stage is not due to a disregard for history, nor does it prove that these new ideas are useless in dealing with art historical problems. Rather, this measure takes into account the idea that the *investigation of events* presents an especially difficult problem (in other areas as well), the solution of which requires careful preparation.

What is needed, first, is an improved knowledge of the works. *If we do not understand the works, then we also do not understand how the course of events has changed,* and then we do not understand the events themselves.[17] Practical work has shown that an exceptionally wide-ranging knowledge of individual works can decisively clarify our knowledge of the relevant course of events.

Second, we need a *clarification of our ideas about events in general* — along with a clarification of related concepts such as "force" (as the source of change), achievement, "evolution." All of the concepts are indispensable and are widely used in research, whether explicitly or implicitly, but they are so vaguely defined that the concept of "evolution," for example, has lost its precise meaning and is used indiscriminately to mean development, events in general, movement, and change. We can accelerate this process of clarification by incorporating results from other areas that are relevant to problems that arise in the investigation of any course of events.[18]

I would only like to add here that the new concept of the work of art outlined above implicitly entails a new view of events that points up the inadequacy of a currently widespread view of art historical events. According to this view of events — which results from a material interpretation of works — *new* works (works with new properties) are simply added to the old, while old works remain unchanged. It has been observed, however, that even a single work with new properties brings with it a new "attitude," and this newly developed attitude brings about changes in the properties — and in the relative value — of *all* works, even previously existing ones. At the same time, there are changes in the environment surrounding works considered " works of art " (in the valuative sense of the term); the constellation of objects that this attitude considers as "motives" changes, and much else besides. Thus, a nearly geometric view is replaced by a dynamic view.

The complete revision of our ideas about events, together with the new material results acquired through the investigation of works, will produce a historical picture that is essentially transformed, both in its general outlines and in its details.

Historical questions have been temporarily deferred in order to allow for the unhindered development of these necessary conditions for new historical work.

d. Above all, the study of art is concerned with two sorts of sequences of events: events connected with the emergence of new attitudes, and events connected with the emergence of the individual concrete work of art associated with a given attitude. It is thus concerned with a phylogenetic and an ontogenetic course of events. (It is also concerned with the course of events during which the material artifact was produced.)

Art history has hitherto emphasized the investigation of concrete sequences of events of the first sort. The study of the *ontogenesis of the individual work of art* — the development of the work from its "conception" through its unfinished "embryonic" states to its final state — has not yet progressed much beyond very weak beginnings. Aside from its intrinsic significance, this task is important for the investigation of "great" courses of events, since events that take place during the production of an individual work of art can retrospectively change the "attitude" that originally gave rise to them.[19]

We have thus outlined only a few of the relevant objects of investigation; others will present themselves as we proceed from this provisional foundation.

Relevant Methods

Methods — in the narrow sense — cannot be formulated before addressing particular problems but can only develop in the process of addressing them. Nevertheless, it is possible to set forth a few general maxims. These are determined, first, by the particular nature of the objects being investigated and, second, by the stage of development of the relevant field of study.

So, for example, what we have described as the unique character of the primary objects of the study of art completely precludes an interrogation of the objects according to preestablished conceptual schemata (formulaic methods of interrogation). "I can pose as many questions about things as I like and demand an answer for each, as long as the question is meaningful with regard to the thing." Works of art, *in this respect*, behave not like things but like phenomena. (This does not affect their reality and objectivity; see above.) "Insofar as a phenomenon naturally arose out of a particular attitude, it only has properties specific to this attitude. It is pointless to ask about other properties, and in fact, this immediately leads to a distortion since the question has now changed the attitude itself. So, for example, under certain conditions, the question 'Was that blue light or dark?' (or 'Was the space "additive" or "divisive"?')[20] may be unanswerable. This is not because the viewer failed to 'notice' or attend specifically to these properties but because under the given conditions the phenomenon was not defined according to this line of thought — although this could never be the case for a thing. If you press for answers to such questions, you will end up creating new phenomena for which they can be answered. But then, rather than developing an essential core, you will have falsely replaced one phenomenon with another" (Kurt Koffka). Thus, through supposedly "objective" formal description, the work of art is replaced by something entirely different and is actually destroyed. The unsuitability of these particular methods sharply reveals — this time from a different angle — the unique character of these objects of investigation.

On the other hand, the predominance of certain methods is an expression of the particular stage of development of a given field of study, which manifests itself similarly in other fields of study. Typical of this stage is "the isolation from the immediate demands of praxis,[21] an antitheoretical attitude focused on phenomena, the increased nearness (and concreteness) of the object, greater differentiation from other fields of study and increased safeguarding of methods of consideration, and, finally, the shift from a contraction to an expansion of the area of study." This stage can be described as a transition from the "systematic phase" to the "descriptive phase" and manifests itself similarly in other fields of study as well (Kurt Lewin). Thus it is clear that requirements that Kurt Lewin has developed for the methods of comparative epistemology (the study of fields of study) may be applied point for point to the new phase of the study of art.[22]

Today's most pressing tasks and methods arise out of this situation. I will briefly apply each of the requirements proposed by Lewin to our material. (These sections of Lewin's work should be read in full and carefully considered.)

1. Reflections *about* art or types of art must give way to the investigation of works. Similarly, speculation about the essence of historical processes must give way to the investigation of the properties of concrete historical sequences of events. (For critiques of this programmatic point, see Lewin, p. 78.)

2. For a while, work within the field of art history will energetically emphasize the description of the phenomenological properties of concrete objects, that is, those characteristics directly accessible to perception, in contrast to the previous emphasis on conditional and genetic characteristics typical of the "systematic phase" in all fields of study.

3. The fact that works of art are not biological or psychological but rather "essential" or "ideal" objects — in any case, objects belonging to a specific sphere — should not lead to the general use of radical, absolute distinctions. Even between essential, ideal works that are sharply opposed to each other, one usually finds intermediary essential types, often forming a continuous series of transitions, so that here, too, "pure" cases should only be described as borderline or ideal. This tendency toward constructing absolutes has a distorting effect and prevents the spirit of non-

deductive descriptions based on individual works from emerging.

4. As a rule, the construction of absolutes is only made possible through a rather thoughtless treatment of *examples*. This point is so crucial that I shall cite the relevant passage from Lewin at length:

The example is granted an extraordinarily heightened significance in the descriptive phase. Since this phase, unlike later phases, does not yet have extensive access to other criteria, "exposition by example" is the essential means for proving, or better yet verifying, the correctness of assertions. If examples are truly to fulfill this function, a new spirit of increased rigor and responsibility must guide their use. The example must be dissociated from a procedure all too common in the "systematic" phase, in which an illustration derived from a singular, isolated type is treated as evidence of a much more general type; the extreme cases of this procedure already appear astonishingly lax.

Above all, one must consider whether or not counterexamples can be found that demand a restriction on the generality of the assertion or prohibit it from being made altogether.

This in no way supports the claim, which is thoroughly unfounded in the so-called empirical sciences as well, that a general statement can only be verified through a majority of similar cases. However, the definition of a general type must not inadvertently raise qualities specific to the type represented by an example to the level of essentials. As banal as this requirement may sound, it is for that very reason difficult genuinely to fulfill it, and the majority of faulty descriptions today are based on a false estimation of the area validly covered by the example employed, regardless of whether this area is overestimated or underestimated. (The occurrence of the latter is not at all seldom and has led to deep-seated errors.) The naive treatment of the example that overconfidently sees only its positive, confirming function must be replaced by a method that also recognizes the example's negative function, which is to call attention to errors. As a general requirement, we should consider the area covered by the example and carefully seek out counterexamples.

Thus general statements will be based not on a majority of similar cases but on a consideration of cases that are as diverse as possible, that is, on dissimilar types of evidence. This corresponds to the increased level of caution regarding "general" (generalizing) judgments — that is, judgments that use the term "all" and not those that make a claim for generality or incontestability — and in no way implies a diminished faith in the example's value as evidence or in the value of the individual case. Rather, the cautious consideration of the area validly covered by the example is the necessary methodological correlate to the conviction that the individual example may provide the basis for apodictic judgments concerning the general type to which the example belongs.

5. We must replace statements about abstract possibilities with determinations of concrete facts.

6. We must take care not to destroy the full and singular concreteness of the individual work in the process of detaching it from its surroundings. What may be considered a "whole" work can only be determined in each individual case.

7. The demand to investigate the concrete individual work does not call for the removal of the individual object from its surroundings, nor does it call for its isolated treatment. Whenever possible, the description of the individual object should go hand in hand with the investigation of *related types*. The most important methodological means of fulfilling this, as well as most of the other requirements discussed, is *comparative* description.

Again, a quote from Lewin (with minor changes) helps to clarify this point:

Instead of characterizing works according to general classifications that can only be arrived at by way of extremely hypothetical generalizations, comparative description makes determinations by contrasting works with other concrete individual works, or rather with types representing "last species." Thus through comparative description we become independent of a broad stratum of otherwise unavoidable theories that are, moreover, especially dangerous because they are difficult to recognize as such.

Determinations made through comparison are essentially relative. A concrete object is measured against others, but it is defined as a member of a particular class. This does not mean that the resulting knowledge will be any less general than the apparently absolute determinations of earlier periods. Rather, this relativity makes possible an incomparably more precise and thereby much more reliable description.

The comparative method is extraordinarily productive, above all, as a heuristic principle. For often, important qualities that would otherwise remain hidden first come to light through comparison with other closely related works.

Comparative observation forces us into close proximity with objects and sharpens our view of the valid range of examples by marking out the borders of related types. It thus provides an essential safeguard against the current and largely unavoidable tendency to work with irreconcilable antitheses — that is, against the danger of thinking in terms of absolutes.

The intentional use of comparative description is probably the most effective aid against the extraordinarily common equivocations and other errors of terminology that find false similarities among essentially dissimilar works and all too often wrench apart closely related works through diverse nomenclature. For it is the task of comparative description to mark out the entire field of relationships and to designate the individual type as the member of a series in which every intermediary step can be determined. This reveals previously imperceptible connections between distant elements in a series and often leads to a thoroughly transformed view of various properties of the individual element as well. This clarification of relationships — between particular properties in different works or in the position of certain works or processes within more comprehensive totalities — is precisely the focus of comparative description.

The conscious emphasis and detailed discussion of the question of "equivalence" is one of its most essential features. This applies to properties, processes, and works at every level and may concern functional as well as morphological equivalences. The careful discussion of these problems is an important safeguard against misleading terminology or appearances, and, furthermore, it compels us to consider the individual in association with its respective connections.

Finally, the comparative method provides antispeculative, "non-theoretical" description with a path along which scholarship can advance step by step, with each new step functioning as a confirmation of those which preceded it. It prevents description from disintegrating into an incoherent conglomerate of concrete individual facts. The future development of the study of art history will take place against the background of comparative description, and the consistency and accuracy of its practice will determine how quickly this field of study will find its way from the spirit of "systems" to that of quiet, objective scholarship that (at least for the time being) often appears to be more narrow-minded.

8. The attitude toward pure description presently necessary in the study of art is not a permanent feature of the field but only a characteristic of this new phase. The study of art cannot always limit itself to establishing the phenomenal characteristics of objects but must advance to the investigation of conditional genetic

relationships. For the study of art, description is not the last but the *first* task of rigorous investigation.

9. In order to accomplish its most relevant tasks — above all, to clarify the function and interconnection of the so-called parts of a work — the second study of art will intentionally and with good conscience practice the *thought experiment*, which was hitherto utilized only surreptitiously.[23] But it will also use corresponding caution to enlist the conclusive *real experiment*. A study of art conceived as the *study of culture* cannot refuse knowledge derived from similar endeavors, as, for example, Werner has done in his theoretical investigations of language.[24]

Cooperation with Other Fields of Study
The collaboration of the study of art with other fields of study is objectively necessary for a very simple reason: the spheres of investigation cannot be cut off from one another. Even in the field of art history as it stands now, certain unavoidable questions are posed that are rooted in structures of interrogation proper to other fields of study and that, without recourse to the collective knowledge of the relevant discipline, can only be answered insufficiently or incorrectly.

Cooperation is only possible if the individual identity of a field has been so firmly established that there is no fear that contact with other fields of study might bring about a dissolution of its own objects and methods of consideration. For works of art can *also* be considered "expressions" of a personality or character type, manifestations of a national spirit or zeitgeist, forms of understanding; artistic phenomena can be placed in the service of the psychology of individuals or types, general humanistic and epistemological studies, and much else besides. But there has also been the danger that the autonomous consideration of the work of art as work of art might be forgotten.[25] "Psychologism" is not the only but merely the best-known derailment of an autonomous study of art. The foundations outlined here protect the study of art from such a deviation so that it may safely interact with other areas.

The principle guiding this interaction must be to enlist outside results *only* when they are securely established in their own field of study and when they demonstrably contribute to the resolution of a concrete problem within the study of art.

The study of art at its present stage needs other fields of study primarily to back up its own research — it is to this end that we have enlisted Gestalt theory and experimental and phenomenological aesthetics, for instance. But even more important, the study of art needs other fields of study in order to eliminate certain prejudices that have previously hindered its own research. This new theory of scholarship can reveal characteristics that until now were falsely viewed as permanent features of the field of art history to be typical features of a particular developmental stage in new fields of study. The fact that, in all of these cases, we have considered ideas belonging to a particular theoretical position was not due to unilateral partisanship for this direction, but of course it was also not entirely arbitrary. In fact, *every* idea and observation that help us better to solve or even to see a particular problem should be welcome.

Enlisting outside results will become even more important than it is in the present stage when we progress beyond description to explanation. The new psychology already holds a wealth of knowledge waiting to be put to use in an explanatory study of art.[26]

Art historians of the old school often misunderstand the first signs of this need for cooperation (with the new psychology, for example), as well as any expression of the new tendencies we have described, as a call to make the study of art more "naturalistic." This suspicion is based on entirely superficial features, such as more frequent citations from writings outside the study of art and the use of certain phrases. In reality, the new position has already energetically broken away from certain "naturalistic" views that still significantly influence the work of art historians who enthusiastically advocate an anti-naturalistic program as individuals. The new position has broken away from the view that works of art can be investigated like things (although this view has defiantly persisted in the face of all different ideological orientations); it breaks away from the idea that an individual work of art belongs to its natural group in the same way that a biological individual belongs to its species; and it is also on the verge of freeing ideas about art-related events from unconscious "naturalistic" prejudices. Incidentally, the approach that we have rejected along with this adjective has been superseded in and partly through the natural sciences as well. There is no valid reason to oppose the consolidation of various attempts to gain knowledge about the intellectual product, "the full explanation of which constitutes an eminent goal not only of the humanities but of the natural sciences as well" (Allesch).

First Results

The approach to individual aesthetic products and the methods we have described are more than merely "theoretical," as is confirmed by various results that this process yields after only a few steps. Insofar as we consciously foreground the investigation of the individual work and particularly its pure description, these results belong first and foremost to a descriptive study of the work of art and, in fact, to the *general* study of art. Although they are based on the concrete individual work, these results are valid for all constructs of its type. They are clearly significant for the solution of other tasks facing any study of art. We will enumerate them in an unsystematic and partial list:

1. The *levels of meaning* in the work of art. In the individual work of art, regardless of its level of internal unity and consistency, not everything is related equally closely to everything else, but there are different levels of interdependence, of meaningful necessity, and of relative contingency (just as there are in the structure of the "larger world"). Typical complexes of relations develop, each of which can be understood as arising from *one* central structural principle. Furthermore, these complexes stand in a determinable structural relation to one another, whereby certain complexes typically presuppose others and are in this sense positioned "over" them. This warrants the use of the term "levels."

This first, primitive idea, which we have presented in an extremely simplified form, may still be further developed (cf. Werner's *Formanten*).[27]

2. Artistic *substances*. It is not possible — even within an individual level of meaning — to account for everything in purely formal terms; a complete description also requires determinations of substance (a "what" along with the "how").

In the specific case of the work of art, this may correspond to the general contention put forward by Adolf Meyer in regard to other areas of investigation — namely, that every scholarly theory arises out of rationalism and empiricism and, further, that it is impossible to dissolve rationalism into empiricism, or vice versa.

The scope of this observation is demonstrated by the fact that when one attempts to work out historical constants or invariants (of a national or regional type, for example), invariable artistic substances appear alongside the purely formal constants that previously constituted the primary objects of investigation.

I can only touch on this here and refer the reader to Otto Pächt's investigations of historical constants.[28]

3a. The *dynamic character* of the aesthetic construct (its immanent, relative value). Not only factual information can be gathered from the work, but also the final condition toward which the work "aspires" — its "ideal" — as well as its distance from this final condition toward which it is moving.[29] This observation of "dynamic character" (Koffka's term[30]) can be carried out just as directly as the observation of other properties: for example, that the work is not stable, that it aspires to a "better" condition, that it is "bad." These "values" are not merely deduced or somehow felt; rather, they are just as immediately perceptible as the rest of the work. The work's "dullness" or "insipidity" is just as immediately perceptible as its "blueness." Of course, this is only valid for the *work seen with a particular attitude*; if the attitude is changed, the dynamic character (the immanent value), as well as the other properties of the work, will also change. Something that was bad when seen with one attitude may be good when seen with another — within reasonably established limits.

Of course, we still have not addressed the differences of rank and value that exist among various attitudes.

Incidentally, there appears to be yet another meaning of the term "work of art" (beyond the naive confusion about the artifact). According to general terminology, only *successful* artistic products are considered works of art. This fails to recognize that the character of the artistic organization of form is expressed in its unsuccessful works no less than in its successful ones.

3b. The *physiognomic character* of the work. Like the "dynamic character" of a work, its physiognomic character can also be rigorously determined through pure observation. The qualities of "sadness," "severity," "tenderness," and so on are not merely the emotional associations of viewers but are objective properties of a work understood in a particular way that are only valid in reference to a particular attitude (basis of expression). The situation here is — with minor changes necessitated by the subject matter — identical in principle to that described by Werner in his work on linguistic physiognomy.[31] But for us, this state of affairs is perhaps even more significant, since in most if not all cases the "physiognomic approach" is the attitude *demanded* when considering works of art.

4. The *transcendent character* of the work of art. The individual work points beyond itself to other manifestations of the same formal organization as that which it appears to represent. Again, these further possibilities are not speculative but are directly experienced in the analysis of a given work.

This observation is difficult to communicate in abstract form, but it will become important for attribution and for the establishment of the natural ordering (the last species) of works of art.

5. The *orientation* of the work of art. Regardless of its degree of aesthetic unity, the work carries within itself traces of its prehistory and the seeds of future transformations. At least some of its properties can only be understood by considering that this state was reached by way of particular previous states and is itself a transition to subsequent states. (By looking at a color scale, for example, one can often tell which color level has been superseded.) Of course, this property is quite distinct from the "dynamic character."

This sense of orientation is of great importance to the investigation of the events that gave rise to the works.[32] Only in this way is it possible to make the leap from individual works to real events without stumbling. Real events can never again be reconstructed on the basis of individual, neutrally self-contained works.

Consequences of Reorganization
The new tendencies justify themselves directly in the resolution of problems intrinsic to the study of art and indirectly in that through them this "organism" becomes more securely established, more distinctive, more structured, and more differentiated.

1a. By producing objects proper to itself, this "organism" maintains an immutable core; and by proceeding on the basis of these works, it establishes its characteristic aspect. It distinguishes itself among other approaches to art objects as a "study of art as the study of *art*."

1b. By eliminating elements that do not yield new knowledge, this core is made smaller, but it is also newly strengthened; the areas in which scholarly activity merges with other ways of dealing with the same objects are restricted to certain peripheral zones. This results in the eradication of all literariness and the renunciation of all statements that have no direct connection to the objects of investigation but are merely tacked on. An approach based on observation limits the effect of emotional factors, which so easily and imperceptibly find their way into all speculation. As this process advances, it will become easier to distinguish serious investigation from the dilettantism that superficially imitates it. The further this intellectual organism consolidates itself as scholarship, the more its subsequent development will be motivated and guided by endogenous, intrinsic forces, and the more independent it will be from the fluctuations of the "zeitgeist."

1c. Concrete work has shown that certain problems can only be resolved after first resolving other problems that have naturally arisen alongside them. In this way, the conception of the natural boundaries of this field of study and its internal structure are transformed through the research itself, rather than through abstract reflection about these matters. For instance, it organically incorporates a "general study of art" and a theory of artistic value that were until now artificially separated and long subject to speculative treatment, and thereby gives these areas an incomparably broader empirical foundation.

On the other hand, not all of the connections in this field of study are equally close; within it there exist entire, largely autonomous subfields. The independence of individual disciplines (such as the ahistorical study of works as opposed to art history) becomes more pronounced, and again this appears not as a postulate or theoretical thesis but in the practical work of scholars. This does not contradict the idea that autonomous disciplines exist in dynamic relation to each other — they are mutually dependent (as we have already demonstrated in passing), and they develop alongside and through each other. In this way, the conception of the structure of the field is more broadly clarified, and this in turn has a favorable effect on its praxis.

The same holds true for the auxiliary disciplines of the study of art: diplomatics, textual criticism, restoration procedures, and so on. Since the individual work of art is granted greater significance than ever before, a greater emphasis will have to be placed on the meticulous restoration of the "artifact's" original external condition. We can expect an increased level of precision and a higher estimation of "philological" methods (which are more easily neglected in the "study of art from above").

2a. This new approach will lead to the creation of new organs and new forms of scholarly work. The *monograph* — not so much the biographical monograph, since there is no guarantee that the empirical individual is also an aesthetic individual, but rather the monograph focusing on individual works of art or on closely related "natural" families of works — is emerging as a major new form of scholarly examination alongside those commonly used until now.[33] Since each sentence in this type of monograph must justify itself in relation to a work that stands immediately before us, it also cultivates a new spirit of concrete rigor and responsibility.

2b. Since broad areas of the study of art have not all been treated with the same rigor, and yet we cannot trace the larger connections without an attitude based on this sort of detailed examination, we must supplement the form of the monograph with overviews of broader, but once again, naturally bounded groups of objects; we must strive for an overview of all the problems in the relevant area rather than for hasty resolutions. We need a *productive understanding of the gaps in the structure of knowledge* and of the broader relations among problems. There is now a greater emphasis than ever before on posing meaningful and precisely formulated questions, and the presentation of questions is itself becoming an independent and productive form of scholarly investigation.

2c. Finally, as a framework for these investigations of the smallest details and the largest unknowns, we will employ far-reaching "constructions" (constructive models of historical events, for example) as long as they are available, or, if absolutely necessary, we will establish new ones, while recognizing their provisional function and purely hypothetical significance. At the same time, we will try to keep hypotheses to a minimum, and we will grow less dependent on them as work based on observation advances.

3. Since this tendency toward rigor, concreteness, and proximity to the object makes it impossible to produce an "overview" of the entire area covered by the study of art (as was still possible, and even requisite, not long ago), a demand for summation is emerging. In the epoch of the study of art that is now drawing to a close, nearly every leading art historian had begun to erect or had at least planned out his own complete overview of the study of art, which was necessarily both internally inconsistent and irreconcilable with the frameworks of other overviews. In the second study of art, now, and actually for the first time, studies of art (art histories) are being replaced by *the* study of art (art history), which is being shaped through collective work. This is retrospectively exerting a strong demand for the standardization of terminologies and the verification of methods and results.

This inner collectivism (which is the natural social form of all scholarship) should also manifest itself externally, through the gradual abandonment of the individual scholar's isolation and through the formation of small, cell-like work groups.

Since even a preliminary adaptation of more rigorous formulations exposes most of the old points of contention as false problems, we may expect that the theoretical differences among existing schools will gradually diminish.

4. All of these things exact very specific requirements from those scholars striving to bring about change and to call forth a new type of art historian. The first type to die out should be the art historian with a bad conscience — the type who was really convinced that works of art should not be investigated but only "experienced" but who proceeded to investigate anyway, only badly. This type should be followed by those one-sided talents who take their capacity for aesthetic reproduction to be a scholarly achievement in itself. Meanwhile, this capacity would be subject to an even higher standard — in much the same way that scholars of music are expected to have a certain minimum and demonstrable talent for reproduction — although we would also expect it to be supplemented by the very different capacity for dispassionate scholarly observation and logical, conceptual thought. And finally, those scholars for whom the investigation of art was merely a means for satisfying other ambitions (such as philosophical or humanistic interests) will give way to those for whom the knowledge of artistic phenomena is of primary and indispensable interest.

This slow, careful method of working requires patience and a certain phlegmatic temperament; however, the naturally broad frame of reference surrounding the tasks at hand and the commitment to a comprehensive penetration into the "depths" of objects will prevent a total preoccupation with trivialities. In general, the type and hierarchical position of scholars would be determined by a "good" combination of antithetical capacities held in a taut balance: scholarly productivity and aesthetic reproductivity, concrete observation and abstract thinking, and so on.

Finally, the almost limitless plasticity of the "facts" in this area poses less of a threat to preconceived opinions than the rigid facts of other areas of investigation, and therefore demands that the scholar strictly curb his desire to see things the way he would like them to be.

5. This new basis will — eventually — greatly facilitate a scholarly "popularization" of results without making concessions to bad journalism.

Without abandoning its own interests, the newly developing study of art can fulfill a long-deflected legitimate expectation on the part of the art public. The layman naturally expects the study of art to satisfy his desire to derive something from the individual work that will organize his own chaotic experience and make it clearer and more meaningful. He is looking for "attitudes" with which to approach works of art — and that is precisely the cardinal problem of the new phase of the study of art. As a result of this coincidence of interests, it will be possible to abandon those surrogates that were previously called on to appease this expectation with a false sense of satisfaction. It is not necessary to kindle an abstract emotion as long as the viewer is made to experience — through his knowledge of works — their inherent emotive powers. And since, according to this view, more advanced knowledge both presupposes and results in new and "better" perception, this sort of popularization will consciously reorganize the viewer's perceptions (as today's good popular literature already attempts to do), rather than imparting disparate "insights" about the works or fragmentary bits of intellectual knowledge dissolved in an emotional fog. This sort of popularization will thus strive for *organization* — with the closest proximity to the object *and* to life — in an area that was previously restructured only incidentally and haphazardly.

Beginnings of a Rigorous Art History
The field of art history sketched out here was not *devised* by us; rather its beginnings are already *present* everywhere in the current field. The new tendencies that we have discussed were not formulated on the basis of hypotheses about future developments in our field of study but encountered in the study of art as it presently exists. Through pure observation, we can ascertain not only its present state but also the direction in which it is moving.

While it would be useful to point out which "schools" within the current study of art have given rise to these beginnings, we cannot take that as our task here. There are hardly any directions that have not somehow helped prepare the way for this reorganization.

Aside from those groups that feel no inner demand for change, the greatest obstacle to the reorganization and further development of this field of study is presented by those groups that have suppressed this desire through false satisfactions.

The emergence of the new tendencies can be accelerated, above all, by a clear understanding of the present situation. This understanding will come about, in turn, through a comprehensive transformation of the system of value in the realm of scholarly activity: through a *new appreciation of methodological self-consciousness* and through the confident expectation that far-sighted reflection on one's own activity will not hinder but rather will promote "life," even in scholarship. "La pensée peut précéder la vie: elle contribuera par là même à la redresser" (Ramon Fernandez, *De la personnalité*). Only this conviction renders an endeavor such as ours meaningful; the resonance of our endeavor depends on the acceptance of this conviction.

Notes

1. See Sedlmayr, review of Karl Tolnai, *Kritische Berichte zur kunstgeschichtlichen Literatur* 1 (1927–1928), p. 24.

2. Compare Hubert Schrade's view of iconography to that of Louis Brehiér in *Kritische Berichte* 2 (1928–1929), esp. pp. 198ff. Also see the review by Wolfgang Stechow in the same volume, p. 187.

3. Max Wertheimer, *Über Gestalttheorie* (Erlangen: Weltkreis-Verlag, 1925), pp. 3–4.

4. The possibilities of cartographic-statistical methods for the history of form have not yet been exhausted, for example, and physical and chemical means of reconstructing the original condition of objects, as well as their consequences for making attributions, are only beginning to be used.

5. Heinz Werner, "Studien über Strukturgesetze V (Über die Ausprägung von Tongestalten)," *Zeitschrift für Psychologie* 101 (1927), pp. 179ff.

6. G. J. von Allesch, "Die ästhetische Erscheinungsweise der Farben," *Psychologische Forschung* 6 (1925). See also Sedlmayr, review of G. J. von Allesch, *Kritische Berichte* 4 (1931–1932), pp. 214–24.

7. Paraphrase of statements in Heinz Werner's "Über die Sprachphysiognomik...," *Zeitschrift für Psychologie* 109 (1929).

8. See Benedetto Croce, "Einige kritische Grundsätze..." (1919), German translation by Julius von Schlosser, *Wiener Jahrbuch für Kunstgeschichte* 4 (1926), p. 16.

9. Cf. Hans Jantzen, *Der gotische Kirchenraum* (1927), reprinted in *Über den gotischen Kirchenraum und andere Aufsätze* (Berlin: Mann, 1951), pp. 7–20.

10. *This* is why it is so important to note as much as possible about the objective condition of works. See Sedlmayr, *Die Architektur Borrominis* (1939); (reprinted Hildesheim: Olms, 1973), p. 22.

11. See Hans Jantzen, "Zur Beurteilung der gotischen Architektur als Raumkunst," *Kritische Berichte* 1 (1927–1928), p. 18.

12. See Sedlmayr, "Fischer von Erlach: Gegenwärtige Erkenntnislage," *Kritische Berichte* 1 (1927–1928), p. 120, and *Die Architektur Borrominis*, p. 22.

13. See Max Wertheimer, *Schlußprozesse im produktiven Denken* (1918), re-

printed in *Drei Abhandlungen zur Gestalttheorie* (Erlangen: Philosophische Akademie, 1925).

14. Kurt Koffka, "Zur Theorie der Erlebniswahrnehmung," *Annalen der Philosophie* 3 (1922), pp. 375–99.

15. See Guido Kaschnitz von Weinberg, *Gnomon* 5 (1929), p. 205.

16. See, for example, Heinz Werner, *Die Ursprünge der Lyrik* (Munich: Reinhardt, 1924), pp. 5–7.

17. See Otto Pächt in *Kritische Berichte* 2 (1928–1929), p. 164.

18. See, for example, Kurt Lewin, "Gesetz und Experiment in der Psychologie," *Symposion* 1 (1927), and the general discussion in Lewin, "Vorsatz, Wille und Bedürfnis," *Psychologische Forschung* 7 (1927).

19. See Sedlmayr, review of A. E. Popp, *Kritische Berichte* 2 (1928–1929), pp. 187–97, esp. p. 190.

20. This is my adaptation.

21. In our case, these would be the demands of museum praxis, for example.

22. Kurt Lewin, "Idee und Aufgabe der vergleichenden Wissenschaftslehre," *Symposion* 1 (1927).

23. For examples of thought experiments, see Paul Frankl, "Systematik und Erlebnis," *Kritische Berichte* 1 (1927–1928), p. 101, as well as Sedlmayr, "Gestaltetes Sehen," *Belvedere* 8 (1925), p. 71.

24. Heinz Werner, "Die Rolle der Sprachempfindung," *Zeitschrift für Psychologie* 117 (1930), p. 230.

25. See Werner Ziegenfuss, *Die phänomenologischen Ästhetik* (Berlin: Collignon, 1928), pp. 102ff.

26. I am thinking, for example, of Heinz Werner's work on the problem of "feeling" (*Empfinden*), E. M. Hornbostel's investigations of "optical inversion," the examination of "eidetic phenomena" by E. R. Jaensch and his associates, or H. Volkelt's observations concerning the "art" of children.

27. See Sedlmayr, "Gestaltetes Sehen," pp. 66–73, and "Zum gestalteten Sehen," *Belvedere* 9/10 (1926), pp. 24–32. Also see Hans Sedlmayr, "Pieter Bruegel — Der Sturz der Blinden," *Hefte des kunsthistorischen Seminars der Univer-*

sität München 2 (1957), reprinted in *Epochen und Werke* (Mittenwald: Mäander, 1977), vol. 1, pp. 319–57.

28. Otto Pächt, "Gestaltungsprinzipien der westlichen Malerei des 15. Jahrhunderts" (1933), reprinted in *Methodisches zur kunsthistorischen Praxis* (Munich, 1977), pp. 17–58; "Design Principles of Fifteenth-Century Northern Painting," no. 6 in this volume.

29. Mikhail Alpatov, "Eine byzantinische Reliefikone des Hl. Demetrios in Moskau," *Belvedere* 8 (1925), pp. 34ff.

30. Kurt Koffka, "Psychologie," *Die Philosophie in ihren Einzelgebieten* (Berlin: Ullstein, 1925), pp. 599ff.

31. Werner, "Über die Sprachphysiognomik," *Zeitschrift für Psychologie* 109 (1929).

32. See Sedlmayr, *Kritische Berichte* 2 (1928–1929), pp. 189–90, in which this property is still designated by the general term "dynamic character."

33. That is, the monograph of *structure* is emerging as a major new form of scholarly examination. See Sedlmayr, *Kritische Berichte* 2 (1928–1929), pp. 187ff.

Translated by Mia Fineman.

Otto Pächt, "The End of the Image Theory" (1930/1931)

Otto Pächt (1902–1988) wrote a dissertation on narrative in medieval painting under Julius von Schlosser in Vienna (1925). In the late 1920s, Pächt and his innovative colleague Hans Sedlmayr were rereading Alois Riegl. Pächt prepared a bibliographic appendix to the new edition of Riegl's Late Roman Art Industry *(1927) and edited the innovative journal that he and Sedlmayr had founded together, Kunstwissenschaftliche Forschungen. Pächt published few direct statements about art historical method. In 1963, while in exile in England, he published an essay on Riegl. The summa of his thinking on method is the long title essay in* Methodisches zur kunsthistorischen Praxis *(1977), a text assembled by his students from lecture notes.*

"The End of the Image Theory" was published in Kritische Berichte zur kunstgeschichtlichen Literatur, *a progressive new review journal edited by Pächt's close friend Bruno Fürst. The piece is an attack on poeticizing attempts to render the aesthetic qualities of works of art in prose. Pächt saw this tendency creeping into art historical scholarship. The essay points to the contradictions in Pächt and Sedlmayr, who themselves held an idealist view of the singularity and eloquence of the work of art and yet admired the scholarly rigor and dry, restrained prose styles of Riegl and Schlosser.*

Chapter Four

The End of the Image Theory

(1930/1931)

Otto Pächt

There is a way of describing works of art that gives the impression that they have been reproduced with poetic means, illustrated in words. To be fair, one must credit this procedure with contributing not a little to the popularization of art history. Though this may be a dubious merit, one can at least say that it meets an active need of our time. In contrast to the high prestige that poetic description enjoys, the theoretical foundation of the approach is rather slight, for it necessarily presupposes a concept of scientific truth — truth as faithful reflection, as imitation of reality — that has become untenable since the advent of modern epistemology.[1] Every science starts first with a conceptual grasp of its subject. Concepts, however, are no substitute for and not reproductions of the object under scientific examination; they are signs and symbols from which one must select to convey intelligibly something of the essence of the designated object.

If one seriously undertakes the poetic reproduction of a work of art, one intends in principle nothing other than the transposition of artistic content from one aesthetic medium to another. In the first place, such a translation is a purely artistic task; it presupposes the rare gift of a poetic craft, it requires aesthetic production — not reproduction. One would be asking of scholarship, in one of its most elementary and routine activities, to rely on the accidents of poetic inspiration and the grace of lucky moments. For now, we are completely ignoring other unavoidable difficulties, such as the delicate problem of how, in rendering the work into a necessarily heterogeneous style, to avoid subjectivity in interpretation and preserve the incontrovertible postulate of scientific objectivity. Here we want only to consider the real purpose of the transference from the visual into the linguistic sphere. Apparently, it is to give the artistic content a form in which sense and meaning are easily grasped. In rationalistic prejudice, then, one believes a *literary* product to be more easily accessible to critical reflection because its means of expression, language, also serves as the voice of critical intelligence.[2] Even if it were so, that would not relieve us of the obligation of strictly scientific description. We would have the same task to perform on the poetic version as on the original — only once removed. And through just this step, by which one had thought to have brought the original closer to understanding, one eliminates its specifically artistic values, which lie in the purely visual. For it is just these values in an accurate translation that would have to be replaced with equivalents from the linguistic art. Thus they can never be described. The cumbersome maneuver misses its actual aim; the works of visual art are not made to speak in their most authentic voice.

Poeticizing description occurs in this extreme form only in the works of those outside scholarship.[3] Yet even in scholarship, there are powerful currents with a disturbing affinity for the "image theory." These tendencies, because in practice they are accorded such significance, are our subject.

One can evaluate every trend in scholarship in two ways: by the positive results that its methods have achieved (and since in our case the method proves itself incorrect, the judgment must be unfavorable); and by its symptomatic significance as the expression (even if very inadequate) of some fully serviceable, fundamental ideas and correct partial insights. From this latter point of view, a far more positive assessment of our case is possible.

In the most recent period of art historical scholarship, two different camps with regard to the problem of description have emerged.[4] One camp wants to derive descriptive concepts from the individual object itself and believes that this is the only way to do justice to the full, concrete visual content of the phenomenon. The other wants to arrive at a perhaps only approximate description by differentiating a few basic concepts yielded by deduction. Here description is more a determination of the place to be assigned to the particular object within a given general system of order. The methods advocated by the first camp appear to possess the advantage of adequacy to the object. However, it is not clear how rigorous conceptual interpretations could be developed out of this and how concepts gleaned from several of these individual descriptions could be brought to the same plane. Nevertheless, until now one saw here a necessary prerequisite for implementing most of the operations of the historical and comparative disciplines of art history. The other method — starting from a fixed system of references — guaranteed its own scientific format from the start. However, that method had trouble overcoming a certain distance from the object. And since, according to the usual view, history should, if possible, concern itself with the unique, here the charge of a priori construction, of the ahistorical, threatens, while the opposing camp must content itself knowing that its positions will not be viewed as scientifically binding. It is necessary to get beyond this rigid either-or of the two standpoints.

The opposition between the two methods has sharpened almost to the point of contradiction because most supporters of systemless description feel obliged to keep themselves as unfettered as possible, free from any reflective attitude, in order to let the work of art have its effect on them, pure and undiluted. To consider the object with complete impartiality and naïveté is, however, an unfulfillable desire. This desire reveals a total misrecognition of the essence of perception in general and of the apprehension of the work of art in particular.[5] The supporters of free description would be correct in their self-isolation against any intellectualizing influences if in the process of perception objects stood out as if on a sheet of blank paper. Then it would make sense to keep the sheet white — the mirror entirely clean — so as not to cloud the image appearing there. In reality, the situation is quite different. We could not apprehend an object, and indeed anything from the external world, if we did not bring to it a certain disposition, a certain attitude toward form. Decisive for the realization of a phenomenon, and a co-determinant of its final form, are not only the external objective data (the constellation of stimuli) but also fundamentally the state of the reception apparatus, which is strongly formed by prior experiences, that is, external as well as internal conditions. If this is true for any object from the external world, how much more significance must be assigned to the central factors in apprehending a work of art, which emerges out of its material substratum — the art object (*Kunstding*) — to become an artistic creation only through a particular attitude.[6] Very different phenomena result from different attitudes toward the same object — above all, they are phenomena of different quality. Only in the adequate attitude is a truly good phenomenon — that also permits good description — possible. To be sure, every attitude can be adapted; and, moreover, a pressure toward a specific interpretation lies in the work of art itself, so that the final phenomenon emerges in a continuing interaction between the central and the peripheral factors. However, there is no guarantee that this goal will be attained without our participation, that is, through passively maintaining our original attitude, an attitude in a necessarily arbitrary relationship to the object under observation. It is the duty of a scholarly discipline actively to pursue the adequate attitude; that is, the discipline must be greatly concerned with the methodological problem of working out certain procedures that will favorably influence the process of perception. Whoever resists such an attempt at methodological advancement in aesthetic receptivity, because here he sees the danger of rationalistic distortion, must recognize that he is not keeping himself impartial, as he might think, but rather maintaining his prescientific, vulgar psychological views, namely, views from a previous state of knowledge that had permeated general opinion. Without being aware of it, he reacts with this deficient and obsolete attitude to the newly presented object.

We must examine this latent attitude more closely. In order to capture the individual clarity of the concrete object in words, one searches for appropriate linguistic images. This search creates the inclination to discover everywhere similarities between the artistic object, its properties and components, and the things and phenomena in our environment for which we have pithy linguistic expressions readily at hand — especially those that enhance the aesthetic phenomenon. What enhances value is again determined by the prevailing fashion, the changing taste of the times. Depending on whether one stands closer or farther away from expressionism, one prefers the realm of "coiled," "fiery," the "convulsively wound up," "primordial," or "cubic." Within this framework, however, free thought is given the widest field. The more imaginative one is, the more striking similarities one will find; the more easily one can associate any possible image, the more suggestive will the description seem. This associative and thus eminently arbitrary and subjective procedure is already discredited by the known fact that one can project, with some complacence, anything whatsoever onto a picture, sculpture, or ornament. And the situation remains unchanged even when the linguistic image is conceived purely as a comparison intended to elucidate concrete facts through confrontation with something already known. The danger of offering a completely misleading and irrelevant interpretation, under the suggestive power of this linguistic image, has not diminished.

One should not misinterpret our remarks to mean that we regard the use of pictorial expressions (vivid characterizations) in description as altogether inadmissible. Just one point should be clarified: everything depends on reacting to the work of art with the correct images. Only as long as one was convinced that the phenomenon to be described stood firm and unchanging, as well as independent from each beholder, could one believe that the argument was actually about whether to use more concretely vivid or more abstract expressions. The subject of the description was supposedly agreed on. The whole thing seemed nothing more than a question of terminology, a purely formal matter of scholarly presentation. But if one frees one's view from this rigid orientation and recognizes that it depends on which phenomenal state of affairs one has to describe, then the terminological difficulties seem to be resolved. (In fact, it is not a terminological problem.) The quality of the description is dependent on the quality of the described phenomenon. If I have a thoroughly formed phenomenon (far removed from the chaotic or fragmented), it is very easy to describe. For then perception itself is no longer blurred (diffuse or complex), blind and dumb, but articulated, and thus intelligent and knowing, in the truest sense of the word "meaning-full" (*sinn-voll*). One has to evoke then only this meaning, the internal order of the aesthetic phenomenon, and the image itself begins to "speak."

This is not to say that there are no purely terminological problems. Yet these were not the cause of the great differences of opinion and confusion. Indeed, terminological difficulties will not become visible and relevant until one has decided on a conceptual formulation. At that point, where one is looking for signs that can be clearly assigned to art historical objects, the question of whether to use colloquial language will become acute. Words usually have an exceptionally blurred and indeterminate content; they have several meanings. Even if it is clear in a concrete individual case which meaning is intended, it is nevertheless very dangerous to operate with such concepts, for the omitted meanings of a word unwittingly resonate with it, and indeed can replace the intended meaning. Vice versa, different words are often used for the same concept. All of these problems can be remedied with strict definition and an exact determination of the conceptual and semantic content. A separate scientific language however — for this is what terminological questions require — can only be the aim of research that fundamentally refuses to achieve effects through language outside the domain of scholarship, therefore deliberately renouncing any illegitimately gained popularity.

Until now we have essentially been thinking about the description of an *individual* work of art; as soon as phenomena of a supra-individual type — common and central attributes of a group of related works — articulate their "style," the situation is different. If one inspects the efforts in this direction in the recent literature, one notes that true conceptual interpretations arise much more frequently and that one is generally moving in much greater proximity to concepts.

It is not difficult to find an explanation for why this happens: the object of the description is already a product of structured seeing. In order that the principle of the formation, the characteristic in a mode of representation, the orderliness (regularity, lawfulness) of the phenomenon, the style of a work, can be grasped, the clarification process of perception must already be well developed. Moreover, the task of clarification is set in such a way that understanding should be achieved; it automatically tends toward the realization of meaningful phenomena.

Even in this area, one frequently encounters the inclination to achieve, at any cost, vivid characterizations heavily saturated with pictorial content. Not so much intuitionist as scholarly-technical motives can be held responsible for this. One requires from the characterization of a stylistic phenomenon that in its full, concrete vividness, as well as in the name given to it, it is easily remembered. One searches, therefore, for the pithiest possible linguistic image, a vivid formula, with which one hopes to make oneself rapidly and thoroughly understood. So, for example, the handy term *Kastenraum* (box space) was chosen to characterize the peculiar late-medieval pictorial representation of architecture. Certainly, these odd structures superficially resemble a box or a crate or, even better, a sentry box. Of course, that is not to say that the artists imagined their heroes living in such shelters. Everyone knows that the expression *Kastenraum* is only to be understood figuratively. The point of comparison is the narrowness of the shelter as well as the barrenness of the space. But this comparison means nothing for the pictorial interpretation in question (the feeling of a closeness of space does not occur in this artistic world, does not constitute representational content); it is derived from a non-immanent aesthetic system, in fact from the standpoint of a naturalistic observer. Thus hidden behind this widespread term lies a pure convention; at most, one can accept this term as a comforting mnemonic aid (as a nickname, a nom de guerre). A good description should be more. It must emerge from the center of an immanent aesthetic frame of reference and articulate the essential structural characteristics of the object. The description is formed not from an external point of view, not on a mere similarity, but on an inner grasp of the coherence of the whole. Only then will the description be not an arbitrarily attached label but a true conceptual symbol that serves as a base of operations for any further research.

In those cases when such a different approach to the problem of description is adopted, out of quite different intentions, the linguistic image, the strongly, sensuously flavored expression, is always preferred. In my opinion, this demands another kind of explanation. There must be something in the essence of the linguistic image that makes it so valuable; the linguistic form itself must guarantee very special effects. It is that immediacy with which the emotions are addressed during that lingering in the sensual sphere of expression. As soon as one sets to rationally penetrating, judging one's emotional experience, all of its original purity is lost. Any admixture of reflexive categories jeopardizes, or at least hinders, the complete realization of the emotional. Thus the qualities that are most valued in description are not those that provide a faithful translation (reflection) of a concrete objective content but those that guarantee an undisturbed, direct transferal of emotional content. This factor seems to be more or less emphasized in all of the types of description discussed, usually interwoven with the other elements but always included. Once again the problem has revealed itself as basically a material one: it involves a very different level of experience that art historical representation is striving toward. This especially applies to the extended circle of readers interested in art history — with whose needs scholarship has been so concerned that it has lost sight of its own requirements and objectives: one would rather have a vivid sensation of the work of art than a clear conception of it.

In a recent psychological study, Heinz Werner showed that the experience of one and the same phenomenon can pass through different phases; that is, not only can one have different phenomena from the same object, worse and better, but the phenomena themselves can reoccur in quite different ways.[7] Werner proved the possibility of a transformation in the experience of the same object, a transformation leading incrementally from a purely objective perception to (although still referring to the object in some manner) a fully subjective feeling in the sense of a vital, physical realization. "There are objective ways of experiencing on different, higher levels; at the least, the objective viewing of an object is to be distinguished from a very different way of perceiving, which we want to call, to use a good colloquial expression and the usage of romantic psychology, above all Herder, 'feeling'" (*Empfinden*). According to Werner, four states are to be differentiated in the transformation of experience, with a gradual blurring of the opposition of subject and object (with the sequence understood purely in the sense of an ordering of the phenomena). The phenomenon moves from a distanced opposition ever increasingly toward the center; it is then fully assimilated; finally the phenomenon fills the consciousness entirely: a sound, a color are now, so to speak, physically felt. The latter is perhaps a very intensive but scarcely a differentiating and articulating way of experiencing. And it is only too clear that descriptions that want to communicate from this level must incline heavily toward pictorial comparisons and expressions in which the emotional sphere predominates. It is equally clear that only a faithful illustrative process, if possible without the intervention of conscious rational activity, seems capable of preventing damage to this experiential content, so sensitive to any conscious operation.

But how does it happen that one stumbles upon just these realms of experience that naturally pose the greatest difficulties for scholarly work? The reasons are not hard to find: one knows that access to a work of art is gained only from very particular attitudes that differ from ordinary attitudes toward everyday things and that such access proclaims just those emotional ways of experiencing as a specifically aesthetic behavior.[8] On the other hand, the level of experience of precise and articulate perception, serving a more objective, purposeful grasping of the external world, is abhorred. Or more correctly: out of the inability to keep aesthetic perception separate from the perception of things, and out of the fear of sliding into an attitude directed toward objective, purposeful apprehension, one rescues oneself through the pure "feeling" of aesthetic objects. This position shows considerable similarity to what Moritz Geiger describes in his *Zugänge zur Ästhetik* as "internal concentration," which he contrasts, as the impure failure of an authentic experience of art, with the solely admissible "external concentration."[9] Here, in observing the widespread resistance to experiencing art in external concentration, we come upon the last and deepest root of all the mischief that has impeded the development of art history into an exact science. How should the history of art secure its proper object if the processes that are meant to deliver it actually offer an ersatz for sensations of a very different nature? One is against the true aesthetic attitude because the true aesthetic need is never fully present, because an intellectual involvement with art is supposed to furnish a substitute for religious experiences that are no longer achievable, and because in recent times the increasingly widespread aesthetic receptivity signifies a transformation of religious receptivity. But the aesthetic experience can only become a real equivalent of the religious when it remains within the sphere of pure feeling, which is distinguished by an especially high degree of intensity and a particular emotional proximity. Thus the art historian who will most purely meet the expectations of the art historical community will be the one who seeks to convey the strongly emotionally tinged content of this sphere and promises to supply the listener or the reader with a direct rendering of its phenomena.

Purely theoretically, the representation and communication of phenomena from this zone of experience are by no means insoluble, even if hugely difficult, problems. But the endeavor is dangerous in practice because the situation almost automatically becomes the occasion to skip over completely the level of perception. It is in fact a basic condition for the realization of purely emotional sensations that the phenomenal stimuli be presented in a properly fragmented manner. Lack of differentiation is a constitutive characteristic of such phenomena. What a temptation not to allow it to come to clarity! Thus phenomena of this latter category are indeed presented to the public; but there is no control for whether it is really the artistic structures, and not some surrogates, that have become the emotional data. The works of art in that case serve as points of departure for arbitrary emotional associations. In this way, the historian and his public obtain nothing that they do not already latently possess, except that they now wish to find it sanctioned as artistic value by history. They have, as Benedetto Croce says, "allowed the object to disappear in favor of the work of art" in order to "smuggle their infinite longing for happiness into such well-calculated and well-defined works," and then "to extract that which they have put into it as the revelation of a superior spirit."[10]

Notes

1. Cf. Moritz Schlick, *Allgemeine Erkenntnislehre*, 2nd ed. (Berlin: Springer, 1925), pp. 55ff. In addition, with direct reference to the specifically historical-theoretical problem, see Alfred Vierkandt, "Gesellschafts- und Geschichtsphilosophie," in Max Dessoir (ed.), *Lehrbuch der Philosophie* (Berlin: Ullstein, 1925), p. 919.

2. The correct thought hiding behind this bias, when fully grasped, leads necessarily to the discovery of the inner contradictions of poetic description and its insufficiencies. Even this "illustration" is only possible once the words — those too are grounded in aesthetic intentions — have a conceptual core, even if the conceptual content is indefinite, diluted, and in flux. An illustration merely in sounds of words would be impossible. Thus the musical reproduction of a work of visual art would appear pointless.

3. For example, in Wilhelm Fraenger. Nowhere, however, is the position under criticism more absurdly pursued than in a recent attempt at a methodological justification. What Heinrich Lützeler, in *Formen der Kunsterkenntnis* (Bonn: Cohen, 1924), invents as postulated ideals for descriptions belong to those improbabilities by which reality still manages to surpass the most lively imagination. For example: "Thus the description is shaped by the same laws as the picture. The descriptive word is able to illustrate the artistic form in a very concrete sense. In Wölfflin, one can only guess at the possibility, not point to it as reality. We find it as reality in several perfect descriptions by Winckelmann. If Greek statues were lost to us, in the sound of the words Winckelmann devoted to them (!) we would still have a sense of their grace and clarity and their noble simplicity and silent grandeur" (p. 68).

4. Cf. the study soon to appear in *Kunstwissenschaftliche Forschungen* 1 (1931) by Hans Sedlmayr, "Zu einer strengen Kunstwissenschaft" ["Toward a Rigorous Study of Art," no. 3 in this volume].

5. The following comments are nothing more than a condensed report on the doctrine of perception as it has been developed by Gestalt psychology [see, above all, Kurt Koffka, "Psychologie," in *Die Philosophie in ihren Einzelgebieten* (Berlin: Ullstein, 1925), pp. 559ff., and Koffka, "Zur Theorie der Erlebniswahr-

nehmung," *Annalen der Philosophie* 3 (1922)], which offers crucial information on this point as on many other methodological problems in art history. The fundamental significance of modern Gestalt theory for the development of art historical thought was first recognized and applied to our discipline by Hans Sedlmayr.

6. Sedlmayr, "Fischer von Erlach: Gegenwärtige Erkenntnislage," *Kritische Berichte* 1 (1927–1928), p. 118.

7. "Das Problem des Empfindens und die Methoden seiner experimentellen Prüfung," *Zeitschrift für Psychologie* 114 (1930), p. 152ff.

8. Thus an aesthetician, Emil Utitz, characteristically called the specifically aesthetic approach postulated by him *Gefühlsanschauung* (emotional vision).

9. See Moritz Geiger, *Zugänge zur Ästhetik* (Leipzig: Der Neue Geist, 1928), pp. 12ff. Especially in individual traits, the approaches described by Werner and Geiger agree completely, so that one could view Werner's study as the psychological explanation of Geiger's phenomenology of aesthetic pleasure. "An anecdote may illustrate the effect of true inner concentration: one tells the story of how the famous actor Garrick once placed a bet that he would succeed in captivating a theater audience with his recitation of the alphabet, without them noticing what was actually being recited. Garrick won his bet: his vibrating voice alone moved the audience to tears, producing feelings in them to which they sentimentally succumbed. This is typical internal concentration." And: "All emphasis rests on the feeling that is evoked without too much consideration of the appearance of the object that brought it about" (p. 16).

10. See Benedetto Croce, "Zur Theorie und Kritik der Geschichte der bildenden Kunst," translated and with an introduction by Julius von Schlosser, *Wiener Jahrbuch für Kunstgeschichte* 4 (1926), p. 38.

Translated by Tawney Becker.

Structure Analysis: Practice

Guido Kaschnitz von Weinberg, "Remarks on the Structure of Egypt-ian Sculpture" (1933)

Guido Kaschnitz von Weinberg (1890–1958) was born, like Otto Pächt, in Vienna and studied classical archaeology at the university. He wrote a dissertation on Greek vase painting (1913). Between 1923 and 1932, he lived and worked in Rome as an assistant at the Archaeological Institute and in the Vatican collections. Here Kaschnitz studied Roman art and read Alois Riegl intensively. In 1929, he wrote an important review of the new edition of Late Roman Art Industry. *Kaschnitz was the most dedicated disciple of Riegl, and he was quickly recognized as such by the somewhat younger art historians back in Vienna. His major essays in the structure-analytical mode were written in the 1930s while he was teaching in distant Königsberg. "Remarks on the Structure of Egyptian Sculpture" appeared in the second number of* Kunstwissenschaftliche Forschungen.

Typically Kaschnitz summoned forth entire world-historical schemata from the close analysis of a few key monuments. In this essay, he argues that Egyptian sculpture treated mass not as an artistic content in its own right, as ancient Near Eastern sculpture had, but as a metaphor for nature. Although it often appears to capture the look and feel of reality, Egyptian sculpture was actually entirely metaphysical in its ambitions.

(Source: Guido Kaschnitz von Weinberg, "Bemerkungen zur Struktur der ägyptischen Plastik," Kunstwissenschaftliche Forschungen 2 [1933], pp. 7ff.; reprinted in Guido Kaschnitz von Weinberg, Kleine Schriften zur Struktur 1 [Berlin: Mann, 1965], pp. 15–37.)

Chapter Five

Remarks on the Structure of Egyptian Sculpture (1933)

Guido Kaschnitz von Weinberg

The method of *Strukturforschung* in art history — whose real founder is Alois Riegl — may lead us into areas that until now, surprisingly, have been hardly investigated. I am thinking in particular of the ancient Near East and Egypt. The reasons for this neglect seem to lie in the peculiar kind of art historical method that the preceding century elaborated and brought to perfection. Heinrich Wölfflin's "categories of vision" will get us nowhere in the Near East. It can be shown that such "forms of seeing," inherited mainly from Greek and Classical culture, remain foreign to the Near East in general and to Egypt in particular. Art there means the immortalization of very specific claims or the realization of a new world grounded in particular notions of religion and the afterlife. Art can thus only be understood by starting with that *meaning (Sinn)* that served as the point of departure for those realizations. The main reason for this is that we do not grasp such a meaning, once detached from our aesthetic attitude, as something objectively given that must then be objectively assessed. Hence, for the time being, perhaps the only practicable route is *Strukturforschung*, a route that does not proceed from the complex of the aesthetic and the pure experience of form but that tries to grasp the construction and the operative power of artistic creation objectively. Since the method of *Geistesgeschichte* remains unpromising, *Strukturforschung* is the only way any progress can be made — and without relying on that complicated physiological-psychological process out of which the impressionistic experience of art develops its concepts. Such concepts enable us to grasp only the *relations* between a work of art and a modern viewer and only those relations that have always been strange to the Near East and therefore represent only the attitudes of modern viewers, which, in the present case, are unimportant for us. An investigation that is oriented along formal impressionistic lines, just as much as one governed by aesthetic considerations, would mislead us or produce distorted ideas. In Near Eastern art history, neither the conceptual forms nor the conceptual equipment found in a modern study of art plays any role that could serve as a point of departure.[1]

The concept of structure is closely related to the *Kunstwollen* (artistic will) described by Riegl, if we understand that term in its most useful sense. We are dealing with manifestations of a certain "will of a supra-individual kind, standing opposed as a normative force to the individual."[2] If one takes representational art as a man-made metaphor for the world, the divine, and the human bonds at work within it, then structure is the operative form of that force that, in art, stands symbolically for cosmic or divine energies as they are reflected in our interpretation and imagination.[3]

It is important to stress the metaphoric character of artistic structure. This metaphoric character has in European art very little to do, for example, with the material construction of a marble or bronze statue, and thus is fundamentally distinct from architectonic structure. Here the static laws of construction and durability are nearly always identical with the artistic goals they serve. In Greek temples, accordingly, the entasis of columns or the swelling of the echinus derives exclusively from the effort to confer artistic expression on structural forces that in fact reside, in one form or another, in the technical construction of the build-ing.[4] With sculpture, however, it is a matter not of a metaphor of the static energies operative in a statue but rather of *symbols* of an external perceptible world. And on this point, the essence of the sculpture of the ancient Near East differs markedly from the interpretations of Greek and later Western art. While, as I have said, the metaphor in Greek sculpture assumes an entirely fictive character, that is, it does not conform to the actual static position of the respective statue, metaphoric forms in the ancient Near East are at all times the expression of actual static relations. A statue in the round from the Near East achieves its effect from its present mass, and the artistic metaphor develops out of that specifically controlled force of gravity on matter that determines the form taken by the volume.

This lack of fictive elements in ancient Near Eastern sculp-ture needs to be related as closely as possible to internal tenacity and the consequent lack of optical form for reasons that cannot be fully discussed here. But even beyond that, everything to be said about artistic structure in Near Eastern sculpture remains in the realm of the metaphoric, and hence of the metaphysical, even if here the will to form encounters matter in a manner foreign to Euro-pean art. Neither the difficulty of translating creative visions into stone nor the question of whether these visions possess a struc-ture that qualifies them for admission to the perceptible world plays any role at all, because in the ancient Near East one is only concerned with the realization of pure Being in matter. For rea-sons I shall shortly explain, such a translation follows effortlessly. The Near Eastern artist is not familiar with the agony of creation.

We are led out of these theoretical questions and suggestions and into the historical development by the question of how the creative will approaches matter. More precisely, how does the creative will ever come to terms with the laws of matter, that is, with the notion of mass that leads to corporeality? It has not been sufficiently recognized that an important problem hides behind this question. The prehistoric evidence alone — and here I do not include the Paleolithic, for particular reasons[5] — shows beyond question that Europeans were not able to take this step by their own power. One can claim with certainty that Europe would never have produced sculpture on its own. The capacity for operating in a creative, representational fashion, directly from a sense of corporeality, is entirely un-European.

The Neolithic European, just as much as his west and central Asian neighbors, lacked any capacity for achieving an artistic metaphor of his mental world, for he had no access to the realm of corporeal awareness. But there remains that impulse or *will to action* generally characteristic of the artistic urge of European peoples. It is the source of the decorative character of purely European–west Asian art, such as that found in late Neolithic vase ornament.

We do not know how in the very earliest periods the ancient cultures of the Near East and Egypt succeeded in bestowing bodily expression on their will to shape forms. One suspects, however, that the relative poverty of the prehistoric development in the Near East is closely connected to the sudden transition to bodily, that is, pictorial formation. Presumably, the primary content of this evolution, which for us, as was mentioned, seems somewhat erratic, was the *identification of the will to shape with the notion of mass.*

It is difficult today to obtain a proper idea of the unusualness and significance of this step. It would seem obvious to extend the matter-of-factness with which the modern sculptor takes up his clay and marble to the developmental possibilities of entire cultural realms. If one rightly rejects that idea, however, one is compelled to suppose that all civilized societies, with the exception of those in the Near East, not only were incapable of such an identification with the element of physicality but at times even met it with resistance. Indeed it seems that even today contemporary Europeans, cut off from the South, tend to turn once more to a superficial and ornamentally oriented mode of formation. For this, the specifically anticlassical and anti-Italian development of German expressionism has given us sufficient clues — ones that in their nature seem to point back to the late European Neolithic period.

It is unclear, however, whether one ought to conclude from this the existence of an original, fundamentally different inclination on the part of the inhabitants of the Near East or whether in their case external circumstances diverted development in other directions. This enormous change seems to have happened quickly and smoothly, to judge from the comparatively small remains of the pre-Sumerian period in Mesopotamia. This would seem to support the former theory.

The creative factor in the artistic evolution of the Near East consequently lies in the fact that the *will to creative action identifies itself with the concept of mass*. It also lies in the fact that — more simply if less precisely expressed — this urge subsequently reproduces bodily or three-dimensional expression, as it were, out of itself. The essential point is that the urge to shape at no point entered into an opposition with the concept of mass, as it did in Europe; the artist did not *struggle*, but rather from his physical awareness he *unfolded* in an inexhaustible abundance.

The peculiarity of this situation only becomes completely clear when one compares it with the nature of non-Eastern sculpture. Here occurs the second configuration of the will to form with respect to mass — the only one, at any rate, that is still conceivable. In this case, the urge to shape, in accordance with its particular character, is unable to produce in bodily form. As has been said, that will would have remained perpetually in the realm of superficial shaping had not the idea of mass — indeed shaped mass, although that is not the main point right now — been introduced to it through the intervention of the Near East. There emerges a relationship of will to mass thoroughly different from that of the Near East, one for examples of which we could appeal to middle Minoan, Mycenaean, and early Greek art. In this case, it is necessarily *from the outside* that the will to shape approaches the bodily — an element completely alien to it at the outset, yet one toward which it is propelled by an intense attraction. The likelihood that such an attraction arose directly from the inability to create physically cannot be explored here. Whatever the case may be, everything is propelled toward conflict, because the will must come to terms one way or another with the foreign element. The conflict lies in the attempt to penetrate the reluctant mass and to turn it completely into the bearer of its own nature.[6] From this conflict arises the tension characteristic of European sculpture and the lack of tension characteristic of Near Eastern sculpture. In one form or another, the conflict is always noticeable in European art. Only European art has this problem. The Near East is free of any problematic in the same way that it is free of all conflict. The struggle over form remains necessarily foreign to it.

In both European and Near Eastern art, the transition to bodily shaping brings with it a very important ancillary phenomenon. I am referring to the adoption of organic form. As long as the will to shape was denied bodily expression, what it shaped was, over and over again, exclusively itself. Beginning with the basic rhythms of ornament and progressing to a more or less substantial degree of distinctiveness, it made perceptible the temperament and nature of its being, without, however, at any point abandoning surface or giving up the uniformity that lay in the direct symbolizing of the abstract drive through a similarly abstract line.[7]

No matter how the will to shape arrives at the transition to sculpted representation — whether the idea of mass is introduced into it, as in Europe, or it generates it itself, as in the Near East — such a promotion to the realm of the bodily can only take place in the form of a *metaphor of the sensory world*. It is clear that the attempt at an abstract sculpture has no more justification as an end in itself than the adoption of an ornament. The decoration of vessels is now replaced by the interpretation of the world through the will to shape. The bond with the reality of the object to be decorated that is present in ornament is now supplanted by reference to the world's sensory existence. The will to shape manifests itself in the form of a Being that is alien and through which that will now achieves self-expression in the artistic sphere. In actual fact, however, the metaphorical world of artistic forms that arises in this way represents no more than the manifestation of this will to form at its realization.

The emergence of objective motifs in art can only be understood as a symptom of the transition to bodily shaping. Alternative explanations — whether the emphasis is placed on the struggle to represent the sensual world or on the longing to raise the will to shape to sculpted expression — remain pointless, since what we have here are merely two aspects of the same process. Such is the interpretation — if we choose to confine ourselves to Egypt — that we must give above all to the oldest Egyptian "palettes" (Curtius, *Antike Kunst*, p. 24).

The relation of the shaping will to the idea of mass lies at the basis of the transition of visual art to a corporeal manner of representation. And indeed in the Near East, as I have already mentioned, this concerns a process whereby the urge assimilates itself to the nature of mass perfectly and *without conflict*. In other words, *shaping takes place in the spirit of those laws that form the basis of the idea of mass*. The extent to which such laws become distinct and to which the process of shaping gives rise to changes occurring within the bounds of those laws determines the extent of the freedom and capability for action of the will to shape.

Any consideration of ancient Near Eastern plastic structure must start from this realization. It is, of course, impossible to reconstruct the psychological and creative processes that ultimately led Egyptians of the predynastic period to progress from simple ornament to plastic representation of the perceptible and organic world. The only road open to us is to try to infer from the kind of permanently fixed mode of representing bodies and space the processes that — hidden to the artist — lie at the basis of such psychological operations.

It belongs to the essence of Near Eastern art, as we have already remarked, that the will to make forms does not act in opposition to mass. What is at issue in such an arrangement can only be the activation — in an artistic, that is, metaphoric sense — of energies present in mass, whereby in each case we must understand as the object of the metaphors both the will to shape itself, and more or less far-flung elements of the material world, for, as we have seen, each presupposes the other. Thus it remains the task of the Near Eastern artist to modulate the energies of mass in such a manner that they may operate as a symbol of organic life as well as of the creative temperament.

What, then, are the forces latent in mass that the sculptor transforms into that mysterious vitality that forms the basis of the artistic structure of every Near Eastern work of art?

That energy that gives to bodies what we call mass is gravity. The aim of gravity is — to put it somewhat crudely — to transform the earth into as smooth a ball as possible. Therefore, whatever has shape cannot assert itself without coming into conflict with gravity and thus can only do so by means of the strength or cohesiveness of its material.

It is in such a conflict — in the constant endeavor of gravity to destroy the coherence of matter and therefore form — that the source of the Orient's artistic structure lies hidden. To turn the inherent tension and dynamic resulting from this conflict into a symbol of organic vitality is the task of the Near Eastern sculptor.

From this there emerges a fundamental characteristic of Egyptian structure — if we may for the moment restrict ourselves to that: organic nature must be symbolized through energies whose purely *inorganic* physical nature cannot but be clear to everyone. Hence the utterly perfect rationalism of Egyptian art and the total absence of any real formal imagination.[8] *The will to shape identifies itself with the idea of pure Being*; that is, it gives up its own qualities and enters *a state completely devoid of energy*.

But in predynastic art and even in the early period of the Old Kingdom, this process has not yet come to this. Because the will to shape clothes itself in gravity's system of laws and nowhere opposes it, space — of which the forms of Egyptian sculpture are a corporeally distinct part — must correspond in its structure to the laws of *gravity*. One may imagine that in the course of development that extends more or less from the crouching terra-cotta woman in Berlin (figure 5.1) to the famous statue of Khasekhemui in Cairo from the Second Dynasty (figure 5.2), the predynastic art of Egypt unconsciously distilled out such an idea of space, so to speak, as the product of the clarifying construction of forms. But more lies in this idea of clarification than can be grasped by the word alone. The physicality exuded by the exuberantly swelling *physis* of the terra-cotta figure is still determined by the experience of mass perceived through the senses. The drive to confer on ideals an unchanging shape transforms itself into mass. The mass is really present, and it is from its weight, perceptible to the senses, that the figurine derives all that it possesses by way of vitality.

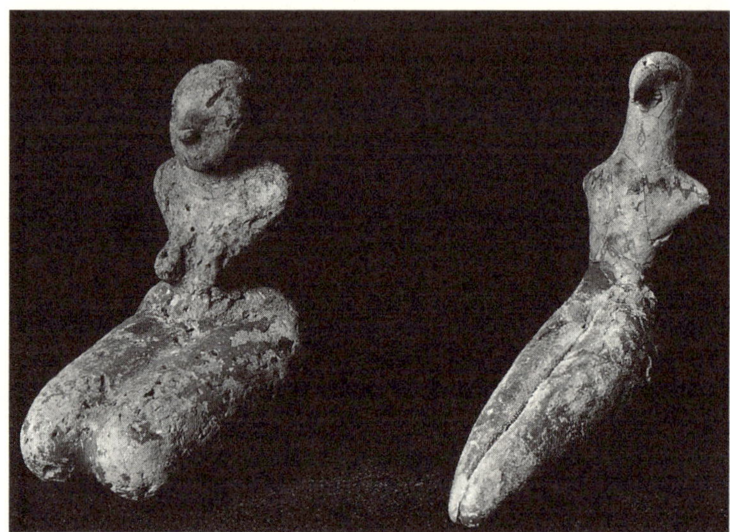

Figure 5.1. Terra-cotta figures of kneeling women, Staatliche Museen Preussischer Kulturbesitz, Berlin (Foto Marburg/Art Resource, NY).
Figure 5.2. Seated statue of Khasekhemui, Ashmolean Musuem, Oxford University.

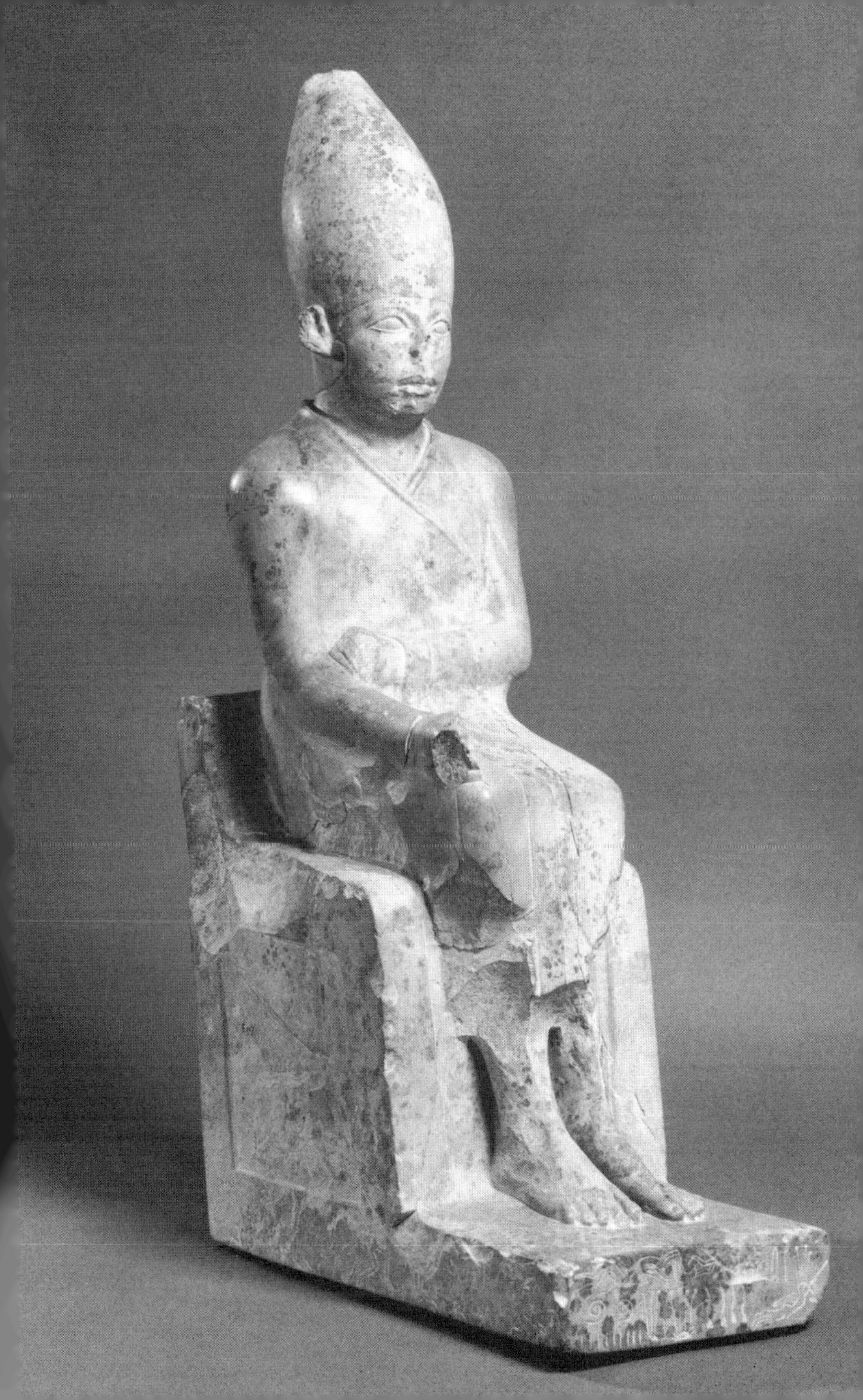

In the statue of Khasekhemui, what we experienced in the kneeling woman as a bodily symbol of fleshy exuberance, and what we can still recognize in the sculpture of the First Dynasty, retreats into a rigorous system of concise, defined forms and sharp lines. What we feel — rather than recognize with rational clarity — as typical Egyptian style has in this case revealed itself with an excess of angularity that is almost painful. A geometrically dry and rational system of the most acute forms has succeeded in proliferating abundance. This much is obvious from simple observation. What stands behind it determines the character of the entire ensuing development of Egyptian art.[9]

With the illumination provided by this important background, we are in a position to attempt to distinguish step by step the individual phases of this interesting process. Here we can only refer to one transitional monument, the granite statue of a sitting man in Naples (figure 5.3),[10] in which the previously mentioned sharp forms of the mature style, the edges and lines of a rigorous system, seem for the first time to emerge from the compact nexus of an organic mass. On close consideration, there can be no doubt about the significance of the process behind this change in appearances. The fact of the matter is that, in the figure of Khasekhemui, the urge to form now no longer hypostatizes itself in simple abundance, as with the terra-cotta of the crouching woman: it has retreated from exuberant heaviness into a system of lines, curves, and ledges, while what we previously recognized as mass seems to have shrunk, almost as if its entire nature, its entire power, had transformed itself into this system of formal signs under which it has vanished.

With this, we have come perhaps a step closer to the explanation of this remarkable process. What has occurred? To begin with, it is obvious that there was a major decrease in the *sensual*, inherent, tangible, and weighty symbolism of the figure. The

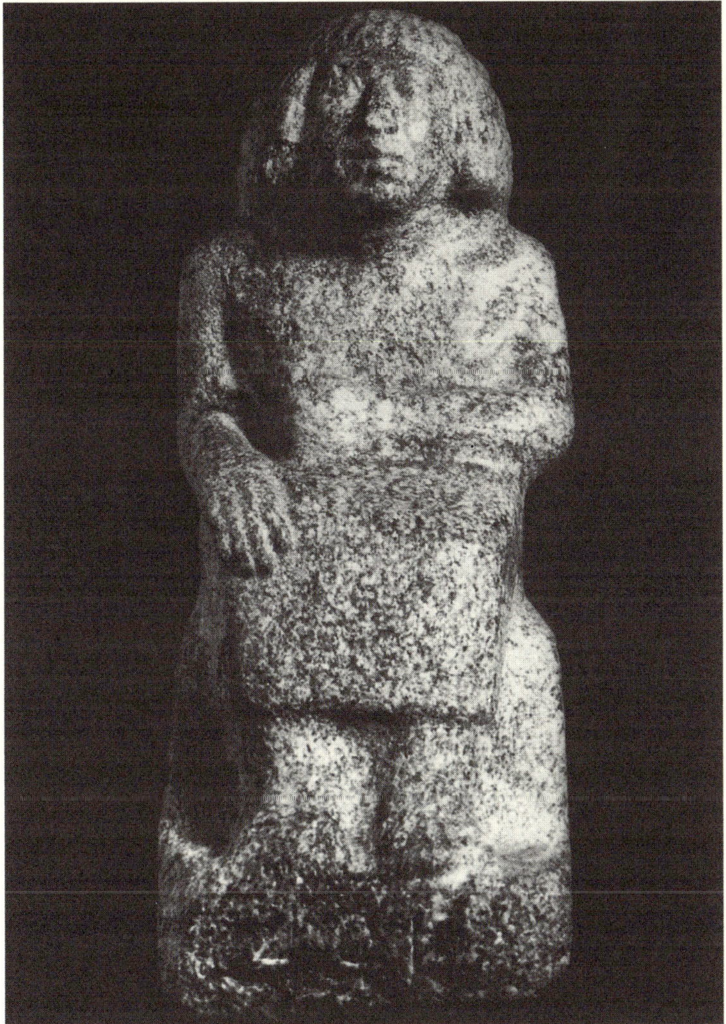

Figure 5.3. Statue of a seated man, Museo Nazionale, Soprintendenza
Archeologica, Naples.

really present mass, which in its weight and volume constituted the basis for all forms in the case of the crouching woman, has been replaced by signs undoubtedly derived from it[11] — signs, because these forms can no longer be conceptualized as the sensual manifestation of heaviness and therefore cannot be developed directly *out of the matter* under the guidance of the will to shape, but rather can only, as it were, be *imposed* as a disposition of the matter that bears the forms but no longer produces them by directly nurturing them.

This process is perhaps best characterized as the *transfer of a structure previously immanent in the work of art to a metaphysical sphere.*

If one tries to reduce this process to its bare epistemological basis, it may become easier to grasp and comprehend in its essence. In mathematical terms, this change in the basis of artistic structure would correspond to the derivation of the spatial coordinate system from the simple idea of gravity. Here, too, what we experience is nothing other than an abstraction and the endeavor to distill the *permanent* from the bewildering abundance of sensory phenomena. This undertaking succeeds, but what the physicist is left with as the result of his efforts no longer has sensual reality but rather belongs to metaphysics. In a sphere that no longer has anything to do with reality as seen and felt, he develops out of the *plumb line* of the coordinate system a *transcendental space* in whose invisible structure the real world no longer has any share; for objects may indeed be imagined in it in accordance with their volume, yet their actual existence cannot be conceived in a space of this kind, which is devoid of energy and thus metaphysical in nature. Indeed, the force of gravity, bound as it is to the sensory object, cannot be accommodated in this space and would repeal the space's metaphysical character.[12] Since gravity is a physical affair, causality, the idea of time, and the possibility of change would immediately enter into this space, which would contradict the absolute idea.

I shall not expand here further on the origin of the three coordinates of this realm, which we call height, breadth, and depth, inasmuch as it is general knowledge. They should be understood as the intersections of three planes, two of which go through the plumb line and all of which are perpendicular to each other. All of these planes refer to the force of gravity in their layout — the first two because they run through the plumb line itself and the third, which extends horizontally, because it is the geometric locus of all those points whose potential gravity is the same. Thus the horizontal plane is distinguished from all the remaining planes with respect to gravity by the fact that it is only there that pieces of mass can execute a movement that is neutral to the force of gravity — a movement, accordingly, in which none of the components works either for or against the purposes of gravity. But all of these particularities are, it must be stressed, now only relations of a pure metaphysical type and no longer signify any actual connection to gravity. In this realm, they now have only a purely symbolic value and create no opposition to the abstract nature of the coordinate space.

The concept of spatial structure that has arisen in this way in the mind of the physicists corresponds in large part to the composition of those systems of space that science calls Euclidean or "real" and geometrical. This is a space of three dimensions, whose coordinates are infinite and stand perpendicular to each other, whose curvature is constant and equal to zero. In form, it is identical to that notion of space that we are able to develop exclusively from the data supplied by the sense of touch — a notion, however, that in reality is thoroughly permeated by the perspectivally conditioned phenomenon of visual space and remains unilluminated. For our purposes, it is especially important that this space, while directionally bound by its perpendicular coordinates, is still thoroughly lacking in energy and is hence metaphysical. In this regard, it moves beyond physical space, which is filled with energy and matter. Its derivation, then, presupposes a conveyance, from the realm of the physically determinate to that of the metaphysical, of everything in it that is conceived as real.[13]

What interests us in this process of scientific cognition is not merely the fact that the concept of space hereby obtained corresponds in its appearance to the concept of space that forms the basis of works from the Fourth Dynasty to the Twelfth Dynasty in ever more explicit fashion but also the essence of the derivation in and of itself, whose parallel in the field of art is represented by the rise of Egyptian artistic structure in the early dynastic period. This essence consists in the *intellectualization of properties and processes perceptible to the senses*, in the *transformation of a sensory fact into its metaphysical form*. It is a matter no longer of weight perceptible by means of sight and touch but rather of the *system of laws* deduced from it, which in the mind comes together to create the idea of a transcendental space in Euclidean form. A new sphere opens up — one in which the mind embeds reality; a sphere into whose metaphysical state the mind conveys life in order to possess it, preserved in this manner, as an element of scientific thought. What is left, once this process has been completed, is *that which has become* (*das Gewordene*), the preservation of all life in *form* (*Gestalt*).[14]

The issue here is exactly this transferal of reality to a transcendental realm. What interests us is the course of that process whereby the perceiving mind produces an imaginary space in order to give its forms permanence. The route traveled by Egyptian art from its origins to the strict stylistic exactitude of the Twelfth Dynasty must have been similar. This is not the place to evaluate this intellectualization in Egyptian art. That it clung to a certain frigidity in its unparalleled absolutism, indeed that it gave expression to the most vehement rationalization of human experience that has ever occurred, will not be called into question. Yet it seems to me that to deny the metaphysical character of Egyptian art, as Wilhelm Worringer has done, is unwarranted.

If one tries to get a clear picture of the historical process whereby the sensual nature of the predynastic structure was conveyed into the realm of metaphysics, then one perhaps arrives at the following considerations: in the beginning, there was the experience of the energy-laden force of mass and the attempt to reproduce the taut fullness of flesh by means of these energies proper to matter. It is the weight caused by this gravity that is so powerful in the voluminous thighs of the clay figure of a kneeling woman in Berlin, which we have already mentioned several times.[15]

In the subsequent development, there occurs that transformation of the artistic metaphor's means into the metaphysical, whose parallel in the scientific epistemological sphere I have just tried to outline. The endeavor to symbolize the animated energies of organic bodies in massively curving forms is gradually abandoned. Increasingly from this point on, the aim becomes manifestly no longer that of achieving a metaphor of the organic world through the representation of abundance but one of abstracting and rendering self-sufficient the formal relations of mass resulting from that representation — a process that one may best characterize as the *passage of the sensual existence of mass into its metaphysical form*, in other words, into its *system of laws* (cf. the development from figure 5.4 to figure 5.5).

Often in the history of art, we witness the loosening of the inner unity of mass and form. In Europe, we encounter it for the first time in the late Minoan period. In that case, however, it was a unity of an entirely different type that disintegrated. What gradually died away were the vital energies of a conflict between mass

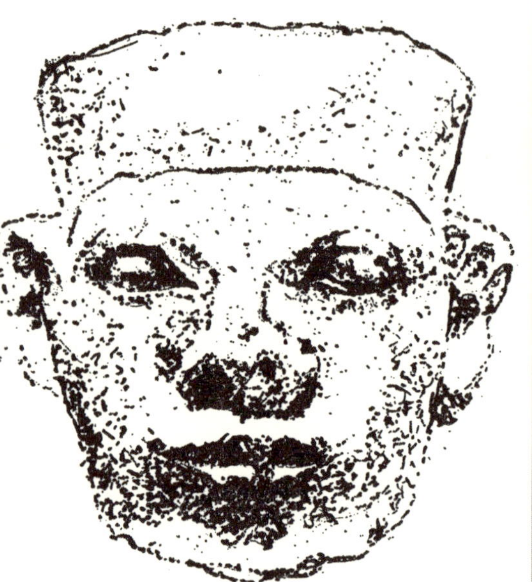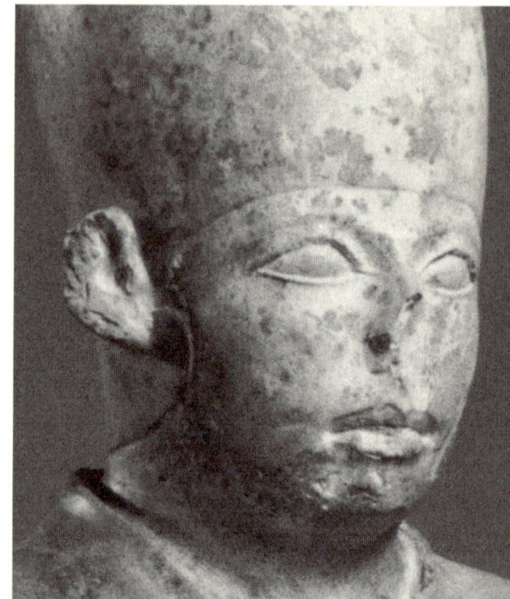

Figure 5.4. Head of a king of the First Dynasty.
Figure 5.5. Head of Khasekhemui, detail from seated statue, fig. 5.2, Ashmolean Museum, Oxford University.

and the urge to shape. Mass was permeated by a force that never had the ability or inclination to identify itself with mass in the way characteristic of the Egyptian will to form. Thus, the forms that again became autonomous in the late Minoan period, while they bear the signs of this conflict, have, by virtue of their autonomy, lost any connection with the system of laws pertaining to mass, because they did not in fact originate in this mass, as in Egypt. Instead, they returned, worn out, to that large reservoir of the purely ornamental world of forms from which, many centuries earlier, they had come.

In Egyptian art, such a process is impossible. There the shaping will had identified itself with corporeal energies and energies of mass and came into play only in the formation of the concept of mass. The form — or, more precisely, the will to form — cannot be readily separated from mass in the case of Egyptian art, since, on the whole, it was in the form of mass that it first became perceptible. The process of transition to the realm of metaphysics — the causes of which lie buried in the mysteries of the development of the Egyptian — is obliged to confine itself to the elimination of mass's perceptible Being, yet without ever being able to detach itself from the actual essence of the notion of mass, an essence which lies in its system of laws. In other words, the remarkable influence of the material mass, thanks to which, in predynastic sculpture, form achieved expression, is now replaced by dependence on the *idea* of mass — on the system of laws that gradually evolved out of the sensual existence of mass. Therein lies the transcendental character of that art which, in the era of the first dynasties, emerged from the primitive nature of the oldest period in the Near East. Thus, too — in a manner that could scarcely have been otherwise — form remains dependent on the *concept* of mass, and the fundamental Near Eastern character of Egyptian art is preserved. This link to mass refers not to the phenomena of gravity and volume, however, but to the laws developed out of them and thus to the metaphysical symbols of mass.

Yet even these laws are intelligible only with the aid of the senses. I have already tried to explain what is meant by these laws: the system of right-angled coordinates or, better, the concept of space, which first becomes accessible to thought with the help of the coordinate system. The concept of such a space, derived as it is from gravity, first emerged through the elimination of the active energy belonging to gravity, thereby dispensing as well with the concepts of becoming, of change, and indeed even of time itself. This space is the symbol of pure Being. Everything that enters into it becomes timeless and is immune to every alteration. Herein lies the key to understanding Egyptian structure. Its first high point occurs in the works of the Twelfth Dynasty.

This space determined by its coordinates should not be looked at with strictly physical eyes. We wish to call it, with reference to its absence of energy, the *existential space* or the *coordinate space*.

Yet how may the idea of form find perceptible expression in Egyptian art if, exactly like an abstraction, it is incapable of advancing to the world of bodies and of perceptions on its own? This question is justified, for we must always remember that the metaphor of organic nature now no longer comes into being by means of a sensory medium, namely, mass, but that, along with the transference of mass into its metaphysical representation, there also occurs, in parallel fashion, a corresponding transformation of the artistic metaphor. Henceforth in Egyptian art, it is, therefore, a question no longer of the *form of perceptible matter but rather of the making visible in matter forms whose construction has taken place in a metaphysical realm;* this matter, however, has played no role in the process of creating forms. Thus in Egyptian sculpture, matter is only the bearer or mediator of form; it *helps* form to appear but with respect to all form-representing energies preserves a perfect *neutrality*. Mass has vanished. The stone no longer has weight in an artistic sense. It is the *medium* of existential space, whose sole task is to allow the form to become perceptible in the essence of this space, which is abstract in itself.[16]

Such a transformation offers a simple explanation for the remarkable incorporeality of Egyptian sculpture, which stands in such curious contrast to its origins. The metaphysical character of Egyptian sculpture lies in the fact that it is more *form that has become stone* than *matter that has been given form*. The stone is not so much *formed* as the *bearer* of form — form that *was not wrested* from it forcibly and with much effort but rather that is *inscribed* on it. Its importance for the form is simply what it is also for the hieroglyph: the stone is the medium of signification.

Closely connected with the metaphysical nature of Egyptian structure as it has just been explicated is its total lack of energy. The force of gravity is dependent on matter, and it vanished in Egyptian art together with the concept of mass. The space, derived from gravity yet free of its influence, is entirely lacking in energy and is thus an eternally calm abstraction in which only that which is equally calm can have a share. This accounts for its perfect *homogeneity* and its absolute *timelessness*. It is in the complete absence of contact with the coming-to-be and passing-away of the natural world that Egyptian art, whose existence is dependent on such a space, expresses its metaphysical character perhaps most clearly.[17] But this dependence affects only the form, which is alone capable of possessing a metaphysical character. It does not include the matter — the stone, the mass in itself, which, as I have said, here serves merely as the phenomenal medium, yet out of which the form itself never develops.

Because this artistic spatial conception of the Egyptians is absolutely devoid of energy, it possesses the attribute of *immutability* — of *pure being*. Whatever enters into it also immediately enters into the condition of eternal *conservation*, which represents the *true basis of Egyptian art. Everything organic is immediately stripped of its vital energies, which at the same time carry within themselves the causes of their future decay.* Its *form* alone — by its entry into the essence of this existential space, by the elimination of every transitory element — is, so to speak, *mummified* for all eternity.

In Egyptian art, then, the concept of space cannot be derived from an interrelation of bodies, as, for instance, in Greek art. Because the concept of mass no longer has any validity in Egypt, it is on the whole no longer possible to come to grips with Egyptian space on the basis of materials alone. This space is devoid of energy because even forces, if they are to be expressed sensually, are dependent on matter and mass. Whatever goes for the real world cannot be avoided by the artistic metaphor. The entasis of Doric columns in its fictive nature is nevertheless the expression of a force actually at work in the pillar. Greek space is pervaded by forces that *take effect* in mass and that symbolize organic vital forces and tension in the fictive form of *conflict*. There can be no question of this in Egyptian art. Force that has to take effect in mass, even in the fictive aesthetic phenomenon, signifies *change, passage of time,* and *death,* and it is precisely from these things that the Egyptian seeks to liberate himself. The Egyptian frees his forms of matter and thus of all energies — of all problematics that symbolize not only the impulse of momentary life but also its endless setting of goals.

Egyptian sculpture is perhaps best characterized as the *integration of the organic with the nature of existential space,* which functions as the focal point of the integration; that is, it may be understood as the fundamental structural level that absorbs the organic into itself without itself undergoing any relaxation or change in its structure.

But at what cost does the organic gain entry to this sphere of permanence, a sphere that has so little in common with its own innermost, time-dependent nature?

If the metaphorical image of man, animal, or plant should emerge in this metaphysical sphere, it can only do so by means commensurable with this sphere itself. Mass and the fictive expression of its indwelling energies are irreconcilable with the nature of this idea of space. The representation of vital, striving existence is, therefore, also ruled out. So, too, is everything that for us constitutes the concept of *personality* — the concept of a *center of life* that governs the functions of the other parts and members.[18] What is left is the *exterior vessel of life,* the *form* freed from the forces that it generated, from the marks of growth and of development, and hence ultimately from the notion of *causality*, which signifies unending movement and eternal change.

In this way, the organic is freed from all vital mutability — disemboweled, as it were, and purified of those elements that contain the seeds of future decay. It becomes saturated with what we experience as the essence of existential space — with that system of laws that rises from inorganic sources and that, in contrast to the forces of organic nature, possesses unvarying permanence and universality. Of their former organic nature they retain only the lifeless signs and of causality, only its goal; the having-become, the form. In the having-become, however, the multiplicity of life is bound together into a unity through the laws of being.

If in daily life we speak of *form (Gestalt)*, then location and *movement* are inseparably joined to it. Movement originates here in the will, which allows the forces belonging to the organic context to function and points in specific directions; movement is both the activity and the meaning of organic life and is inseparably linked to *causality*. But if, in this case, movement — for example, the movement of human limbs — can only be imagined together with the notion of the powerful muscles that engender it, then a context is encountered that cannot find access to the sphere of Egyptian art. For what is, is at rest, and any movement — all Becoming — is unimaginable in it.[19] Agglomeration and dissolution, concentration and relaxation are concepts that become possible only in connection with mass — gatherings and dispersals of forces that originate only in matter and in opposition to it and that can consequently be manifested only fictively, that is, symbolically, as formed mass.

If movement now — as was the organic body before — is freed from everything that binds it to its origin, to its sensual nature, to causality and thus to its impermanence — if one frees it from all accidents of light, which Egyptian art typically knows nothing of because light would have to function as a symbol of variability — then nothing remains except its visible sign: *direction*. The transition to metaphysical existence is achieved in this way. *Movement in Egyptian art is thus without body and energy*. It is the *shape of movement* that is engraved in the stone, which meanwhile has nothing to do with its form.

As a symbol of transience, the route leading from cause to effect, which is basically identical with active force, has no place in Egyptian existential space. Consequently, the figures move not only in a space that is free of gravity but also in a sphere that excludes every nexus of forces of the sort that one inevitably associates with the notion of human and organic individuality. More precisely, causal connections are grasped in terms of their results, as *forms of movement*, gestures, namely, the *having-become*. As a consequence, the character of any movement — that of the human body, for instance — can only be recognized by the interrelation of vectors that are devoid of energy, hence, by the relation of the human body to the functional orientation of gravity and thus to the perpendicular coordinates. In this we may recognize the metaphysical manifestation, in Egyptian art, of the conflict between organic elasticity and gravity that determines the existence of organic entities in nature. Here the conflict has become energy-less *form*.

How precisely this comes about can be illustrated by the example of a raised arm in a relief representation and its relation to the corresponding process in reality (figure 5.6). The higher the arm is held and thus shifted from its normal position with respect to gravity, the stronger the effect of this gravity in the natural world and the greater the strain to conquer it through the use of muscles. Egyptian art now strips the natural process of its dynamic and physical content with the aim of freeing its constructions from the system of causality and thus from mutability and the passage of time. *The conflict between gravity and muscle power no longer finds expression in aesthetic form.* The causal connection between the contraction of muscles and action is severed. What remains is the *result of this conflict of energy* or rather *its metaphysical form (Gestalt).* Their relation to the symbol of gravity, that is, to the vertical dimension and more generally to the coordinate system of existential space, accordingly represents the metaphysical interpretation of that elastic relationship that we are in the habit of seeing as a conflict between muscle power and gravity in its kinetic components. In a manner consistent with the metaphysical realm of Egyptian art, this conflict of forces is symbolized exclusively geometrically and therefore without energy. In the present example, this is achieved by means of the angle at which, above all, the arm follows the plumb line, that is, the vertical axis of the static coordinate system. In its most basic sense, this angle is the *metaphysical form of the causal link between energy components and action.*

The result is the geometric aspect of Egyptian sculpture — what has been called its cubism. In sculpture in the round, the

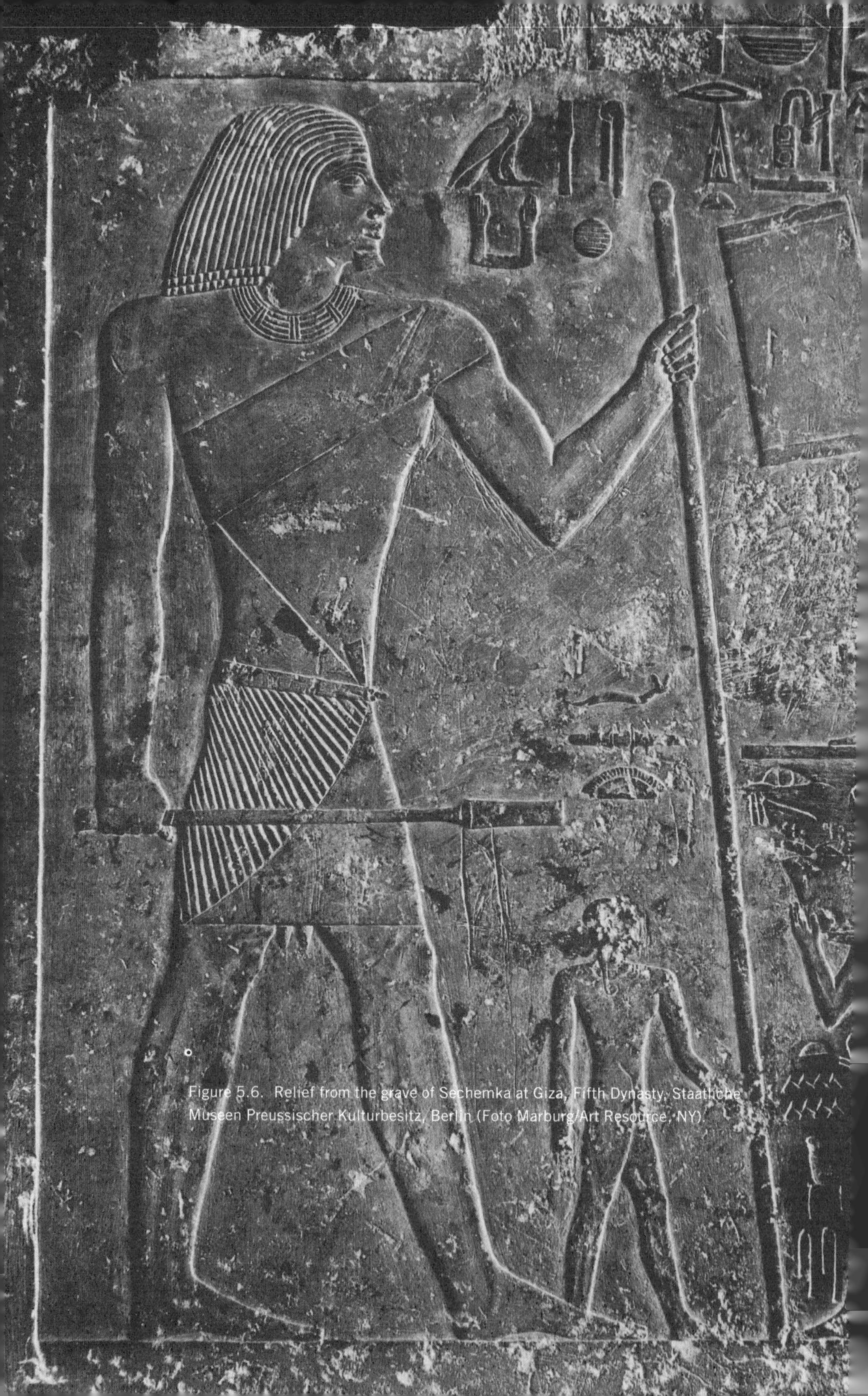

Figure 5.6. Relief from the grave of Sechemka at Giza, Fifth Dynasty, Staatliche Museen Preussischer Kulturbesitz, Berlin (Foto Marburg/Art Resource, NY).

geometry of the relief naturally becomes stereometry. The symbol of the corporeal therefore comes to stand in the same relation to the coordinate planes as earlier the linear outline in the relief stood to its axes. For the symbol of corporeal form, this does not in itself imply any necessary bond whereby, for instance, such forms, as one might well suppose, would inevitably approximate the simplest stereometric elements — a cube or a ball, for example. But if this does occur, it does so in the attempt to shape the essence of the realm of bodily symbols as clearly and intelligibly as possible by means of the simplicity of the relation to the symbolic elements of that space to which they belong, namely, to the coordinate planes.

In fact, however, this increase in comprehensibility in the sense of a stricter stylization also possesses an expressive character that should not be overlooked, yet which, owing to lack of space, I can only touch on very briefly here. This much is clear: the stronger the connection with the coordinate planes emerges, thus the more the form becomes assimilated to basic stereometric shapes, the stronger will be the manifestation of the link to that unchangeable essence of Being that is represented by coordinate space. With the degree of stylization, then, diminishes above all the receptivity to naturalistic details of the surface phenomenon; all the more prominent, however, becomes the *eternity–content* of the figure. That this circumstance also guided the Egyptians, at least unconsciously, is shown by the distinction in stylization between everyday animals and those that have been divinized — a fact to which Walter Wreszinski has drawn my attention (figures 5.7 and 5.8). The ordinary animals admit into their organization an abundance of natural, that is, organic, detail; their corporeal being, their appearance, is meant to be transferred into the realm of existential space as precisely and naturalistically as possible. The divinized animals are meant to express the eternal character

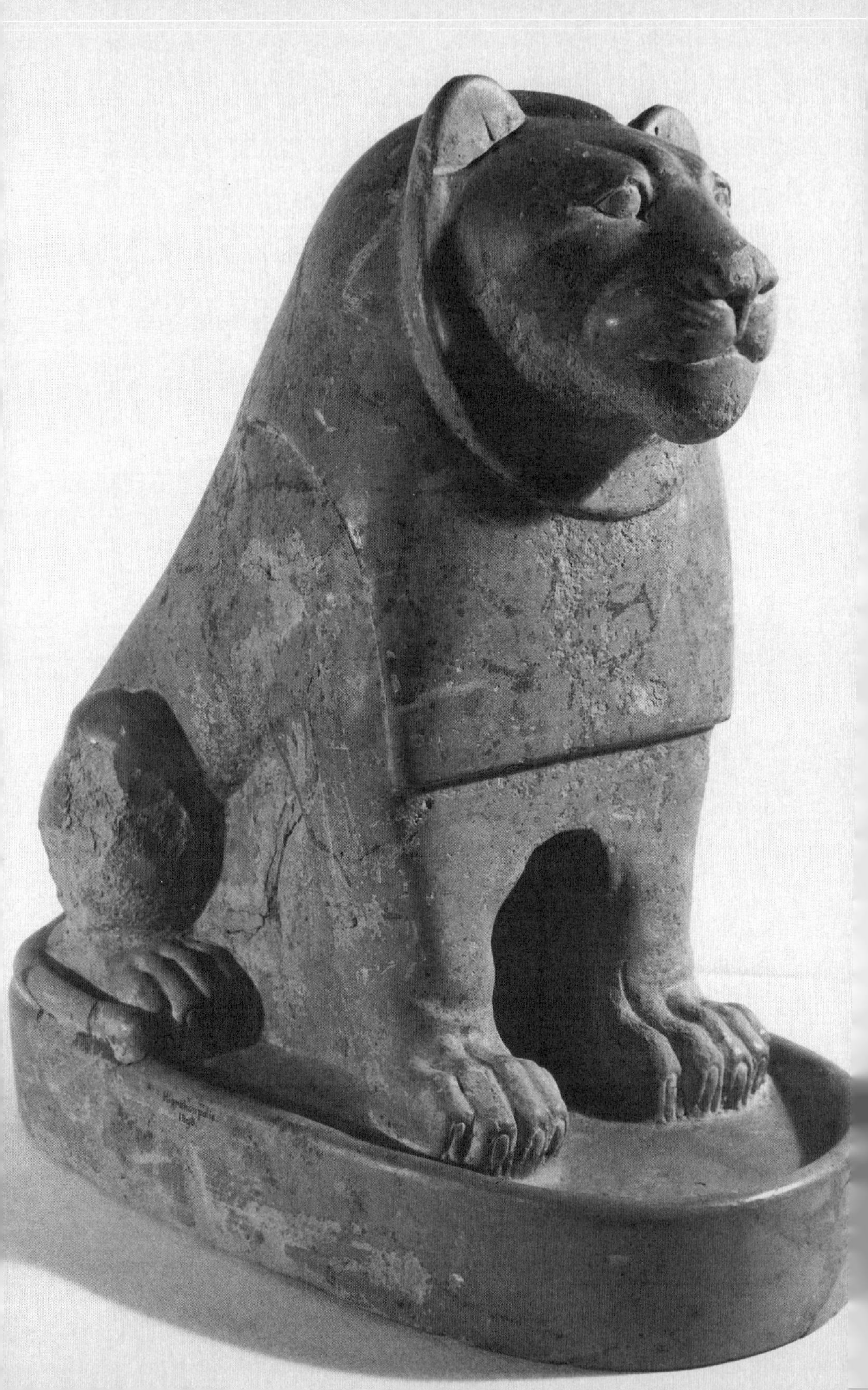

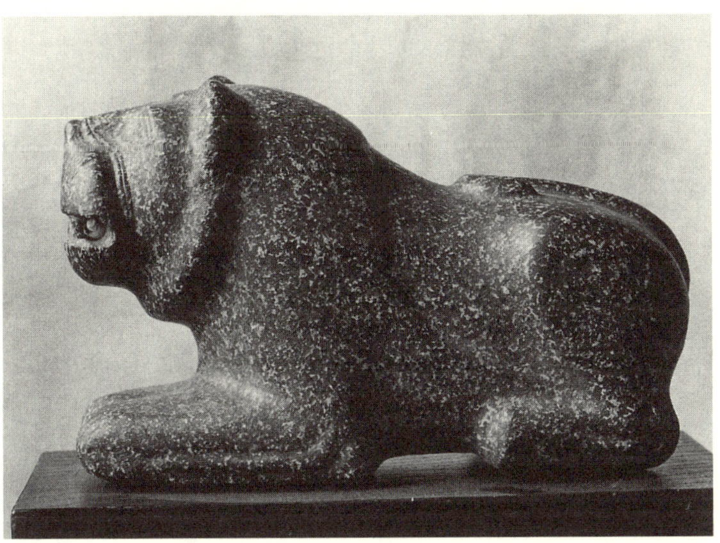

Figure 5.7 (opposite page). Statue of a seated lion from Hierakonoplis, Ashmolean Museum, Oxford University.
Figure 5.8 (above). Statue of a reclining lion, Staatliche Museen Preussischer Kulturbesitz, Berlin (Foto Marburg/Art Resource, NY).

of divinity; thus greater importance is attached to the most emphatic possible display of the connection to the coordinate planes of existential space than to the inclusion of naturalistic particulars, which would only disturb this impression. The same observation accounts for the stronger stylistic restraint of royal and divine figures in constrast to statues of ordinary men, among which the least restrained are those of slaves and barbarians.

Let us, however, return to movement, whose reinterpretation in the metaphysical sphere of Egyptian aesthetic space can still furnish us with important insights into the essence of Egyptian structure.

We have already established that the form of movement becomes conserved in direction, while the symbols of life have retreated into their imperishable signs. This movement's function is given permanence by its liberation from all matter, from its sensory manifestation, from everything that causes change and is subject to change, with the result that only the sign of movement, freed from all causality — that is, the shape of the movement — remains. Hence the most vehement movement on Egyptian reliefs is also immersed in the most perfect calm. Here nobody struggles with a goal, no one seeks to overcome or to break through the confinement of his natural existence. All tragedy, all guilt, is excluded here, and the conditions of life require no more explanation or justification than the shape of movement and Being in general, which has no acquaintance with problems.

If movement and thus force are symbolized in direction, then the *human will* must also necessarily express itself in the shape of movement. We must now ask how this time-bound element of human existence gets transposed into the form of an eternal value, because only as such is it able to find accommodation in the existential space of Egyptian art. As a metaphor of its finite existence — thus more or less in the same guise in which the will makes its appearance in Greek art — the human will cannot gain access to Egyptian space without bursting it open with its energetic content. As we have already established, a representation of force in its causal form of expression as energy-filled movement is unable to find a point of entry into an existential space that is devoid of energy because there is no place in a timeless existential space for energy as a dimension of time. Thus if *direction* remains explicable as the *shape of the will*, as already noted, it manifests itself in the previously considered attachment to the perpendicular coordinates, and so with the plumb line, although only with respect to those elements that arise from the conflict between gravity and vital force. But this conflict always takes place in the sphere of personality; hence there continues to cling to it something of the character of an individual entity, a character that on its own could find no purchase in the timeless eternity of Egyptian space and would render impossible the composition of coordinated ranges of representation. Thus there is still another link that binds the will to the structure of existential space in Egyptian art. It is through the *endless* nature of this bond that the activity of the particular first acquires the character of a final goal, situated in timelessness, that transcends all local events. It is this that first binds the particular to the general, this that first removes from the *form* of action its individual limitedness and fuses it with the form of a higher unity, with the *shape (Gestalt)* of a universal will that permeates every Egyptian work of art even in the smallest details.

The infinitude and timelessness of all Being, which Egyptians wished to confer on their images, can be captured not in borders but only by means of the link with that directional grouping of an endless number of horizontals that in its own right once more refers to the infinite, where its goal lies (figure 5.9).

Here, in spite of all metaphysical considerations, lies clearly the rationalism of Egyptian art, which seeks to clothe even its

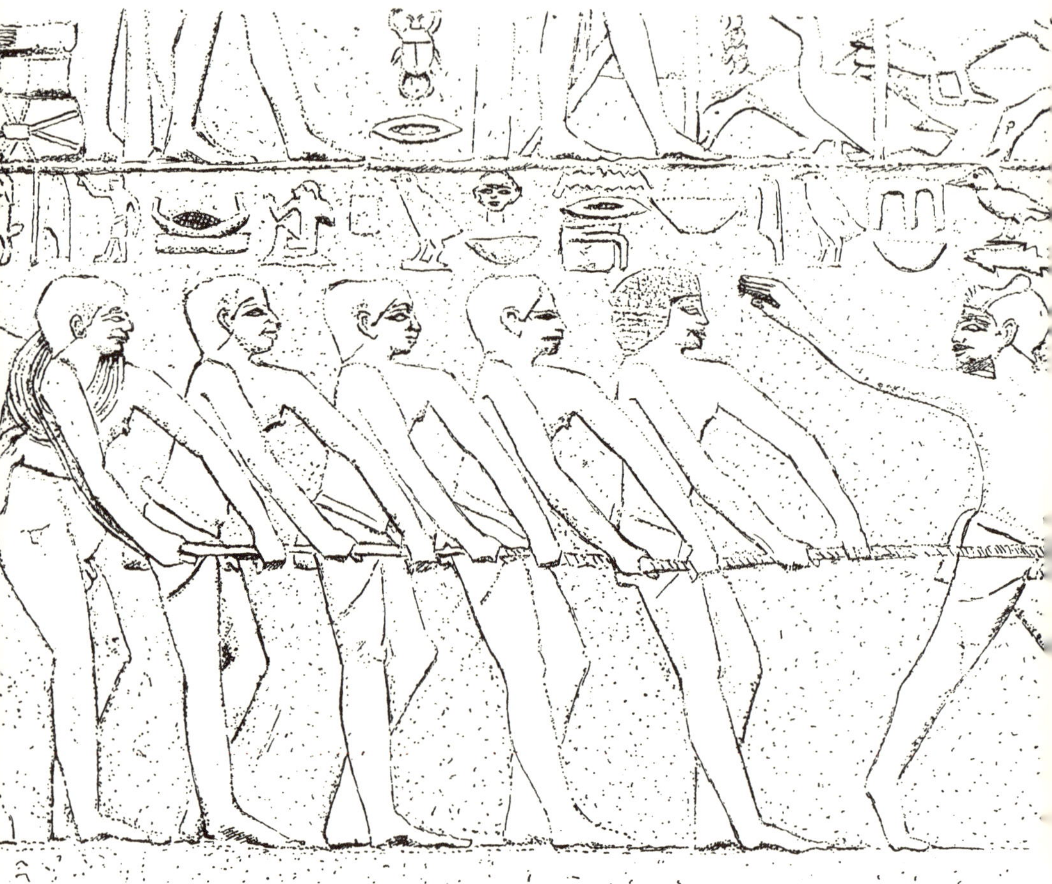

Figure 5.9. Relief from the grave of Neferseshempta at Saqqara, Fifth Dynasty.

belief in eternity in the forms of geometrically unequivocal signs.

If one examines any Egyptian relief with this in mind, one perceives that nowhere is there a form that is not firmly embedded in this *directional constraint of horizontal bundles of rays*. The famous relief from a grave in Giza, now in Berlin, which we have selected as an example (figure 5.6), shows this constraint no more and no less than any other Egyptian relief from the Old Kingdom to the latest period. To emphasize only the most prominent elements, we find there the direction of the glance, the shoulder line and its prolongation to the ends of the thumb of the left hand, the lower border of the aprons, the connecting line of the knee, and finally the ground line of the legs. Between these, however, less significant horizontals can be perceived. One is aware of them and anticipates them more than one sees them; together with the verticals, they create a formal grid out of which the forms seem to have composed themselves, and this grid, nearly invisible but nonetheless palpable, constitutes the visible sign of the structure of Egyptian existential space.

In this way, every figure on every Egyptian relief is bound together in the direction of its action in the same group of horizontals. Activity follows on activity, shape on shape, and all of them are incorporated into the rhythm of the group of horizontals, which must be understood as an emblem of the infinity and timelessness of space. And thus the actual *form* of its will always lies in the same timeless remoteness that for the Egyptian was the symbol of eternity. *It was the binding of the individual form of action to infinity — an infinity that extinguished all individual expression — that first guaranteed the eternity of that form.*

Thus these horizontals are always in reality nothing other than the coordinate of the *fourth dimension* — time — which in this case, in an existential space in itself timeless, can be understood no longer as the symbol of causality but only as infinity. Direction turns into the shape of movement and thence, finally, into the shape of time and of becoming, remaining anchored in unchangeable existential space by virtue of the fact that here it points toward the infinite as defined by the group of *horizontals*. Hence all movement emerges as mere direction, not by starting from the causal or the finite; it neither measures time nor is defined by time but is embedded in the timeless infinite and in the horizontals of the fourth dimension. The symbolic significance of this is that all movement is, as it were, flowing away in time and with time and that it thereby suspends time and thus preserves it within itself. In this realm, there is no arising and no passing away; everything takes place at the same time — a time in which the causally conditioned event does not stand out and must consequently make its appearance as something whose becoming has been completed as a mere form. For this reason, we seek in vain in the representations on Egyptian reliefs a spatial composition in a modern sense. The only spatial connection is direction, flowing through all the forms of action, as the shape of time; in this stream these figures swim, so to speak, and by the stream they are assembled into a unity that, while it manifests itself spatially, possesses no intrinsic spatial value.

With this comment on the liberation of Egyptian art from the notion of a *temporal limit*, these remarks on the structure of Egyptian sculpture must come to an end. The Egyptian artist is, above all, a kind of *conservator of life*. The foundation of his art lies in the *integration of the organic world with an existential space derived from the inorganic*. This process frees the organic from all matter, which is subject to change and to which consequently the transitoriness of all form must be attributed. The surface of things remains unaffected by this transition to a metaphysical sphere so long as this surface itself is taken as something incorporeal and as pure appearance — an appearance that, although it adheres to the matter, still represents, as it were, its outermost, infinitely fine epidermis. Once it has been liberated from the causal limitations of matter, no obstacle blocks its entrance into Egyptian existential space; and its insertion into the infinitely fine structure of the existential grid indeed presupposes a transposition into the uniform rhythm of this network, yet without any deformation of its variegated and manifold appearance. This explains Egyptian art's often baffling *naturalism of surfaces.*[20]

In summation, the most conspicuous feature of Egyptian structure remains the fact that matter, or rather mass, has no share in its construction. The will is not active in and through matter, and form does not arise as the expression of such activity. The sculptor does not *form*, rather he seeks to *conserve* in stone whatever is valuable in life. Matter does not express anything, but is only the medium whose function is to allow the form to become perceptible in existential space. Stone is in a way the materialization of this space. It performs for the Egyptian's metaphysical world of forms the same service that a screen does for a slide whose origin it had nothing to do with. The structure of Egyptian sculpture thus has a fully *immaterial* character. Although it manifests itself in matter, matter has no share in its construction. Forms appear in stone, but nothing joins them to it aesthetically. Therein lies the metaphysical character of their manifestation.

It is perhaps worth noting that the concept of aesthetic structure in Egyptian sculpture, as it has been tentatively developed here, has nothing to do with a proper interpretation of the Egyptian world of forms, of the sort Hans Gerhard Evers in his book *Staat aus dem Stein*, and to some extent Worringer, have attempted. The experiment undertaken here to determine what lies at the base of the formal manifestations of Egyptian sculpture, what its elementary historical foundations are, what powers and means it had at its disposal, and to what basic laws the will to shape had to yield is far from any scholarly historical project. What is apprehended by this experiment is only the lowest stratum of the properly aesthetic, even if this stratum is perhaps more powerful and more significant here in Egyptian art than in most other phases of development of European and ancient Near Eastern art. These are, in a sense, the most global preconditions to which every Egyptian sculptor is subject, from the Old Kingdom on, and which leave the individual will less room to maneuver than in other artistic traditions. All particular manifestations realized within these constrictions remain outside the scope of this inquiry; indeed, in my view, these manifestations cannot be interpreted on the basis of the approach adopted here. The explication of the Egyptian world of forms is only possible if one adopts the method prescribed by its own origin, namely by starting with the demands and objectives that characterized the mental and religious disposition of the Egyptian people and their transformation in the course of history. Only the general sphere of such spiritual presuppositions is reflected in the structure of the work of art. The content of these mental and religious dispositions and the nature of their association with the formal expression to which they lead cannot be inferred from structure. Nowhere has this content been adduced.

When confronted with the problems of plastic structure raised here, questions of the *organization* of sculpture's active form, which until now have been placed in the foreground by art historians (Schäfer, *Von ägyptischer Kunst*), seem to me to lose some of their importance. It must be admitted that that approach was essentially shaped by the way the problem was posed. Because my inquiry has nothing to do with aesthetics, and because the aim is not to "experience" Egyptian art — moreover, in my view, the very notion of experience was foreign to the Egyptians, at least in its modern sense — it is at the most the causal dependence of this modern aesthetic experience on the essence of the structural construction that plays a certain role. What this means is that the essential task of Egyptian art is the translation of the organic world into a realm whose derivation from the inorganic promises to bestow the value of eternity on transitory life but also that Egyptian art *completely lacks elements of the moment of action, at least in the sense in which we tend to ascribe it to Greek art. The conservation of life in existential space* constitutes the actual *creative* moment of Egyptian art, in which the specific kind of *active form* plays no integrating role.

From the arrangement of certain Egyptian monuments of funerary sculpture, we know that there was, in many cases at least, no thought given to an optical reception or to anything of this sort that might approximate our own optical aesthetic experience. Yet because every visualization, whether or not aesthetic goals are pursued, can only proceed in the form of reproduction proper to our senses, which are also those of its creator, the symbolization of the existential space of Egyptian art must also be of this sort. That is to say, this symbolization must above all correspond to the laws of our own capacities for optical reception.

The character of coordinate space, the space that comes closest to the metaphysical conception of space found in Egypt, cannot as such be grasped in optical terms. The thought process connected with the optic equipment of our bodies transforms that space into a perspectively constructed visual space, which completely changes the nature of the coordinate space and distorts or altogether suppresses its data. For this reason and only for this reason, visual space cannot be used for the symbolization of Egyptian coordinate space. "Perspective" means reference of the represented object to the viewer, and such a reference must necessarily be absent from the symbolization of existential space, which is foreign to any contact with the finite, the unique, and the transitory. Existential space, together with the world presented in it, is self-sufficient; in its structure, it is neither the object nor the creation of the individual, as is presupposed with perspective. Its world is an end in itself and has no practical goal lying outside of it.

In the organization of Egyptian sculpture, the issue can only be one of transferring imaginary existential space into the forms of reception of the eye in such a way that nothing essential in its character is changed and the aims of its activity — which lie in timelessness and are thus in themselves already fulfilled — undergo no destructive deflection through an admixture of elements of momentary and transitory life. But this can only happen if all of the data of this space appear in those elements that we have adopted as our aids in imagining existential space, namely, the system of coordinate axes or planes, as the case may be, that can be drawn through these axes. Thus it follows that all the data of an Egyptian sculpture in the round must refer to these planes. In the explanation of the active form, we have also characteristically reached the same result that we had previously reached in the analysis of the structure itself. The form of the optical appearance thus agrees perfectly with the picture that we previously had of the integration of existential space through the organic nature immortalized in it. The result is, as we have already indicated, that existential space and active form are identical in Egyptian art; or, more properly, there is no specific active form whatever.

These relations are similar, but more complicated, in reliefs. The data of a sculpture in the round may refer to all the planes of the coordinate system; but in a relief they must crowd together on the flat surface of a single plane. Here, of course, just as with sculpture in the round, the question about the organization of these data is no longer one of structure; this question has been answered comprehensively and usefully in the cited works of

Ludwig Curtius, Heinrich Schäfer, and Gerhard Krahmer. Just as it previously entered into coordinate space, the form must now spread out in the plane — in the reduced element and symbol of this space. The form must shift its essence as much as possible into the operative field of this plane, from which it cannot escape. There is thus little sense in constantly wishing to make direct inferences from the form in an Egyptian low relief to its organic model in nature. For Egyptian sculpture is never a *copy* of nature; indeed, it is only even a metaphor of nature in a very conditional sense. It is a *conservation* or, if one prefers, a petrification or mummification of the organic world and of life, as well as, above all, of its religious associations. But this conservation takes place not in the forms of the relief image itself but rather, as has already been amply explained, in a metaphysical realm into which one would first of all have to convey the relief image insofar as one is concerned to understand the represented forms. Egyptians, for whom such a conceptual world was the norm, could thus never be in a position to take offense at the dislocations and deformations involved in the representation of organic entities. *For Egyptians, the question was solely whether formal signs were sufficiently available to guarantee the reality and completeness of the object and of the metaphysical action connected with it.* Any inclination to evoke or maintain an illusionistic impression was evidently very remote. For Egyptians, the *illusion of eternal stability* sufficed.[21]

Hence the representational surface of an Egyptian relief is also merely stone and as such is exclusively a symbol of an element of existential space. It is not meant to *simulate* any space. It is itself the *materialization of a coordinate plane*, or, more precisely, of two such planes of existential space, and is therefore able to assimilate only the significant content of this space. Thus it contains no instructions about a conception of space in the modern sense — that is, no data that might refer to visual space. It certainly does not originate in any *art of seeing*, even a special kind of seeing, as has been supposed. It is, rather, exclusively a *function of the metaphysical power of imagination*.[22] Its goal was to conserve life by translating it out of its organic nature into the lawfulness of an inorganic sphere and thus to fix it forever as something *having-become*. In this bold and rationalistic attempt to dissolve Becoming into an idea of Being, nothing could remain of the former beyond its *form*. This form alone, together with its magical content, remained imperishable and thus became a symbol for a world beyond in which life did preserve its *form* but otherwise vanished entirely in the timeless and spiritual existence of the otherworldly realm.[23]

In this sense, Egyptian art is the supreme attempt to overcome death in that it attempted to fix life within a space that identified itself with time — by completely assimilating it, so to speak, as a new dimension and thus paralyzing it in its finite operation.

So interpreted, the Egyptian attitude stands in explicit contrast to the modern period. In modernity, it is space that must be overcome by time — an endeavor that in the end drives the sensation of ephemerality and of the temporal limitation of all existence to a tormented extreme. In Egypt, it was through the conquest of space through time that the wisdom of the East sought and found eternity and the consciousness of unchanging Being and its totality, to the extent that this goal lies at all within the grasp of human nature.

Notes

1. Art historical research has concerned itself only very little with Egypt. Fundamental studies in this field are (besides many studies by Friedrich Wilhelm von Bissing): Ludwig Curtius, *Die antike Kunst: Ägypten und Vorderasien* (Wildpark-Potsdam: Athenaion, 1923), and Heinrich Schäfer, *Von ägyptischer Kunst*, 3rd ed. (Leipzig: Hinrichs, 1930); cf. Hans Gerhard Evers, *Staat aus dem Stein* (Munich: Bruckmann, 1929). These remarks owe a particular debt to critical engagement with the work of the late Gerhard Krahmer, *Figur und Raum in der ägyptischen und griechisch-archaischen Kunst* (Halle: Niemeyer, 1931), and the work of Wilhelm Worringer and Friedrich Matz, particularly "Zur Komposition ägyptischer Wandbilder," *Jahrbuch des Deutschen Archäologischen Instituts* 37 (1922), pp. 39ff. Cf. also Günther Roeder, "Vorgeschichtliche Plastik Ägyptens," *Ipek* 2 (1926), pp. 64ff.

2. Cf. Hans Sedlmayr, "Die Quintessenz der Lehren Riegls," in Alois Riegl, *Gesammelte Aufsätze* (Augsburg: Filser, 1929), pp. xviii ff.

3. The idea of structure developed here deviates from the principles of the Vienna School in many respects — though, in my view, never in any essential way. This can be explained by the fact that it is derived from the same tradition (Riegl) but was developed without connection to the circle of *Kunstwissenschaftliche Forschungen*. The position of the present work may be most readily understood as a consequence of the point of view lucidly presented by Sedlmayr in "Die Quintessenz der Lehren Riegls," xviii ff. I am in any case certain that any still appreciable differences in conceptualization and aim will in time get blurred.

4. Cf. Ludwig Coellen, *Der Stil in der bildenden Kunst* (Darmstadt: Arkadenverlag, 1921), p. 41.

5. This period, which is governed by unique conditions, must be dealt with elsewhere, so far as the structure of its art is concerned.

6. This European attitude was described very well in a limited sense for the baroque period by Erich Jaensch, "Fechners Grundlegung der Ästhetik und die Wendung von Psychophysik zu organischer Psychologie," in *Festschrift Ludwig Klages* (Leipzig: Barth, 1932), pp. 107f.

7. All of this, of course, concerns ornament — which in central Europe, apart from sporadic southern influences, is always abstract — only in its structural essence and has nothing to do with the actual goals of the ornamental representation, whether they are magical or decorative in character. On this subject, see also the apt comments by Dagobert Frey in "Das Kunstwerk als Willensproblem," *Bericht des 4. Kongresses für Ästhetik und Kunstwissenschaft* [*Beilageheft zur Zeitschrift für Ästhetik und Kunstwissenschaft* 25 (1931), pp. 231ff.], and Ernst Strauss, "Über einige Grundfragen der Ornamentbetrachtung," *Zeitschrift für Ästhetik und allgemeine Kunstwissenschaft* 27 (1933), pp. 33–48.

8. See Curtius, *Antike Kunst*, p. 109; Worringer, *Ägyptische Kunst* (Munich: Piper, 1927), p. 31, passim.

9. Worringer, *Ägyptische Kunst*, p. 7.

10. Bissing, *Denkmäler ägyptischer Skulptur* (Munich: Bruckmann, 1911), plate 3.

11. Cf. Walter Strich, *Der irrationale Mensch* (Berlin: Schneider, 1928), pp. 108f.

12. Views on what is meant by the notions transcendental and metaphysical differ widely. In my opinion, one can speak of the metaphysical character of an artistic structure if the means with which it works, or the elements to which it refers, are not accessible to the senses; e.g., when one characterizes Egyptian space as a sensory symbol of the general nature of Being. In this sense, of course, a certain metaphysical character must be granted to all art. Nevertheless, in this case, I think it makes a difference whether, as in Greek art, the will to form operates through the material in expressing the absolute or whether, as in Egyptian art, its metaphysical existence becomes visible only in the material. Material in Egyptian art, as will presently be shown, is not an element of artistic structure.

13. Ewald Wasmuth, *Kritik des mechanisierten Weltbildes* (Hellerau: Hegner, 1929), p. 156.

14. "Something similar occurs with offerings to the dead, which become mere images." Cf. Balthasar Pörtner, *Die ägyptischen Totenstelen als Zeugen des sozialen und religiösen Lebens ihrer Zeit, Studien zur Geschichte und Kultur des Altertums* (Paderborn: Schoningh, 1911), vol. 4, p. 5.

15. Cf. Richard Frydmann, "Vertikaleinfühlung und Stilwillen," *Zeitschrift für Ästhetik und Kunstwissenschaft* 24 (1930), pp. 126ff.

16. "What he (the Egyptian) inscribed in the stone were his riddles, 'his hieroglyphs'" (Hegel, *Philosophie der Geschichte*).

17. Worringer, *Ägyptische Kunst*, p. 11.

18. Hence the paratactic nature of Egyptian art, which Krahmer, *Figur und Raum*, pp. 10ff., has clearly established.

19. "Egyptian outlines have a perfect form of being but no form of becoming" (Worringer, *Ägyptische Kunst*, p. 64).

20. Flinders Petrie probably has something similar in mind when in *The Arts and Crafts of Ancient Egypt* (Edinburgh and London: Foulis, 1923), p. 8, he speaks, first of all, of the "endurance" for which Egyptian statues were worked and goes on to say that upon this quality "was built a rich and varied character, reflected in the elaborate and beautiful sculpture which covered, but never interfered with, the grand mass of a monument"; cf. also Worringer, *Ägyptische Kunst*, p. 34, who, in my opinion, unconvincingly interprets in the opposite sense an observation that is in itself correct when he allows nature among the Egyptians to be revised by an "externally derived system of laws."

21. Cf. Evers, *Staat aus dem Stein*, pp. 63f.

22. "The figure thus never becomes a mere image in the sense of something viewed and calculated only for the beholder; rather it retains, as the active bearer of life, a factual reality" (Curtius, *Antike Kunst*, p. 197); cf. also Evers, *Staat aus dem Stein*, pp. 1ff.

23. Strich, *Der irrationale Mensch*, p. 111. Already Goethe criticized the timelessness of Egyptian art, for which he wanted it banished from museums to curiosity cabinets.

Translated by Brian Fuchs and Amy C. Smith.

Otto Pächt, "Design Principles of Fifteenth-Century Northern Painting" (1933)

This essay, which appeared in the second issue of Kunstwissenschaftliche Forschungen, *earned Otto Pächt the* Habilitation, *the right to hold an advanced university position. The year it was published, 1933, he got a job teaching at Heidelberg, but the Nazi regime prevented him as a Jew from taking it. Eventually, he found work in England, at the British Museum and finally at Oxford. Pächt's two main areas of expertise were manuscript illumination and fifteenth-century northern panel painting. His first book was on early Austrian panel painting (1929). "Design Principles of Fifteenth-Century Northern Painting" exemplifies Pächt's sweeping, systematizing vision of Western art history and his tendency to classify form in national or geographical terms, which his American friend Meyer Schapiro reproached him for. But it also puts on display his keen, creative eye. The essay analyzes the relationships between figure and ground in early Flemish, Dutch, and French paintings. Pächt argues that northern painting was driven by a constant negotiation between spatial illusionism and the patterns generated by the projection of three-dimensional form on the picture plane. Pächt's formal analyses undermine the conventional interpretation of Renaissance art as the triumph of pictorial illusionism.*

(Source: Otto Pächt, "Gestaltungsprinzipien der westlichen Malerei," Kunstwissenschaftliche Forschungen *2 [1933]; reprinted in Otto Pächt,* Methodisches zur kunsthistorischen Praxis *[Munich: Prestel, 1977], pp. 17–58. ©Michael Pächt, Munich, 1995.)*

Design Principles of Fifteenth-Century Northern Painting (1933)

Otto Pächt

Introduction

"If the history of art wants to occupy a position among the humanistic disciplines commensurate with the significance of art in the life of peoples and individuals, then it must treat the problem of the development of modern painting primarily as an aesthetic problem. And when it comes to expressly naturalistic art, as opposed to the decorative art of the Middle Ages, there can be no doubt which problem occupies the beginning stages of modern painting like no other and contains above all the key to the evaluation of artistic achievement: the conquest of the third dimension."[1] If I have selected precisely these lines out of the extensive literature on the development of spatial representation in early Netherlandish and early French painting, it is because in them we hear the explicit assurance that the object of investigation will be an aesthetic problem. This claim, which lies as an unproven assumption behind all investigations into the origins of modern painting, is one we must examine more closely.

The thesis that the problem of reducing three-dimensional space onto a two-dimensional surface plays a decisive role in the emergence of modern painting — to which, in itself, one might perfectly well subscribe — contains an ambiguous message. There is a *technical* (representational) problem and there is an *aesthetic* problem of reducing space onto surface. Paradoxically, despite his profession of exclusive interest in the development of painting as an artistic discipline, the writer just quoted focused solely on advancements in the solution of technical problems.

Now, it shall certainly not be claimed here that as soon as artists began to represent the world in perspective every technical problem was solved immediately and easily. Any unbiased consideration teaches one main lesson: that the path toward perspectival correctness was blocked not so much by inadequate (technical) ability as by *positive compulsion*, namely, the pressure *to project three-dimensional space onto the surface in such a way as to yield an aesthetically relevant order*. When it comes to the reduction of space onto surface in art, still another condition must be met besides the demand for perspectival and general representational (reproductive) correctness. The forms achieved through projection — the optical equivalents of the (intended) three-dimensional reality — must at the same time be conceived as parts of a pictorial structure whose rule system has still hardly been investigated. We can say only provisionally, in fact, that it is a system of laws operating in the plane surface. *Every element belongs simultaneously to two different systems of reference.* Yet crucial for the character of the image as a work of art is that it is only within a specifically aesthetic system that the visible elements form a unity. And that means that the exactly accurate portrayal, the mechanical reproduction, can always result in errors, inconsistencies, or contradictions. For only the other reckoning, the aesthetic system, is meant to come out even. The unity of surface organization must be preserved, even at the cost of the coherence of the spatial order. We see now how misleading it is to speak of the space problem as the central problem of modern painting. *Here, too, the specific realm of the aesthetic rule system is the surface* (admittedly the imaginary surface of the optical plane).

Only recently has scholarly research again become conscious of the significance of the surface for perspectival painting. At first, to be sure, scholarship did not recognize the implications of its discovery. It sought to demonstrate its validity only for certain periods and styles (High Renaissance) without addressing the question of whether the central aesthetic problem of modern painting might not lie locked in the problem of surface design. A further obstacle to a correct understanding of the situation seems to me to lie in a too narrow interpretation of the concept of surface organization. For instance, some have tried to discover beneath the surface of the representation a sort of secret pictorial ornament, gladly imagined as a figure (such as a star or rosette) characterized by a certain geometrical regularity or especially suggestive form, which is then usually assigned a specific symbolic meaning.[2] The interpreter thus believes he has uncovered the deeper symbolic significance of the work of art, inconspicuously woven, by means of these ornamental figures, into the external representational meaning. Most such interpretations have been dismissed. One senses that the actual (deeper) symbolic content of an image, its formal symbol, as it were, cannot be so superficially and arbitrarily bound up with the pictorial structure, in the way the cat in a picture puzzle is intertwined with the lines and forms of the landscape. And in fact it is difficult to see how the form of a surface ornament containing its own objective meaning (for example, a palmette) could be reconciled with the image of a spatial world of objects in a more than superficial and random way.[3]

Still another direction of study, which must be taken far more seriously, operates with the notion of surface organization (called "pictorial motif" by Theodor Hetzer). Yet even here the term is used more in the ordinary sense of composition.[4] Composition, for these scholars, means roughly the retrospective adjustment of a spatially conceived physical world with the final effect of a pleasing arrangement on the surface of the picture. Here, too, one is thinking more of a secondary, ornamental unification on the picture plane.[5]

If analysis is not to inflict violence on works of art, one may not approach them with the expectation of discovering pure surface patterns that retain meaning as regular geometrical figures or other symbolic forms even when abstracted from the level of physical and spatial significance. Furthermore, one cannot expect to encounter two distinct, as it were, superimposed systems of rules but rather must try to imagine the operation of a double rule system: that is, to see and understand surface and spatial values in an intimate, mutual penetration. Any pictorial analysis, then, must take the following statement as a maxim: *surface and pictorial space must not be investigated separately*. The central aesthetic problem of this art cannot be grasped if one goes on thinking about spatial illusion in the old, extra-aesthetic sense. Nor can it be grasped if — as though to compensate or supplement the spatial illusion — one continues to extract through analysis an aesthetic value belonging not to artistic categories but to purely decorative ones. The theories called on to supplement the basic assumptions have functioned, then, only as a superficial corrective to a false, outmoded point of view that remains at its core unaffected.

One cannot recognize that peculiar double rule system that distinguishes all postmedieval perspectival painting (and not only that of western European schools) either through speculative considerations about the essence of the new art or through its historical derivations from earlier styles.[6] We have arrived at this (we believe) crucial realization through the quite specific and highly concrete observation of a double meaning in all projective form, which we shall discuss in detail in the next section. Our theory is valuable primarily in that it enables us at last to recognize as necessary and meaningful to the overall artistic intention those characteristics of early Netherlandish painting that appear most disconcerting to our own perceptual habits and that until now have only been evaluated negatively (namely, as inadequacy of representational technique). But we may not stop with that. It is important to recognize the operation of the double rule system throughout the entire structure and to organize the visible data in a uniform way from that point of view. In this way, the immediate artistic experience is preserved, while at the same time we become aware of it more deeply as a carefully and thoroughly formed phenomenon.

If one goes in the other direction and attempts to analyze surface composition and spatial composition separately, the artistic phenomenon falls to pieces. Any statements made at that point are abstractions pushed heedlessly into the place of the lost phenomenon. They may appear first as an organizing schema whose primitive, rigid regularity can be brought into a meaningful connection with the rich and nuanced visible presence of the image only with violent manipulations. Or they may stand as a *perceptual*, concrete idea, which likewise can be associated with the content of the picture only through complete lack of interest in an artistic order. By saying this, I do not wish to claim that those who have analyzed works of art according to this dualistic procedure have not had specifically aesthetic experiences before the great early Netherlandish paintings. But still, it is most likely that this was possible only so long as scholars confronted the works as amateurs. The intention to describe, as we know from psychology, transforms the phenomena themselves.[7] And a certain danger lies in the fact that with insufficient care the original phenomena may be replaced with less worthy ones. The "objective distance" of many descriptions stems from the fact that the objects themselves have changed — that the statements relate to phenomena less rich in artistic content and thus distinct from those purportedly in question. It is not the viewer's inadequate relationship to the painting that is to blame for such an error (indeed this error is hardly a necessary one, nor is the conceptual recognition of artistic phenomena completely impossible). Rather, his inadequate ability to become conscious of the content of his own experience is responsible. An important part of scientific activity must be the attempt to overcome and reconcile the inherent dichotomy between one's role as an experiencing person and one's role as a scholarly analyst through the critical perception of one's own experience.

The Southern Netherlands

The Segment of Reality as Formal Whole

The assumption that the central problem of modern painting is the problem of space demands substantiation. The correlate to this assumption is the definition — wholeheartedly accepted in the literature — of the modern framed picture as a segment of reality. To have established this conception of the picture is supposed to be the epochal historical achievement of early Netherlandish painting.[8] But just as was the case with the basic assumption, we must ask of this related idea whether it in fact is able to direct our investigation further toward genuinely artistic problems.

The concept of the segment of reality originates in the objective world. Reality as the painter's object means, in this case, the visible world and is conceived as something whole and infinite, only a limited portion of which appears within the picture frame. But whether a segment is given to us phenomenally as well remains uncertain. Indeed, as an artistic form, the segment of an object need not always appear as fragmentary or in need of completion.

It would not occur to anyone, for example, to define the artistic character of a sculptural bust as merely the segment of a larger whole. Along the same lines, it would be wholly conceivable that the fragmentariness of a picture that seems from an objective, concrete standpoint to be a segment of reality would not enter our consciousness — at least so long as our eyes understand how to follow the artistic intention of the design process.[9] If we wish to speculate about pictorial representations as artistic constructions, then in each case we must inquire whether the objectively fragmentary quality manifests itself in perceptual equivalents as well. For even in naturalistic styles, the qualities that emerge from the so-called natural experience of perception are still extra- or pre-artistic facts. They can enter into the picture only by means of a particular translation which we shall call formation (*Formung*).

Now, early Netherlandish painting introduces no identical formal sign to stand for the segment of reality. To be sure, the imaginary space within such paintings can be continued and completed outside the boundaries of the picture. But this can happen only when one imagines that space as abstract, free from the corporeal, material forms it contains and that appear in the picture. Even if some of these forms become visible as fragments within the picture frame, the optical equivalent of the physical world on the pictorial surface (that is, all of the projective forms) produces something whole and complete in itself to which nothing can be added or taken away.

To the extent that the *appearance of the three-dimensional physical world is reworked into a two-dimensional construction, a whole emerges from the segment or part.* It was the Netherlandish painters' decisive achievement — tantamount to a discovery — to have gleaned the means to this transvaluation from the process of projection. Thereby they could safeguard the unity of the picture.

The Double Nature of Projective Form

Within the projection of any object a quality of spatial illusion lies concealed. At the same time, however, the object's silhouette contains a pure surface quality (for example, a circular tabletop can project itself on the surface as an oval). In early Netherlandish painting, these silhouette figures (ovals and such) suddenly relate to each other as surface forms. At the same time — and quite independently — the corporeal beings and objects to which they correspond (that is, whose projections they are) appear contained in an all-around spatial context. Thus the *pictorial world is subjected to two heteronomous ordering principles.* The realm of one extends beyond the pictorial boundary, allowing the spatial context to continue across the edges of the picture; at the same time, the surface cohesiveness of the silhouette values creates a closed unity of its own. One rule system, valid only within the pictorial frame, merges with another obtaining even beyond it.

This *double rule system* — which, for the moment, we have grasped only in general terms — must now be investigated more closely. We still do not comprehend the system of surface arrangement. It is indeed difficult to discern how a proper compositional system can be established for a naturalistic, perspectival painting style.

Let us suppose, for the moment, that the projection (as we understand it) of a three-dimensional physical world onto a pictorial surface would apply to the composition of an early Netherlandish picture. The construction of the pictorial surface would then be completely determined by the floor plan of the pictorial space and by the placement and distancing of figures and objects in relation to the picture plane (or by the standpoint of the viewer). In such a projection, we would observe a fairly haphazard juxtaposition and overlapping of silhouettes, which at one moment would densely cover the pictorial surface and at the next leave it gaping open.

This hardly describes early Netherlandish pictures, for these, even at first glance, produce a totally different impression. The pictorial surface is covered almost completely with the projections of objects; only exceptionally do small empty patches remain. One can thus see the *pictorial field as ground* upon which *physical forms appear as pattern*. These are in fact distributed in such a way that they fill the pictorial ground fairly compactly (at a later point, we shall return to the question of what can be ground and what pattern). If one imagines the internal form of the figures and objects — their modelling — erased so that only their silhouettes appeared on the ground, very few blank spaces would remain between them. What is important in this process is not so much the insignificant surface area of these intervals as the fact that the forms they produce have the character of ground left over from the pattern. That is, they have the character of negative form. (A good example in the Mérode Altarpiece [figure 6.1] is the fire screen pointing upward like a tongue. Enframed by the fireplace roof above, the relatively small slab with its shadows dominates the entire large inner surface of the fireplace.)

The dense filling of the pictorial field (that is, the ground) occurs by means of the strict accommodation of the objects' contours to one another. This linkage binds together forms that are connected neither spatially nor in an objective, contextual relationship and that often even possess completely distinct positions in space. The simple juxtaposition of objects on the surface — which, as a projection, need not imply their spatial proximity — can thus create a sort of cohesion.

Let us return to our earlier example: the projection of a circular tabletop that produces a form bounded by an oval outline on the pictorial surface (figure 6.1).[10] For the Netherlandish painters, an object's projection becomes identical with such a form; the projection might, say, abut the oval with a shallow curve, then

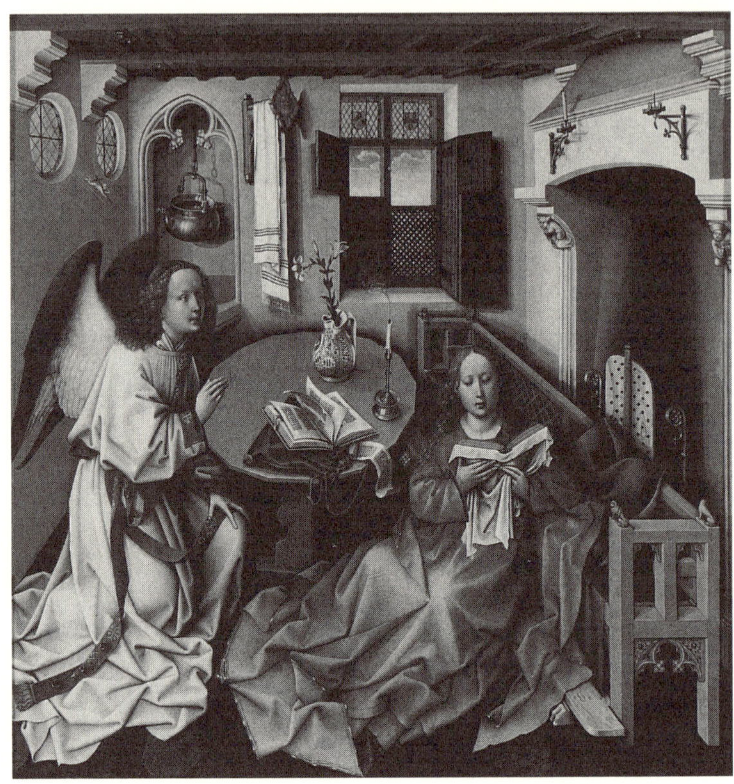

Figure 6.1. Master of Flémalle, Mérode Altarpiece, *Annunciation* (detail),
Metropolitan Museum of Art (Cloisters Collection, 1956. 56.70, NY).

accompany and trace over the adjacent contour with its own outline. For the moment, let us disregard the fact that these parallel outlines can indicate very different things; in one case, that is, a curve is meant to represent something physically flat, and in another, a curve denotes a circle and thus only appears flat in the projective foreshortening. Furthermore, let us set aside the possibility that two parallel lines of equal size could indicate either a short surface or a long but foreshortened extension. The contours remain pure surface drawing and as such exist in an intimate relationship to one another.

This is so, in fact, not only in those places where a correspondence of the outlines results, as it were, fortuitously but throughout the entire image. The projections of objects merge together from all sides, almost without a gap, to form a single, extremely fine uppermost layer on the pictorial field. Of course, this kind of all-encompassing, continuous surface cohesiveness cannot be the accidental outcome of the projection process. It can arise only if the pictorial conception determines the design in accordance with the surface of projection. In order to imagine most clearly how this sort of pictorial thinking works, one must invert the relationship that projection usually assumes in a thought experiment. First of all, in this system no three-dimensional physical world would be projected onto the surface. Rather, one would recognize the screen of the projection surface first, with its configuration of distinctively shaped patches; these patches would then be projected backward as objects and bodies onto the space understood as lying behind the screen. This inverted projection might seem at first a highly paradoxical assumption, but that would be the case only if it were regarded as a mechanical process. We shall employ the pictorially conceived expression "inverted projection" as an auxiliary hypothesis to facilitate our apprehension of Netherlandish pictorial structures. *When one accords primary status to surface order*, one enters the position from which one can successfully reconstruct a Netherlandish picture in visual terms. As long as one clings to the conventional notion of projection, on the other hand, a series of features will remain incomprehensible.[11]

The Priority of Surface Order

Once one has become aware that an early Netherlandish picture is oriented according to two systems of reference, the further observation that these are not equal in value immediately arises. Contrary to all expectations, the rule system governing the surface proves itself decisive wherever a conflict emerges between the two ordering principles.

IMPACT ON THE SPATIAL ORDER

The priority of surface order becomes apparent, above all, whenever it conflicts with the demands of spatial illusion. Among the fundamental conditions to which, according to general conviction, the emergence of spatial illusion is bound, that requiring that all objects be seen and reproduced from a single, unified vantage point is particularly important. For the early period of Netherlandish painting, viewers usually miss this unified standpoint and therefore refer to imperfect perspective.[12] Individual objects, for example, offer themselves to our gaze from a completely different angle from that which generally functions in pictures. The objects appear distorted, since they tend to be depicted in a view from above (as if from a highly elevated viewpoint) rather than from a normal standpoint. The cause of this distortion, however, is not inadequate perspectival competence but the artistic design principle of the *horror vacui*; this demands that the pictorial field be completely covered with the projections of objects in a single, continuous surface rapport. In order to achieve this, the contours of the silhouettes must be fitted firmly against each other. There emerges thus a *pressure to align the neighboring outlines*, which now and then distorts the silhouette (projection) itself and conditions the — for our naturalistic habits of seeing — disruptive shifts in perspective.

Admittedly, that explanation does not adequately describe the actual design process. We must now imagine the process of formal construction as entailing the determination of the projective form's shape by the negative space between the neighboring surface projections (and, of course, vice versa). A concrete three-dimensional object would then be sought to conform to that remaining silhouette shape. And so it can even be claimed that both the selection of objects and the choice of viewpoint in which they appear depend fundamentally on the shape of the silhouettes.

It is not only individual objects that tend to be displayed in a distorted perspective in early Netherlandish paintings. In many cases, the entire lower section might be presented in a view from above, while the upper half of the picture appears in a straightforward view, for example the *Annunciation* of the Mérode Altarpiece (figure 6.1) or the landscape with the *Adoration of the Lamb* in the Ghent Altarpiece (figure 6.2), with its supposed break in style.[13] Even the view from above in the picture's lower half, moreover, need not always be unified; figures observed more from above can be juxtaposed with others seen emphatically from across the space (such as the Annunciate Virgin next to the angel in the Mérode Altarpiece). But to describe Netherlandish pictorial order simply as a combination of normal view in the upper half and view from above in the lower half of a picture would still hardly be adequate. Nor would this order be more comprehensible if one were to presuppose two vanishing points instead of one — to say nothing of the fact that this shift of viewpoints would still demand explication. Only when one acknowledges the interrela-

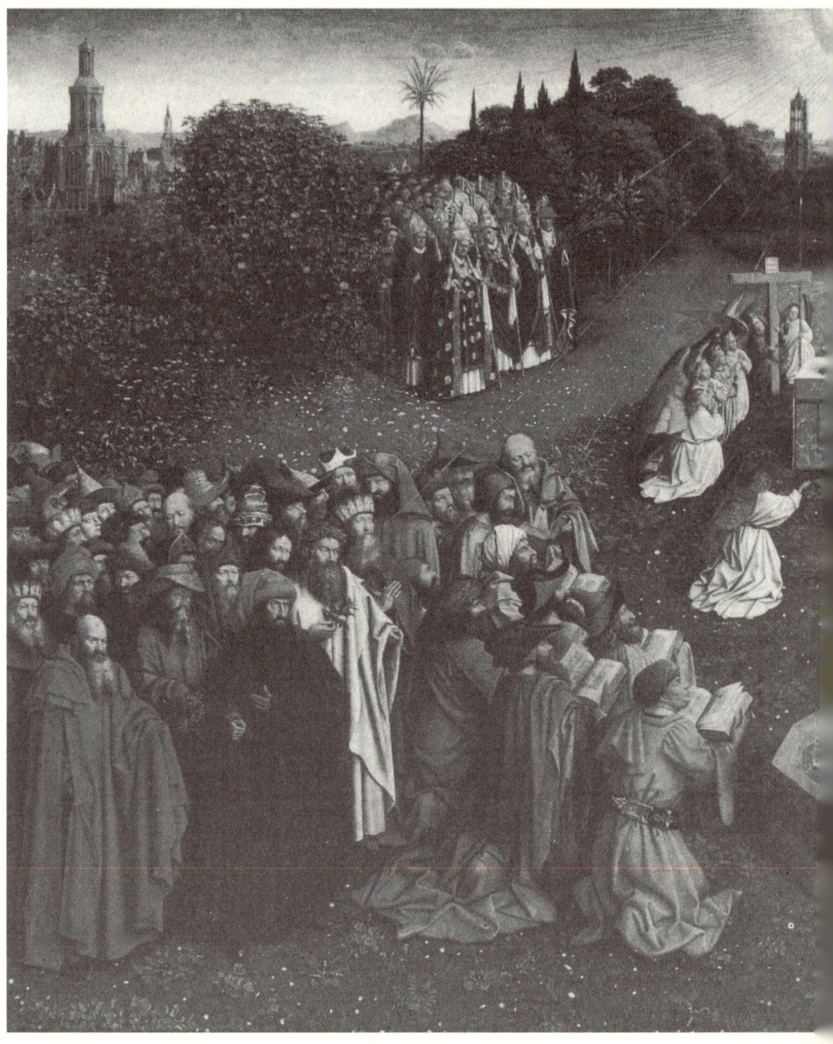

Figure 6.2. Hubert and Jan van Eyck, Ghent Altarpiece, *Adoration of the Lamb*, central panel, St. Baafskathedraal, Ghent (© St. Baafskathedraal and Paul M.R. Maeyaert).

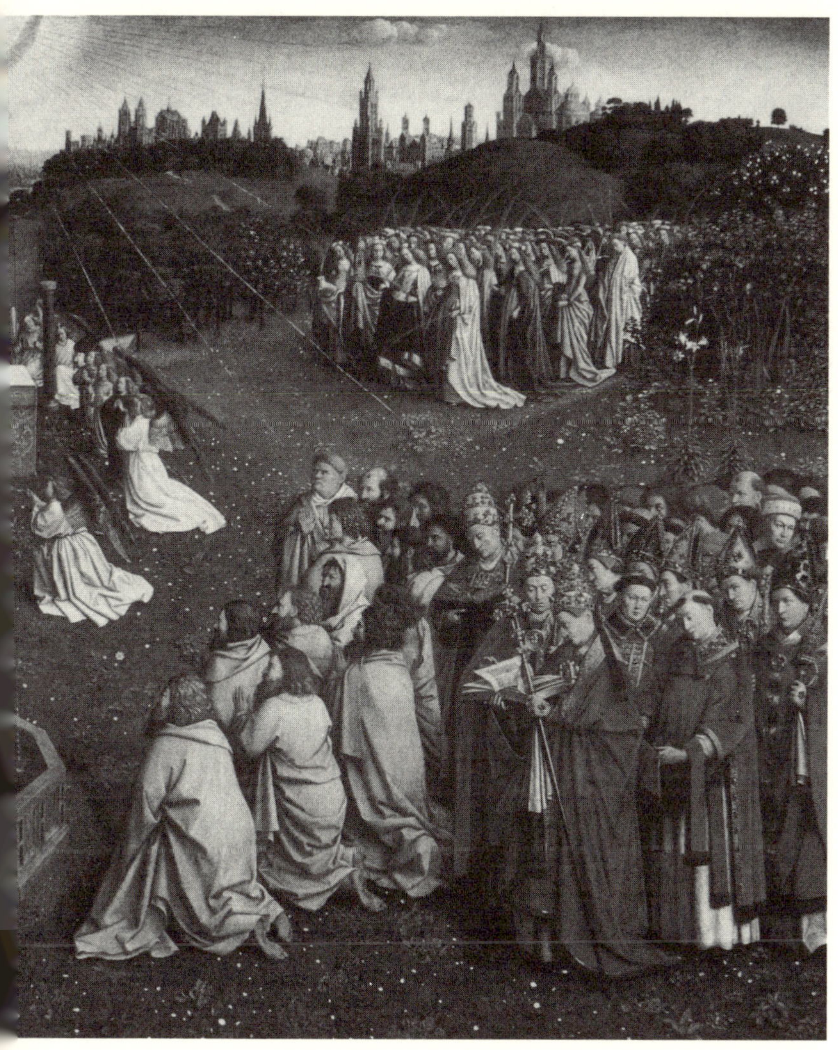

tionship of the object projections on the pictorial surface, while recognizing the picture's composition from that continuous cohesion of the silhouettes on the surface, does the shifting viewpoint gather significance in each particular case. For if the rule of pictorial organization demands an intimate, gapless conjunction of silhouettes, then only those projections will be judged most suitable whose objective form is directed primarily upward, toward the plane parallel to the picture surface. Preferably, these would include everything that stands upright: the erect human form; the far, enclosing wall of an interior room; or, outdoors, a row of hills or the silhouette of a city delimiting the gaze at the horizon. According to the laws of natural vision, things at the horizon and in the distance already appear flat, lacking three-dimensional volume; they join together in the form of a unified *veduta*, that is to say, as pure aspect. Wherever a two-dimensional rendering already lies close to natural visual experience, the surface value of the projective form need not be determined solely by artificial means. Everything appears more natural within the upper part of the picture because the model is more suited to compositional needs there. For the Netherlanders, nature already has, as it were, something artificial about it.

In contrast, the projections of objects whose extension in height occurs on a vertical surface plane (as is the case with the tabletop in the *Annunciation* of the Mérode Altarpiece) must be stretched downward and laterally if they are to become useful components of the surface pattern. By means of this stretching (which appears to us as a visual distortion), the projective form acquires an orientation toward nearby object silhouettes and thus forms an immediate point of connection to them. Wherever the cohesion of the surface pattern threatens to crumble — which is the case in every collision of vertical and horizontal spatial orientations — the effect of the horizontal thrust is weakened.

This enables the gaze gradually to glide through the extension of the projected area further over the surface. Thus the viewer transfers the sensation of the uninterrupted cohesiveness of the visible world all the more spontaneously to the spatial order. The continuity of the surface connections arouses the illusion of spatial unity. It does not, at any rate, allow us to become aware of the fact that the spatial continuum we perceive is composed only of fragments.

The viewing of all early Netherlandish pictures (and not just the oldest) would be simplified considerably if the spectator would change his approach to them. First, he should allow his imagination to proceed not from the actual spatial distribution of objects thought to be projected secondarily and mechanically onto the picture surface but from the organization of the surface itself — which is, to be sure, always understood as a surface for projections. He will facilitate his viewing further by attempting to read the picture from top to bottom or, to be more precise, from the rear enclosing wall or backdrop (that is, a surface lying parallel to the picture plane, which the projection alters in format but not design), across the contiguous details on the picture surface, and finally outward into the space. He would still always be guided, of course, by the directional components of spatial depth and picture plane.

Expressive Value of the Surface Relationships
Until now we have become acquainted with only the negative consequences of the priority of surface order (the disruption of spatial relationships, the interruption of the so-called illusion of reality, and so on). We will achieve a still more comprehensive understanding of the character of the Netherlandish pictorial structure only when we take an overview of the expressive possibilities of a painting style which organizes the pictorial space outward from the projective surface.

Because the artist regards the cohesiveness of individual projections as most important, *the pictorial space cannot contain as many objects as the contour relationships might accommodate, that is, as many objects as there might be standpoints in the picture space. Rather, there exist only as many as can appear as juxtaposed projections within the pictorial field.* Since moments of overlapping play a relatively subordinate role, one might say that *in essence the capacity of the pictorial space is dependent on the surface's capacity for projections.*

This rule does not at all apply only to the Master of Flémalle and his contemporaries. It is a functional rule of the Netherlandish pictorial imagination itself and is therefore barely affected by advances in spatial treatment. Thus, for example, the right half of the central panel of Hugo van der Goes's Portinari Altarpiece (figure 6.3) is composed in exactly the same way as the corresponding half of the Mérode Altarpiece. The lower, diagonal boundary of the group of shepherds joins precisely with the upper diagonal of the group of kneeling angels. The group of shepherds is composed not behind the angel group but above it. This line of contact corresponds to the backrest of the wooden bench in the Mérode Altarpiece: it is a diagonal that leads simultaneously back *into* the picture and, within the pictorial field, upward. Because the projection of the shepherd group can begin only above the heads of the angels, the space behind the angels remains empty. This occurs, however, without our noticing this gap or perceiving the space there as less densely animated.

The qualities of fullness and figural solidity on the surface conceal the partial emptiness and lack of precision in the spatial conception: the strangely altered viewpoint in the Mérode Altarpiece appears as the complete compression of the pictorial space. In this instance, the specific moment of illusion characteristic of early Netherlandish painting becomes tangible. *Peculiarities*

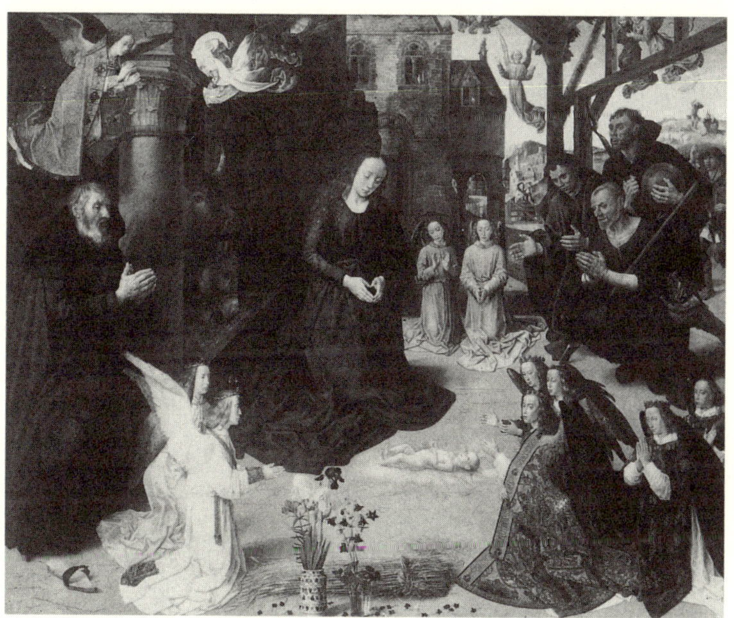

Figure 6.3. Hugo van der Goes, Portinari Altarpiece, *Adoration of the Shepherds*, Uffizi, Florence (Alinari/Art Resource, NY).

of viewpoint confront us as essential qualities of reality. To say it another way: formal properties, or expressive features of the pictorial pattern, function as characteristics of subject matter.

This is simply the other side of that general functional rule that demands that nothing become visible in a picture that does not appear translated into an expressive surface value. The impression of a crowd is achieved not through the simple reproduction of objects or bodies pushing tightly against each other in space but through the tight conjunction of their projections on the pictorial surface. Likewise, any kind of spatial relations can be fully apprehended only if they allow themselves to be expressed in equivalent surface referents. Distance, for example, is perceived only when our gaze has to travel on the picture surface (the actual distance suggested by the path of the gaze plays an insignificant role in the process). The Netherlandish painters were well aware that, even in places where only the visual aspects of phenomena were to be pictorially captured, those aspects had to be translated into a particular artistic medium (the medium of the painted surface). And so they made it their task to find the perceptible surface equivalents for an abundance of phenomena from the visible world.

The Netherlandish design principle had still further-reaching consequences. Through certain constellations of projections on the surface, relationships within the physical world could be manifested — relationships of a not directly visible nature and therefore not possible to portray through mechanical reproduction.[14] So perfect is this hegemony of the surface order that through it spatial, physical expressions can be transformed even into their opposites. With the help of the projections' contact on the surface, things that are distant can be conjoined in such a way that one senses immediately that they belong together. Conversely, spatial proximity can be made completely ineffectual in

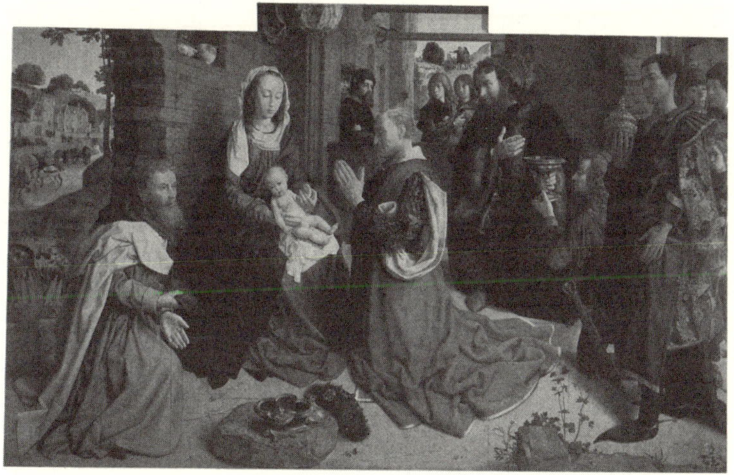

Figure 6.4. Hugo van der Goes, Monforte Altarpiece, *Adoration of the Magi*, Staatliche Museen Preussischer Kulturbesitz, Gëmaldegalerie, Berlin.

outward appearance, so that, for example, two figures might seem emphatically distanced in spite of their actual closeness in space. To cite another case: whenever our gaze must progress upward from one figure to another — for example, in the Monforte Altarpiece of van der Goes, from Joseph to Mary (figure 6.4) — we sense that the one figure is subordinate to the other, regardless of the fact that they may appear on exactly the same level in space and that there may be no external sign of subordinate relationship.

Ultimately, a particularly rich scale of expressive possibilities was developed through the very fact that the conformity to two systems of reference was directly and openly employed as a representational characteristic. Beneath the order of the surface pattern, an objective, physical cohesiveness (or at least the beginnings of such) remains perceptible. This cohesion is totally disengaged from meaning, so that the divergence or tension itself now becomes part of the pictorial content. To the most significant of these tensions — that between the spatial segment and the autonomy of surface pattern — we shall return in another context.

Organization of the Pictorial Pattern
Let us turn once again to the problem of surface order itself. The cohesiveness of silhouette values on the surface is what we are calling pictorial pattern. By that we understand a collection of formal qualities, generated by nonobjective factors, that lends the pictorial representation the character of a uniformly self-contained whole. The impression of completeness is grounded first of all on a particular accentuation of the picture's edge, through which an internal picture frame is created, and second, on a system of weight distribution among the silhouettes of objects.[15]

Wholeness and Unity

A pictorial pattern whose individual units are projective forms — which create the most diverse silhouette shapes — does not, of course, end at the picture's edge in such a way that all the contours run parallel to the outer borders. At the lower edge, an approximately straight boundary line, rich in forward and backward leaps, tends to take shape. Wherever excessively large gaps threaten to remain, they are closed up by filler motifs, such as the bundle of hay that van der Goes interpolates into the circle of figures in his *Nativity* (figure 6.7). And, as always, it is crucial that the vacant spaces remaining on the picture's borders never become forms with their own value but rather retain the character of negative forms. In most cases, the pattern at the lower edge of the picture appears jagged.

The upper and lateral boundaries, on the contrary, are typically fashioned in an entirely different manner. Here, vertically elongated physical forms (doorposts, ceiling beams, the erect contour of a human figure's back) function as enclosing accents while at the same time producing an internal reinforcement of the borders of the pictorial field. This is a much more emphatic, actively located boundary marker than that at the picture's lower edge. There it looks more as if the course of the contours were co-determined by a border against which the objects collide. In return, the considerably more forceful internal frame at the top and the sides tends not to enclose the entire pictorial field without interruption; the painter contents himself here with an only partial execution.

These internal borderlines do not always correspond to the objective edge values of concrete things in the picture. On the contrary: from the very beginnings of Netherlandish painting, the tendency becomes ever more noticeable *to avoid as much as possible a correspondence between formal and physical boundary functions.* The physical form extends beyond the border of the picture and is cut off by the picture frame. The segment of the object that emerges thereby, however, becomes a formal whole through enclosing accents extracted from the internal modeling of the physical form. The boundary of the latter lies immediately at the picture's border. The pictorial pattern ends — as a formal whole — at the edge of the picture.

In the Mérode Altarpiece, the picture's borders correspond to the borders of the chamber depicted (the walls, the beamed ceiling). In Rogier van der Weyden's *Annunciation* (figure 6.5), produced about thirty years later, neither the upper nor the lateral left spatial barrier is to be seen; rather, the picture frame cuts off the field of vision even within the picture's spatial boundaries. A similar line of development can be traced from the Dijon *Nativity* of the Master of Flémalle (figure 6.6) to the Portinari Altarpiece of van der Goes. In his later *Nativity* (figure 6.7), van der Goes even goes so far as to make obvious the segmented quality of the pictorial field through the half figures of prophets at the bottom. But even here the pictorial pattern remains a formal whole. It does not seem fragmentary, does not insist on being completed, and thus in its decorative schema does not manifest the slightest inclination toward a system of infinite pattern. By means of the enclosing accents, an internal frame is demarcated at the top and sides. The beamed ceiling of the interior in the Mérode Altarpiece is replaced in Rogier's *Annunciation* by the horizontal stripes of the bed canopy; on the right, the function of the lateral bounding walls is taken over by the vertical bed curtains and, on the left, by the steeply towering figure of the angel (the wings no longer standing out at a diagonal from the body!). In the example from van der Goes just cited (figure 6.7), on the other hand, the corners of the curtains and the half figures of the prophets create a proper viewing window through which the actual scene is observed. In this case, then, we are dealing with an *explicit* framing of the gaze.

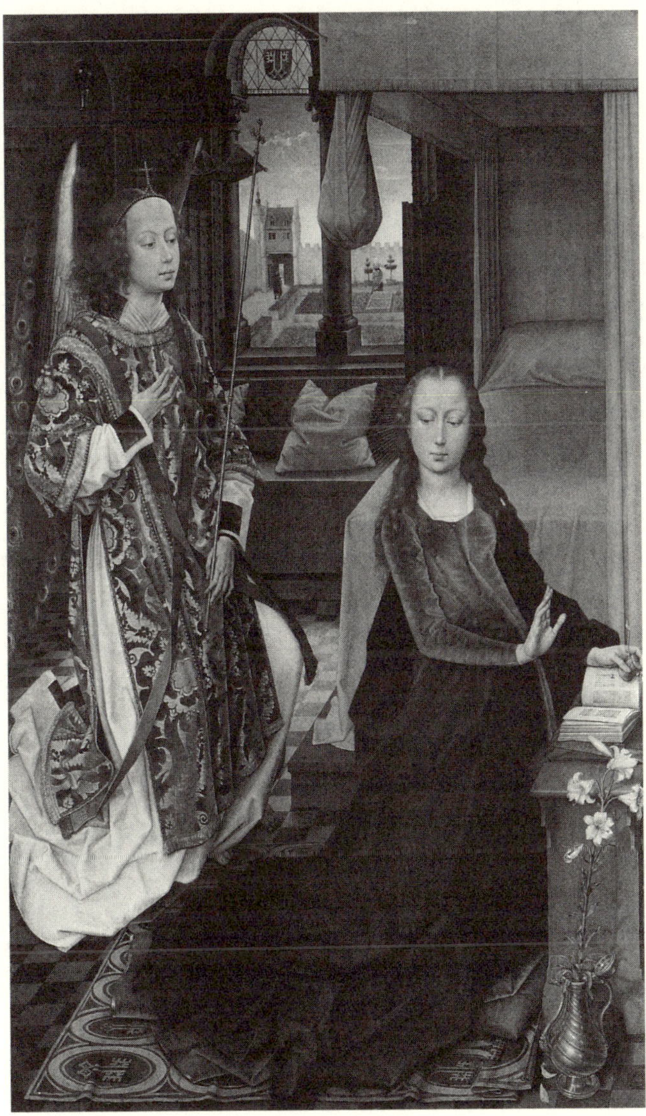

Figure 6.5. Rogier van der Weyden, *Annunciation*, Metropolitan Museum of Art (Gift of J. Pierpont Morgan, 1917, 17.190.17).

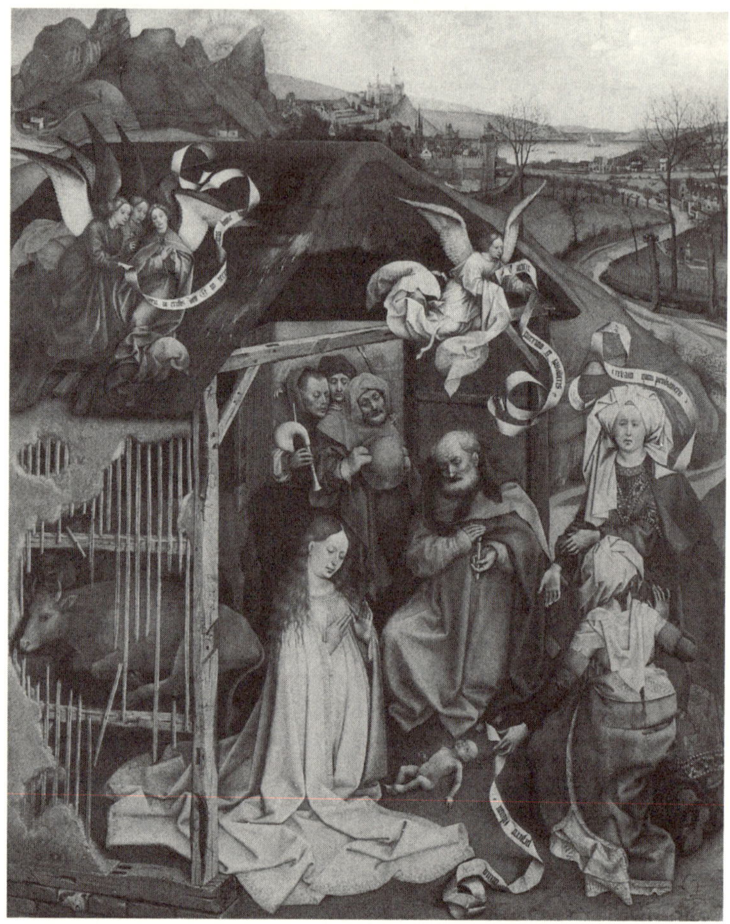

Figure 6.6. Master of Flémalle, *Nativity*, Musée des Beaux-Arts, Dijon.

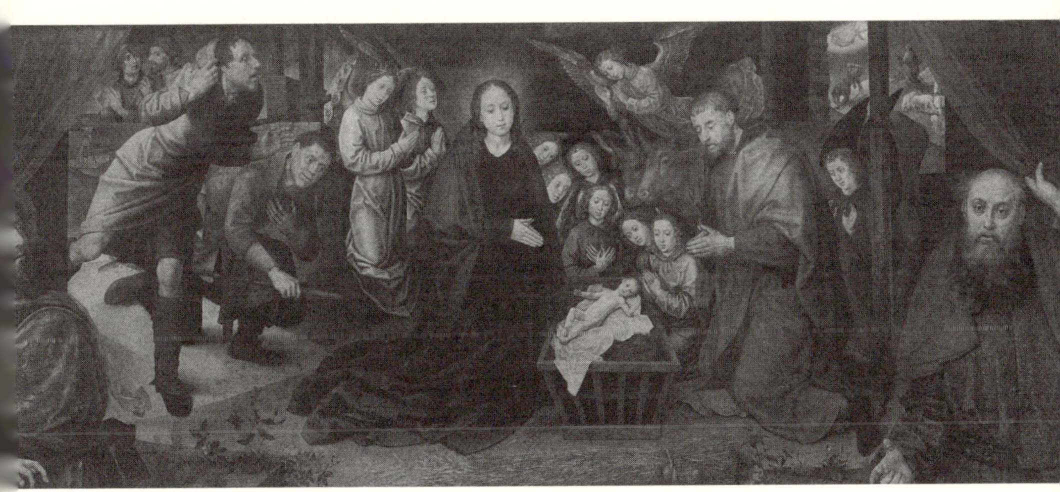

Figure 6.7. Hugo van der Goes, *Nativity,* Staatliche Museen Preussischer Kulturbesitz, Gëmaldegalerie, Berlin.

Throughout the entire development of Netherlandish painting, the relationship between the pictorial pattern and the whole of the picture remains constant. The pictorial pattern and the format of the picture coincide (that is, as geometric figures they are similar, in quantitative expanse nearly identical). *Only the relationship between pictorial pattern and each depicted physical object as a whole is engaged in constant flux.* So, indeed, during the fifteenth century an increasingly incomplete objective representation becomes more and more capable of producing a formal whole.

At the same time, this development exemplifies in essence the movement from conceptual whole to experiential whole, from a primarily intellectual to a primarily perceptual unity. In this sense, the pictorial space of the Mérode Altarpiece is already an excerpt from an intellectual unity. For the Master of Flémalle created the first interior of modern painting by omitting from the fourteenth-century schema for depicting interiors — the outside view of an opened building — all indications of exterior architecture, retaining solely the opening, the view into the interior space.

An internal balance comes to compensate for the exterior disruption of the pictorial pattern. In an earlier passage, we spoke of the consistent density with which object silhouettes cover the surface of the picture. That generalization is valid, however, only in the sense of an even distribution of formal units divorced from the medium of the surface. Since both the number of layers of objects projected on one another at a single spot within the pictorial field and the three-dimensional spatial content of each item can fluctuate significantly, formal complexes of approximately the same surface area can possess distinct values. The picture surface seems more sparsely occupied in some places than in others. This not only stems from the variety of plastic (bodily and spatial) contents underlying the projective forms but also is associated

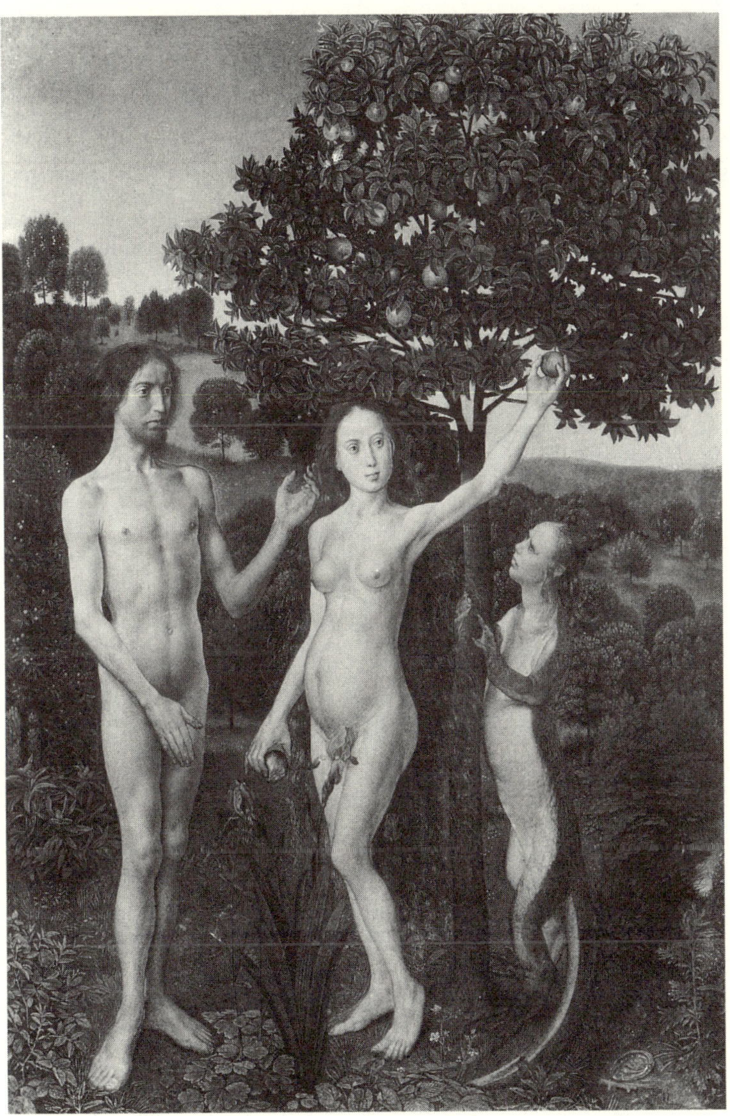

Figure 6.8. Hugo van der Goes, *Fall of Man*, Kunsthistorisches Museum, Vienna.

with other factors (color, precision of drawing, abundance of details, significance of subject matter). Indeed, the specific moments introduced here function not in the same direction but in conflicting directions. The result is an exchange of quantitative and qualitative moments; the surface size of a projection can be set against its plastic value or intensity of color.

In van der Goes's *Fall of Man* (figure 6.8), for example, the figures are distributed such that, were one to consider their plastic value alone, the center of gravity of the picture would be unambiguously shifted into the lower left-hand corner. The upper right-hand corner of the picture, however, acquires weight from the motif of the treetop, with the closed outline of its broad silhouette surface and its dark and therefore "heavy" color (in contrast to the light-colored and thus "lightweight" bodies). With that, the entire picture comes into balance.

The Netherlanders work with a system of balanced tensions that organize the surface so thoroughly that the pictorial pattern as a whole comes to rest. It is a kind of wavering equilibrium. In lateral directions, a perfect balance generally rules (which in no way presupposes an axially symmetrical distribution of formal units). On the vertical axis, in contrast, the center of gravity (in fact, it is a line, as the geometrical locus of all the centers of gravity) is shifted toward the lower edge of the picture. Still, a tension of surface values is the decisive factor in this dimension too — not the gravitation of bodily matter, as in Italian pictures where the ground layer in the lowermost zone is conceived as a support.[16] The lower borderline of the picture can never acquire this significance for the Netherlanders.

Components of the Pictorial Pattern
In describing early Netherlandish pictorial structure, we have until now spoken — for technical reasons and for the sake of

simplicity — of pattern (as the continuous surface cohesiveness of object silhouettes) and ground (as the screen of the pictorial field). Nevertheless, this verbal image must not be taken literally, as if there were a rigorous distinction between pattern units made up of silhouettes of objects and the empty, formless screen of the pictorial field. Such a smooth split is unknown to the Netherlandish pictorial structure. In perspectival painting, it is hardly possible to create a perfectly empty screen in itself (this would necessitate the entire background of the picture signifying nothing but air and sky) and to avoid overlaps completely (although, as we know, the pictorial surface is overlaid by a single layer of silhouettes). These relationships are far more complicated in early Netherlandish painting as well. *Every projective form* (as an element of the pictorial pattern) *is capable of acting as the screen for another projective form.* The simplest example: in the Mérode Altarpiece, the tabletop has the quality of being part of the pictorial pattern relative to spatial boundaries but is, nevertheless, also ground relative to the still life that it bears (figure 6.1). No section of the pictorial field possesses the value of ground or pattern in absolute terms, as was the case in early- and high-medieval painting (where a gold ground or absolutely blank colored surface was used as a screen). In this sense, too, every projective form is fundamentally ambivalent.

Here lie the formal roots of a supremely important innovation in early Netherlandish painting: the equal status, in principle, of human figure and environment. The division of the physical world into elements of a first and second order is lifted, without that compensation achieved by the so-called soft style of c. 1400 through the enlivening of inanimate matter.[17] Here, inorganic, spiritless objects (household effects, furniture) enter into the pictorial pattern's surface rapport with equal status to the human figure, and, conversely, the human figure (as a whole or a part) can itself become a screen, something of the second class. When this occurs, then (on another level than in the soft style) in principle the homogeneity of everything visible is realized.

The fundamental condition for this is that the formal unity can be separated from the physical unity, and that the smaller subunits of the pictorial pattern can be constructed from whole objects or from segments of objects in exactly the *same* way. (Equality prevails, therefore, not only between the organic and the inorganic, but also between the object as a whole and segments of objects.) The same process that on a large scale would bring about the selection of pictorial unity out of a greater physical whole is thus repeated on a small scale. Here, however, it need not be the picture frame that cuts off a part of the whole object by overlapping it, thus providing an opportunity for the creation of a new formal unity; rather, the overlapping occurs through the picture's own internal forms. The part concealed through overlapping becomes a screen just as much as the blank surface of a wall or a background of free-floating air does. The section remaining visible is then rounded off to become a formal whole. In the case of a human figure, this occurs in such a way that a garment's surface (the drapery relief) in the section not overlapped acquires a self-enclosed design, which according to internal logic ends precisely at the point where the figure is overlapped. These overlapped parts then belong to the ground, from which the visible section distinguishes itself as a formal unity. The corresponding physical unity (the human figure) is thus partly pattern and partly ground. As pattern, it latches onto the overlapping figure on equal terms — even, sometimes, continuing the figure on the same plane. Two figures can thus be conceived as bodies staggered behind each other in space, while nonetheless lying as forms on the same plane.

This holds true, for example, for the two female figures on the left side of the Master of Flémalle's Berlin *Crucifixion* panel (figure 6.9). The gathered-up skirt of the figure at the very edge, with a hairpin fold planted like a rampart, delimits the overlapped and thus fragmented lower half of the body's silhouette.

In a certain sense, the part of a three-dimensional object that is visible in a picture is always only a section. This is true even in cases where no overlapping has occurred at all, that is, when the whole object can be seen. To the gaze extending from a single, fixed point, for instance, only *one* side of the human figure can offer itself at any time. The surface of a three-dimensional object visible in a picture is always only a portion of the object's entire surface. Thus, even when a form appears in a picture without any overlapping or concealment, the Netherlanders are not exempt from the primary obligation to transform the raw material of perception, namely, the surface turned toward the viewer, into a formal whole. For the Netherlanders, this becomes a problem unto itself because their naturalistic brand of pictorial narration is not satisfied with representative normal views, such as profile and *en face*. One might say that in their very nature these normative views contain an inherent quality of completeness; in contrast, more unusual positions (three-quarter views, for example) must be artificially transformed into formal wholes. This takes place in the same manner in which that piece of mantle that can be directly seen on the viewer-oriented side yields, through the design of the drapery relief, if not a geometrically regular figure, then certainly a formal whole.[18] As it emerges through projection on the pictorial surface, the formal contour becomes an outer edge, the boundary of a figure centered on itself. Although arbitrary when considered in concrete, physical terms, this boundary becomes the internally necessary culmination of the formal unity. Thus, although in the Berlin *Crucifixion* of the Master of Flémalle, only one section of the mantle of the woman behind Mary can be

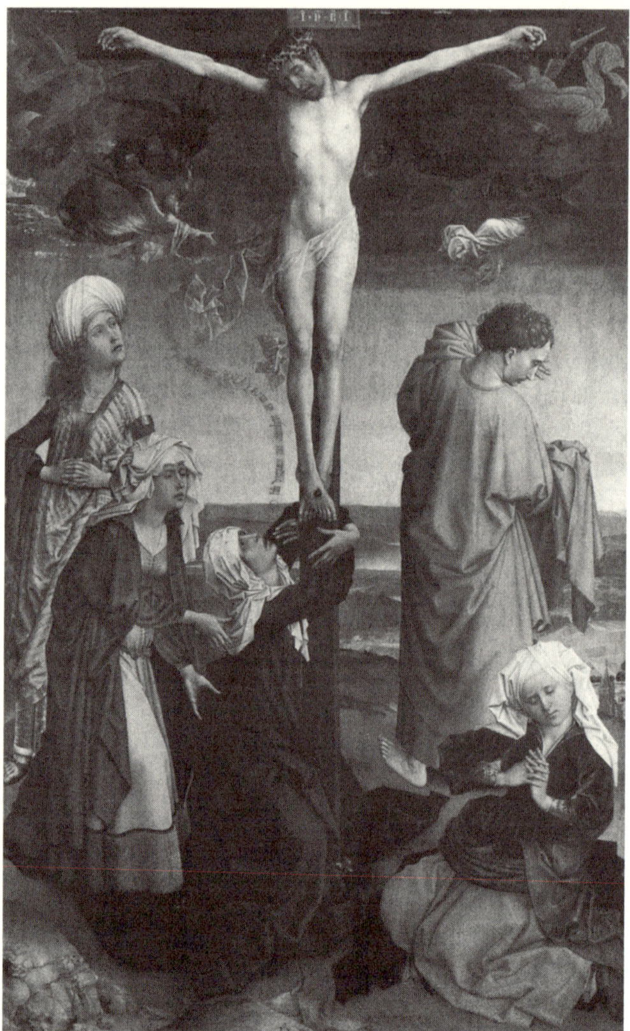

Figure 6.9. Master of Flémalle, *Crucifixion*, Staatliche Museen Preussischer Kulturbesitz, Gëmaldegalerie, Berlin.

seen, the internal design of the drapery relief (radiating outward in the shape of a star) allows a formal whole to emerge.

So far as possible, and with careful respect to these somewhat arbitrary formal boundaries, surface correspondences are sought such that quasi-ornamental configurations develop on the drapery surfaces. As motifs, these are transferable; that is, they help to fulfill the same formal function in often very different contexts (thus, for instance, the drapery motif mentioned above appears again in similar form on the voluminous head covering of the kneeling woman on the right).

Such a *surface-pattern-like design of the internal form represents the necessary culmination of a technique of composing by silhouette values*. In no way would the spatially constructed projections be able to function effectively as silhouettes simply by means of the contiguity and conjunction of their contours. It is only because every element (at least every significant line) of the internal form contains a pure surface value alongside its quality of spatial illusion — so that even the internal design can be read as surface pattern — that we can recognize the contours, too, as edges or boundaries of a surface form.

The Annunciate Virgin of the Mérode Altarpiece can stand as a paradigm. Her left knee is the center of a star-shaped figure whose radii of approximately equal length are made up of short lines running along the picture surface and of foreshortened (long) lines leading into the depth of the image. The outer, enclosing lines appear raised onto the same plane by the star figure — that is, from the interior. The star-shaped radiation of the drapery folds is physically motivated by the outward thrust of the knee against the fabric, through which a concentric stretching and tension of the suppler material occurs.

Design of the Pictorial Pattern

The character of the Netherlandish pictorial pattern (which we now understand as the interrelationship, the entire connectedness, of individual silhouettes) is particularly difficult to apprehend and to describe because, in contrast to the French or German pictorial pattern, it never moves toward easily comprehensible ornamental schemata (elementary planimetric forms, for instance). It contains practically no decorative content that would remain if the individual forms were considered abstractly — as senseless splotches, so to speak — without their concrete, mimetic meaning. It is a pictorial order of a relatively relaxed rule system, the greatest possible contrast to a strictly regulated style. It is an *order that gets by with a minimum of "instructions"* to be followed. Only a very few conditions, which we have already enumerated, must be fulfilled: continuous surface rapport, internal closure of the pictorial pattern, and the creation of equilibrium (a balancing out) in the distribution of silhouette values. Common to these conditions is the quality of great flexibility. Because of this, the *Netherlandish pictorial pattern possesses a tremendous ability to adapt itself to the most varied representational demands.* Because the coalescence into a gap-free, interpenetrating pictorial pattern involves silhouette values exclusively, the physical, contextual relationships are affected only indirectly. Therefore they enjoy, if not unlimited free reign, at any rate the broadest possible room for play. The compositional pressure that seems to intrude in the overall order of things is, in its very spirit, overdetermined to a large degree.

One could also say that it is not the physical world per se but only its outward appearance that must conform to a heteronomous order. This appearance can be completely obedient to its own survival rules and thus come across as an almost embarrassingly objective reportage. Here the subjectivity of all design processes, by means of which both every act of reporting (even when intended to be totally objective) and the unprejudiced act of seeing itself necessarily become active forces shaping the material, is restricted to a minimum. The formative energies act as a light pressure that cautiously colors the visual appearance but leaves the essence of things untouched.

Holland

The elements of design that we have attempted to elucidate with predominantly southern Netherlandish (Flemish) examples are certainly not specimens of that art alone. Indeed, the most basic among them characterize Western pictorial invention in general.[19] Along with its Dutch and French counterparts, southern Netherlandish painting is simply one particular variant of Western pictorial invention.[20] *In all three variants, each form must be observed both in its physical, spatial significance and in its surface pattern; and in all three, the pictorial structure is determined by the double relation between the grouping of the physical objects and the pictorial pattern.* This pictorial pattern itself is nonetheless distinctive in each of the variants, as is, above all, the relation within it between figure and ground.

Disintegration of the Pictorial Pattern

With the Dutch painters, the cohesion of individual projections is ruptured; a close attachment of contour to contour is not a goal. One cannot speak of a *horror vacui* here, for the ground is never fully covered with figure. On the contrary: in broad stretches, this ground becomes visible in all its emptiness and with it, the vast, unfilled space it implies.

In terms of developmental history, the *liberation of the pattern's intervals* takes on the greatest significance: it is the *expression of the fact that open space has become worthy of form.* We must now distinguish the several moments within this process.

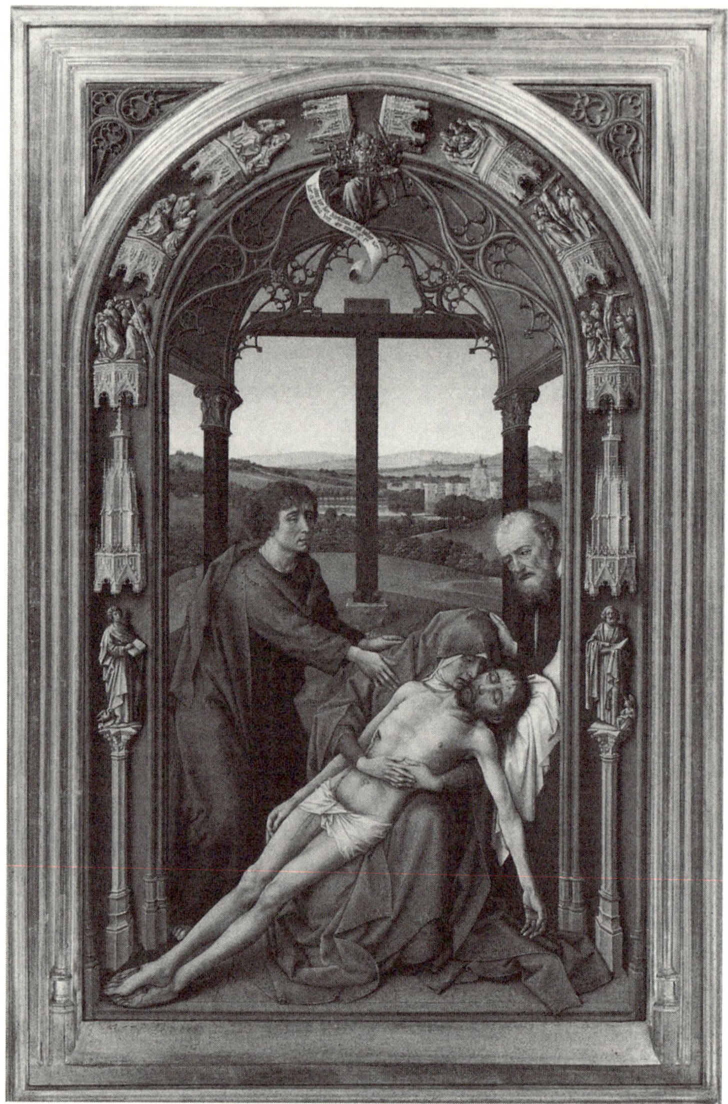

Figure 6.10. Rogier van der Weyden, Miraflores Altarpiece, *Lamentation*, Staatliche Museen Preussischer Kulturbesitz, Gëmaldegalerie, Berlin.

Whereas the southern Netherlanders considered an empty surface an error in the pictorial organization, a hole in the picture surface, the Dutch discovered the aesthetic appeal and eminent representational value of empty ground. In the portal frame of the Miraflores Altarpiece (figure 6.10), Rogier begins filling the niche at the floor level, placing even the lowest jamb figure on a thin pedestal. But Dirk Bouts, while borrowing the same peculiar altar form in his early work (figure 6.11),[21] simply leaves the niche free up to the jamb figure's console, allowing it thus finally to become visible as a niche.[22] The *emptiness* — the expanse, barrenness, paucity of detail — *of a surface* can thus become a *positive value.*

The potentials lying locked in this discovery were first fully exploited by Dutch painting of the seventeenth century, above all, by landscape painting. Of greater importance for the fifteenth century are the consequences that the inclusion of open space had for the depiction of narrative. It must be said in advance that the Dutch worked, almost without exception, with foreign pictorial compositions borrowed from southern Netherlandish painting. That these artists remained unproductive in the invention of scenic contexts is closely connected with the positive sides of their artistic proclivity. Admittedly, this can be grasped only when we have gotten a glimpse into the essence of the Dutch artistic will *(Kunstwollen).*

When a Dutch painter appropriates a southern Netherlandish pictorial composition, he immediately loosens the density of the pattern structure. This process of conversion and reworking usually passes through several phases. In the first phase, the form of the original pattern structure can, as a rule, still be recognized. In the second phase, the individual parts into which the pattern structure has disintegrated are distanced noticeably from each other. But perhaps more important, there remain in the formation of the design no further reminders of the common bond that

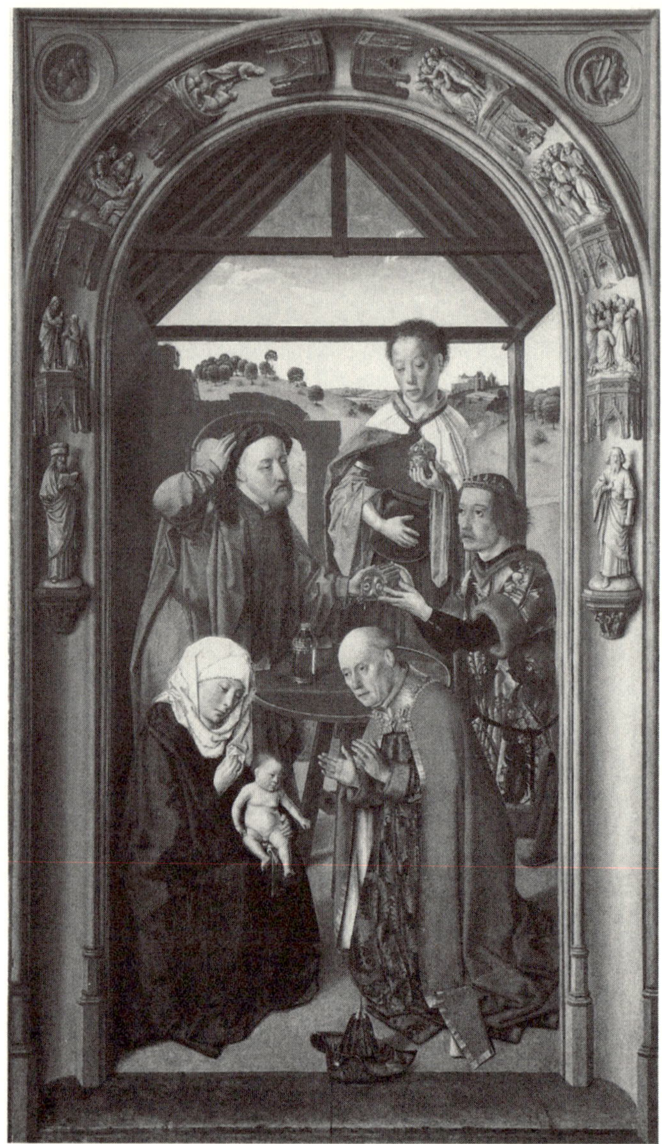

Figure 6.11. Dirk Bouts, *Epiphany*, Museo del Prado, Madrid.

had linked them earlier and that, to a large degree, had determined the composition of the contours.

The following genetic series shall serve as an example: (1) The southern Netherlandish prototype for a series of Dutch Epiphany scenes survives in a faithful copy of a composition by the Master of Flémalle (figure 6.12). (2) The first Dutch rendition is represented by the early work by Bouts at the Prado (figure 6.11). (3) Bouts's late piece, the so-called "Pearl of Brabant," stands as the second version (figure 6.13). In the Prado version, it seems that nothing else has happened than that the left-to-right connection of the pattern (the directional surface movement of the three kings' train) has been transformed into a system of overlapping layers, a staggering of the persons behind one another — as if the scene had needed to be tightly compressed due to its vertical format. But in spite of the narrower pictorial field, the figures no longer adhere so closely together; there is more air between them. The pattern intervals have become significantly larger. One observes, for instance, that the bits of forms above the oldest king's head do not meet up directly, although if one were to push them together their contours would perfectly mesh. This is proof enough that the form of the pattern pieces originated in a strict interpenetrating structure that was borrowed, historically speaking, from the southern Netherlandish painters. The most important consequence of this structural loosening is the spatialization of the pictorial world: when the projections no longer fit tightly together, the forms are likewise no longer pulled back toward the surface. For the first time, objects appear behind one another in a clear spatial arrangement. Were we unfamiliar with the intermediary step represented by Bouts's early piece, it would be difficult to extract from his late work, the "Pearl of Brabant," the original compositional conception, that pictorial invention harking back to the Master of Flémalle. And yet little more has happened than

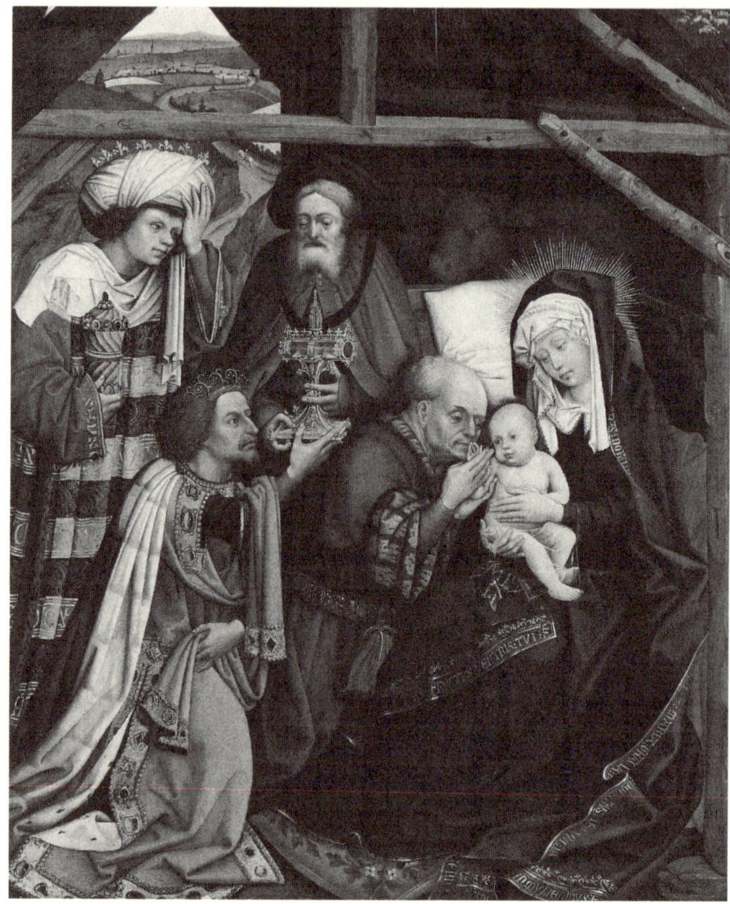

Figure 6.12. Master of Flémalle (copy), *Epiphany*, Staatliche Museen Preussischer Kulturbesitz, Gëmaldegalerie, Berlin.

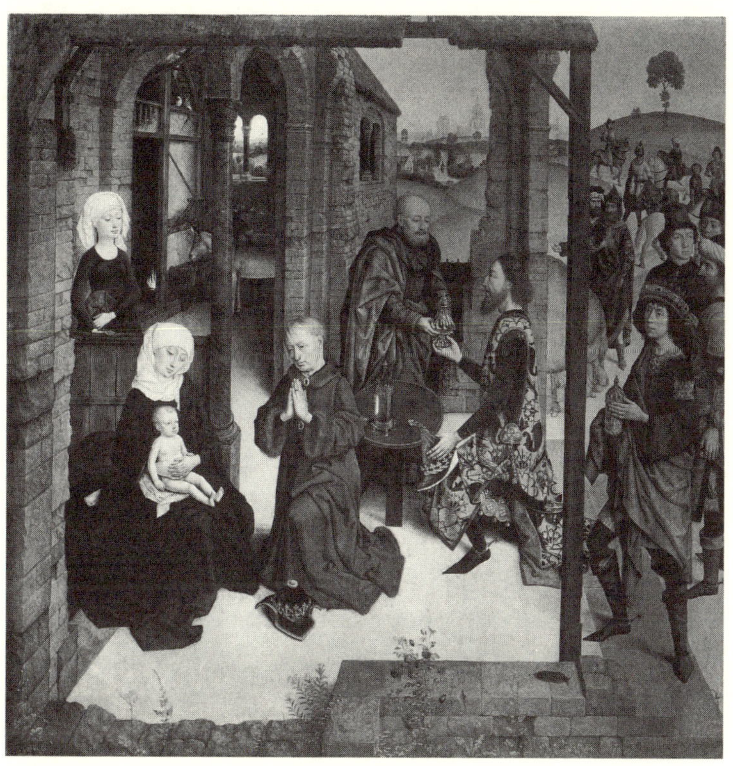

Figure 6.13. Dirk Bouts, *Epiphany* from the "Pearl of Brabant," Bayerische Staatsgemäldesammlungen, Munich.

that a conglomeration of figures (the scene of the Master of Flémalle) has now dissolved completely into open space. The Master of Flémalle had allowed no tiny piece of floor to be seen at the picture's lower edge and at the same time extended the landscape horizon so far upward that the herds of sheep in the right corner could find room only above the stable roof. In contrast, the hat of the oldest king in the Madrid Epiphany can (and should) no longer conceal the empty ground surface between Mary and the king. In Bouts's late piece especially, this little patch of vacant surface has become an empty platform of space pressing far into the depth of the picture; above, bare hilltops and a wide strip of sky peer beneath the ceiling into the stable.

The contrast between Bouts and the Master of Flémalle can in no way be attributed simply to differences in historical style. There are innumerable examples from the sixteenth and seventeenth centuries that manifest the same opposition.[23]

What is decisive for the effect is again not so much the amount of newly visible blank ground as the fact that the *silhouettes of figures and objects themselves are blurry, nearly indistinct.* This phenomenon is based on an extremely optically oriented kind of vision that composes the pictorial surface out of rough patches of color. The inevitable outcome of creating such undefined silhouettes is the absence of any strong congruity between adjacent individual projections, so that the shapes of objects appear starkly isolated. *Here, then, a continuity of ground* — that is, of ambience and empty space — *replaces the continuous cohesiveness of the figural pattern as the defining characteristic.*

The Isolating Verticality: The New Components
With that, the design of the figural pattern undergoes a most essential transformation. Out of the closed wall of figures in Rogier's Escorial *Deposition* (figure 6.14) there emerges, in Bouts's version

(figure 6.15), a scenic construction subdivided by clear intervals into three main sections. Whereas Rogier's composition was based completely on transverse links, Bouts's *Deposition* is more strongly layered vertically. Above all, the central group of the two men with the corpse is steeply erect compared to Rogier's arrangement. But with that, the left-to-right connection is essentially eradicated, so that the lateral groups appear added on only loosely. (Mary and John, for example, are brought in by their gesture toward the dangling arm of Christ, and the group of women to the right, through the forward inclination of the female assistant.) The entire scene thus appears to be composed of three vertical groups tacked in next to each other, producing a sharply triangular composition through the lateral groups' gentle inclination toward the center. The powerfully distinctive, quite rigid verticality of Dutch pictorial structures is not the result of the same gothicizing tendencies that determine the proportioning of Rogier's figures and compositions in the same years. Rather, it is a consistent factor that is necessarily and essentially associated with the Dutch drive toward isolation: the pictorial pattern is meant to crumble into a disconnected juxtaposition of individual vertical strips. An extreme instance of this pictorial structuring can be seen in Bouts's *Justice* pictures (figure 6.16), with their accumulation of isolated verticals and the blunt juxtaposition of tall, elongated figures.

The disintegration of the continuous figural pattern (in our example, the closed wall of figures in Rogier's *Deposition*) into separate, vertically layered formal complexes changes the role of the individual figure within the picture as a whole. The relatively isolated lower elements make up several single figures that have melded into a cumulative, indissoluble unity. If a Rogierian composition consists of emphatically distinct individual actors, then for Bouts the figural group stands as the most important compositional element.

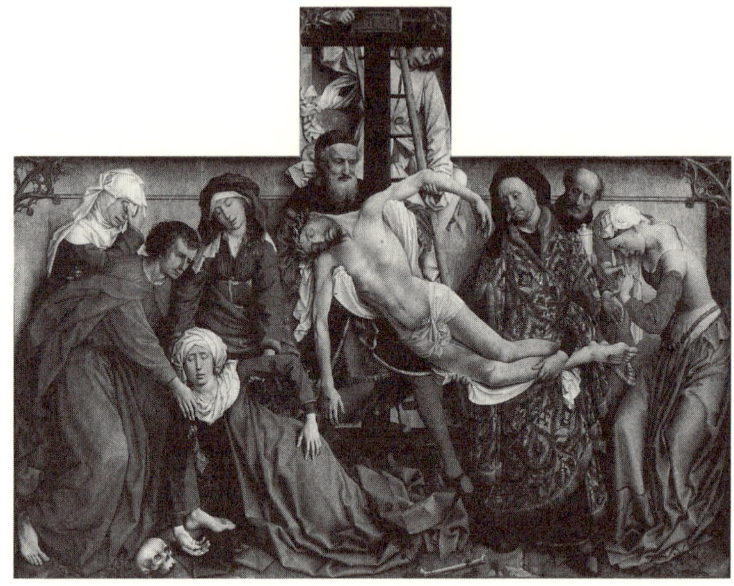

Figure 6.14. Rogier van der Weyden, *Deposition*, Museo del Prado, Madrid.

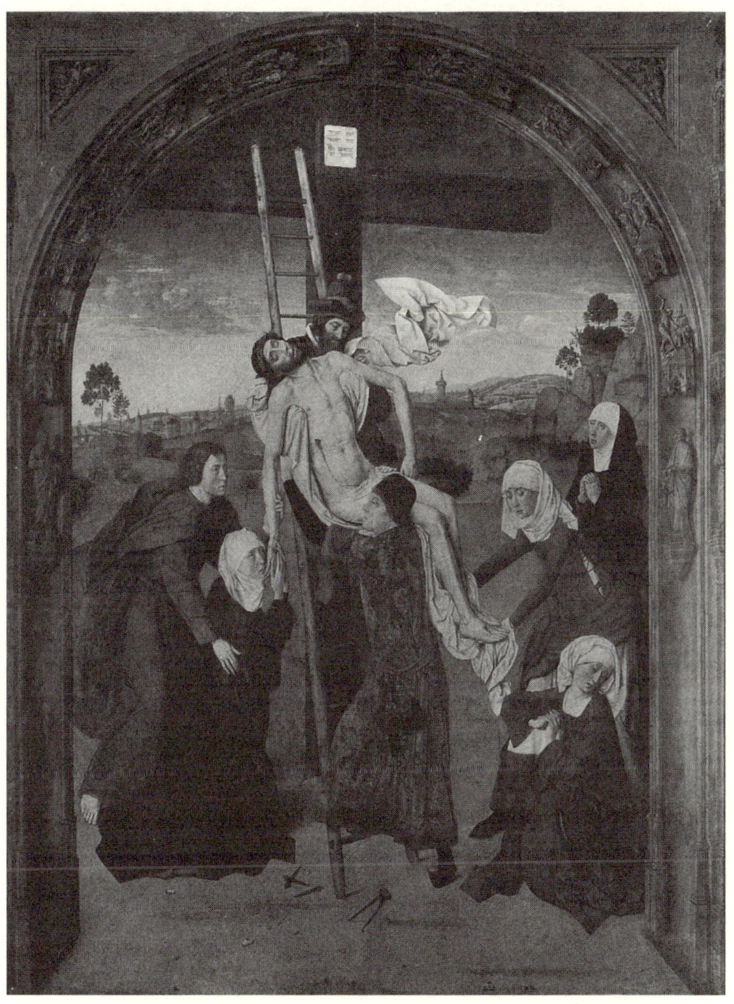

Figure 6.15. Dirk Bouts, *Deposition*, Capilla Real, Granada (© IRPA-KIK, Brussels).

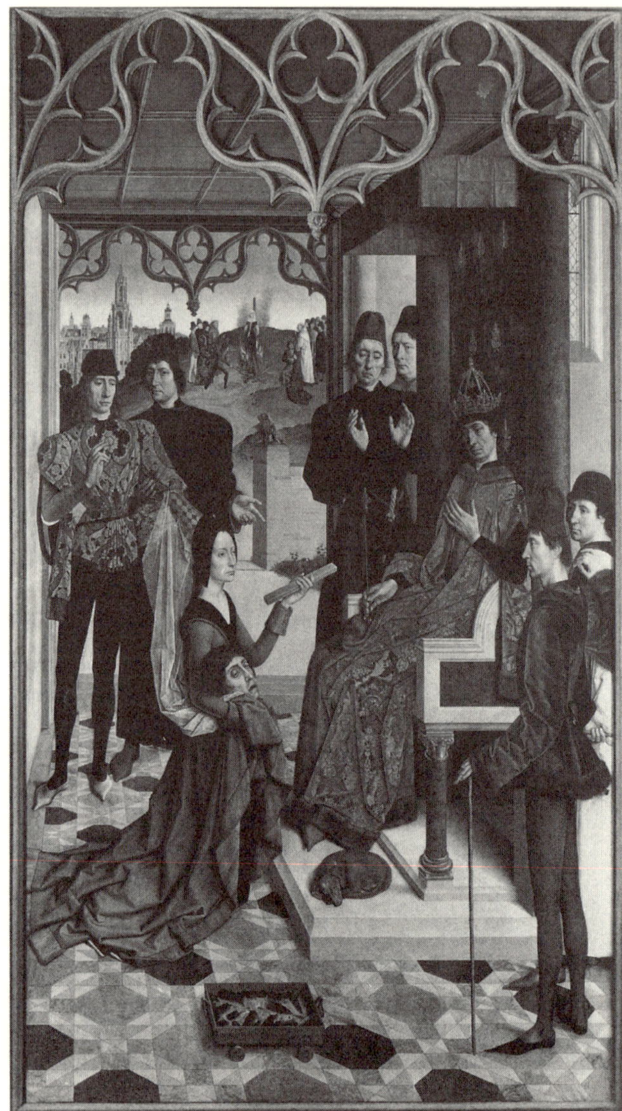

Figure 6.16. Dirk Bouts, "Trial by Fire," from the *Justice of the Emperor Otto III*, Musées Royaux des Beaux-Arts de Belgique, Brussels (© ACL).

Although the Boutsian kind of figure group may originally have emerged as the accumulation of Rogierian figural motifs, it exists phenomenologically prior to its individual components. The group's relative independence is compensated for by a relative lack of autonomy of the individual figures within. A good example of this can be seen in the female group on the right-hand side of Bouts's *Deposition*. The diagonal movement of the central woman creates a bridge to the central group through her forward motion to help remove the corpse. This appears, however, as a secondary deviation from the vertically towering core of the group. The woman's upper body alone, not the entire figure, has loosened itself slightly from the group's alliance.

Examining Bouts's departures from his model in regards to individual motifs, one soon recognizes the common tendency to replace certain elements with others better adapted to the new pictorial structure. This makes possible their fusion into genuine collective unities. We shall now attempt to address the significance of each deviation.

With the hand-wringing Magdalene — the pendant to John, who attends to the collapsing Virgin — Rogier sets a great curve in motion, whose momentum continues into the left side of the picture along the arc of Christ's left arm. As we have seen, Bouts tends to conceive his compositions as a juxtaposition of vertical groups, the flanking pairs leaning toward the center in steep diagonals. He therefore needs a forceful upward-oriented group to form the left leg of his triangular structure. And so, at the place where Rogier has the Virgin sink down in a position perfectly parallel to the reclining S curve of Christ's body, Bouts positions a Mary-John pair borrowed from other Crucifixions, such as the Master of Flémalle's Berlin *Crucifixion* (figure 6.9) and the Vienna *Crucifixion* by Rogier (figure 6.17). These figures direct attention upward toward the top of the cross. Through this appropriation,

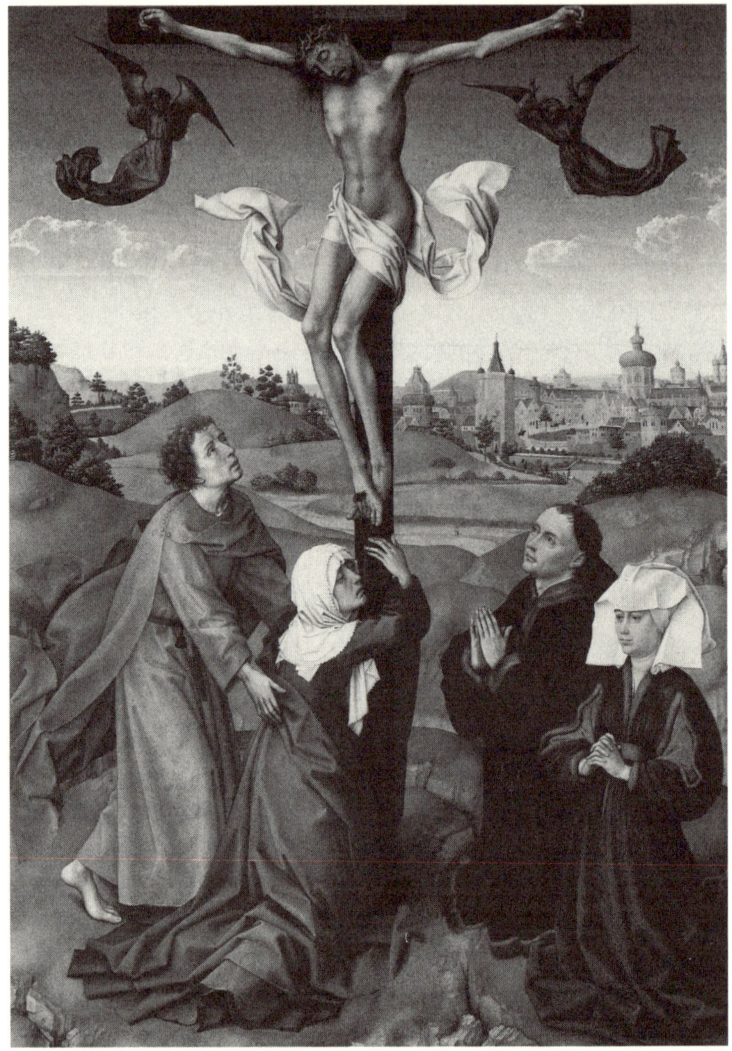

Figure 6.17. Rogier van der Weyden, *Crucifixion*, Kunsthistorisches Museum, Vienna.

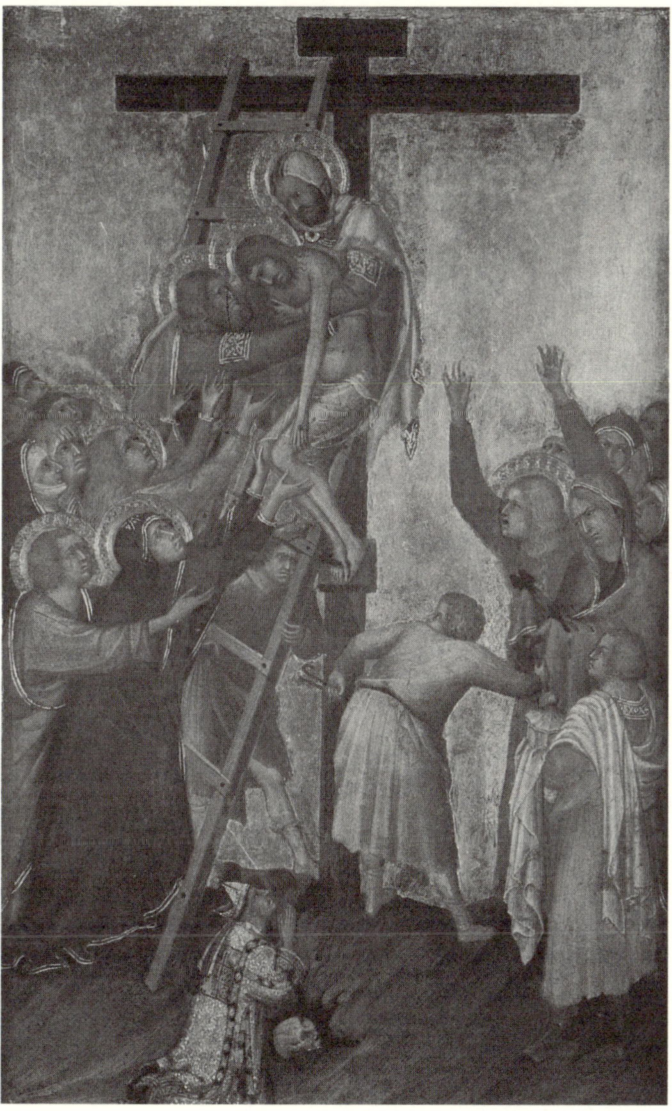

Figure 6.18. Simone Martini, *Deposition*, Koninklijk Museum voor Schone Kunsten, Antwerp (© ACL).

however, Bouts achieves a resemblance more to the fourteenth-century Deposition type, the prime example being Simone Martini's (figure 6.18) as it reverberates in the Master of Flémalle's version. For in the fourteenth-century versions, Mary stretches her arms toward her dead son as she sinks down. This formula flows indirectly, over Flémalle-Rogier Crucifixion types, back to the Deposition. Now, however, it is no longer the Magdalene who serves as the pendant to John but the even more precisely symmetrical woman who leans forward at a diagonal while laying her hands on the drooping body. She, too, can be derived from yet another motif in the Escorial *Deposition*, namely, the woman tending to Mary. But as we have already remarked, Bouts employs diagonal movement only as a (secondary) deviation from a stock-straight, upward-moving structure whose vertical axis is anchored by figures below and above. Beneath the diagonal in this instance, there was room enough for only one kneeling figure, and the lamenting Magdalene under the cross in a *Crucifixion* by the Master of Flémalle proved most appropriate for that spot (figure 6.9). Now the Magdalene must crouch on the ground so that the forward-leaning woman (whom she otherwise would conceal) may become visible. The latter bends forward herself so that we can observe the upper half of the woman standing behind her — a motif also found in the left corner of the Escorial *Deposition*. Every single motif, then, stems from Rogier's or the Master of Flémalle's formal repertoire. Indeed, the entire right-hand group can be seen to have arisen through the compression and overlayering of a diagonal series of steps, such as Rogier had arranged from the unconscious Mary up to the weeping woman on the left side of his *Deposition*. Nevertheless, the structure of such a group as a whole can neither be derived from nor comprehended solely in terms of Rogier's compositional method.

The Substitute for Internal Pictorial Unity

One of the most significant results of the design principle of isolation is that pictorial unity as such dissolves. It is regained by the Dutch only through the introduction of a new factor, in a form fully at odds with other contemporaneous art. Among the southern Netherlanders, the tight conjunction of silhouettes (individual pieces of the pattern) allows a fluid, flowing passage of the gaze over the entire picture surface. In Dutch painting, the cohesiveness of the pattern pieces on the surface has crumbled, and the gaze lacks all instruction for finding its way from one formal complex to another. The continuous cohesion of the southern Netherlandish pictorial pattern, however, is at the same time the optical equivalent of the scenic context, of the existential coherence of the pictorial world. Thus any representation that, like the Dutch type, rejects the formal condensation of the pattern pieces should appear completely disjointed in its scenic quality. And yet a Dutch picture certainly does not lack strong bonds among the persons depicted. It is the illusion of independent conjunction into scenic unity that we do not — and indeed should not — receive.[24]

For the Dutch, individual figures or groups of figures (and thus the individual pattern pieces) create relationships with one another through gestures. These gestures direct attention from one figure or one group to another, thus producing physical, content-bound contact between otherwise completely isolated and distanced formal complexes.[25] These gestures are developed only partially out of the figures' own actions, and even then it is their character as signs that is most clear. Although the movements do appear motivated to a certain extent by the specific situation in which the figures are located, they are at the same time stripped of their narrative meaning. They tend to appear only superficially pegged onto an actor whose facial expression betrays utter lack of interest in his activity. These gestures function most effectively, then, as instructions to the beholder for understanding the isolated groups or single figures as relating contextually to one another.

That this kind of indication is intentional is clearly manifested in those thematic cases where absent narrative action provides no motivation for such mediatory gestures. In this situation, the Dutch painters invented new motifs for expressing content out of a compositional necessity. A new category of persons enters Dutch representations, a kind of speaker (comparable, in a way, to the announcers of baroque theater), meant to compensate for the lack of clearly perceptible connections. Fully indifferent to the proceedings, they function rather as the interpreters and translators of an event. Hence these immediately eye-catching, ostentatious gestures arise. Through them, attention is directed both to the main figures, who otherwise would barely stand out among the dramatis personae, and to the relationships among them, which otherwise would hardly be inferred from the figures' placements and postures. These gestures are aimed at us viewers and not at fellow actors; it is *our* attention that is demanded and steered toward the central proceedings. This can be further ascertained from the fact that neither the demonstrating person nor the person toward whom he gestures actually looks toward the object pointed out. Rather, the addressee usually gazes out of the picture toward the beholder, as in the depiction of Abraham and Melchizedek in the Louvain *Last Supper* Altarpiece (figure 6.19). It is left up to the viewer's, so to speak, complementing and interpolating imagination to activate and complete the figures' cohesion into scenic unity. This act is not immediately perceptible. As road signs for this imaginative process, the gestures attest to the crucial role of the beholder's cooperation in making a picture come together as a whole. The reference to the viewer is completely open: the persons portrayed take direct notice of him. In this instance, the otherwise carefully concealed subject-

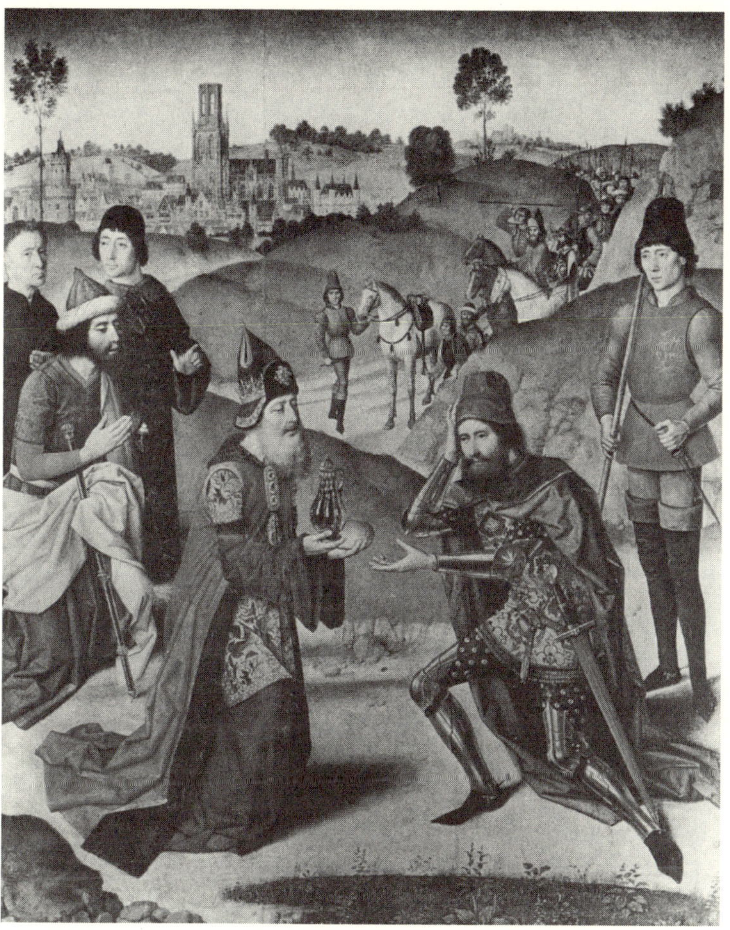

Figure 6.19. Dirk Bouts, Altarpiece of the Last Supper, detail, *Abraham and Melchizedek*, St. Peter, Louvain (Giraudon/Art Resource, NY).

object relationship — the life force of postmedieval artistic design — is deliberately laid bare. No internal pictorial unity exists, strictly speaking — moreover, *this very communication with the beholder becomes the material of representation*, an important element of the pictorial subject matter. In other contemporaneous manners of depiction, even the southern Netherlandish, it is as if the process of viewing arrived at an already existing formal state only secondarily. That is, it is as if we viewers become witnesses to an episode, enacted as if there were no onlookers at all, simply by accident and without ourselves being observed. Whereas in those cases the representation emerges through a kind of secret insider knowledge, in Holland it is precisely the actors' awareness of being observed that determines their attitudes. The pictorial pattern possesses no unconditional existence; it proclaims itself the exclusive product of the subjective imagination.

In Dutch artistic designs, there are forces in effect that differ completely from those of its most closely related school. Even though southern Netherlandish painting works with purely visual values — silhouette values — there are still other relationships established, links created, and compositional connections produced — in short, active formative energies — that ultimately create the tight weave of the pictorial pattern. In Holland, on the contrary, there exists a purely passive, distanced viewing process that mirrors the disconnected juxtaposition of unrelated details on the surface. Significantly, in this type of design, whose principles allow for no absolute pictorial unity, the originality of creation lies more in the production of a new kind of unity, one that involves the spectator, than in the invention of connections or a distinct pictorial pattern. We can now, perhaps, understand why the Dutch created no formal tradition of their own in the fifteenth century (that is, no closed, genetic series can be constructed solely from Dutch works of art), but preferred to appropriate both pictorial composition (that is, proper pattern schemata) and individual motifs from the southern Netherlanders without influencing the latter. They never themselves became creators of a style in any substantial way.

France

The third variant of the northern European representational mode, the French, diverges from the normative southern Netherlandish manner of design onto a completely different route from the Dutch. If a maximally loosened pattern distinguishes Dutch pictorial structure, so an abstract, ornamental schema characterizes French painting.

In French pictorial design, too, the double value of an object's contour plays a central role. For the moment, this may be demonstrated in a simple example. In the Limburg brothers' "April" picture (figure 6.20), the line formed by the garden wall continues that formed by the back of the flower-gathering woman in a perfectly parallel course. The steep line of the bending woman's back, which rises up freely over the ground, and the diagonally stretching garden wall, a boundary that moves back across the ground, project a single diagonal. This result seems not coincidental. Even within the most objectively diverse representations, the diagonal confronts us over and over in French pictorial organization. This predilection for the diagonal is explained by its particular ability to lead the gaze simultaneously inward to the depth of the pictorial space and outward along the surface of the picture. If the entire pictorial field can be plowed through by a *system* of such diagonals, then both pictorial space *and* the picture surface are organized by it. All of the compositional endeavors of French painting are directed toward that goal.

This manner of painting brings together the lines of contact between contiguous object projections in their entirety, thus creating

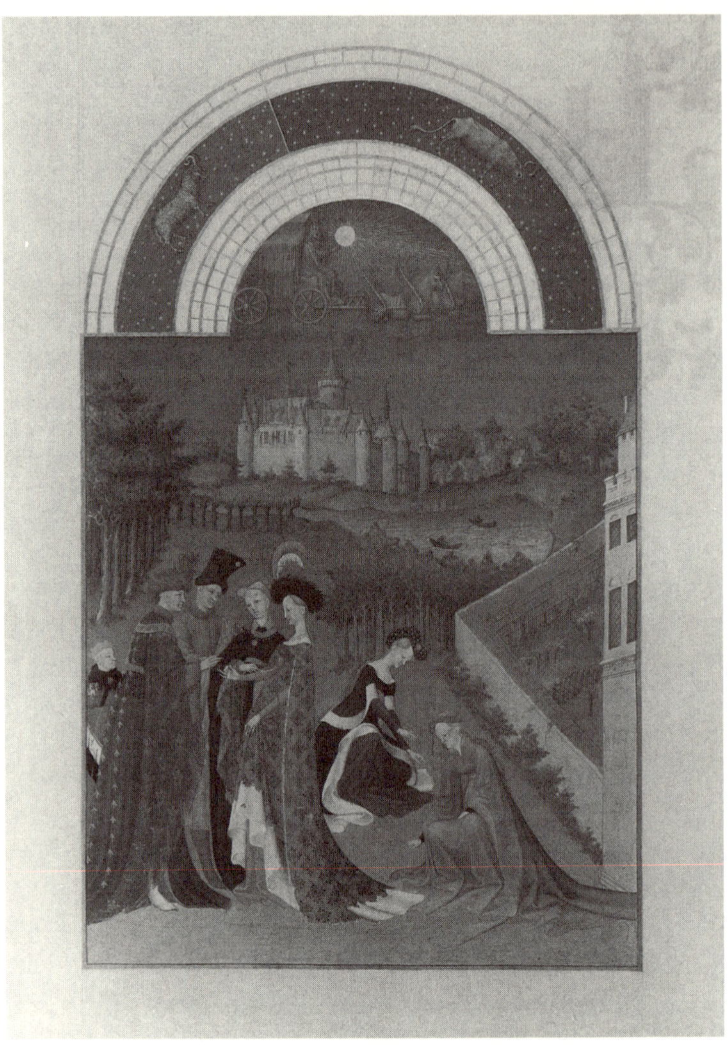

Figure 6.20. Limburg Brothers, *Très Riches Heures du Duc de Berry*, fol. 4 verso, "April Landscape," Musée Condé (Chantilly/Giraudon, Paris).

a tightly woven network on the pictorial surface. The inconspicu-
ousness of the seams secretly running through a Netherlandish
painting is of the utmost importance in that it allows our gaze to
glide without friction over the entire surface pattern and allows
the depicted image to retain the character of being confronted
fortuitously by our gaze. In a French picture, on the other hand,
the seams are asserted openly. And whereas the configuration of
these lines would produce a completely irregular form among the
Netherlanders, French compositions take care that the network of
seams forms itself into as geometrically regular a schema as possible. Very often, the pictorial field is arranged in the form of a
rhomboid grid; that is, the pattern preferentially utilizes a system
of diagonals. Less frequently employed schemata are the circle
and the oval, which, in this instance, are actually special cases
of the rhomboid schema, namely, rhombuses with curved rather
than straight sides. The seams, then, form a single line: in just one
stretch our gaze is led deep into the pictorial space and then back
to the surface, toward the upper edge of the picture and down
again to the bottom.

That this network of lines confronts us in so pointed a fashion
stems from the fact that wherever the picture's seams lie objective
forms of a linear or band-like character appear. In landscape pictures, these are the courses of rivers, canals, walls, avenues; in
figural narratives, they are serial arrangements, regular seating
orders, and the like. Because the boundaries of projections coincide with the factual boundary markers in the outline of the
pictorial stage, the network of seams takes on a highly concrete
character. *The regularity of the pictorial plan and visual organization of the picture are reinforced through the regularity of contour
relationships in pictorial space.*

French pictorial design, with its overarching tendency toward
a rationally, strictly regulated structure, achieves its purest fulfill-

ment whenever the relationship of items in space is already determined by the action of an organizing force — that is, when the influence of human *ratio* can be perceived not only in the phenomenal form but also in the essential form. That is why the favorite theme of French painting is the *cultural* landscape within the landscape picture, the subject of countless calendar pictures in Book of Hours and history scenes (figure 6.21). For the French, the object of depiction is never a chaotic nature but rather a tamed one, captured in rationally comprehensible forms.[26] Even Paradise (and the French would probably contend that this, as the most pure creation of God, is just as it should be) is, for the Limburg brothers, an enclosed garden that appears as a circle on the picture surface (figure 6.22). And as late as the seventeenth century, Jacques Callot sees hell no differently. Among figural representations, the favorite themes are arrangements of social order (figure 6.23). Judicial assemblies, festive ceremonies, even the holy legends and other religious materials are perceived as images of worldly activity, images of life encompassed by social conventions. In his "Epiphany," Jean Fouquet allows the train of the kings to restrain a military parade (figure 6.24), while a vision of heavenly majesty appears as a meeting of Parliament (figure 6.25). *A cultivated world is the subject matter of a rationally regulated pictorial structure.*

Among northern European design principles, the French manner of representation is the most limited in its realm of application. It requires considerable accommodation on the part of the objects; here the portrayal of life manifesting itself in its randomness is impossible (nor, indeed, is it probably desired). Should this manner find itself forced to illustrate a subject not suited to its demands, the minimal adaptability of these structural principles leads to a marked decline in quality. When the Limburg brothers allow the "Fall of the Rebel Angels" (the division of good and evil, the great cosmic turmoil!) to proceed according to the dictates of a strictly decorative rule, the representation takes on a ridiculous effect (figure 6.26). One might call it a purely contrived solution.

In French pictorial conceptions, a curiously rigid quality inheres.[27] In the stereotypical recurrence of the rhomboid surface pattern in countless representations of widely diverse content, we recognize that the *pattern is firmly fixed prior to each scenic invention: that is to say, it is a predetermined pictorial plan.* The macrostructure of the picture surface exists, as it were, even before any scenic interpretation or concretization of objects. Otherwise, it would be impossible to dissect the surface into approximately equal-sized fields or parts of fields (whole, half, or quarter rhombuses). Projections of objects are then poured into these individual fields so that they must conform and adapt to the preconceived schema of the pictorial field's division. The projection of crowds is better suited to this than the projection of the single human form, because the former can effect a process of closure into regular surface figures (figure 6.23). Still, the pictorial ground can remain free from every object projection covering it if the boundaries of the fields are anchored by concrete markers (walls, barriers, furrows in the land, channels of water). *Between the physical world and the organization of the visual surface there reigns, so to speak, a pre-stabilized harmony. The constructed aspect of this order, however, remains hidden through the self-evidence with which the regular design of the picture's appearance takes shape. The beauty of the view seems to contain nothing subjective if it is assumed that the same organizing spirit that has constructed the pictures is governing the structure of the visual world itself.*

That which we perceive as a construction possesses an unlimited truth content for the French. In essence, there exists the same phenomenon that Max Scheler described in another con-

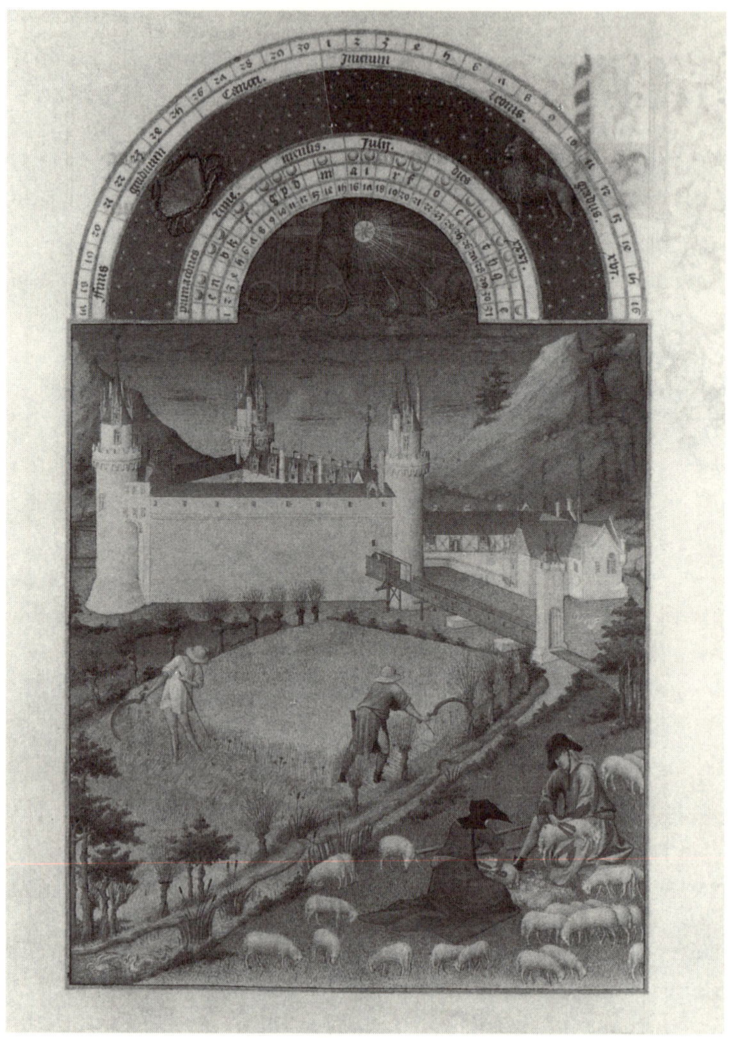

Figure 6.21. Limburg Brothers, *Très Riches Heures du Duc de Berry*, fol. 7 verso, "July Landscape," Musée Condé (Chantilly/Giraudon, Paris).

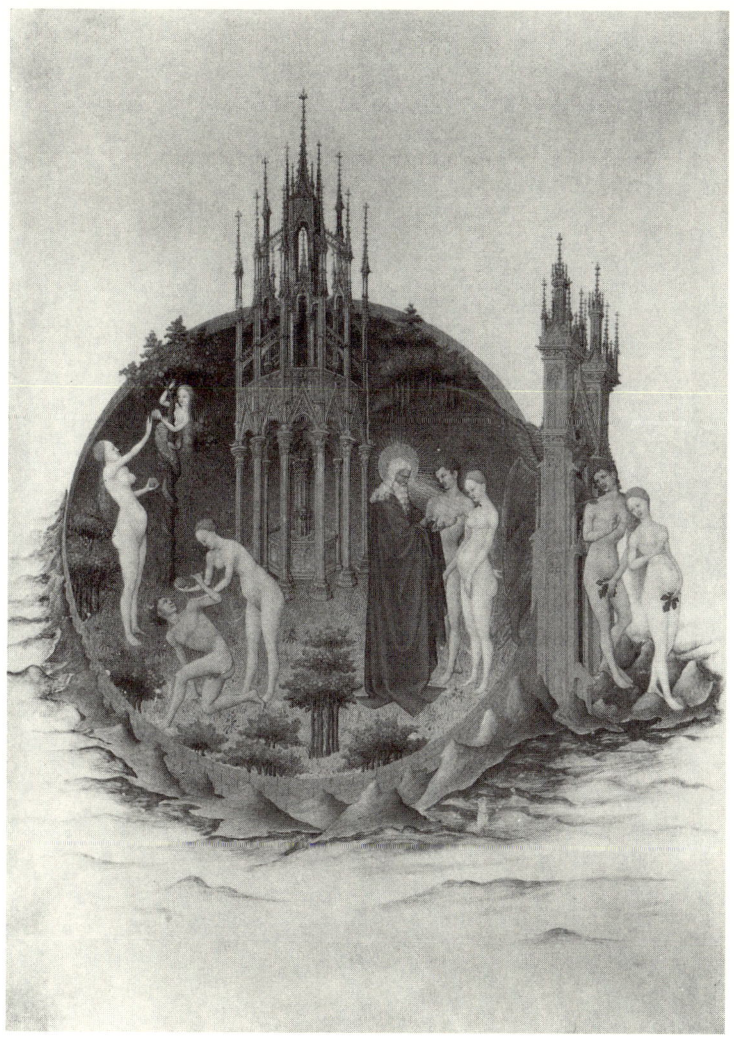

Figure 6.22. Limburg Brothers, *Très Riches Heures du Duc de Berry*, fol. 25 verso, "Paradise," Musée Condé (Chantilly/Giraudon, Paris).

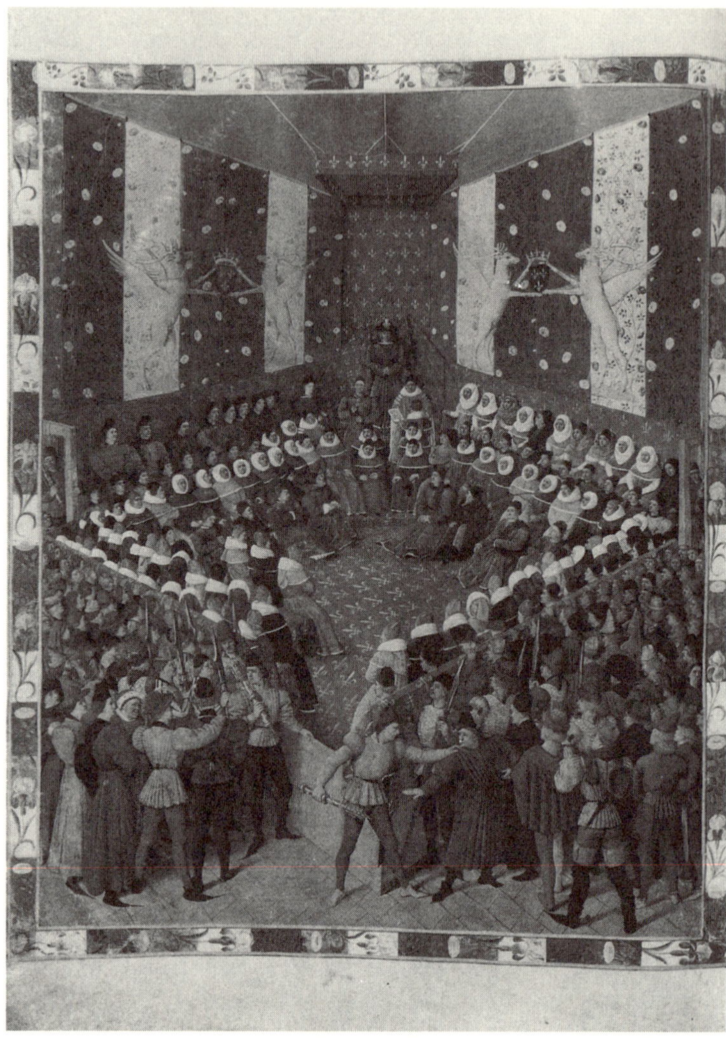

Figure 6.23. Jean Fouquet from Giovanni Boccaccio, *De casibus virorum illustrium*, cod. Gall. 6, fol 2 verso, "Judicial Court of Charles VII," Bayerische Staatsbibliothek, Munich.

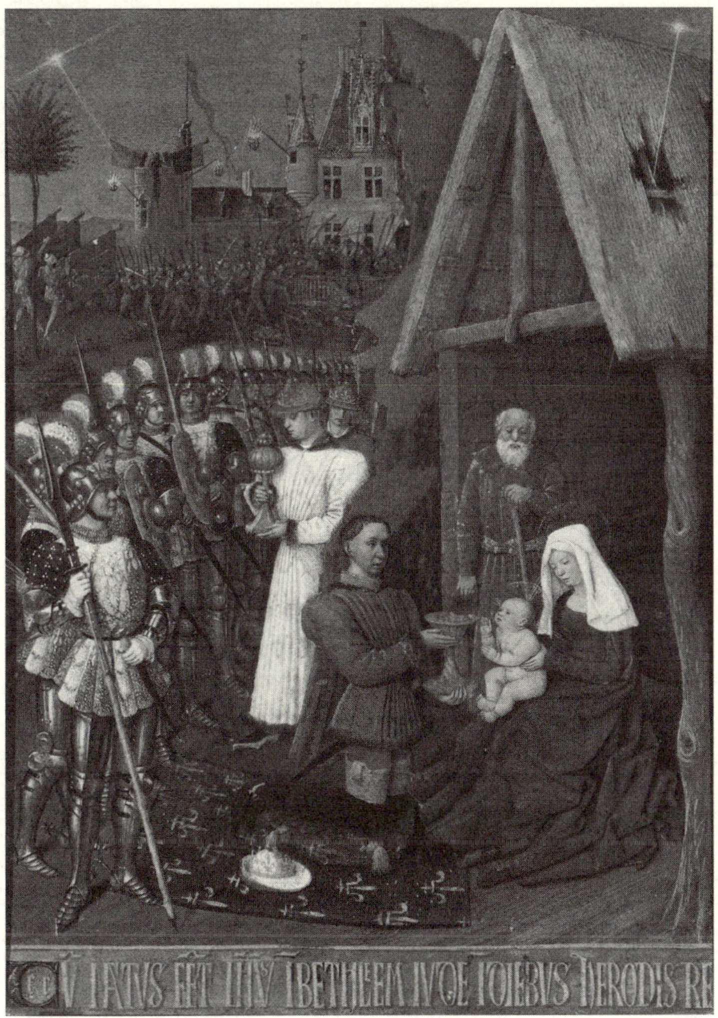

Figure 6.24. Jean Fouquet, *Book of Hours of Etienne Chevalier*, "Epiphany," Musée Condé (Chantilly/Giraudon, Paris).

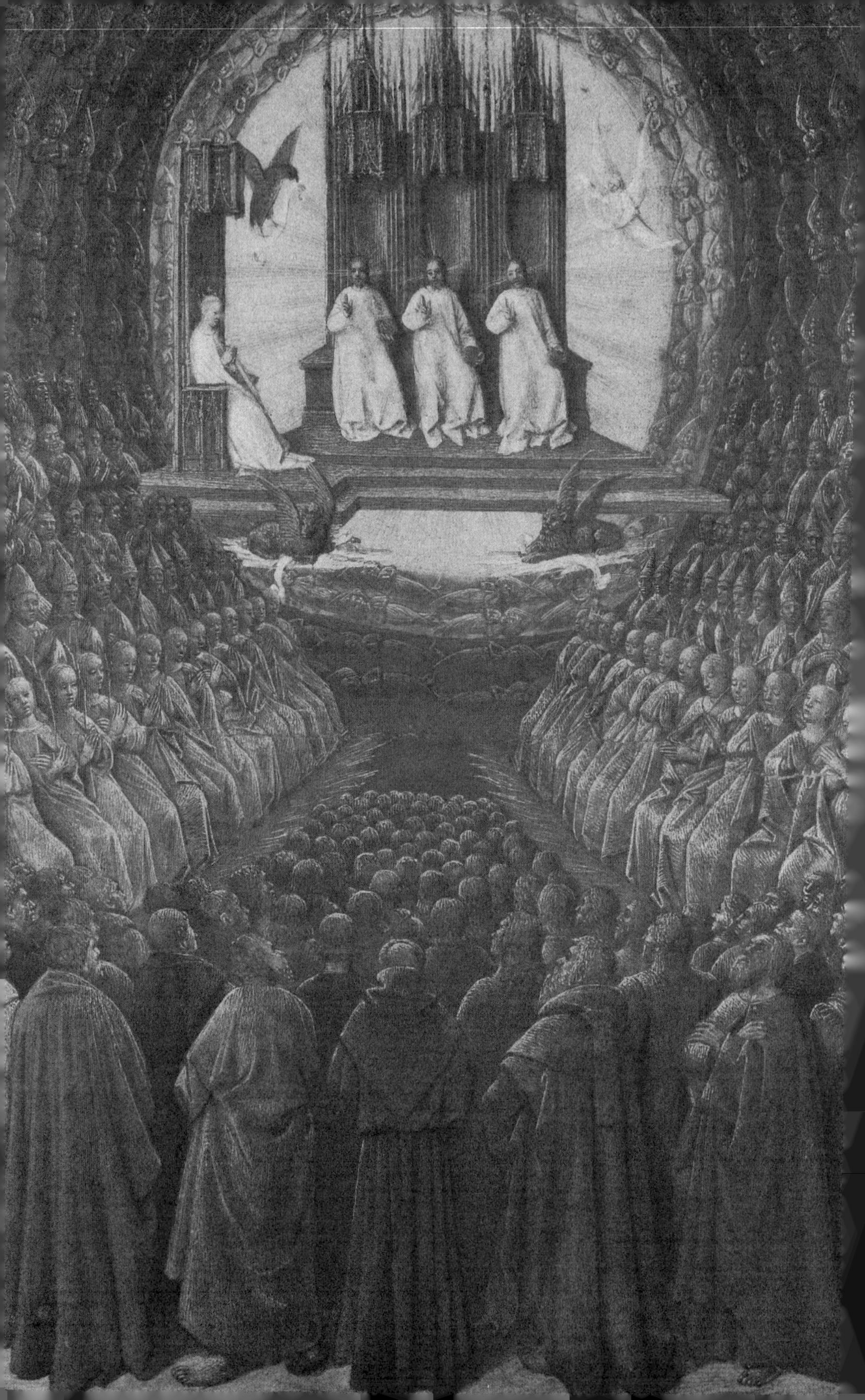

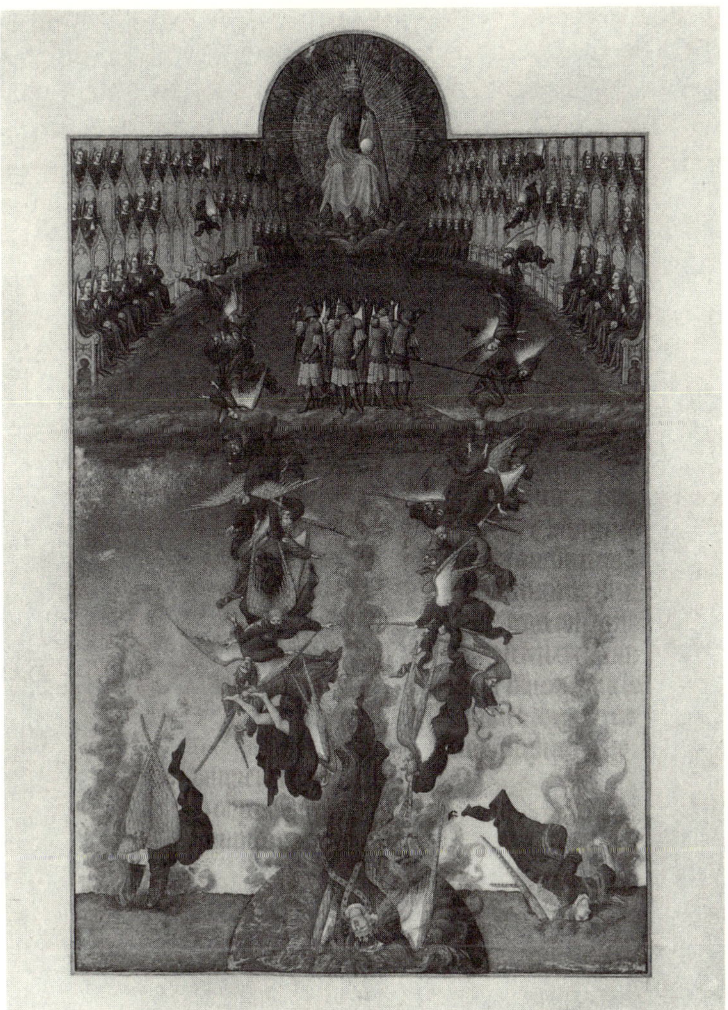

Figure 6.25 (opposite page). Jean Fouquet, *Book of Hours of Etienne Chevalier*, "Vision of Heavenly Majesty," Musée Condé (Chantilly/Giraudon, Paris).
Figure 6.26 (above). Limburg Brothers, *Très Riches Heures du Duc de Berry*, fol. 64 verso, "Fall of the Rebel Angels," Musée Condé (Chantilly/Giraudon, Paris).

text: "We are inclined to view that which they (the French) call clarity in the sciences and philosophy and which, along with their greatest thinker, Descartes, they so eagerly equate with Truth as the wholly unobjective assumption that the world is created in such a way that it can enter into human understanding easily and completely. What to them is 'Truth' to us is simply a subjective, human need."[28] We should not neglect to emphasize, of course, that the demands placed on truth content in both cases are fully different in nature.

The pictorial thinking of the French seeks to allow the most unshakable regularity to crystallize itself with no apparent pressure. The moment in which the pictorial order captures the physical world without violence still lies contained within the French pictorial structure. The rhomboid network in which the physical world is trapped possesses all the characteristics of the geometrical schema of infinite rapport. It is cut off by the picture's edge in such a way that pieces of the pattern are amputated all around. Thus it never reaches an end and can be continued on all sides as far as one likes. Even when objects appear as segments through such overlappings (in particular at the edge of the picture), they are never transformed into formal wholes. Here the fragmentary quality is immediately visible. For the order of the pictorial world extends even over the picture's boundaries, asserting itself as the segment of a larger whole. The concept of order, having emerged as an absolute, universally valid principle, is thus able to free itself from the notion of a strictly delineated design identical with the pictorial field. *Hence the segment of reality as such becomes worthy of form* — without first having to be formally transvalued. Although the visible world is caught firmly within the mesh of an inflexible network, the prison is never really locked; therefore, our eye glides quite unexpectedly into that organization, which presents itself all the more convincingly as an inevitable fate.

A series of significant consequences results, in France, from the strictly predetermined nature of the pictorial pattern, that is, from the prescribed quality of the pictorial plan.

First: *The minimal variability of a pictorial pattern determined a priori often makes it impossible to accommodate the individual illustrative requirements* in a more than superficial manner. French painting has only a very few schemata at hand; the particular representational content must adapt to its form, for better or for worse. French pictorial imagination is aware only of the following alternatives. On the one hand, a strictly decorative organization can be employed whereby every detail is precisely fixed in the overarching picture plan. The static nature of such perfectly regular pictorial structures is almost exclusively suited to pure descriptional depictions of situations or representative narrative ceremonies (for example, the vision of heavenly majesty). On the other hand, a partial deviation can be made from the norm of an otherwise fully intact, strict organization if an ongoing event or process must be represented. For events and changes can appear to the French pictorial imagination only as a partial loosening of so rigid an order, like the removal of a building stone from its solid enclosing structure whereby the tectonics of the whole remains unshaken. The preeminent example of this may be the "Coronation of the Virgin" by Fouquet in Chantilly (figure 6.27). The stage is subdivided in a strictly decorative and symmetrical way by the perspectivally foreshortened lateral walls, which are made up of angelic choirs, and by the frontal, tripartite throne for the Divinity in the center. Of the three identical seated figures, the outermost one on the left has risen to crown the kneeling Virgin. The act of crowning has the effect, within the entire stage set, of being a gentle splintering away from the regular, symmetrical organization. And yet, in this kind of arrangement, it is immediately obvious where within the whole structure the loosened

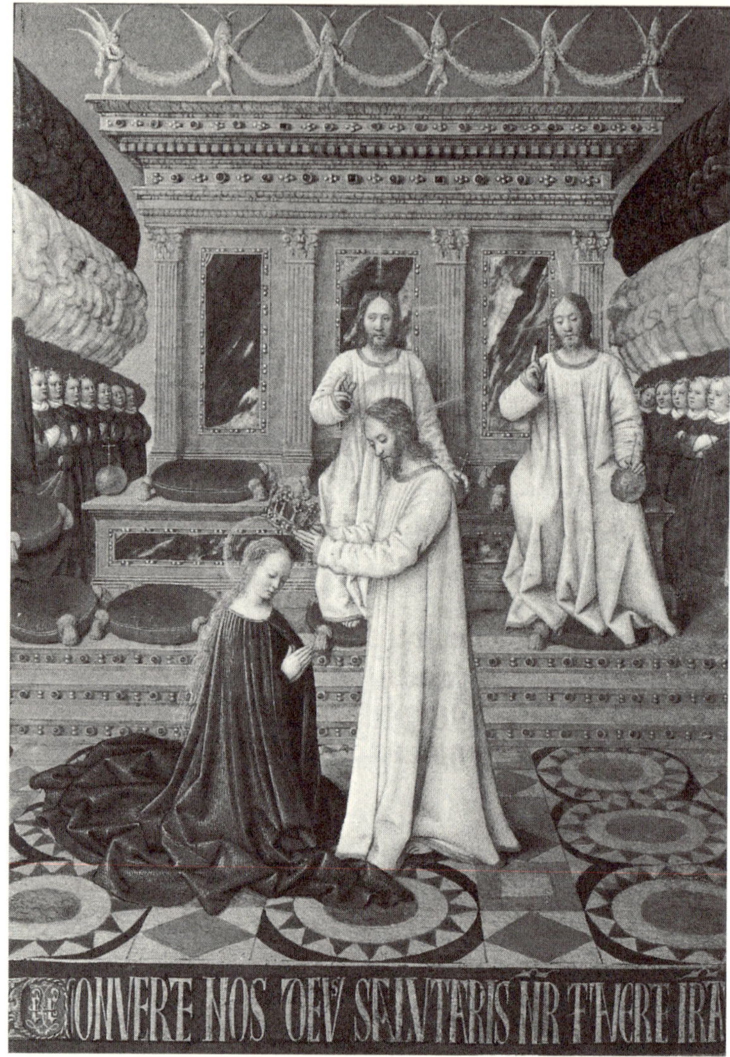

Figure 6.27. Jean Fouquet, *Book of Hours of Etienne Chevalier*, "Coronation of the Virgin," Musée Condé (Chantilly/Giraudon, Paris).

member belongs. The disturbance of organization leads not to a disorderly, chaotic state but to an organization with gaps, which always strives to refill those holes. Change or process is, for Fouquet, the disturbance of a stable order, of normal conditions. And in fact the disturbed region, typically selected off the axis, remains isolated; the movement does not encroach on the surrounding areas.

Second: *If the schemata of the pictorial pattern display minimal compliance and adaptability to special representational demands, so they are, at the same time, subjected relatively little to historical changes in style.* The rhomboid form of the patterning of the pictorial field is identical for the Limburg brothers (figure 6.21), for Fouquet (figure 6.23), and, two hundred years later, for Callot (figure 6.28). Because the French pictorial pattern is worked out so precisely, the consistent quality is apparent here most of all. It is manifest in a concrete form, with its formal framework visible everywhere. The same pattern schema is always, as it were, simply replenished with various contents. A constant basic schema exists in other national styles as well but remains hidden behind its individual, concrete treatment. What remains the same is simply a system of basic relationships, and therefore the superficial resemblance of the various handlings is slight. For the French, in contrast, the basic schema is less latent by a degree and has a concrete, ornamental character. Thus the constant and the variable elements here are always clearly divorced.

That means that, for the French, tradition possesses a visible form. Originality of invention applies only to the interpretation of the basic schema — to variations on the theme and not to changes in the schema itself. The artistic problem poses itself to the French in the strict form of a mathematical problem in which the value of the individual factors might change but the form of the question stays the same.

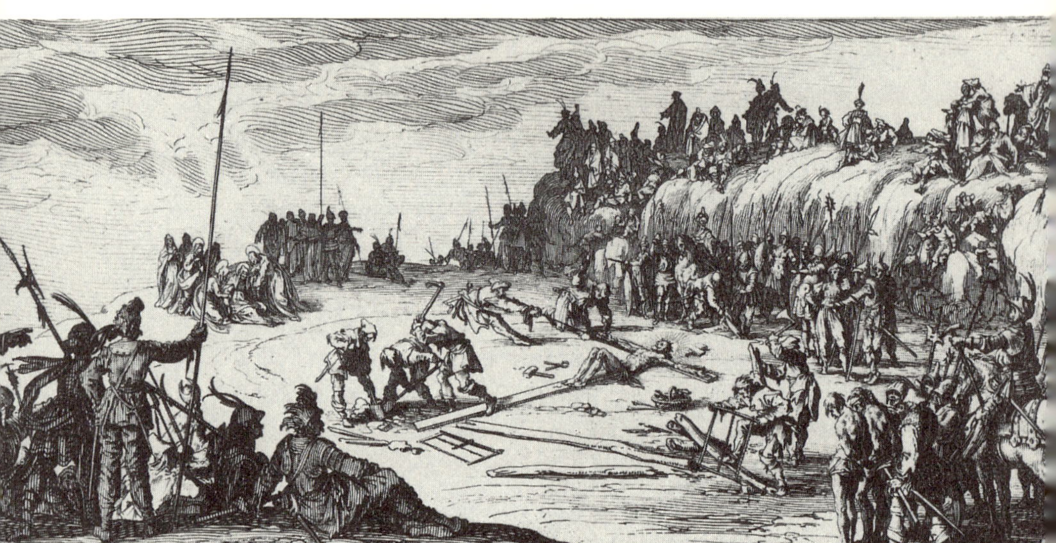

Figure 6.28. Jacques Callot, *Nailing to the Cross*, engraving, Graphische Sammlung Albertina, Vienna.

This unwavering adherence to a consciously dominating basic form, of course, also determines the way French painting appropriates foreign styles or alien artistic achievements. For the same reason that only a limited circle of themes was worthy of taking form in French painting, this mode is only to a small degree receptive to general stylistic developments and foreign ways of seeing. Pictorial structures could be borrowed as a whole only once they underwent transformation into a rational, decorative mode. Netherlandish compositions, developed in relatively free form, could be adjusted to conform to regular organizations only partially. French art opened itself to the influence of early Italian Renaissance painting — to those very trends in which the order of the crowd held primacy over the concentrated organization of the individual figure (Fra Angelico, Jacopo Bellini) — so much the earlier.[29] Considerably more important for fifteenth-century French painting than the example of specific Italian pictorial compositions, however, was the integration of Renaissance architectural forms into the physical world of pictures. Buildings with straight, even timbers must have been welcome primarily because, when foreshortened, they yielded pure diagonals in the very simplest way. Furthermore, this architecture contained regular, rectangular wall surface divisions, which, when situated parallel or orthogonally to the picture surface, delimited the desired regular (square or trapezoidal) pattern fields (figure 6.28). France could borrow overall pictorial structures from Italy only later, in the sixteenth century. For by that time, a style had developed there that transplanted spatial values to the surface and leaned heavily toward the constructive: mannerism.

NOTES

1. Friedrich Winkler, "Reisefrüchte I," *Zeitschrift für bildende Kunst*, n.s., 31 (1919–1920), 202.

2. I refer here primarily to the works of Hans Kauffmann, such as *Rembrandts Bildgestaltung: Ein Beitrag zur Analyse seines Stils* (Stuttgart: Kohlhammer, 1922).

3. See also Ludwig Münz, "H. Kauffmann, *Rembrandts Bildgestaltung*," *Kritische Berichte* 2 (1928–1929), pp. 199ff.

4. Theodor Hetzer, *Das deutsche Element in der italienischen Malerei* (Berlin: Deutscher Kunstverlag, 1929). Hetzer's works are, I believe, best understood as an opposition and reaction to that epoch of art historical research that acknowledged only "spatial composition" in works of postmedieval painting. Hetzer has drawn attention again to "surface composition." Strictly speaking, however, there is never just the one or the other. One can "compose" only in reference to both domains.

5. Hetzer, in fact, provides an excellent formulation of classical pictorial structure when he says: "The sixteenth century loves to create forms that, while conveying an appearance of nature, nonetheless are at the same time ornamental surface constructions of an autonomous character ..." (p. 37). The general artistic attitude that allows this coincidence to become possible at all, however, is never elucidated.

6. Most intellectual-historical interpretations flounder in the dangerous waters of speculation; see most recently that of Karl Tolnai, "Zur Herkunft des Stiles der van Eyck," *Münchner Jahrbuch für bildende Kunst*, n.s., 9 (1932), pp. 320ff.

7. See Kurt Koffka, "Zur Theorie der Erlebniswahrnehmung," *Annalen der Philosophie* 3 (1922).

8. I refer to, among others, the discussions of Erwin Panofsky, "Perspektive als symbolische Form," *Vorträge der Bibliothek Warburg* (1924–1925), pp. 271–78. [*Perspective as Symbolic Form*, trans. Christopher S. Wood (New York: Zone Books, 1991)]. The views represented in this treatise, too, seem to me to proceed from mistaken assumptions. Nevertheless, due to a lack of space, a debate with Panof-

sky's important attempt to solve the problem — by claiming that a still higher meaning is assigned (along with its immediate significance) to the spatial design of the postmedieval picture — must be reserved for a later occasion.

9. Hans Jantzen, "Alois Riegl, *Gesammelte Aufsätze*," *Kritische Berichte* 3 (1930–1931), pp. 65ff., has shown that a series of Heinrich Wölfflin's "principles" for grasping artistic facts also proves itself unsuitable because — just as in our case — the form of the thing is chosen as the point of departure for the construction of the principle. The fact that Wölfflin chose these pairs of principles seems doubly peculiar, insofar as he recognized very well — as numerous passages of his principles testify — that what is involved is a quasi-segment rather than a genuine one, that is, the illusion of a segment. "In the seventeenth century the filling has lost touch with the frame. Everything is done to avoid the impression that this composition was invented just for this surface. Although a *hidden congruity* of course continues to play its part, the whole is meant to look more like a piece cut haphazardly out of the visible world" (p. 132) [Heinrich Wölfflin, *Principles of Art History: The Problem of the Development of Style in Later Art*, trans. M. D. Hottinger (New York: Dover, 1950), pp. 125–26]. And on page 137 [131], we read: "In the tectonic style, the filling relates to the given space, in the a-tectonic the relationship between space and filling is *apparently* adventitious." (Emphasis mine.)

10. Here and in the following passage, one should keep in mind the example of the Mérode Altarpiece to imagine the perceptual content.

11. It is necessary at this point to counter yet another possible misunderstanding. When we describe the Netherlandish principle of pictorial design as a kind of inverted projection, some readers may find our discussion deficient in its treatment of the signification of the object of projection. The fact that we do not touch on this point could be falsely interpreted as our deeming further discussion superfluous, since in a naturalistic art such as early Netherlandish painting only a piece of "nature" could ever figure as an object of representation. In actuality, this question remains unelaborated here simply because in a second, developmental-historical part of this study, which will appear later, it shall be demonstrated that the model for early Netherlandish painters — at least as con-

cerns the whole of the picture — was never "nature" but rather a historicized structure of motifs. Moreover, we would like to maintain, there is no such thing, strictly speaking, as an artistic practice consisting only in the "seeing" of an already complete, preexisting "nature."

12. Trapped in the error that this has to do with a specifically artistic problem, an extensive literature has busied itself with investigating when and by whom linear perspective was discovered, and likewise when the so-called empirical perspective was transformed into an exact perspective. These inquiries certainly have their merit; however, one must not attribute to them a significance that cannot by nature apply to them. Only a confusion of representational-technical problems with purely artistic ones can lead to such grotesque conclusions as those that characterize, among others, the writings of Joseph Kern, for instance in "Perspektive und Bildarchitektur bei Jan van Eyck," *Repertorium für Kunstwissenschaft* 35 (1912), pp. 60ff. Kern regards the discovery of the rule of the vanishing point as an *artistic* act of the first rank. Because he sees this rule put into practice for the first time in a picture by Petrus Christus but does not want to concede primacy to this second-rank master, he must take refuge in an awkward, contrived hypothesis in order ultimately to credit Jan van Eyck with the decisive contribution.

13. As is well known, the observation that the landscape in the Ghent *Adoration of the Lamb* splits into two parts portrayed from distinct viewpoints marks the starting point of Max Dvořák's large-scale attempt to distinguish the respective roles of the van Eyck brothers in producing the Ghent Altarpiece [*Das Rätsel der Brüder van Eyck*, rev. ed. (Munich: R. Piper, 1925)]. Dvořák sees the landscape of the central panel as the conjunction of an old-fashioned landscape tapestry and a modern horizon landscape. Thus it seems inevitable to him that the parts played by the two brothers should be delimited accordingly. The assumption that representational-technical differences in attitude — such as the maplike delineation of an expanse of depth on the surface and the reproduction of spatial depth by means of foreshortening — must necessarily be oppositions in style is still an undisputed axiom, even in Dvořák's later works.

14. One must keep in mind here that the obligatory themes of early Nether-

landish painting were religious subjects, that is, imaginative material not only of an invisible but of a specifically supersensory nature.

15. In addition to that, of course, on the closure of the representation in subject matter. The idea that the entire imaginative content contained by a picture should inherently form a unity is, to be sure, completely unfounded. It is largely to blame for the fact that the question of where the artistic unity of a picture lies, or whether in every case there even is such a unity, remains for the most part unaddressed.

16. Only in mannerism does even Italian painting arrive at a devaluation of the picture's lower edge. Typically enough, that very style stood under a strong northern influence and was in turn seized upon by western European painting with incomparably greater enthusiasm than any previous Italian style.

17. On the situation in the soft style, see the discussions in my book *Die österreichische Tafelmalerei der Gotik* (Augsburg: Filser, 1929), p. 9. On the equilibrium between things organic and dead matter, see also Bruno Fürst, "Beiträge zu einer Geschichte der österreichischen Plastik in der ersten Hälfte des 15. Jahrhunderts," (Ph. D. diss.: Leipzig, 1931), pp. 38ff.

18. The term "figure" is used here in the sense in which Gestalt theory speaks of figure as opposed to ground. I avoid using the word in this sense elsewhere, in order to exclude the possibility of confusing it with the meaning of "human figure" — an obvious danger in this study.

19. For the fifteenth century, I am employing the designation "southern Netherlandish" and not "Flemish," because artists of Walloon background also belong to this school (among them one of the most important, Rogier van der Weyden). One can only speak of "Flemish" painting in the strict sense after Antwerp took over as the prime location of artistic development (around 1500), allowing the hegemony gradually to be transferred from the French to the Flemish portion of present-day Belgium. I use the term "Dutch" in the same sense as did Max Dvořák in *Das Rätsel der Kunst der Brüder van Eyck*, pp. 269ff.

20. When I refer here to "French (or southern Netherlandish or Dutch) pictorial invention," that does not mean that all works of early French painting exhibit the French pictorial law system (as discussed here) in the same way. The

statements made here apply primarily to certain central groups of images in which a specific attitude toward the "pictorial problem" is manifested especially pointedly. At the same time, it should be emphasized that the works of great artistic personalities in no way represent an exception from the overarching norm. Rather, in their consistency, they stand as particularly impressive embodiments of the pictorial laws in question.

21. To my knowledge, it has never been noticed or discussed that all representatives of this altar form either stem from Spain or are there today. This could be because Spanish patrons desired an accommodation to the retable forms familiar to them and that it was for this reason that these peculiar constructions emerged.

22. It is typical that Rogier, in his later *Saint John the Baptist* Altarpiece, compensates for the strong tendency toward verticalization by doubling the jamb niches on both sides. The portal frames are then constructed with a narrower pointed arch. Although the outer jambs thus appear filled out with a column, the vacancy of the inner jambs is not highlighted, since these are almost completely concealed by the figures within the scene.

23. One might think, for example, of the transference of the composition of Rubens's Antwerp *Deposition* into Rembrandt's picture in Munich.

24. See Alois Riegl, "Das holländische Gruppenporträt,"*Jahrbuch der kunsthistorischen Sammlung des Allerhöchsten Kaiserhauses* 23 (1902), pp. 75ff (reprinted Vienna: Österreichische Staatsdruckerei, 1931). In order to avoid misunderstanding, we should point out here that Riegl's "internal unity" does not apply to that which, further below, we shall designate "internal pictorial unity." By "internal unity," Riegl understands the continuity brought about by the depiction of psychic effects; the unity of the physical, tangible appearance (which is much closer to our "internal pictorial unity") he calls "external unity."

25. We are coming — albeit from the opposite direction — to conclusions similar to those Riegl reached in his observations on the Dutch group portrait in *Das holländische Gruppenporträt* (p. 85): "The integrating element that nonetheless makes [distinct figures] appear as a unit again lies in the onlooking individual: in the pictorial concept it was called attention: in composition it is called

space" [from passage translated as "Geertgen tot Sint Jans' 'The Legend of the Relics of St. John the Baptist,'" trans. Stephen S. Kayser, in *Modern Perspectives in Western Art History: An Anthology of Twentieth-Century Writings on the Visual Arts*, ed. W. Eugene Kleinbauer (Toronto: University of Toronto Press/Medieval Academy of America, 1989), pp. 135–36].

26. One may well be reminded here of a formulation in the well-known book by Friedrich Sieburg, *Gott in Frankreich*: "The Frenchman desires to comprehend even nature as a part of himself."

27. Winkler in "Reisefrüchte I," p. 204, offers a characterization of Fouquet that turns the true state of affairs upside down: "Therefore his figural compositions are uniquely diverse"; "Next to Jan van Eyck, Fouquet is the one artist who repeats himself the least"; "as multifaceted as nature itself."

28. Max Scheler, *Die Ursachen des Deutschenhasses*, 2nd ed. (Leipzig: Wolff 1917), p. 105.

29. See, for example, Fra Angelico's frescoes at the Vatican, in Frida Schott-müller, *Fra Angelico*, Klassiker der Kunst (Stuttgart: Deutsche Verlags-Anstalt 1911), figs. on pp. 198 and 203.

Translated by Jacqueline E. Jung.

Hans Sedlmayr, "Bruegel's Macchia" (1934)

This essay was Sedlmayr's Habilitationsschrift, *the work that earned him the right to hold an advanced university position. In 1936, he succeeded his teacher Julius von Schlosser as professor in Vienna. The essay analyzes a group of works by Pieter Bruegel the Elder, including the paintings* Netherlandish Proverbs *and* The Blind Leading the Blind *and the drawing* Beekeepers. *"Bruegel's Macchia" stands as the most imaginative set piece in structure-analytical method. Sedlmayr extrapolates the crisis of mid-sixteenth-century Europe from a single formal feature: the blot or color patch that Bruegel used to describe human forms. Bruegel's shapeless figures — described by Sedlmayr with cruel detachment — symbolized the atomization of society and the alienation of the individual. Sedlmayr explicitly compares Bruegel's compositions to the montages of the surrealists. In Sedlmayr's pessimistic reading, Bruegel foresaw the unarticulated, despiritualized society of modernity, a society bereft of an ideal. In the Bruegel essay emerge the first outlines of Sedlmayr's 1948 polemic against modern art,* Verlust der Mitte (Art in Crisis: The Lost Center).

(Source: Hans Sedlmayr, "Die 'Macchia' Bruegels," Jahrbuch der Kunsthistorischen Sammlungen, *n.s. 8 [1934], pp. 137–60; reprinted in Hans Sedlmayr,* Epochen und Werke, *vol. 1 [Vienna: Herold, 1959], pp. 274–318.)*

Chapter Seven

Bruegel's *Macchia* (1934)

Hans Sedlmayr

I

In an incisive essay, Benedetto Croce has drawn attention to a theory of the color patch — the *macchia* — published by the Italian writer Vittorio Imbriani in 1868 in a little book titled *La quinta promotrice*.[1] According to this theory, the *macchia* is "the image of the first *distant* impression of an object or a scene, the first and characteristic effect, to imprint itself upon the eye of the artist, whether he has actually laid eyes on the object or scene, or glimpsed them in his fantasy or memory. It is the springing point, *the characteristic*...[2] brought forth by the particular grouping of variously colored persons and things. When I say *distant*, I do not mean literal distance so much as the moral distance[3] we experience when we have not yet registered the perceived object in all its detail, a process that can only take place after extended immersion and devoted attention."

Between this picture of the first impression, explains Croce, and the completed picture, precisely defined in all its details, lies the entire artistic process: "To complete a picture, to perfect it, means nothing other than a strong *inner* approach to the object, a clarification and consolidation of that which pierced our eye as a brilliant flash. Should, however, that first harmonious accord be lacking, then execution and completion, however distinguished they may be, will never move us inwardly, will never arouse any feeling in the viewer at all, whereas the plain *macchia, without any further objective definition whatsoever*, is fully capable of arousing such a feeling.

"This theory of the color patch," continues Croce, "must certainly be divested of many eccentricities; and one must always bear in mind that the *macchia* is not objectively located in the things themselves but is instead a creation of the artist who may later believe he has found it in the objects onto which he has transferred it." This necessary correction and qualification of Imbriani's thesis notwithstanding, one must marvel with Croce "that such an approach in art criticism was not developed further, that it could, instead, disappear without a trace. The author himself must not have fully grasped the significance of what he had attempted."

Croce's view has prompted me to publish an essay whose main points were drafted before I learned of the article on Imbriani. Taking issue with an interpretation of Bruegel that takes his work to be philosophical "ideograms"[4] — corresponding to that "ideomania" of painters which Imbriani criticized — I argued that one cannot understand the importance of Bruegel's pictures without starting from their particular "form," in which and through which they signify something quite specific. At that point, my strongest argument for this position was that one can clearly derive the larger portion of Bruegel's preferred pictorial motifs from the pictorial conception of his pictures, from "pure" pictorial form — from precisely what Imbriani called the *macchia* — if one understands them correctly; that one can also identify that general atmosphere — Imbriani's "feeling" — in which the various pictorial objects appear immersed, lending them their particular shade of meaning in a way that can only be expressed in images; and moreover, that the pictorial contents revealed by an examination of

Bruegel's *macchia* submit to an intellectual unity that neither I nor anyone else had noted before.

The possibility of this inner affinity between a given, characteristic *macchia* and particular pictorial contents — even though the color patch is not an objective quality of things — is something Imbriani also accepts. He too knows that a *macchia* always evokes the same feeling and with it certain pictorial ideas, to the exclusion of all others: one particular *macchia*, for example, could "never [show] draped figures, never male figures, never a picture of lascivious nudity."

II

Bruegel's pictures are in a certain sense particularly suited to prove Imbriani's theories, for in a curious way they embody, even in their finished state, that first distant vision.[5] To reconstruct the "color patch" from which the finished picture emerges, one need not, it seems, artificially disregard the concrete meaning, shutting down, as it were, one's mental faculties. Instead the picture itself, or, more precisely, one of the two basic components into which it falls of its own accord, shows a tendency to shed its manifest content and to appear to the viewer purely as a lively pattern of color patches. Without any activity on our part, simply through steady, passive viewing and extended attention (and for some viewers immediately), the human figures of typical pictures by Bruegel begin to disintegrate, to fall into pieces and thus to lose their meaning in the usual sense. When this process has reached its peak, one sees instead of figures a multitude of flat, vivid patches with firmly enclosed contours and unified coloration that all seem to lie unconnected and unordered, beside and above each other in a plane at the front of the picture. These are, so to speak, the atoms of the image. Yet this metamorphosis does not affect the entire composition. The deep landscape space in which the figures stand shows no such tendency to disintegrate or to lose meaning; and even when the figures' tendency to fall apart begins to encroach on parts of the larger composition, the latter resists. It is paradoxical to see how two pictorial domains, completely opposed in nature, fall asunder as if one had taken a finished landscape showing the strongest spatial illusion and then scattered throughout it figures pieced together out of flat patches of color.[6]

The overall impression that arises in this way, and that the viewer experiences as astonishing and disturbing, is thoroughly characteristic of nearly all of Bruegel's paintings (albeit with certain deviations in the large figural compositions). It is Bruegel's specific *macchia* that evokes this impression.

There can be no doubt that the effect achieved by Bruegel was fully intentional. The impression I have described could hardly have arisen if Bruegel had not undertaken certain modifications of the manner in which pictorial structure was understood in earlier but closely related painting, modifications that represent an abandonment of certain "achievements" of the early sixteenth century. These modifications all serve a common — and at first sight incomprehensible — purpose. So that the figures fall easily into colored patches, they are "composed" out of homogeneously colored, sharply delineated partial planes. This makes the figures conspicuously flat, less plastic than the strongly receding space in which they take position. As a result, they are connected to their spatial environment in an oddly unsteady, precarious way; they tend to jump out of the space in which they are placed and into a picture plane that is farther forward. Where they accumulate in this zone, the frontal space is transformed and seems to become flatter. To facilitate this loosening from their space, the figures are isolated from the surrounding field by hard contours; and for this reason, the shading that connects a body with space is avoided.

From the standpoint of a Renaissance *macchia*, where none of this can be found, even in pictures showing great distance, these qualities are simply serious deficiencies. So too are other qualities that I have not mentioned here, such as the strange expressionlessness of the faces. Yet in light of the descriptive abilities that Bruegel displays so brilliantly in the landscape portions of the pictures, it is impossible to interpret these characteristics as mere clumsiness.[7] The round cakes covering the roof at the upper left of *Netherlandish Proverbs* (figure 7.1) do not follow the sharp spatial shift of the roof's surface; instead they remain, regardless of the bend in their support, unforeshortened and on the same unified plane as the disintegrating figures. The only explanation for this curious motif, I feel, is that Bruegel has indicated in the picture itself that it is to be visually taken apart into separate patches. The motif is only an exaggerated expression of what otherwise occurs in the picture in a more hidden way.

But what is the meaning of this extraordinary process of disintegration? The way to the answer lies in the following question.

III

Let us take the *macchia* I have described in Bruegel's work as a given. For which pictorial motifs, then, is it the "given," natural form? The answer that follows presents an unsystematic and incomplete list of such subjects. In Bruegel, as with all great artists, there is an inner correspondence of form and content; the one is created for the other.

1

Objects likely to become part of this *macchia* are those whose planar projections result in clear, self-contained, unified patches or that can be assembled out of such patches. In other words, shapes that approximate the simple geometric elements: circles, spheres,

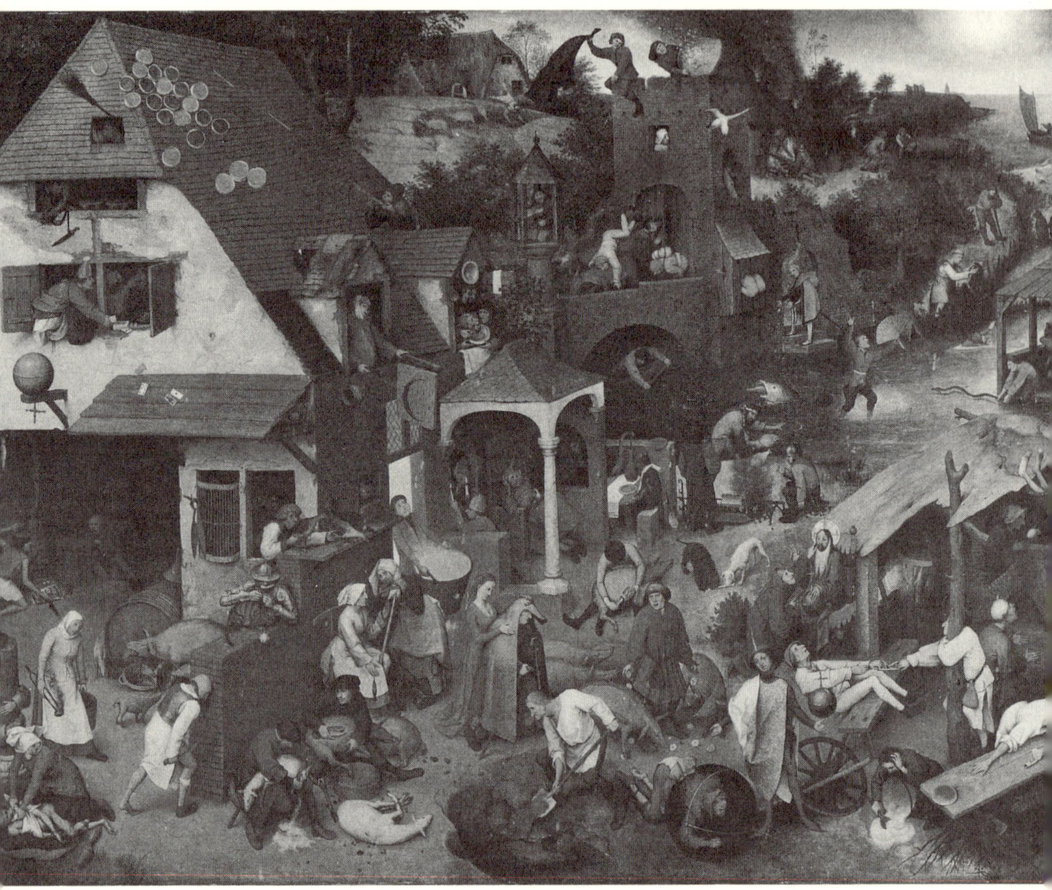

Figure 7.1. Pieter Bruegel, *Netherlandish Proverbs*, Staatliche Museen Preussischer Kulturbesitz, Gëmaldegalerie, Berlin.

ovals, cylinders, cones, and cubes.

In the realm of inanimate nature and human implements, this includes disklike shapes of all sorts. And their number in the pictures of Bruegel is legion: wheels and rings, bowls, plates, and pans, pots and cauldrons, sieves and containers, caps and hats, helmets, shaving bowls, mirrors, dials, oculi, peacocks' eyes, drums, the bases of columns, covers of barrels, sections of tree trunks, cannon barrels, and so on ad infinitum. (The drawing *Allegory of Pride* is particularly rich in the variety of such disklike things.) Then globe-, sack-, and bladder-like forms of all sorts: cannonballs, marbles, globes, balls, sacks, bags, purses, loaves of bread, bagpipes, snail shells, pomegranates, and so on. Conical forms: baskets, pitchers, beehives, bells, bell copes (see again *Allegory of Pride*). Ovals: eggs, shells, bellows. Cylindrical forms: casks, buckets, kettles, lanterns, columns, chopping blocks, tree trunks. Square or cubical forms: tabletops, doors, books, chessboards, trunks, strongboxes, building stones, dice.

As for the human body, Bruegel favors not the articulated nude or delicately draped figure of classical art but the clumsy body of the peasant, clad in stiff cloth, and especially peasant children. It is here one enters the world of the peasant, so significant for Bruegel not only from the point of view of his *macchia* but also for other reasons that I shall enumerate. Similarly appropriate are round heads with a minimum of internal detail, where eyes, nose, and mouth appear as mere points, as on a snowman. The ideal would be a body with a primitive sack-like form and without extremities. For such a sense of the body, the monstrous corporeal masses of cripples are an ideal object of representation, and in *Netherlandish Proverbs* and *The Misanthrope*, bodies are inscribed in spheres.

The painting *The Land of Cockaigne* is a treasure trove of such forms: cakes, bowl, plate, pitcher, tabletop, eggs, the round heads and the barrel-shaped bodies of the gluttons, the pig and the cactus consisting of six disks and nothing more (the classic formula, so to speak, of this object). Another collection of such forms is the plundered shop in the print *The Peddler Robbed by Apes*. But they are present in hardly fewer number in many other pictures.

2

To facilitate the disintegration of figures, the individual parts out of which they are composed must be separated from each other as clearly as possible. This leads to a preference for objects that are, by their very nature, piecemeal and patchwork and that tend to fragment. Thus the clothes of the peasants are not chosen with a uniform taste but are thrown together by chance, just as the "motley" costumes of *The Battle Between Carnival and Lent* are improvised out of everything imaginable. The dappled torsos of the horses and cows fall by themselves into such patches. In the visions of madness (and dreams), we see how heterogeneously composed, fragmented creations — "condensations," to use the specialized term — come together and then dissolve, as in *Dulle Griet* (Mad Meg).

Alternatively, positions and movements of the individual bodies are sought that show the separation and independence of the limbs: the prisoners' feet separated from their bodies by the stocks in *Allegory of Hope*; the awkward movements of the dancing peasants in *Peasant Kermis*, which have been criticized as "poorly drawn"; and the contortions of epileptics. Only the legs remain of the figure who falls into the barrel in *Allegory of Gluttony*, only the upper body of the one who falls through the ice in *Skaters in Front of Saint George's Gate*. They all appear mutilated, and the cripples in fact are.

In its intentions, this disintegration of form corresponds in the real world to the process of destruction. In Bruegel's pictures, the

330

motifs in which forms are broken, shattered, fragmented, or torn are countless: cracked eggshells and splintered tree trunks, burst sacks in *Elck* (Everyman), splintered strongboxes and smashed chests in *The Battle of the Money Chests (and Savings Pots)*, the breach of the fence in *The Parable of the Good Shepherd*, the splitting open of bodies and the self-mutilation of the demons in *The Fall of the Magician*. Related to this is the motif of ransacking in *Elck* and, in a way that will only be completely intelligible later, the view into the bowels of things, be they human or animal viscera, bags or chests, or the body of *The Tower of Babel*.

3

Figures are completely closed off from each other and from the space that surrounds and connects them. Their separation in outline is the visual equivalent of spiritual "detachment" and isolation. The guests of *Peasant Wedding Feast* remain mute and numb, unable to communicate their feelings; hardly any show emotional contact with the others. They behave almost as if in accordance with an atomistic theory of society. In the bustle of *Children's Games*, each child plays alone. The most magnificent expression of a character who is completely shut off from the surrounding world occurs in the visionary *Beekeepers* (figure 7.2). The superficial subject of the picture — which perhaps relates to the larger theme of the seasons, like so many of Bruegel's works — is turned into a profoundly pessimistic allegory of the nature of mankind. These faceless men are the counterpart to another grand portrayal of the "faceless" to whom the outside world is closed off: *The Parable of the Blind*.

In *The Blind Leading the Blind* (figure 7.3), there is only an external connection between isolated bodies. As in *Children's Games*, they stick to each other like "burrs." They move as if mechanically linked, "blindly" chained.

331

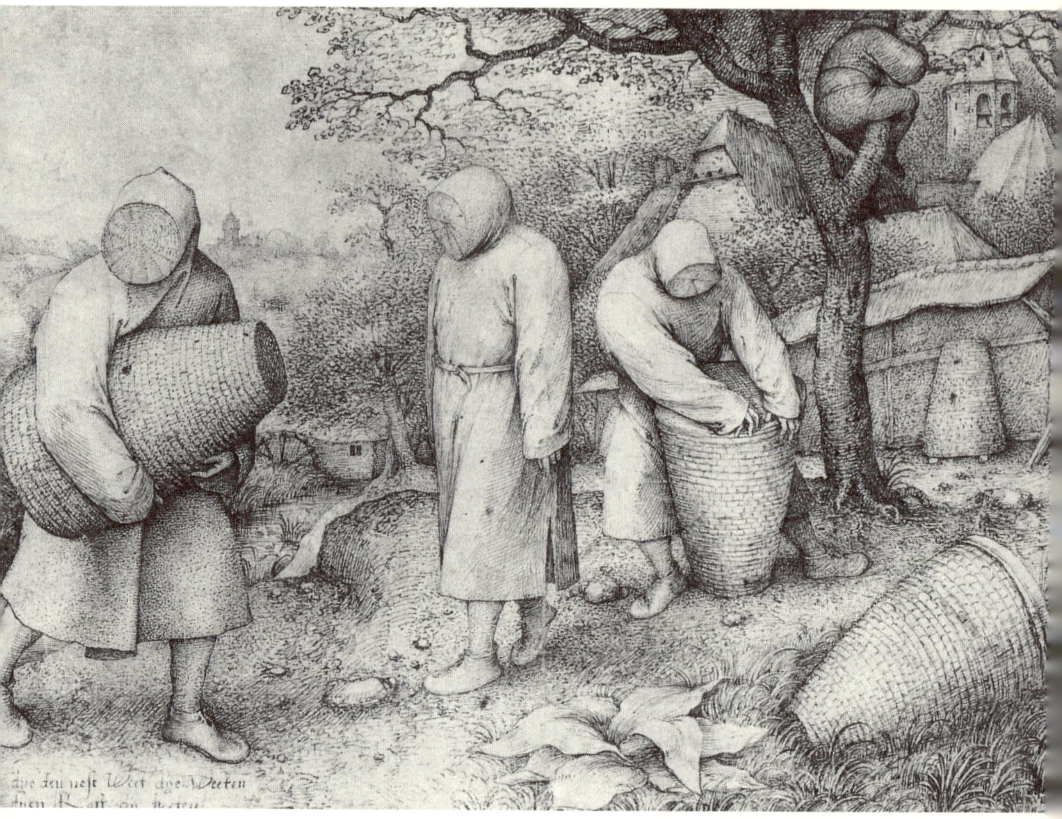

Figure 7.2. Pieter Bruegel, *The Beekeepers*, Staatliche Museen Preussischer Kulturbesitz, KdZ 2713 (© Kupferstichkabinett — Sammlung der Zeichnungen und Druckgraphik, Berlin).

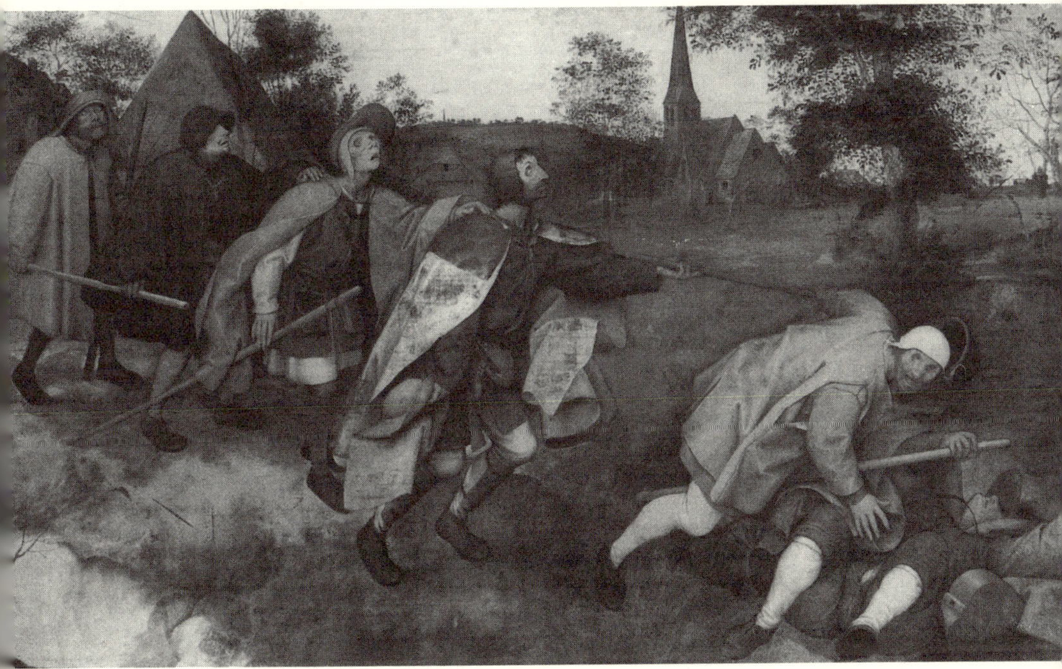

Figure 7.3. Pieter Bruegel, *The Blind Leading the Blind*, Museo Nazionale
Capodimonte, Naples.

4

Bruegel's *macchia* consists of a multitude of similarly isolated patches. This predestines his form to the depiction of the "mass" —be it a mass of piled-up things, as in the little shop in *Elck*, or a mass in the sociological sense. This latter appears in a singular way: as the sum total of individual, unconnected "elements" that are governed by blind powers. This is the favorite theme of nearly every picture of Bruegel's containing small figures: the constructed masses of *The Battle Between Carnival and Lent* and *Children's Games*, the fantastic dying mass in *The Triumph of Death*, the mass murder in *Massacre of the Innocents*, the military mass in *The Conversion of Saint Paul* and *The Suicide of Saul*, the mass phenomenon of the tumult in *Christ Carrying the Cross*, and the battle of all against all in the mass drunkenness of *The Feast of Saint Martin*.

5

The mass of color patches is unordered and seems thrown together. Furthermore, the color patches seem to engage in a random sort of movement; they seem to swim around in all different directions. In the material world, this corresponds to the disorder of bodies and things that can be intensified into the state of "tumult," of "commotion," and finally of fully senseless *chaos*; so too does the disorderly and chaotic form of movement. Both are intimately related to the phenomenon of the mass.

Chaotic motion develops wherever the movement of individuals in a multitude is not determined by a common, shared purpose, where instead individuals proceed following their own instincts, seemingly unconcerned with others. Many of Bruegel's pictures exhibit something like the Brownian motion of particles, for instance *The Battle Between Carnival and Lent* and *Children's Games*. Now a form can be imposed on this disorderly, decom-

334

posing movement by forces intervening from outside; the movement can be steered in a given direction. That could be called guided chaos. Thus the procession in *Christ Carrying the Cross* moves toward its goal in an elliptical curve shown by the red coats of the horsemen who form the train, while all around this "red thread" the greatest pandemonium develops. And thus the chaos of the mass brawl over the wine in *The Feast of Saint Martin* converges "of its own accord" into a strict Italianate conical composition.

On the other hand, disorderly movement is magnified into *senselessness* where there is no direction in the action of the mass's individual parts: *The Feast of Fools* and above all the senseless doings of the animals in *The Peddler Robbed by Apes* are ideal objects for this *macchia*. The end result of such activity is the state of chaos, the "jumble" of *Elck*.

This character of senseless accumulation and chaotic upheaval appears, taken to its extreme, in those visions of madness where every sense of coherence breaks down, where things and their meanings are taken apart and destroyed, where they permeate each other and swim around like undigested material: the absolute chaos of *Dulle Griet*. What has become representable in this picture, thanks to Bruegel's characteristic *macchia*, is not madness and its manners but the very structure of a mad world — something that other forms of modern painting could not capture even approximately.[8] Only in the most recent art, in the work of the expressionists and in particular of the surrealists, do similar possibilities exist.

1 to 5

Bruegel's *macchia* strikes a certain expressive register — Imbriani would speak of "feelings" — that resonates only in specific objects and specific subject matter. This "register," or set of expressive

335

values, or, to use the name suggested by Johannes von Allesch, these "intentions," would encompass the following categories: the clumsy, dull, unarticulated, and primitive; the fragmentary, pieced together, and disintegrating; the self-contained, isolated, and atomistic; the mass confusion, upheaval, and chaos. These "characters" form a sort of bridge between the bare *macchia* and certain subjects that combine with the *macchia* to form a unity that can be separated only artificially. And because Bruegel's *macchia* emerges, as Imbriani says, from a unified vision, the manifest subjects "summoned" by the *macchia* fuse together into a strong intellectual unity. Of course, this is not evident at first glance. What could be the common denominator of the preferred motifs that we have identified — peasants, children, the deformed (cripples, the blind, epileptics, fools), the mass, apes, and madness?[9] They are all manifestations of life in which the purely human borders on other, "lower" states that threaten, dull, distort, or ape its substance. Primitives — a hollow form of human; the mass — more raw and primitive than the individual man; the deformed — only half human; children — not yet completely human; the insane — no longer human. These are liminal states of humanity in which and through which the nature of man is cast into doubt. And they are the very subjects — I mention this only because it illuminates from yet another angle the inner unity of these areas — to which modern anthropology has turned its attention in recent times, as if it were possible to grasp the nature of humanity precisely in these liminal states, states in which man enters into other realms. (One thinks of studies of the psychology of primitives, children, the mentally ill, the crowd, apes, and the intoxicated.)

6

In Bruegel's work, the deformation we have considered thus far affects exclusively the human world. To this the world of nature is in every regard opposed.

Appropriate for the receding background against which the medley of patches stands out, therefore, are objects whose forms are exactly the opposite of those we have discussed, forms that are the least closed and that are most completely dissolved into the surrounding space. Thus, for example, vegetation of a kind that lies as far as possible from the compactness of the figurative is preferred: not the patchy crowns of thickly foliated trees but a defoliated landscape or a "haze" of leafless branches. In the rare instances where closed forms do appear — the cypresses in *The Conversion of Saint Paul* — they are placed at the edges and rendered light and airy by their shading.

7

The ideal here would be for no part to exist independently, for the form of every part only to be intelligible from the state of the whole: a dynamic and organic continuum instead of an atomistic and mechanical structure. The closest approximation of this ideal is perhaps *The Magpie on the Gallows*. The twisting of the trees and even the uprights of the gallows can only be discerned in the streaming movement of the whole, which, in turn, is only visible in the individual trees, just as the water's current can only be seen in the grass and algae that it sets into motion. Even the few individual figures that remain here join in this primary current that suffuses space and nature alike: the dancing peasants turn like leaves in the wind. (In this picture, the dualism of the pictorial elements is almost completely resolved, which I will have more to say about presently.)

6 and 7

In opposition to the human world, which resists the viewer's empathy and turns him away bewildered and disturbed, nature is

337

open to empathy, to a sort of dynamic sympathy that has become foreign to us. Karl Tolnai rightly emphasizes that the principle fusing together all of nature into an inner unity is not air — which is merely an external medium — but the embodiment of all the forces visibly holding sway.

8

The dualistic division of the pictures into figurative patches and spatial ground requires that both components be sundered from each other as sharply as possible and that no connection between them be allowed. Such a connection is created primarily by shadow or chiaroscuro, and then by aerial perspective as the coloristic fusion of things in space. For this reason, aerial perspective affects the figures in Bruegel's pictures conspicuously seldom, although it does prevail in the natural realm. And in Bruegel's pictures, almost without exception, shadow is eliminated in ways that are either realistically explained or unexplained and unconvincing. (The low level of illumination also explains, in turn, the scant modeling of figures through color, shadow, and light, in other words, their patch-like quality.) The shadow is *plausibly* absent in the case of natural illumination provided by an overcast sky, in the diffuse light of semi-illumination. What appears as the indeterminate, shadowless twilight of imaginary spaces in the early engravings is given a positive turn in the paintings: the gray sky of *Children's Games* and *The Battle Between Carnival and Lent*, the overcast sky of *Christ Carrying the Cross* and *Return of the Herd*, the misty sky of *Massacre of the Innocents* and *Hunters in the Snow*. By contrast, the shadow is *implausibly* absent in, for example, the engraving *Summer*. Although the sun stands high in the sky, veiled only lightly by haze, the reapers cast weak, unconvincing shadows. In all of Bruegel's work, the sunlight is most direct in *The Fall of Icarus*.

338

IV

Multa pinxit hic Brugelius quae pingi non possunt.
— Abraham Ortelius
For verses are not, as people think, feelings — but experiences.
— Rainer Maria Rilke

That these pictorial qualities, with all their seeming "deficiencies," were *consciously* cultivated by Bruegel is proven by the fact that the motifs that follow naturally from them are consistent and coherently related to each other. But the question with which the second section ended — "What is the meaning of this extraordinary process of disintegration?" — is not yet answered. Only the answer to this question can allow us to understand why Bruegel preferred precisely these subjects.

The answer, or rather the beginnings of an answer, lies in the description of the total experience that these pictures convey, contained there just as the expressive content of Bruegel's motifs is contained in the description of the *macchia*. In the curious process that takes place as one views these pictures, the logic of entire portions of a picture breaks down and the objects represented seem strange, as does the entire picture. For the viewer, this process is accompanied by the experiences of shock and disturbance, in sensitive viewers even of anxiety and something approaching fear.

And with that, the decisive word can be spoken, the word that holds the key to an understanding of both Bruegel's characteristic *macchia* and his characteristic motifs and that encompasses them both from yet another perspective. The word is *estrangement*.[10]

This experience is familiar to everyone as a timeless possibility of perception. It can be induced by certain psychological conditions.[11] Then even familiar words suddenly lose their clear and stable meaning; they become empty and sound as if they belong to a foreign language. To the extent that this occurs, their purely sensuous tone, devoid of meaning, becomes more intense; it seems that one has never heard them before. The same experience can occur with gestures, facial expressions, movements, and so on. Movement frozen in a snapshot, for example, can take on this estranged, incomprehensible character. It must, however, be caught or arrested: we always experience this process of becoming strange as something that takes place in the object that captures it. It must not be confused with the subjective experiences that accompany it in the person who witnesses this transformation.

Bruegel's painted oeuvre begins with this fundamental phenomenon of an estranged world. In his first typical work, *Netherlandish Proverbs* (figure 7.1), it is the world of language that is "turned into image" and thus presents itself as curiously estranged. This painted image is the visualization of the boundless world of fantasy hidden in the "imagery" of language. Who still thinks about the images embodied in proverbs? Language perpetually surrounds us with a world of images that is no less scurrilous, absurd, insane, uncanny, and comical than the fable world of, say, the series *The Seven Deadly Sins*, which owes its existence to the pictorial fantasy of the painter.

The Battle Between Carnival and Lent shows another of these estranged worlds, that of *masks*. There the familiar shape of man is transformed into a bizarre, strange and demonic, ridiculous, and at the same time terrifying form.[12]

The mask — this "most profound deception" that disguises a form and changes its meaning — is, as it were, the essence of this process of estrangement concretized as a device, a process that can take hold of any object or event whatsoever. Even without the aid of the device of disguise, everyday things can be made to appear no less fantastic and bizarre, suspicious and unfathomable than the masked actors representing "Carnival." Such an active attitude consists in shedding all knowledge of the usual and self-evident sense of the course of everyday life, acting as if one knew nothing of the meaning and function of persons and things — an artificial and abstract attitude. Then the everyday world discloses its hitherto concealed fantastic qualities.[13] The first and classic product of this estranged vision turned onto the everyday is *Children's Games*. If one disregards what children's games are, and what they mean for us and for children, then what children do when engaged in these games is as absurd, uncanny, and suspicious as the behavior of a band of lunatics or other beings incomprehensible to us. There are monsters with ten legs and three heads. The blindfolded boy looking for a pot with a staff is reminiscent of an executioner, the stilt walker of a cripple, the contortions produced by the games of epileptic seizures, the strange toys of magical apparatuses — the whole scene is one of "indescribable mania." The extraordinary example of the estrangement of the everyday is, however, the deeply uncanny picture *The Beekeepers* (figure 7.2).

This aura of estrangement has a unique effect where it lays hold of a story, in particular a religious one. There the estrangement can be achieved simply by looking at a scene as if it were an everyday event, as if one knew nothing of its religious significance. Thus one looks at *Christ Carrying the Cross*, for example, as if one did not know which particular carrying of a cross is depicted. Bruegel's picture shows, so to speak, the sociological aspect of public martyrdom as it could happen at any time, even in the present: the representatives of judicial authority, the order of the place of execution, the gaping crowd, here and there children and barking dogs, and somewhere in the throng, hardly visible, the delinquents. Only subsequently does one see the fragmented scene seemingly patched into the foreground showing the holy personages in the traditional form of Passion pictures from the previous century. Only through this sort of added caption is the picture revealed as the incomparable martyrdom of Christ and not the martyrdom of any ordinary mortal.

If one considers estranged vision the central phenomenon of the art of Bruegel, then the relation of this to the painter's favorite subject matter is immediately visible. The worlds of primitives, children, the blind and cripples, the crowd, madness, and apes are precisely those liminal worlds "in which the nature of man becomes dubious, and dubious precisely because it is alien." Yet at the same time, a multitude of individual motifs that typically appear in Bruegel's work finds a simple explanation. One can see them all as means of evoking this aspect of estrangement in the viewer. Let me specify some of these "means."

The human figure becomes alien, is viewed anew and with suspicion, when it is malformed or disfigured. Therefore, exaggeratedly fat and thin, crippled or contorted bodies are an eternal motif in the pictures of Bruegel. Bodies that are not deformed seem strange as a result of unusual situations, as an effect of "disguising," or when viewed from behind. Hence the countless repetitions of this motif: there are pictures by Bruegel that consist almost entirely of figures seen from behind. In his drawings *naer het leven* (from the life), he studied quite precisely the singular way forms can lose their meaning.[14] The reduction of expression in the heads serves the same purpose. The face and its expression form an emotional bridge between us and other men and prevent us from seeing others merely "from the outside," like objects.

The faces of foreign races whose expressions one does not understand have the uncanny effect of masks (which of course mask primarily the face). In Bruegel's work, either faces are expressionless, like the peasants' dull, wooden faces, or expressions are indeterminate and indifferent, like those of the children, expressions that are impossible to differentiate and seemingly empty.

Everything that can bear expression is minimized, above all the eyes.[15] The faces betray nothing of what goes on behind them; they are mute. This phenomenon reaches its extreme in the rigid faces of the blind men, which almost seem to be natural masks; in the "faceless" figures whose countenances are hidden beneath hoods, helmets and protective masks or covered by things they carry (the bag carrier in *Allegory of Prudence*, the beggar pulling a smock over his head in *Allegory of Charity*); and in the oft-repeated, intentionally "misdrawn" motif of the basket carried on the head, a basket that seems to grow atop the neck in place of the head. Of eleven figures in the foreground of the engraving *Summer*, only two faces can be seen, and both are hardly more expressive than a potato.

With the human body, the process of estrangement often goes through many stages. First inhuman things are invoked: animals, plants, inanimate objects such as puppets or empty clothes. The cowering girls in *Children's Games* look like water lilies, the subjects of *The Cripples* like a family of poisonous mushrooms (Max Dvořák), the subjects of *The Beekeepers* like wandering tree stumps, hair like the fringes of the hats beneath which it wells forth (Tolnai). It would be easy to continue with such examples. In the end, however, the human form is deprived of this metaphorical meaning, and it appears as simply a structure of colored patches. What is man, when one looks at him "from without"? A few colored planes with a bizarre contour. As this process continues, however, colors and forms, now emancipated from the sense they once bore, assume an unknown, independent life, exactly as the word emptied of its meaning strikes a new and strangely enchanting chord.

The same phenomenon of estrangement can occur in the realm of human movement. Here the experience occurs when the motion is, by its very nature, distorted and abnormal — the motor equivalent of malformation. Epileptics writhe in pain the way branches of a tree clutch at the sky; cripples crawl like snails. The unpracticed, unsteady movements of ice-skaters, the reeling of drunks, the groping and staggering of blind men, the contortions of a juggler on the line, the mechanical trotting of animals are just such "strange" movements. This experience can be artificially induced by the deliberate isolation of a single phase of movement from those preceding and following in the completed action that forms its natural context (this is the experience of the snapshot). The motions seem strange, "mechanical," "like those of automatons."[16]

The inanimate and normally inexpressive things of the human sphere — utensils, houses, ships — gain vitality to the same degree that vitality is drained from things that are usually alive.[17] This process of reversal occurs of its own accord when one is confronted with obscure objects, as in the lair of *The Alchemist*. It can also be artificially induced by a "simile," as, for example, in *Allegory of Gluttony*, where the limp bagpipe in the fork of a branch is suggestively compared to the plucked chicken hanging nearby, thus when a "lifeless" object looks like a killed creature. (I would call this a *metaphoric situation*.) There are various levels of this reciprocal process. It reaches its high point when lifeless things, usually expressionless, acquire a face and gaze back at the viewer. (This is a primitive experience and an experience of children.) This is precisely the way to make everyday objects look strange and unusual. In almost every early picture by Bruegel, the physiognomy of an inanimate object is carried to an extreme. Hence the anthropomorphic rocks at the right edge of *The Suicide of Saul*, the vacantly staring eye sockets of the bleached horse's skull in *Christ Carrying the Cross*, the peacock feather's malicious gaze in *Peasant Wedding Feast*, the wolfishly staring bunghole of one of the casks in *Massacre of the Innocents*. In *Children's Games*, however, the use of this motif reaches its apogee. Here four caps —

three black and one red—that have fallen to the ground from the heads that wore them form the eyes, nose, and mouth of a grimacing face that "looks at" the viewer and that, once one has seen it, far exceeds the blank masks of the children in the intensity of its expression. It would be quite mistaken to attribute an anecdotal meaning to this motif—seeing the face, for example, as laughing at the viewer. This would be false simply because the expression of the face, as ever with Bruegel, is utterly indeterminate. Instead, the motif represents the classic formula of the two fundamental tendencies in Bruegel's works: the tendency of the figurative to disintegrate, and the tendency of inanimate objects to make faces. Like the cakes on the roof in *Netherlandish Proverbs*, this motif is a visible clue to a deeper understanding of the picture.

In principle, the process of estrangement should not stop when it comes to nature. The most recent contemporary painting gives numerous examples of how nature can appear alien, uncanny, mysterious, and distorted. In places, one can see something similar in Bruegel's work.[18] In general, however, nature does not participate in the estrangement of the figurative; it is instead the background against which this process takes place. (The most superficial expression of this is that nothing in nature is "misdrawn," so that one could think that Bruegel was a brilliant landscape artist but a clumsy painter of figures.) Here, in the landscape, empathy is not rebuffed. Nature does not confront the viewer as something alien; even where it is imposing and violent, threatening and frightening, it seems still familiar and comfortable. Only against the foil of Bruegel's distorted conception of man can one understand the singularity of his conception of nature: the strange fusion of spatial distance and emotional proximity, of global landscape and *paysage intime*. The objects, too, in typical pictures by Bruegel reveal the same rupture that was discovered by a purely formal approach that disregarded their representational aspect: the empathic and closely observed world of nature is home to the alien and skeptically regarded human realm, which has now become dubious and suspect.

Although this estrangement affects only one of the two representational components into which the picture "disintegrates," it nonetheless, in yet another curious way, takes hold of the picture *as such*. With Bruegel's *macchia*, it is almost as if there were a thin sheet of ice between picture and beholder.[19] The picture itself, behaving in a way so singularly different from others, seeming to dissolve and decompose before our eyes, strikes the viewer who sees this process as bizarre and alien. Contemplating the actors in the scene depicted raises the question: "What is man, anyway?" Contemplating the picture itself then raises another question: "What is a picture?" And one could answer: the picture itself is wearing a mask.[20] The superficial purpose of this is to entertain the naive viewer; this "aspect" of the pictures cannot be denied. But behind the mask is hidden a second face about which the first betrays nothing.

Pictures such as these demand a double audience. One audience is optimistic and naive and cannot see these "funny" objects "without laughing" (Karel van Mander). The other audience is pessimistic, aesthetic, capable of seeing through the mask, and yet still enjoys this penetrating vision. It can hardly be a coincidence that such an enigmatic character as the emperor Rudolf II was fond of collecting Bruegel's pictures. Both a simple visual pleasure and a subtle form of contemplation that can grasp, in vision, the problems of the human world have in Bruegel's work an infinite domain. At both levels, every examination of the pictures reveals details that are new and have never before been discovered.

V

The estrangement of the perceived world is a familiar phenomenon of the diseased psyche. "Things no longer look as they did before, they are changed, alien, they look as flat as reliefs": this is one example of the laments that Karl Jaspers cites as typical for this form of mental illness.[21] "Perceptions are so strange, peculiar, phantomlike...." Closely related to this are other pathological phenomena that are rooted in a loss of empathy. In these conditions, everything is dead, meaningless, and alien; one sees others only superficially, with no awareness of them as emotional beings(!).

Art provides a prominent example of the pictorial projection of such pathological experiences that in their extreme forms are accompanied by anxiety: the work of the Belgian painter James Ensor. This has been established beyond any doubt by Wilhelm Fraenger.[22] Significantly, the experience of estrangement and anxiety calls forth here the same motifs that I have identified in Bruegel: the depictions of masks, the mass, unstable space, and panic. With regard to the last two motifs, I would point to a work of Bruegel's — *The Parable of the Unfaithful Shepherd* — in which the feeling of panic (here of an individual) is strikingly conveyed by an incomparable depiction of vertiginously receding space. This same experience lies behind other motifs favored by Ensor: the *skeleton* (for Bruegel the main theme in *The Triumph of Death*) and particularly the *portrait squelettisé* (not incidentally a common mannerist subject), as well as obscenity, which also appears in many pictures by Bruegel. Though they might be determined in yet other ways, both of these motifs strike me as intimately connected with the way the entire sphere of man becomes alien and filled with misgiving. Here we can point to another passage from Fraenger's essay on Ensor, a passage that describes this fundamental fact of estrangement in a way that could be applied verbatim to Bruegel: "Suddenly, from behind the accustomed human faces, bestial features emerge grotesquely; their manners and movements seem depersonalized, like those of automatons; everything about them seems unusual and suspicious."

Ensor's utterly different linear and painterly system — his different *macchia* — colors these motives in another direction (toward the "morbid," which is absent from Bruegel), one that could be traced through the entire fin de siècle. But this does not diminish the relation to similar motifs in Bruegel.

Nonetheless, there are no grounds for assuming any pathology behind Bruegel's production, as one can in the case of Ensor.[23] It is not as if Ensor depicted what really seemed to him a transformed world, while Bruegel's transformation was only fictional. For even "the mentally ill do not consider the world to be truly transformed; for them it is only *as if* everything were different" (Jaspers). Perhaps the difference is simply that pictures by Bruegel are called into being by an act of will, developing and unfolding as one possible vision of mankind, while the vision of Ensor comes unsummoned and inescapable, possessing him.[24] This could be established on the basis of details of artistic choice, but it can be seen clearly enough in the fact that opposed to his "night vision," Bruegel developed a completely different "daytime vision," whose role is filled by "nature." It can furthermore be shown in the way the darker view seems to be formed experimentally and is ultimately resolved and vanquished in a reconciliation of the two pictorial realms. (More on this presently.)

VI

Before Bruegel's time, there was a "style" in which a large number of the phenomena one finds in his work can be observed. It is that tendency of northern art that, to characterize it at first quite superficially, seems to stiffen the "soft style" of the early fifteenth century and that is brought to its extreme in the work of Konrad

Witz and related artists (for example, the master of the so-called Znaimer Altar in the Österreichische Galerie in the Belvedere in Vienna). One can say at the outset that all the symptoms of this rigid "style" can be explained by one central fact. This art is the first since the beginning of the Middle Ages to observe the visible world from a strictly external and only external point of view, purely as a matter of *appearance* and seemingly ignorant of any distinctions but the visible.[25] Now widely considered particularly "realistic," this manner of seeing and representing is completely opposed to the natural way of seeing, which does not shrink from intimacy with the things seen. Everyone can experience what tremendous effort it takes when drawing from life to abandon this natural kind of seeing and shift into that distanced, "cold" mode of observation that yields the "correct" pictorial projection of things, their estranged contour and form.[26]

Almost without exception, all phenomena of this "style," which I shall enumerate from the account provided by Bruno Fürst, can be traced back to this basic approach.[27]

Because the distinction between dead and alive simply does not exist for this type of vision that perceives nothing but the pure, visible form, "living things are drained of their reality and soul; all *things* are set into an intermediary world between the living and the dead. Related to this are two processes: on the one hand, expressions are neutralized and people are made anonymous" — the same as with Bruegel — "on the other, lifeless things are seen as important, are *made* important, and everything inorganic is given a life and vitality of its own. This sense of having a 'mask' is one of the principal expressive qualities of this form of art" — indeed, for this kind of attention takes visible form to be a sort of mask of internal essences. Thus, "from an emphasis on living souls," which for this kind of attention cannot be directly seen, only inferred or induced, "the emphasis is now on rendering visible the 'soulless' mechanics of the phenomenal world." "People cling to each other like burrs" — this, too, is a very good characterization of Bruegel's work. "It is like the mechanical meshing of gears in a machine relying on the most basic physics." And since one cannot see the inner dynamics of things and beings "from the outside," a disintegration into pieces appears as a sort of by-product of this "vision." (Relevant here is also the "citation" of outdated historical forms, which appear "historical" precisely because of one's distance from them. This is as characteristic for the period around 1440 as it is for Bruegel — recall the Passion group in *Christ Carrying the Cross* — and mannerism generally.)

A large number of innovations are introduced to achieve this effect, means identical to those used by Bruegel as vehicles of estrangement. "The accumulation of figures seen from behind, or figures seen only in quarter profile, is striking," writes Fürst — something that one understands as a typical means of estrangement after our study of Bruegel. "Man as a wandering suit of armor," whose closed visor makes the head seem to disappear — on the one hand, the warrior Sabothai by Konrad Witz, on the other, the beekeepers. Fürst writes of "the extreme accentuation of tools and equipment" and also of the motif of "grasping the shoulder of one's neighbor" as a way of establishing contact "to prevent a break in the chain" — the very same motif that will see its most magnificent representation in Bruegel's *Blind Leading the Blind* (figure 7.3).

Despite these many similarities, however, the art of Bruegel cannot simply be derived from the "rigid style," not even his conception of the human figure. For in this style, estrangement is, to a certain extent, only a concomitant to the discovery of the cold, remote view from the outside. Things have visual qualities only; value judgments or inferences about them do not enter into the depiction. With Bruegel, on the other hand, the experience of estrangement stands at the center of his conception of the human world and is given an emotional color. His people look uncanny and strange because, in their essence, *they themselves* are problematic hybrids and alien (if perhaps not downright "bad") creatures. The early development of this vision is to be found not in the style of 1440 but in the work of Hieronymus Bosch.[28]

VII

The idea that the roots of Bruegel's art are to be found in Bosch is a venerable one. Already in 1566, Lodovico Guicciardini wrote of Bruegel as "the second Bosch." This applies, of course, only to certain elements of his pictures — the human realm — but it is true in a deeper sense than has hitherto been assumed. If one sees estranged vision as a central phenomenon of Bruegel's art, then it is this very vision — and not only the themes of specific pictures by Bruegel — that is anticipated in the diabolical and ghostly world of Bosch. Bruegel's estranged vision is the secularization of Bosch's "pan-diabolism"; it is the discovery of Bosch's nightmare vision in the everyday world. Bruegel's *Seven Deadly Sins* are the connecting link in this process of secularization. Here all sorts of "monstrosities of the fantasy" are depicted, but they are invented and therefore, for all their ghostliness, harmless. In the pictures of Bosch, such things are not imagined but are instead deeply believed, "bloody" truth. The hell painted by Bosch is a visible religious reality, and the whole horror of that reality survives its transplantation into our world. The *Seven Deadly Sins* by Bruegel, on the other hand, are invented allegories, and their transplantation into the everyday has to a certain degree only a heuristic value: to teach one to see this world anew and through the categories of the bizarre, the grotesque, and the fantastical. One can follow this secularization process quite concretely in certain motifs, for example that of the mutilated human body. In Bosch's

351

vision of hell, it expresses the agony of the damned; in Bruegel's drawings of the *Seven Deadly Sins*, it returns as a monstrous fantasy laden with allegorical meaning; it is then "found" in the depiction of the everyday cripples; and finally it leads quite innocently to the observation that one can always find mutilation when one sees the world with alien eyes.[29]

Bruegel could therefore appropriate a part of the middle of Bosch's compositions, transforming it accordingly. Tolnai characterizes many of Bosch's figures as "light, hollow, flat shapes that are smoothed onto the painted surface like colorful shading or transfer pictures"; he speaks of the "unwrinkled smoothness of their finish" and the "thin fiction of their masks."[30] This description could apply to Bruegel's depiction of figures, with the exception of the phantomlike quality Tolnai identifies in Bosch. For Bruegel's figures are certainly not thin fictions: their reality, tangibility, and compactness are emphasized by all means available, although they, too, often have "something dead and hollow" about them. Bosch's archaizing manner of representation — already archaic, incidentally, at the time — is appropriated as a vehicle of conveying the experience of estrangement.

It has long been recognized that Bosch lived on in one side of Bruegel's art; Bruegel began, of course, as a draftsman of works à la Bosch. What has not been recognized, however, is precisely what Bruegel took from Bosch: the experience of an estranged world. In Bosch, the experience of estrangement is merely an echo on the periphery of hell; like the ghostly, the spectral, the sadistic, the obscene, the automatic, and so on, it is part of the infernal agony.[31] But beginning with his paintings, Bruegel draws this into the center of our field of vision; it becomes, as I have said, a sort of visual "heuristic hypothesis" in which the familiar world is viewed with cold interest.

The second great difference between Bosch and Bruegel is

that, for the latter, nature is not involved in the process of estrangement. (The few pictures for which this does not hold, such as *The Triumph of Death* and *Dulle Griet*, are also closest to Bosch thematically; it is significant that their attribution has wavered between Bosch and Bruegel.) This creates a rupture in Bruegel's pictures, one that runs through them at the level of meaning as well as at the level of form.

Pictorial form such as this, discordant and pieced together from elements of two different kinds, was only possible with the advent of mannerism.

VIII

The concept of mannerism, Wilhelm Pinder has written, is still an immature one. But among other characteristics, two have already emerged as essential: discordance and estrangement.

According to Max Dvořák's far-reaching analysis, one fundamental fact of mannerism in the visual arts is "the possibility of choosing varying levels of reality" for the various parts of a picture. The discordance of Bruegel's pictures is a function of this possibility; they have as little to do with the rigid style as does the work of Bosch. It is the principle of the "com-position" of a pictorial whole out of parts of very different substance, the same principle of piecing together evident in the work of Jacopo da Pontormo or in the Palazzo Zuccari.

Pinder considers a "rigidified atmosphere" the "first prerequisite" of mannerism; for him, too, mannerism implies "inner tensions." A rigid or petrified atmosphere: this is clearly identical with, or similar to, what I have called here "estranged vision." Thus it produces an appearance similar to that which we observed as the result or means of estrangement for Bruegel. There we find, according to Pinder, "the contour immobilized, the figure made passive"; "living beings are covered in an inflexible armor";

353

"garments are rigid"; "a shell instead of a body, a mask instead of a face"; "animals' hidden similarity to humans" — this last the reverse of men's hidden similarity to beasts in Bruegel. Furthermore, "mannerism *conceals*." "Here everything seems to be protective." Mannerism never directly represents or openly reveals; typically, it secretly betrays instead. The result of all this is a particular reaction on the part of the viewer and a peculiar emotion accompanying the pictures: the experience of distress and doubt. "Against his will, the careful viewer becomes an examiner, a depth psychologist." And his question is: "What is man, anyway?" This clearly presupposes "a tension between what is said and what is meant" — in other words, estrangement. Or, instead of "estrangement," in the sphere of the visual one could talk of the quality of being "masked." The mask is a conspicuous symbol of mannerism: it renders things alien; it makes their features turn rigid; it conceals the "real" behind something that does not belong to the organism; it arouses doubt, "mixed feelings," fear, and curiosity.

Yet our list of more or less peripheral manifestations, the visible signs of the central phenomenon of estrangement, is not thereby complete. According to Pinder, "a sort of decomposition of colors can occur," "a dissolution toward a cadaverous white." This can perhaps be interpreted as a situation in which pigment and the familiar sense of colors become strange. In Italian mannerism, where the human figure remains dominant, the equation of different spheres of existence that we identified behind the estranged quality of Bruegel's works can appear as an assimilation of the male to the female body; this is mannerism's hermaphroditism, its violation of nature. Or it can appear as a substitution of tactile qualities: bodies of flesh look like stone. Mannerism exhibits an exceptionally refined sense of the varieties of material, precisely because materials are experienced as alien, different, and resisting empathy. We can conclude this brief survey of the typical "register" of mannerism, interpreted in light of common origins, with a number of rubrics: "allegory"; the historical and exotic as alien, curious; the erotic (the opposite sex as alien); the obscene as that which is hidden and to be revealed; the view into the viscera; alien idols; a foreign god; and death, the alien par excellence.

Perhaps one can see a connection between the two characteristics of mannerism that are presented here in caricatured form, interpreting estrangement as the sundering of beholder from the world, on the one hand, and of beholder from the picture, on the other.

Yet despite the numerous qualities they share, Bruegel's estranged vision has no direct connection to mannerism. Mannerism's estrangement is, as Carl Linfert has subtly shown, above all a kind of *deadening*, while Bruegel's is, as we have seen, the secularization of the diabolical. Thus in complete contrast to Bruegel, mannerism is humorless. And then the material that is subject to estranged vision is different. For Bruegel, it is the whole gamut of everyday human life and especially the marginal activities of man, subjects that had been treated without any alienating intention in northern genre pictures long before him. In Italian mannerism (which has given the entire European phenomenon its name), the material that is transformed is essentially "classic art." "Mannerism works with forms that have already been formed," writes Pinder. More decisively, in Linfert's words, "Mannerism appears as the estrangement of the classical itself."

On the other hand, however, the piecing together of a complete picture out of elements of diverse realities is, as far as we know today, a mannerist innovation. Bruegel adopted it directly from Italian mannerism, which he had studied carefully (something that could be established in matters of detail).

Simplifying crudely, one could claim the following: Bruegel first learned the possibility of piecing an image together from several different levels of reality, and perhaps the principle of the masklike picture in general, from the study of mannerist art. His estranged vision of the human world has a separate source (Bosch) and is developed in a direction that only partially corresponds to Italian mannerism. His addition of the tension between nature and the human world is unique in the realm of art but has, in other areas of culture, historical precedents that I shall not address here. This tension creates the potential for a complete dissolution unknown in mannerist art.[32]

IX

Bruegel's pictures do not originate in a process whereby the meaningless *macchia* is first created and perfected in itself, a certain kind of pictorial content then being attracted as if by a magnet or, to put it differently, the available material then being sifted through to catch those that correspond to, that "explain" or "justify," the *macchia*. Such a process is possible only as a marginal phenomenon in "modern" painting, particularly since the nineteenth century (I know of cases where this is taught in art schools as a principle of "composition"). In formulating his theory, Imbriani had just such phenomena in mind. In general, however, the *macchia* and the preferred subjects are formed slowly in a reciprocal process, and the achievement of the artist consists in bringing about a complete harmony of these two spheres, that of "form" and that of "content."

In Bruegel's work, this process is extraordinarily clear. His characteristic *macchia*, which was the starting point of this investigation, developed through the cold fusion of two different pictorial genres that were previously separate in his oeuvre.

We know these two separate genres, which are riveted together after 1559, almost exclusively from drawings and engravings, which are, not incidentally, predominant in Bruegel's oeuvre up until the time of this synthesis. There are drawings in which nature is represented free from human presence; at most there are a few tiny decorative figures lost in the space of the picture. And there are other drawings in which an imaginary space is tightly packed with fabulous, imaginary creatures. Disregarding his specific interpretations, one finds this distinction clearly expressed by Tolnai.

In terms of "form," each group is clearly distinguished from the other and is to a certain extent antithetical down to its details. Tolnai has found an apt expression to characterize these "formal" differences. The pictorial form of the fantastic pictures (*Big Fish Eat the Little Fish*, *Ass in School*, *The Temptation of Saint Anthony*, *The Seven Deadly Sins*) develops according to the "unnatural, abstract constructional principle of assembling and enclosing heterogeneous things"; this patchwork fantasy is also operative in the invention of imaginary creatures and objects. "These places [the mythical kingdoms of the different vices] do not have a structure like that of our world [that is, nature]; they fall into elements." Senselessness reigns. Characteristic is "the equal and persistent urgency of all the elements" — thus, as we have seen above, the principle of the mass. All other traits that we have recognized as characteristic of one of the paintings' two components appear already in these early drawings: "Bruegel avoids contrasts of light and shadow." (What still appears here as the shadowlessness of an abstract fantasy space's mythical and indeterminate illumination becomes later, realistically "explained," the overcast sky.) "The forms of the paintings consist of unified, unbroken surfaces. As much as possible, spatial projection and recession, rising and falling are avoided on the surface. The roundness of forms is not concealed by shading around the edges, nor does this occur by

shadows burrowing into the depth of negative spaces." "The contour encloses the simple, round surfaces of the forms." "Thus the
outline seems simply cut out, while the clothing seems attached
as a shell enclosing the block-like body." Tolnai speaks very per-
ceptively of the "closed-in" block form and the "barrier" of the
contour.

In representations of the natural world in his drawn landscapes, Bruegel proceeds in a completely different way. "Fluffy
shapes [are] picked out of the ground by thin, hairlike lines, hooks,
and dots." As opposed to the assembly of heterogeneous things,
here the dynamically perceived unity of all natural things is re-
created. Tolnai's formulations are not so pregnant here, but they
suffice to make tangible the opposition between these two different pictorial realms. The two genres have completely different
historical precedents. Drawings of the first kind come from Bosch;
they represent a somewhat tamer Bosch, a Bosch with "comical"
accents. The landscapes have themselves two main precursors: on
the one side, the northern panoramic view (*Weltlandschaft*); on
the other, the intimate landscape as it appears in the background
of Venetian paintings.[33] (This is merely a preliminary conclusion
that remains to be investigated in depth.)

The first of the two genres assumes a particular importance.
For it constitutes, so to speak, the schema by which the everyday
human world is later conceived in the pictures after 1559 (and
similarly in the allegorical drawings *The Seven Virtues*, which run
parallel to these pictures). Seen through the lens of this schema,
the everyday is given entirely new dimensions: the bizarre, grotesque, scurrilous, and spectral. The painting *Netherlandish Proverbs* represents the transition; in a certain sense, it still depicts a
fabulous, imaginary world, as do the drawings *The Seven Deadly
Sins*.[34] I have already recounted how this schema discovers and
depicts at first the somewhat trivial vision of the masks and then,

ever more boldly, the fantastic vision of more general phenomena, a progression that leads from *Children's Games* to *The Beekeepers* (figure 7.2). Tolnai seems almost to have recognized this transition from the *creation* of the fantastic (in *The Seven Deadly Sins* of 1556 to 1557, following the example of Bosch) to the *observation* of the fantastic (in the *Virtues* series of 1558 to 1559), yet he was unable to grasp the significance of this insight.

At the same time as the discovery of the fantastic in everyday life (which is thereby alienated) and the development of various means by which to convey this experience to the viewer, the second fundamental tenet of Bruegel's pictures appears: the tension that we have examined above, the visual equivalent of the opposition between nature and non-nature, of the alien existence of the human world in nature. This tension is absent from *Netherlandish Proverbs* (figure 7.1), where, as in *The Seven Deadly Sins*, the landscape stage is still assembled out of separate scenes. The opposition between the homogeneous landscape stage and the fragmentary figures interspersed there is already clear in *The Battle Between Carnival and Lent* and is even more pronounced in *Children's Games*.

In these synthetically produced pictures, color appears in support of the new ideas. On the one hand, it accentuates the experience of estrangement; precisely how this happens would have to be investigated in detail. On the other hand, it intensifies the inner division of the pictures' construction by separating individual figures from the surrounding space, helping them fall into pieces and spin about. By giving the same hue to areas that belong to different figures — the same blue tone, for example, appearing in the torso of one figure, the arms of another, the legs of a third, and the garments of a fourth — the dismemberment of the figures is heightened in a way that can only be achieved by color. Thus prints and drawings are no longer capable of giving the same visual expression to these ideas as can painting. For this reason, the drawings and the prints made from them (*The Seven Virtues*, for example) decline in importance in comparison to the paintings. And a new, minor genre emerges next to the other two: the "small" landscape group of 1559–1562, in which the transfigured realm of nature, the counterpart to the estranged human world of the paintings, is studied.

The years 1558 and 1559 are truly decisive in Bruegel's development. This is when the important ideas come together forcefully, when his characteristic *macchia* emerges, and when he develops from a graphic artist who occasionally paints into a true painter.

Since this entire inquiry has been based on Bruegel's middle period, I need not discuss it in any more detail. What followed was yet another great change, this time less sudden than gradual. The gulf between the heterogeneous pictorial elements is not closed but smoothed over; the rupture heals. This transformation is documented above all in the magnificent pictures of the seasons. Formally, this smoothing over occurs because the unusual qualities that, with a unifying pictorial conception, would seem to be "errors" — the hard contours and the patchy, flat, shadowless figures — must to a certain extent be realistically *justified* or *explained*. In other words, Bruegel has sought out natural conditions, the accurate depiction of which would be in accordance with the principles governing his art. Such conditions can be seen, for example, in *Hunters in the Snow*. The background of snow is a "natural" way to make the figures appear flat, patchy, silhouetted, sharply delineated, and isolated both from each other and from the background; these qualities do not seem unusual or strange because they are grounded in everyday experience.[35] Another way of achieving this balance is similarly based on a natural experience, namely, the way figures farthest forward in a perceived space sometimes seem flatter than those farther back. *Return of the Herd*, for example, makes use of this observation.

Beyond formal matters, the rapprochement between the worlds of man and of nature corresponds to this new "realism." Even humans now appear as creatures of nature. A major example of this is again *Return of the Herd*. Here animals mediate between man and nature. The shepherds with their freckled, leathery skin and heavy movements are compared to the cattle they tend; the cattle in turn are compared to the landscape to which they belong. The backs of the cows "equal" the lines of the hills; their tails are hardly distinguished from the roots of the trees; their spotted skins are in harmony with the general dappled quality of autumn. The "visual metaphor," which we have already recognized as a vehicle of estrangement, leads here to a congruence among man, animal, and landscape.

Nevertheless, even though the torn halves are sewn together, the tear itself remains tangible in the picture: in the formal sphere as a hidden dissonance, in the objective sphere as the demotion of the human to the animal or vegetable. That lends this depiction of nature its great, incomparable melancholy. In the end, nature remains as devoid of human presence as it does in the drawings with which Bruegel began. In *The Magpie on the Gallows*, the tiny figures of the dancing peasants are merely "staffage," as in the early drawings.

Beside these, however, there are monumental human subjects with only a few large figures, foreshadowed in works by Bosch such as his *Parable of the Blind* and made heroic with the means of Italian art. Here, against the foil of a tranquil nature, we see the consummate depiction of the darker side of man: peasants (*Peasant Wedding Feast* and *Peasant Kermis*), *The Cripples* (a group picked out of the small-figure *Battle Between Carnival and Lent*), *The Beekeepers*, *The Parable of the Unfaithful Shepherd*. Thus we can again distinguish between roughly two types of pictures, and the path that Bruegel has followed can hardly be made clearer than by comparing each type with the corresponding pictures of the early years.

Only now can we speak of "heroes" in Bruegel's pictures. His "hero" is on the one hand nature, on the other man at the margin of humanity.

X

There is, to put it somewhat crudely, an "evolution" in Bruegel's art: a division into two types of formation (*Gestalten*), the same division or tension in the individual pictures, then the veiling and resolution of the tension. And, inseparable from the changes in the *macchia*, this evolution encompasses at the same time the story of the gradual development, maturation, and growth of Bruegel's artistic abilities.

This would be not an *art* historical study but an abstract reflection if we overlooked the fact that Bruegel's drawings of the first phase, before 1559, are utterly insignificant as works of art, however amusing they are in their richness of fantastic invention or however impressive in their strong feeling for nature. In retrospect, they are interesting as documents of a great talent that still had to find its own form, that still had to come into its own. There are no *great* works of art among Bruegel's early works.

Many pictures of the middle period — and now we can say, with no risk of misunderstanding, his "mannerist" period — are without doubt quite important. One can, however, say of them what Pinder has said of mannerism in general: they are barred from the final level of genius. In many of them, a pictorial equivalent is found for a very original view of the visual world; yet the means by which this experience of "estrangement" is conveyed to the viewer are too deliberate. One senses a "trick" — as one should.

Bruegel's extraordinary achievement as an artist is that he continued to perfect these means, namely, by making them simpler, so that in the end he could express his vision — and indeed, estrangement here is a *visual* experience — in a completely unaffected and natural way. The greatest achievements, achievements of absolute genius, occur in his last period of approximately 1565 to 1568, thus in the period when he overcomes mannerism (and elsewhere too the entry into or exit from mannerism marks achievements of greatest genius).[36] A consensus as to the pinnacles of his art is as attainable and as necessary as a consensus about the stylistic facts. They would have to include, from his cycle of the seasons, *Return of the Herd* and *Hunters in the Snow* and, from the monumental figural compositions, above all *The Blind Leading the Blind*, then *The Beekeepers* (the picture of the mute, faceless people), the *Cripples*, *Peasant Wedding Feast*, and probably *The Parable of the Unfaithful Shepherd*. The new, deeper understanding of these pictures has brought about a new and higher appraisal of Bruegel: Dvořák, Bruegel's "savior," compares him to Shakespeare and Michelangelo.

To show what in fact constitutes the artistic superiority of these last great pictures over the earlier works, one would have to start from the beginning, taking the analysis of Bruegel's art out of the sphere of generalities and into that of specifics. It seems to me that, among other factors, a harmonization of various "registers" throughout all aspects of the picture would prove itself one of the most significant. Using one example, I would like at least to suggest what I mean by this.

The intense effect of *Hunters in the Snow* seems to me to be the result of just such a bringing of different "voices" in the picture into a great harmony. One "voice" ringing through the whole picture in various ways is that of *rigidity* or *stiffness*. The outlines of the figures are already rigid; rigid too are the lines of the rigorously diagonal composition. The branches of the trees stand stiffly in the frost; man and animal are stiff with cold; the water of the ponds and streams stiffens into ice; the landscape itself is rigid with ice and snow. All movements look rigid against the white of the snow; and the bird in the air stands out as if frozen for a moment in flight. Related to this is a second "voice," that of *cold*. The color harmony of black, green-gray, and white is itself cold. The sharp and clearly delineated lines have a cold effect. Everywhere one sees the real cold of winter in which the people huddle. Added to this is the *mute* and the *silent*. There is no face that would speak to us: the hunters are contracted with cold, the dogs are silent, the crows sit mute, the snow muffles distant noises. The picture has not silenced the objects; the objects are themselves in reality so. Finally, there is the voice of the *muffled*. The figures are packed into their warm winter clothing; the houses and mountains capped and covered by the white masses of snow. Winter transforms the "face" of nature. Rigid, cold, silent, mute, muffled: these voices resound together; they converge into unison; they "describe" winter, and they "describe" death. Common to both winter and death is the experience of estrangement. But the death-like quality of winter, and the physical estrangement that accompanies it, is cathartic: it feels not terrifying but familiar, comfortable, intimate.

Here Bruegel's *macchia* succeeds in rendering features of winter visible in a way that no other *macchia* could. An impressionistic *macchia*, for example, could never allow the visualization of the "rigidity" of winter, for it does not recognize hard lines and silhouettes. Impressionism would prefer to depict winter's color and light, but this takes winter as a mere pretext and misses its "essence" completely. And a *macchia* that is not rooted in the experience of "estrangement" could never capture this quality in a season that can transfigure the landscape overnight like a mask. The vision of winter that makes such a profound impression in this picture is entirely conditioned by the fundamental characteristics of Bruegel's art: estrangement and its particular characteristic *macchia*. And "winter" is, in turn, an ideal, even predestined subject for this *macchia* — a *macchia* that was of course firmly established *before Hunters in the Snow*. This affinity is already signaled in *Massacre of the Innocents*, where the snow helps make the dappled medley of the scene plausible. But the complete coincidence of *macchia* and subject matter is only achieved in *Hunters in the Snow*; and this is why it is by far the greater work of art.

We can see something similar in other pictures, *Dulle Griet*, for example. And as a sort of cross-check, one could explore pictures such as *The Tower of Babel* to see why they have no deep impact.

Of course, such experiments serve only to indicate the artist's achievement; they are in no way evidence in themselves.

XI

To avoid confusion, I have ignored certain phenomena that would have to be considered if one wanted to extrapolate this short sketch into a proper theory of Bruegel's art. For until the fundamental fact addressed by this investigation is established, a consideration of these other phenomena would only cloud the issue.

Such matters would include a thorough consideration of Bruegel's colors. The few references above concern only the general function of color, not specific choices and their significance. This inquiry would have to be quite far-reaching, and therefore I prefer to omit it entirely.

One would have to investigate Bruegel's pictorial organization or "compositions" and, closely related to this, his choice of viewpoint and format. Bruegel prefers austere organizational schemata based on simple, nearly geometric forms: circles, ellipses, cones, diagonals, and especially fan shapes. These strong schemata yield various effects, depending on whether they are combined with the spotted chaos of the small-figure pictures, with the large, uninhabited landscapes, or with the monumental figures of the late depictions of human subjects. Applied to Bruegel's typical subject matter, the rigor of these compositions, familiar from Italian paintings, has a paradoxical, discordant effect: to Dvořák, the picture of the *Cripples* looked for this reason like a "*parody* of the Italianate pyramidal composition."[37] In its original context, this compositional schema usually had a static effect, but it is often strangely set into motion by Bruegel: the *Cripples* crawl centrifugally apart; the pyramid in *The Feast of Saint Martin* is thrown together out of individual bodies. In some pictures, this leads to space itself being set into motion: the space seems to rotate. Circular compositions are suited to this — a wonderful example is *The Land of Cockaigne* — and even better are the fan-shaped compositions. The result is an impression similar to the experience of looking out the window of a moving train, where the train seems to stand still and the landscape seems to rotate about a distant fulcrum; sensitive observers feel a mild vertigo. In other words, space becomes *unstable*; and one recalls how the experience of unstable space in Ensor is inseparable from the themes of the mass, the mask, and panic. And thus space assumes qualities that are, from the perspective of normal experience, *alien* and disquieting. The motif of rotating space is strongly suggested already in *Children's Games*; it returns in *Peasant Wedding Feast*, where the two men carrying serving boards form the tangents and the table the radius of an arc; and it is wonderfully joined to another fan motif formed by the rays of the sun in the print *Summer*. There is a compelling illusion of rotating space in the gripping image of spatial recession in *The Parable of the Unfaithful Shepherd*; it is similar in the apocryphal picture *The Peddler Robbed by Apes* and present in more moderate form in *The Blind Leading the Blind* (figure 7.3). Not coincidentally, the motif is always associated with subjects in which the experience of *danger* is central.

Finally, a third phenomenon would have to be considered. Any one specific picture — *Hunters in the Snow*, for example — can mean very different things, just as any represented object can have a variety of meanings. (For example, a body without a head can mean "chest," "beheaded," "headless," and other things as well.[38]) Even where real things of the outside world are shown in all their vividness, Bruegel's pictures, without exception, never mean to suggest specific individual objects. His pictures depict, for example, not an individual landscape that could be identified with a place-name but rather a type. To a certain extent, this is the exact opposite of what occurs in the Middle Ages, when a specific town might be referred to but can be characterized only generally, perhaps using the same pictorial schema that is also used to represent other towns. Bruegel paints not an autumn landscape but autumn itself; not children playing games but the games that children play; not men who are blind but the blind as a species of man.

For such an account, the history pictures assume a special significance; they are, in any case, unique. They appear as "timeless" events that are only secondarily, through the addition of details that "designate" a scene, characterized as a particular episode or case of something that could occur anywhere, at any time. *Christ Carrying the Cross*, *The Suicide of Saul*, *Massacre of the Innocents*, and *The Conversion of Saint Paul* are examples of such eternal possibilities, and the situation is only slightly different in *The Fall of Icarus*. With such an approach, a portrait cannot be made as a portrait. Unlike the figure beside him, Bruegel's self-portrait bears individual features, and thus, like the history paintings, it becomes a particular episode of a timeless event: the *Artist and Connoisseur*. (Here too we see a composite out of two levels of reality.) Even Bruegel's scenes of nature aspire to general validity; in other words, where a specific mountain or a specific town, castle, and such appears, it is the type or species that is seen, the epitome, say, of the castle.[39]

This subordination of images to general meanings often gives the pictures a peculiar hidden symbolic resonance. This is part and parcel of the principle of the masked picture.

A historical investigation into specific pictorial means — formats, uses of color, techniques, and so on — would contribute a great deal to an understanding of Bruegel's pictorial form. Such a task could build on the many existing observations, which could, of course, be augmented.

Many of the specific pictorial means used by Bruegel come, quite naturally, from the same sources out of which he developed his entire way of thinking and the *macchia* that corresponds to this. Thus Bruegel took not only the estranged vision from Bosch (eliminating, at the same time, the diabolical element) but also the figures' smooth planarity, which is intimately associated with this and which makes them seem so "hollow" and "dead." Bruegel also borrowed a multitude of specific inventions, though he seldom took them over literally. The list of Bruegel's mannerist borrowings remains to be compiled; Dvořák's general suggestion has not yet been followed here.

Some of Bruegel's pictorial means, however, are derived from sources that have little to do with his own "vision" in the deeper sense. For example, his late, horizontal-format paintings in which a very few monumental "genre" figures are shown against the background of a tranquil village landscape are foreshadowed in a striking way in the works of the so-called Brunswick Monogrammist. Yet this artist, whom Ludwig von Baldass first brought to our attention,[40] utterly lacks the profundity of Bruegel's estranged vision. The most important suggestion for an understanding of

Bruegel's pictorial means is perhaps Gustav Glück's remarks about the art of tapestry.[41] Here the tapestry-like quality of Bruegel's pictures, which spontaneously reveals itself in the course of a straightforward, impartial description, is explained by a concrete historical connection with Burgundian tapestry making. Glück describes a characteristic of Bruegel's that "is conspicuous in all of his paintings, even those of his mature period, and that, thanks to his incomparable art, lends the paintings a hitherto inconceivable stylistic greatness: the lack of painterly values, gradation, and modeling of solid bodies. Figures are completely flat and not conceived plastically; the essence of his perspective is linear draftsmanship and not cubic composition." Glück's description is fully compatible with the description of *one* of the constituent pictorial elements given at the beginning of this study, namely, that of the human figures. Glück goes on to conclude as follows: "If he [Bruegel] worked in an age when chiaroscuro and a sense of the three-dimensionality of bodies dominated, he is clearly ...[42] reverting to an archaic style, just as he also reintroduces costumes from earlier ages. *His art of the plane is based on the style of tapestries and on its surrogate, watercolor painting on canvas.*"

This statement is undoubtedly correct. And it is all the more convincing in that it explains not only the anachronisms he mentions but also the standardized horizontal format of Bruegel's pictures and even some of the pictures' technical peculiarities. Moreover, the subjects most often depicted in tapestries are to an extent the same as those Bruegel preferred: "poor people" who can be viewed as curious or comic figures.

Yet with this discovery — one of the most important in all the research on Bruegel — the real question of the meaning this reversion to an archaic style had for Bruegel is in no way answered. Nor does it explain why he adhered to this style only for the depiction of human figures, while using a completely different and more modern style for the landscape environment in which the figures appear, a style that incorporates gradation and modeling and that works with smooth transitions and aerial perspective. This fusion of two modes of representation is the true characteristic, and the true paradox, of Bruegel's pictures. Though few Burgundian tapestries survive, one can safely state that such a fusion is completely absent from that type of work, in which the field surrounding the figures is shown in the very same planar manner as the figures themselves.

It is these two questions, until now unanswered and indeed unposed, that this study has sought to answer.

Tapestry is an art for a courtly audience for whom the representation of peasants had the charm of the *alien* and the comic. The peasant was alien to the buyers of these tapestries, but alien only in an empirical and sociological sense, not in the absolute, graphic, profoundly human sense of Bruegel. Nevertheless an uncultivated audience can see and enjoy Bruegel's pictures in the same way the Burgundian court saw those tapestries.

Notes

1. Benedetto Croce, *Kleine Schriften zur Ästhetik* (Tübingen: Mohr, 1929), vol. 1, p. 249. For the presentation and translation of these works, German art history is indebted to Julius von Schlosser.

2. Here I have omitted the words "in the effect of light," which delimit the phenomenon too narrowly.

3. We would be more inclined to speak of "intellectual distance" (*geistige Ferne*).

4. I refer to Karl Tolnai [Charles de Tolnay], *Die Zeichnungen Pieter Bruegels* (Munich: Piper, 1925).

5. When I speak here and later of Bruegel's pictures in general, as types, I am thinking in particular of that group of multifigural paintings with which his painted oeuvre begins: *Netherlandish Proverbs*, *The Battle Between Carnival and Lent*, *Children's Games*, and so on, where the painter's specific *macchia* first develops decisively. Section IX of this essay will discuss the transition between these and both the later and earlier works.

6. "Dispersed throughout the scene like the pattern of a carpet," as Max Dvořák describes it in "Pieter Bruegel der Ältere" (1920), in *Kunstgeschichte als Geistesgeschichte: Studien zur abendländischen Kunstentwicklung* (Munich: Piper, 1924), translated as *The History of Art as The History of Ideas* (London: Routledge, 1984).

7. As does Axel Romdahl, who believes he can explain the planarity and the clumsy outline of the animals in *Return of the Herd* by Bruegel's limited experience as an animal painter. See "Pieter Brueghel der Ältere und sein Kunstschaffen," *Jahrbuch der kunsthistorischen Sammlungen des Allerhöchsten Kaiserhauses* 25 (1905).

8. To experience the inseparability of *macchia* and theme quite concretely, one might try to imagine this subject matter put into another pictorial form.

9. One might also add "intoxication" (*The Feast of Saint Martin*).

10. *Entfremdung*, the German word used here, can also be rendered as either "alienation" or "making strange," and Sedlmayr takes full advantage of the several implications of this word, which was central to both the social and literary theory of his time — TRANS.

371

11. For example, repetitive, monotonous recitation of the same word causes it to shed its meaning; while staring at something causes it to shed its visual sense.

12. One thinks here of the wonderful depiction of this experience in Rilke's *Die Aufzeichnungen des Malte Laurids Brigge* (Leipzig: Insel-Verlag, 1910), which contains a rare collection of various experiences of estrangement.

13. In the very conditions of life, Bruegel "seeks and finds the grotesque and bizarre," writes Dvořák. "Reality transforms itself into Utopia," observes Wilhelm Fraenger very astutely in *Der Bauern-Bruegel und das deutsche Sprichwort* (Erlenbach-Zurich: Rentsch, 1923).

14. This is why "figures are dominated by their garments, usually, in fact, consumed by them." Tolnai, "Beiträge zu Bruegels Zeichnungen," *Jahrbuch der Preussischen Kunstsammlungen* 50 (1929).

15. "Even physiognomic interest must yield to this obstruction," writes Dvořák. In fact, both physiognomic reduction and obstruction are a result of this making strange.

16. Both Dvořák and Fraenger have noted this in Bruegel's figures. Tolnai, too, has observed this characteristic without delving into its source: "Bruegel creates not only the congenital grotesqueness of malformation but the phantom grotesqueness that insidiously accompanies even the most usual human motions." "In the paintings, the figure is nothing but a clearly defined gesture isolated from the before and the after of the action, as if its entire existence were frozen into a gestural silhouette."

17. "Even lifeless things seem to come to life," notes Dvořák.

18. For example in the *View of the Tiber*.

19. As superbly noted by Tolnai: "The separation between the space of the viewer and this *strange* pictorial realm remains unbridgeable, however close this realm draws." Here we even see the word that reveals the route to the source of Bruegel's visions.

20. This masked quality — in his own words, looking like a herm of Silenus — has been keenly felt by Tolnai. But he seeks the second, hidden meaning of the picture in a zone that, from the point of view advanced here, seems still superficial.

21. Karl Jaspers, *Allgemeine Psychopathologie*, 3rd ed. (Berlin: Springer, 1929).

22. Wilhelm Fraenger, "James Ensor: Die Kathedrale," *Die graphischen Künste* (1926–1927), pp. 81ff.

23. As a biographical contribution to an understanding of the sources in Bruegel's art of "estrangement," "masks," and so on, one might cite van Mander's anecdote that Bruegel liked "to frighten people, even his own friends, with specters and strange noises."

24. From a purely psychological point of view, it is safe to assume a different level of corporeal illusion in the visions behind the pictures of Bruegel and Ensor.

25. As Wilhelm Pinder has written (I am paraphrasing from memory): representing a prophet once meant transfiguring oneself in the sublime state of prophecy; it now often means merely imagining how someone looks reading or writing.

26. Later in the historical evolution of art, color becomes problematic in a similar way.

27. Bruno Fürst, "Beiträge zu einer Geschichte der österreichischen Plastik" (Ph. D. diss., Leipzig, 1931).

28. See Charles de Tolnay, *Hieronymus Bosch* (French ed. Basel, 1937), especially the conclusion, p. 51.

29. The chaotic pictorial form of Bosch, which is secularized by Bruegel, was originally reserved for a single type of picture: representations of hell (see, for example, the Eyckian panel in the Metropolitan Museum of Art, New York). Nothing similar appears (for this reason) in antiquity.

30. See his unpublished dissertation "Hieronymus Bosch" (University of Vienna, 1925).

31. Tolnai has correctly noted these components of the art of Bosch: "The home world (*Weltheim*) becomes an alien world," he writes in one passage; and thus, I would add, it becomes uncanny (*unheimlich*), because it is a world rendered unstable by demons. In another passage, he speaks specifically of "estrangement of the surrounding world."

32. Wilhelm Pinder has seen the symptoms of mannerism in a way that is as yet unsurpassed. See Pinder, "Zur Physiognomik des Manierismus," in Hans Prinzhorn (ed.), *Die Wissenschaft am Scheideweg von Leben und Geist. Festschrift Ludwig Klages zum 60. Geburtstag* (Leipzig: Barth, 1932), pp. 148–56.

With his incisive remarks about "the possibility of choosing different levels of reality," Dvořák is the first to have developed a theory of mannerism ("Pieter Bruegel der Ältere," pp. 219ff.). Pinder then followed with the important idea of "imposed form" (in lectures from 1927 on), but this idea cannot properly be distinguished from the phenomenon of classicism; he later introduced the characterization cited above. I myself have asserted that the dualism of mannerist compositions and their resistance to any system are of decisive importance (see "Skizze des Manieristischen," in *Die Architektur Borrominis* (Berlin: Frankfurter Verlags-Anstalt, 1930), pp. 152ff.) These rudiments of a theory are developed in a very promising direction by Ernst Gombrich in a dissertation on Giulio Romano written at the Second Art Historical Institute, Vienna, titled "Zum Werke Giulio Romanos," (*Jahrbuch der kunsthistorischen Sammlungen Wien*, n.s., 8 [1934], pp. 79–104, and n.s., 9 [1935], pp. 121–50), and especially in a work on the Château d'Ecouen written in 1933 by Carl Linfert. Linfert's ideas have contributed decisively to the development of this essay.

Nikolaus Pevsner's work on mannerist painting, *Die italienische Malerei vom Ende der Renaissance bis zum ausgehenden Rokoko, Handbuch der Kunstwissenschaft* (Wildpark-Potsdam: Athenaion, 1928), and Ernst Michalski's work on mannerist architecture, "Das Problem des Manierismus in der italienischen Architektur," *Zeitschrift für Kunstgeschichte*, n.s., 2 (1933), pp. 88–109, are lacking in a synthetic overview of mannerism; they consider only its isolated symptoms. For this reason, the richness of mannerist architecture is hardly visible to Michalski. On the problem of mannerist architecture, compare my essay on Michelangelo's Area Capitolina, "Die Area Capitolina des Michelangelo," *Jahrbuch der Preussischen Kunstsammlungen* 53 (1931), p. 266, supplemented by the confrontation with the Capitol of Della Porta, "Das Kapitol des Della Porta," *Zeitschrift für Kunstgeschichte*, n.s., 3 (1934), pp. 264–74, and the work by Gombrich mentioned above. With his fruitful notion of "disturbed form," Gombrich has discovered the mannerist nature of architecture previously misunderstood.

The survey by Friedrich Antal, "Zum Problem des niederländischen Manierismus," *Kritische Berichte*, 1/2 (1928–1929), pp. 207ff., which is commendable in drawing attention to the rich material hitherto ignored by art historians, attempts to organize this material according to affiliations and influences by studying isolated, abstract stylistic characteristics and superficial formal motifs. The result is a grotesque caricature of an outdated history of styles in the worst sense of the term.

Mannerism's theoretical self-reflexivity is presented with sovereign clarity in Julius von Schlosser, *Die Kunstliteratur: Ein Handbuch zur Quellenkunde der neueren Kunstgeschichte* (Vienna: Schroll, 1924), pp. 338ff.

A good introduction to the basic phenomena of both mannerism and the art of Bruegel is offered by the direction of contemporary art that calls itself surrealism, the strangely estranged vision of which also revives the piecing together of parts from different realities (the principle of montage). In an essay on the painter Giorgio de Chirico, Jean Cocteau, one of surrealism's adherents, characterizes the movement's central tenet as follows: "True surrealism consists in showing the surprising things custom conceals beneath its cover and prevents us from seeing. One's name no longer has a human form. None of us can hear it. But when a messenger wakes us by shouting it in the hall of a hotel, when a cashier asks for it, when pupils mock it in class, it happens that they tear away the cover of this name, detached from us, solitary and singular as an unknown object." "De Chirico shows us reality by making it strange. He is a painter of alien landscapes" (Chirico nous montre la realité en la depaysant. C'est un depaysagiste). And further, on the work of Picasso: "Picasso's work is disguised, masked." Cocteau, *Essai de critique indirecte* (Paris: Grasset, 1932).

33. These sources have long been recognized.

34. The painting was produced after the drawings of the *Sins* were "assembled, in all probability, solely out of puns and proverbs" (Tolnai). Though painted in 1559, the same year as *The Battle Between Carnival and Lent*, *Netherlandish Proverbs* is older compositionally.

35. Winter itself, in a way, produces Bruegel pictures. A village skating

pond seen from a bird's-eye view is, potentially, a permanent Bruegel picture as it naturally contains essential ingredients of the "typical Bruegel": the sharp separation, patchiness, and flatness of the figures; the mass and its confusion; the muffling up against the cold; the grotesque movements, poses, and contortions that seem unnatural and unaccustomed; and finally the "petrified atmosphere" in more than one sense.

As I quickly leafed through the illustrations of *Das Burgenland, seine Bauten und Kunstschätze* (Vienna: Schroll, 1929), an "artistic topography" edited by Dagobert Frey, I thought I saw in the snow-covered cemetery of figure 63, with its jumble of gravestones, a painting by Bruegel or his school. The photograph of the cemetery showed a related *macchia*.

36. Michelangelo is a case of the former; El Greco, Cervantes, and Shakespeare of the latter. See Pinder, "Zur Physiognomik des Manierismus."

37. The unmediated confrontation of two separate spheres is one of the essences of parody. I cannot go beyond this observation here.

38. See Kurt Koffka, *Zur Analyse der Vorstellungen und ihre Gesetze* (Leipzig: Quelle und Meyer, 1912), section "Vorstellung und Bedeutung," esp. p. 258.

39. This has also been recognized by Tolnai, who, however, misrepresents the matter when he speaks for example of the *Urberg* (ur-mountain). This implies something mythic or Platonic, which is quite foreign to Bruegel.

40. Ludwig von Baldass, "Die niederländische Landschaftsmalerei von Patenir bis Bruegel," *Jahrbuch der kunsthistorischen Sammlungen des Allerhöchsten Kaiserhauses* 34 (1918), pp. 111–57.

41. Gustav Glück, *Bruegels Gemälde* (Vienna: Schroll, 1932).

42. Here I have left out Glück's equivocation — "unconsciously or perhaps consciously." Certainly Bruegel knew that he was archaizing.

Translated by Frederic J. Schwartz.

Fritz Novotny, passages from Cézanne and the End of Scientific Perspective *(1938)*

Fritz Novotny (1902–1983) was born in Vienna and studied art history at the university under Julius von Schlosser's rival Josef Strzygowski. He wrote a dissertation on Romanesque architectural sculpture in Austria. Later he was named curator and eventually director of the Österreichische Galerie in Vienna. Novotny published several important essays on Cézanne as well as the book excerpted here. He did not write explicitly on methodology, but his Cézanne book is in some ways the purest and most thoroughgoing example of Strukturanalyse. *The book is a detailed analysis of the almost imperceptible departures from correct linear perspective in Cézanne's landscapes. Cézanne's modernity — and his difference from the impressionists — lies in the estrangement and anxiety generated in these pictures by the tension between scientific illusionism and artistic willfullness. The book had a powerful impact on Meyer Schapiro and other Cézanne scholars.*

The two passages translated here are drawn from the first part of the book, on space in Cézanne's landscapes. They are taken from the sections with the headings "Distortions of Scientific Perspective" and "The Construction of Space in Relationship to the Total Formation of the Picture." The second part of the book discusses Cézanne's relationship to postimpressionists and neo-impressionists like van Gogh, Gauguin, and Seurat; to cubism; and in general to the rest of the history of Western painting.

(Source: Fritz Novotny, Cézanne und das Ende der wissenschaftlichen Perspektive *[Vienna: Schroll, 1938], pp. 32–47 and 91–103.)*

Chapter Eight

Passages from *Cézanne and the End of Scientific Perspective* (1938)

Fritz Novotny

That feature of the pictorial section just mentioned, the size of the section in the distant landscape, is already conducive to this phenomenon [that is, Cézanne's apparent indifference toward the expressive spatial possibilities of the selected landscape views].[1] This is because a narrow section of distant space is so far the only kind of pictorial section that is capable of altering the objective appearance of the represented portion of the landscape without also making deviations from natural linear perspective necessary. A kind of reduction of space is thus achieved as the main effect of this choice of section, even though it does not at all affect the actual spatial structure of the picture: the distant landscape in the representation is less deep than in the natural model. This means not that it has less spatial substance but just that, with regard to the extension of depth, the represented landscape differs from the motif, assuming the motif can still be identified today. As has already been said, viewed in itself, even this method of narrowing space should be regarded as a very cautious one that, as an aesthetic value, cannot be grasped directly from the picture but only in comparison with the natural model. It does, however, run parallel to a certain tendency for forming space that found direct expression in several departures from natural linear perspective.

379

An obvious method of reducing spatial depth is to avoid long, slanted orthogonals or vanishing lines. As already mentioned, Cézanne uses this method much less than a superficial, summarily remembered impression of his landscapes would lead one to assume. Still, the way in which he handles these vanishing lines, with respect to their capacity to create space, does in the end result in the expected reduction of space. In fact, in Cézanne's landscapes, we often find a kind of hesitation in the movement of the perspectival lines. The representation of the garden wall in the foreground of *Railway Cutting with Mont Ste-Victoire* (Munich, V. 50, R. 156) (figure 8.1) is a particularly vivid example of this.[2] The wall can barely be recognized as a wall not only because it is not described as matter but precisely because of the absence of small tensions and differentiations that, even with smaller changes in depth, bring about or support the pull of perspectival depth. (It cannot even be inferred with certainty that the equally wide, extended dark-brown strip that is angled slightly at the lower end of the painting represents a *vertical* surface.)

In *A Turn in the Road at La Roche-Guyon* (Smith College Museum of Art, V. 441, R. 539) (Figure 8.2), the edges of roads are sometimes treated in the same way as the perspectival oval of a circular bowl, plate, or pitcher in a still life (for example, V. 496, 512; R. 635, 675, or in the composition of fruit in the famous still life in the Museum of Modern Art, New York, V. 341, R. 418). In other words, the continuous curve is simplified in such a way that it functions as a joining together of straight lines and circular parts; and more or less conspicuously, the ellipses look like rectangular forms with semicircles attached to them.[3] This method of forming perspectival lines in roadways and the like can be found repeatedly, for example, in the landscapes (for example, V. 467, 789, and 1071; R. 538, 889, 457).

The alteration of perspectival lines can weaken their move-

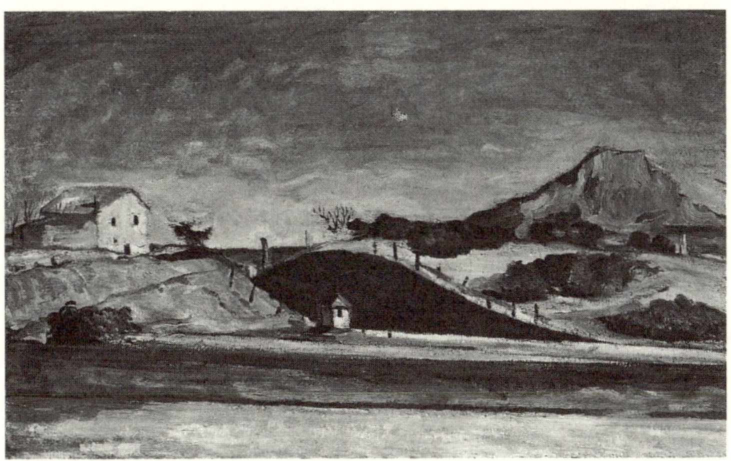

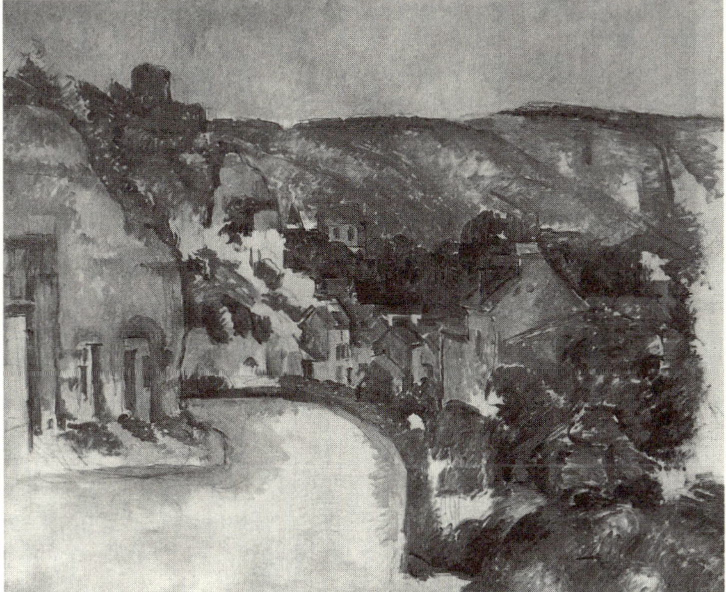

Figure 8.1 (above). Paul Cézanne, *Railway Cutting with Mont Ste-Victoire*, Bayerische Staatsgemäldesammlungen, Munich.
Figure 8.2 (below). Paul Cézanne, *A Turn in the Road at La Roche-Guyon*, Smith College Museum of Art, Northampton, MA (Photo: Stephen Petegorsky).

ment; an interesting case of this is the *Landscape with Mont Ste-Victoire* in Moscow (V. 423, R. 398) (figure 8.3). The pictorial section and the quantitative division within it of foreground, middle ground, background, and sky correspond to the way the landscape motif normally looks (apart from the previously mentioned slight horizontal construction of the angle of view). However, in the foreground terrain, one of the perspectival lines is noticeably altered (compare the photograph [figure 8.4], which, with respect to the foreground, represents the natural impression). As in the painting, the more remote edge of the field, on which the poplars stand today, is positioned parallel to the eye plane. But while in reality the front boundary of this field, apparently a small water channel, moves at a steeper angle in space, in Cézanne's representation it has become almost a horizontal, running close to the picture's edge.

Admittedly this does not take into consideration the specific qualities that contour generally possesses in Cézanne's painting, namely, the characteristic vagueness and especially the lack of tension that signifies one of the most fundamental artistic inventions in his painting.[4] The effect of this lack of tension, which is governed by, among other things, the nature of the object at whose contours it appears, is, as a rule, especially noticeable in lines of flight, since from the outset these are more likely to stimulate the counter-process of an *increase* in movement.

It is not easy to separate such deviations from correct linear perspective from that general peculiarity of Cézanne's line that also comes to affect the lines of perspective. Cézanne's way of forming outlines results not only in the retardation of movement already mentioned but sometimes has still another effect, which occurs most clearly in instances where several contours running in various directions, the main nerves of the total perspectival structure, meet.[5] Here it seems that the diverse angles in which

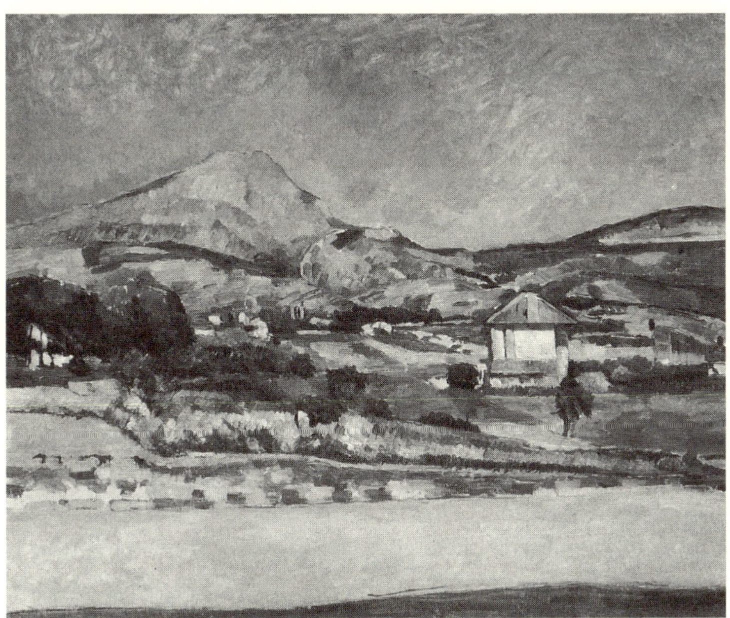

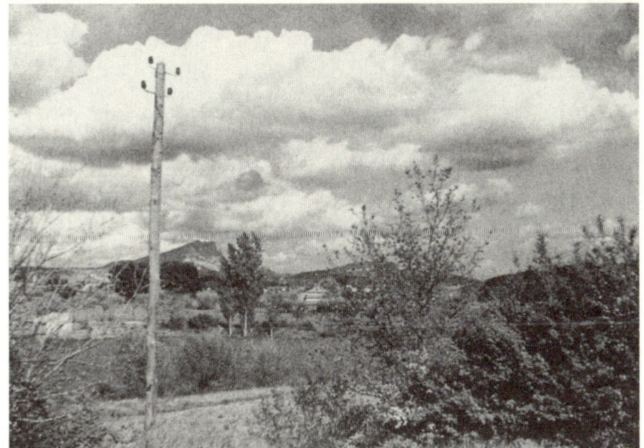

Figure 8.3 (above). Paul Cézanne, *Landscape with Mont Ste-Victoire*, Pushkin Museum of Fine Arts, Moscow (Giraudon/Art Resource, NY).
Figure 8.4 (below). Photo by John Rewald from *Les Sites Cézanniens du pays d'Aix* (Paris: Seuil, 1996).

those contours and their shapes hold together on the surface and in space do not correspond exactly with reality, as if the smallest unverifiable shifts in this system of spatially significant outlines have acquired the absolute necessity and clarity of perspectival classification. This necessity is *the* integrating feature of an exact perspectival reproduction even when there is a great variety of different vectors and only a few extended and parallel contours.

In nature, such a tangle of axes signifies a richness of space. In Cézanne's representation, this simple expansive effect is absent, and such a variety of axes often has an uncertain effect. This effect, which is difficult to describe, can also occur when the linear perspective framework is completely accurate, because it is really just based on a peculiarity of the outlines' form that is projected by the viewer onto the perspectival structure. It has to do then with an unusual formation of contour resulting in a decrease of perspectival exactness and clarity while at the same time achieving a material and spatial structure of extraordinary strength. The cautious joining of surfaces to contours, the constantly changing strength of these contours, the apparent lability but fundamental firmness of the picture's general framework — these are the means that make it possible to shake a fundamental system of linear perspective from the inside out, as it were, to the farthest depth, a system that is to all appearances thoroughly indisputable and that, handled in a different way, allows no doubt as to its accuracy in depicting space. A comparison with the role of line in the impressionist landscape can elucidate the curiousness of this contoured form in its relation to perspective. In its ease and suggestive sketchiness, the impressionist line — in drawing and painting — is also far removed from the perfect consistency of the outlines that run through natural perspectival appearance. However, here the result is not an uncertainty on the part of the viewer about the perspectival constellation; on the contrary, the linear formation makes the perspectival construction absolutely clear. One of the goals of the impressionist depiction of space is, in fact, not only to produce the full intensity of spatial content but also to provide perspectival accuracy through the abbreviated and abstracted forms of a suggestive system of contours. (The concept of impressionism is here intended in its widest scope, encompassing also baroque impressionism. In Rembrandt's landscape drawings, for example, the perspectival sensation is actually a very critical factor of the pictorial idea.)

It is part of the nature of this impressionist method of representation that its linear perspective does not have to be absolutely precise, since it counts on the viewer to complete the picture, often unconsciously. There is a great difference between the so-called deficiency of drawing in impressionism and that of Cézanne. In the impressionist approach, an interrupted outline leaves no doubt as to the complete course it will follow in describing the space and bodies; whereas in Cézanne, faltering and often fragmentary lines give the impression that the perspectival appearance is being grasped elementally, at its roots. This impression arises *after* the superficial impression that the perspectival system of Cézanne's landscapes corresponds to that of the impressionists.[6]

Finally, it can also be determined that the formation of *outlines* through brushwork and coloring brings with it not only that weakening of perspectival intensity but also that "pure" line whose efficacy we sense as if beneath a covering layer, which we attempt to concretize and which sometimes actually becomes unveiled and visible. Even this pure outline, insofar as it comes into consideration at all, seems to dispense with the finest perspectival nuances. In Cézanne's mode of representation, the curve of a body, the volume of a treetop, a row of objects revealed one behind the other by an intersection of curves, such basic facts of perspectival detail are expressed with the scarcest of means, in the mere strokes of the contours. Previously we were only considering the lack of tension and the reduction of a movement that is proper to the converging lines characteristic of larger formats. But the impression of perspectival continuity, of the currents and countercurrents in pictorial relations of space and proportion, depends not only on the picture's predominant main lines but also, and in a certain sense even more decisively, on the sum of all the small elemental parts of the perspectival space.

This characteristic has been described as an effect, while the means with which it is achieved have only briefly been mentioned, and it is hardly necessary to note that it occurs in very different degrees in Cézanne's oeuvre. Sometimes the reduction of the line's perspectival truth value is barely noticeable, so that the form of the outline comes closer to that of the impressionist style. On the other hand, as in the earlier mentioned instances of a multiform, angular system of contours and axes, the perspectival continuum may be called into question, and the structure of axes can appear strange when measured against reality. However, such an effect should probably not be separated from actual deviations from natural linear perspective, and these will now be enumerated.

One of these deviations is a certain aversion to the low point of view.

To be sure, in Cézanne's landscapes, the low point of view does occur, and we cannot speak of a preference or avoidance of one of the points of view, in the roughest classification of the term. This is correct, however, only for this most summary distinction of points of view, defined as the main lines of sight that determine the spatial section, and this requires a more complete account.

The avoidance of the low point of view, when the total spatial phenomenon in the picture would lead one to expect it, can be found in parts of the picture, and is most clearly discernible where straight lines are concerned, above all, therefore, in buildings. The edges of two eaves that form the corner of a roof will, in Cézanne's representation, sometimes not be shown in the obtuse angle produced by a slightly low point of view, which is natural for a building seen from the ground and from a small distance away, but be merged into one of the picture's only drawn-out horizontals. Examples of this kind are the rear views of *Jas de Bouffan* (V. 415, 817; R. 269, 22) and *Mill by the "Bridge of Trois Sautets"* (V. 978, 979; R. 391, 392). However, examples of this sort do not say much in themselves. First of all, there are not many of them, and counterexamples can also be found in which a low point of view is represented to a degree that would occur naturally, as in the group of houses in some views of *Jas de Bouffan* (for example, National Gallery, Prague, V. 460, R. 600 [figure 8.5], or V. 461–464, R. 596, 567, 611, 268), in *Road by Maison Maria* in the Kimbell Art Museum, Fort Worth (V. 761, R. 792), and other landscapes (V. 668, 403, 397; R. 828, 440, 438).

More fundamental to the way perspective is formed in Cézanne's landscapes are occasional inconsistencies within the pictorial space. The painting that was last mentioned — the *Landscape with Houses* in the National Gallery of Art (V. 397, R. 438) — shows such an inconsistency; the nearer building appears to be viewed from a lower point of view than the larger group of houses behind it. In the painting *Jas de Bouffan* in Prague (V. 460, R. 600) (figure 8.5), the difference between the perspectival structure of the group of buildings at the right and that of the large building on the left is less obvious, but it is essential and definitive for the formation of total space. The sculptural, multiform group on the right shows the lines of the gutters from an extremely low point of view, and this allows a rather low-lying eye level to be inferred. The nearly frontal sight of the large house facade on the left does

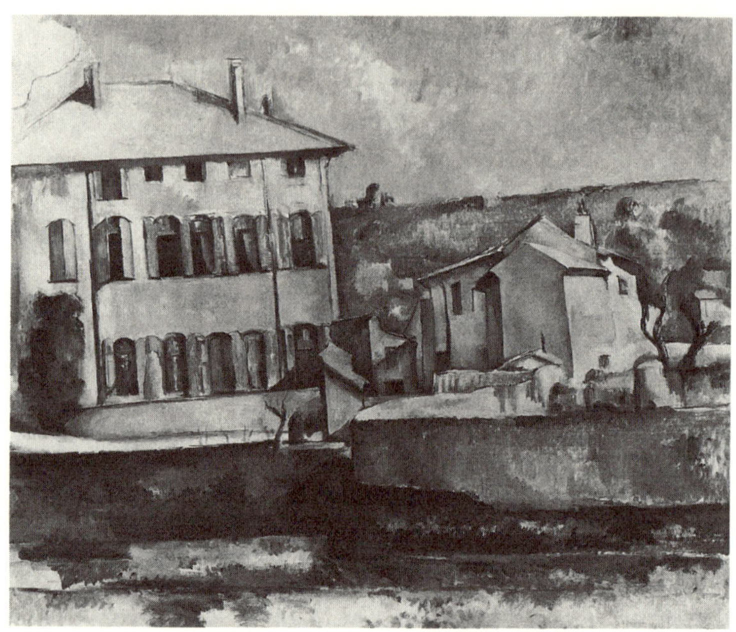

Figure 8.5. Paul Cézanne, *House and Farm at Jas de Bouffan*, National Gallery, Prague.

not, perhaps, contradict this position; nevertheless, this house seems to be depicted from a higher point of view than the buildings on the right side of the picture. The surface of the roof is represented in a perspectival incline that seems too slight, and the low point of view beneath the roof eaves (the angle between two edges that can be so instructive, as in the examples just cited, does not lie within the picture's space) is depicted with an odd indifference toward the demands of exact perspective that exist for just such a situation. Thus, this left part of the painting is perspectivally less "vehement" than the representation of the richly formed block of buildings opposite.

The avoidance of the low point of view is therefore not a general determining property of Cézanne's landscape perspective but, rather, the occasional and more distinct effect of a generic peculiarity that we described at the beginning as a weakening of the accent of the perspective. We have already observed this peculiarity in its most general and ubiquitous manifestation, namely, in the formation of contour. Here we are dealing with a special case of the weakening of emphasis of *linear* perspective.[7] Sometimes it occurs in the same picture in varying degrees, for example, in the *Jas de Bouffan* in Prague.

A peculiarity like that in the *Basin at Jas de Bouffan* (Hermitage, St. Petersburg, V. 167, R. 278) (figure 8.6) is also one of these special cases. In reality, the stone edge of the basin at the rear end of the lion figure forms a right-angled corner, which can barely be made out in Cézanne's representation. The embankment at this site of the waterspout bends so slightly that the edge of the basin appears to be a continuous horizontal in a *single* plane. Even if the perspectival appearance of this corner also reveals a very obtuse angle (compare the photograph of the subject in figure 8.7), there is still a question here of whether this angle has been intentionally straightened. If the eye level to

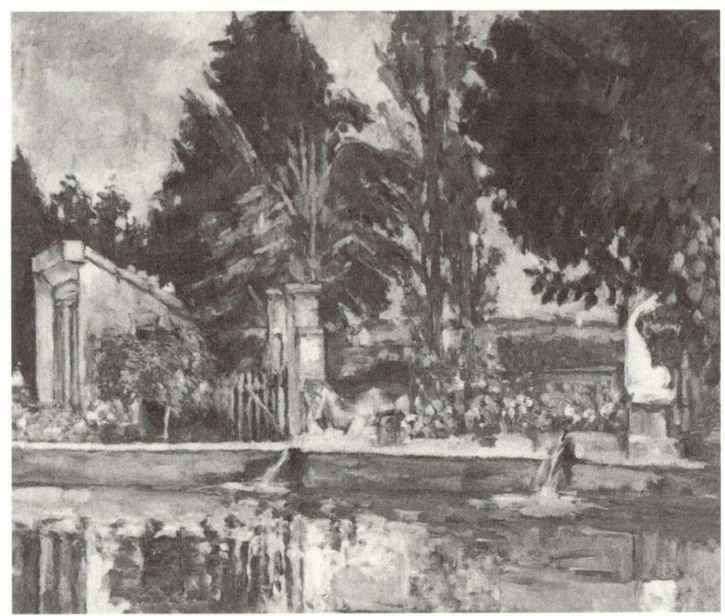

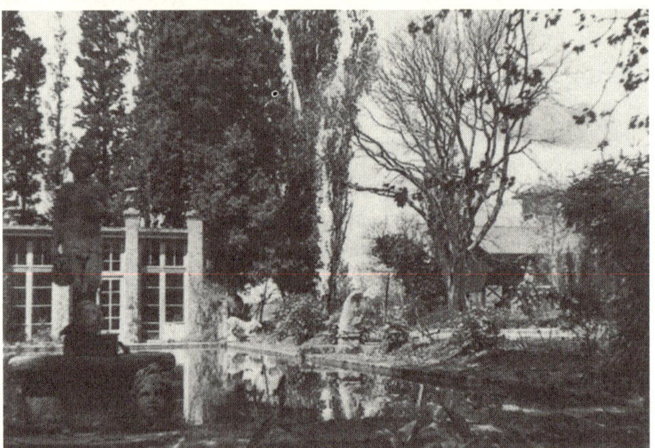

Figure 8.6 (above). Paul Cézanne, *Basin at Jas de Bouffan* from Albert Kostenevich, *Hidden Treasures Revealed* (St. Petersburg and New York: State Hermitage Museum with H.N. Abrams, 1995).
Figure 8.7 (below). Photo by John Rewald from Rewald, *The Paintings of Paul Cézanne* (New York: Abrams, 1996).

which this composition corresponds were to be deduced, then an improbably deep location would have to be assumed, and the overall space of the landscape does not at all express such a location. (The appearance of space produced by such a location would oppose the avoidance of the low point of view.)

The question of whether an angle would be straightened in this way for compositional reasons shall be postponed until a later section.

In a certain sense, it is the apparently exaggerated view from above that forms the counterpart to the avoidance of the low point of view. Like the latter, however, it cannot be considered a constitutive and determining characteristic of Cézanne's conception of space. First of all, it can be added to the kinds of phenomena cited up to now that reduce the pull of depth. *Approach of Jas de Bouffan* (Barnes Foundation, Merion, PA, V. 649, R.617) (figure 8.8) offers an example of this. The two decisive perspectival lines are produced through the positioning of the tree bases on the avenue. Their convergence is decreased so that, in comparison with the natural appearance, the depth of the whole avenue is reduced and the area of land between the trees is seen from a higher point of view. Thus the typical spatial appearance of an avenue formed by high trees is essentially transformed. Not only is the movement into depth curtailed, but also the contrast between the flat area of land and the wall of trees rising directly from this area is decreased, a contrast that is characteristic of the way an avenue like this customarily appears (in other words, characteristic of the view into depth from a normal eye level).[8] (Related examples are: in the view of the basin in *Jas de Bouffan* at the Metropolitan Museum of Art, New York [V. 648, R. 566], the path on the right rises steeply in a manner that is oddly abrupt; in the Moscow painting which was already mentioned, *Jas de Bouffan* [V. 462, R. 567], the avenue on the left contradicts the view of the

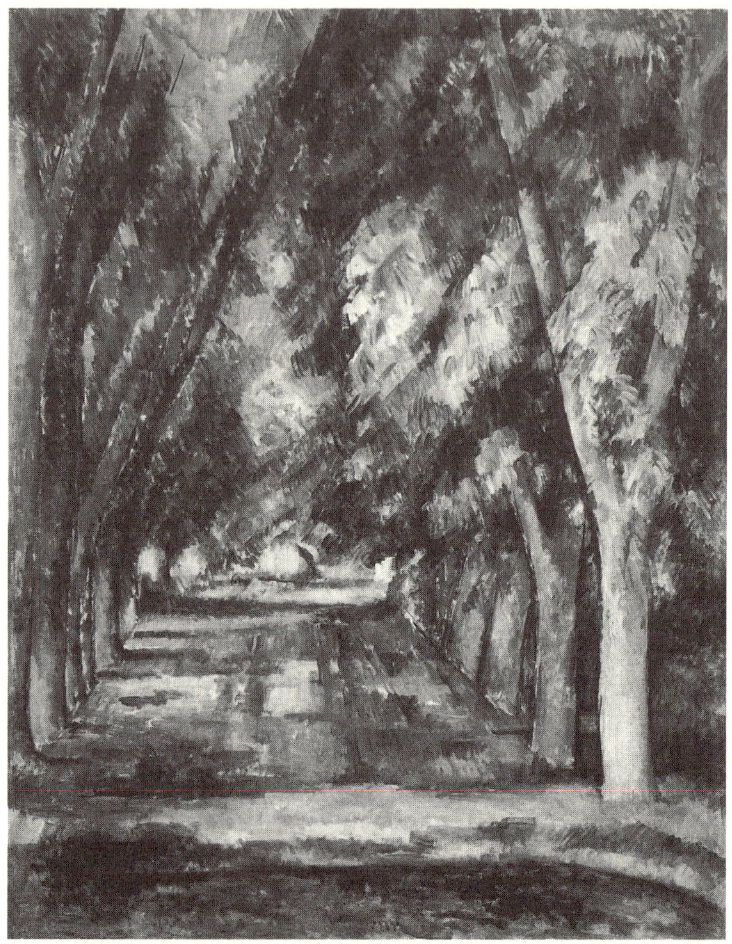

Figure 8.8. Paul Cézanne, *Approach of Jas de Bouffan*, BF#939 Gallery II, Barnes Foundation, Merion, PA (© Reproduced with the permission of the Barnes Foundation™ All rights reserved).

right side of the picture in a way that is perspectivally incomprehensible; and, less glaringly, this same avenue in the spring landscape of *Jas de Bouffan* in the Museum of Art, Rhode Island School of Design [V. 463, R. 611].)

The *reduction of contrast* seems to be a very important feature of Cézanne's general mode of representation. We have first to consider the reduction of contrast in its connection with the weakening of perspectival emphasis.

If we recognize this weakening of perspectival emphasis as a peculiarity that underlies component features like the avoidance of the low point of view, the increased top view, the straightening of angles made by perspectival lines, and the decreased convergence of parallel lines, then it seems to have *its* cause in the reduction of contrast that is a comprehensive, fundamental trait of Cézanne's form.

This reduction of contrast, which relates to the characteristics just now enumerated, generally consists of a decreased perspectival contrast between the sizes of single objects as they recede in space. Of course, it is only a different term for the same phenomenon if we speak, on the one hand, of the reduced convergence of parallel lines, the straightening of the perspectival angle, and so on and, on the other hand, of a reduction in the degree to which the dimensions of individual objects decrease perspectivally. It would be pointless to emphasize this effect of the basic physical and optical law of perspective if it did not admit different *artistic* possibilities of interpretation.

First of all, the *repoussoir* effect of large objects and expanses in the foreground, like a lawn or a surface of water, is diminished. As difficult as this is to establish in an isolated case, a comprehensive overview of a large number of Cézanne's landscapes produces the impression that the dimensional effect of scenery in the foreground, and thus its *repoussoir* value, is not fully exploited.

Cézanne does not avoid using foreground scenery, just as he does not avoid pronounced perspectival lines of depth; on the contrary, an abundant use of such foreground objects is more likely: trees or tree trunks that are cut off by the picture's edge and frame or, like lattices, obstruct a distant view; boulders, bushes, and the like occur so frequently in his paintings that it is not necessary to cite specific examples. The process of painterly formation, a process to which these foreground pieces of scenery are also subject, is analogous to the deceleration in the movement of perspectival line (such as the weakening of spatially significant outlines discussed earlier) in that the proportions between distant objects and those in the foreground are often not clearly established for the viewer of the picture. Together with reductions of spatial contrast, as we saw, for example, in *Approach of Jas de Bouffan* (figure 8.8), this uncertainty about the perspectival relations of size leads to just that impression of a decrease in differences of size. The *Landscape with Mont Ste-Victoire, Seen from the Approach to Château Noir* in the Cleveland Museum of Art (V. 666, R. 900), represents a clear example of this. The treetop in the upper-left part of the picture and the objects in the foreground at the picture's lower edge are more important for framing surfaces than for creating space, even though, apart from the representation of detail, they would be more suitable for creating space simply according to their arrangement.[9] The effect is quite similar in many other cases where the foreground frames a distant landscape.

If a series of motifs is examined in comparison with nature, proceeding from this impression that perspectival differentiations in size are not fully utilized, then a typical formative process is revealed. In many cases, opposing degrees of size have been altered so that perspectivally large foreground objects have been made a bit smaller or, conversely, objects in the background of the picture somewhat larger. One of the most pronounced examples of this kind is *Mont Ste-Victoire, Seen from Bibémus*, which towers in the background over a rock cleft in the middle ground (Baltimore Museum of Art, V. 766, R. 837) (figure 8.9).[10] The mountain is noticeably enlarged in comparison with the boulders in the middle ground. If one measures the visible mountaintop, from the peak to the right corner of the large, convex boulder at the left of the cleft, against the horizontal stretch of this boulder, it turns out that, in reality, that mountaintop corresponds to about two-thirds of this horizontal stretch. In Cézanne's painting, the scale is altered so much toward the opposite, that the horizontal span is substantially *shorter* than the vertical one.

Such a large increase in the size of the distant mountain mass, which was also particularly heroicized in this painting through the formation of contour, is apparently rather isolated, at least in Cézanne's mature art (in his mature art, the winter avenue in *Jas de Bouffan* in the Minneapolis Institute of Art [V. 476, R. 551] still heroicizes the mountain). In the early period, similar instances can be found in the paintings of the "Railway Cutting": in the Munich picture with the view of Mont Ste-Victoire (figure 8.1), and in the painting in the Barnes Collection with the oversize tower of St. Sauveur Cathedral visible between the two hills of the land cutting (V. 42, R. 89). In all other cases where Mont Ste-Victoire is enlarged, either this is achieved not at all at the expense of the perspectival expansion of objects lying nearer in space but only by a narrow section in the manner already described or the enlargement of the mountain is less than that in the picture from the quarry. It must also be considered that although a perspectival enlargement of the mountain is discernible in Cézanne's painting, perhaps because he measured by sight, the form of the mountain also *appears* larger in the overall section from nature than it actually is according to perspectival proportions. That this appearance, which also determines normal seeing,

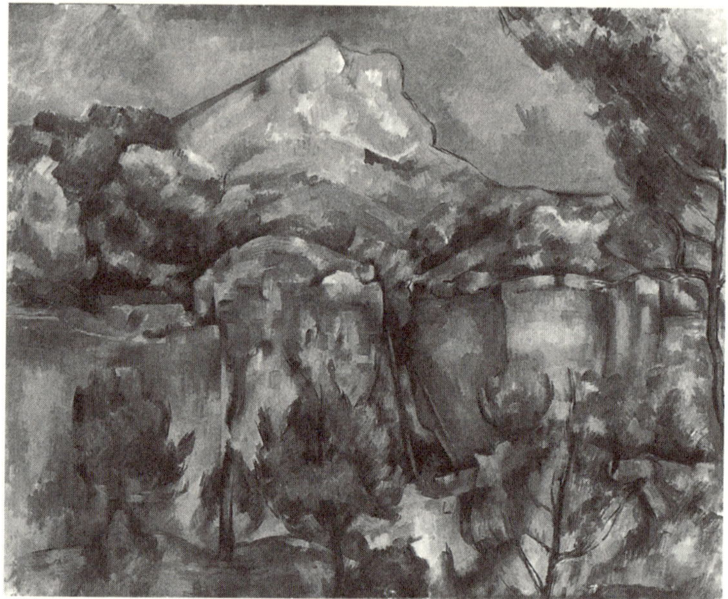

Figure 8.9. Paul Cézanne, *Mont Ste-Victoire Seen from Bibémus*, BMA 1950.196, Baltimore Museum of Art: The Cone Collection, formed by Dr. Claribel Cone and Miss Etta Cone of Baltimore Maryland.

is more decisive for Cézanne than the exact perspectival proportions is obvious and, in any case, less indicative than the reverse would be. Such cases, as for example in the landscapes of the park entrance to Château Noir, are therefore ruled out with regard to the problem of perspectival increases in size. There remain only those in which a certain degree of dimensional excess is surpassed. Besides the works already mentioned, this is true of Mont Ste-Victoire in the background of *Road by Maison Maria* (V. 761, R. 792) and in the background of *Mill by the "Bridge of Trois Sautets"* (V. 979, R. 392) and in the watercolor with the bridge at Gardanne, in which the far church tower and houses are significantly enlarged (V. 912, R. 248). In any case, not many more instances of this kind can be found, even if we include those works in which the enlargement of distant mountain forms relates to the elevation of distant parts of the terrain (for example, in the watercolor with the mountain range of Pilon du Roi in the background [V. 909, R. 246]).

This phenomenon is accompanied by a more significant contribution to the formation of pictorial space, insofar as it operates literally from the other side, namely, from the foreground. Just as objects in the distance are represented larger than in reality when measured against the middle ground and foreground of the landscape's space, so also are foreground objects in Cézanne's paintings occasionally made smaller.

In the *Forest Interior with the Millstone* in the Philadelphia Museum of Art (V. 768, R. 763), the millstone's size is reduced from what would be perspectivally appropriate. In a landscape from the park of Château Noir in the National Gallery, London (V. 787, R. 880), a large boulder in the foreground is smaller than the boulder lying deeper in space (although not to the degree that would be inferred from the photograph of the motif in John Rewald and Leo Marschuetz, "Cézanne au Château Noir," *L'Amour de l'Art* 16. 1 [1935], figure 18).

This weakening of the space-creating power of single foreground objects can now only be demonstrated in a few surviving cases, and it was certainly never frequent in Cézanne's painting. Moreover, it must be considered not for itself alone but as only one form of expression of an overall perspectival foreground weakening. In comparing many motifs with nature, the previously mentioned impression of a perspectival reduction in foreground distances can also be recognized as a truly quantitative decrease in foreground space. This is connected with the formation of the spatial section. The fact that, as explained above, Cézanne usually chooses the "normal" sectional size of the distant landscape but often decides on a smaller angle of view can now be amended: the smallness of the section is usually achieved at the expense of the picture's lower foreground. Thus in several landscapes with Mont Ste-Victoire, for example, the effect of the mountain's size is somewhat intensified, but not because the upper edge of the picture is moved deliberately toward the mountain peak, that is, not because so little sky is depicted that the mountain's size seems to have deviated from the impression given in nature. Rather, the narrowing of the partial view occurs, so to speak, from below. The effect produced in this way can perhaps best be described as a kind of sinking of the picture's foreground. It is difficult to establish by comparing photographs of the corresponding motifs, but an overview of a large number of motifs as they appear in nature makes it completely clear.

This reduction of the foreground results in the picture's objects being pulled closer, just as does generally the small section. Clear examples of this feature are the view of the buildings in *Jas de Bouffan* in the National Gallery, Prague (figure 8.5), in which the wide expanse of lawn in the foreground corresponding to the standpoint of the viewer is incorporated into only a relatively small part of the pictorial section. The same phenomenon can be identified in the Munich picture *Railway Cutting* (figure 8.1), painted from a nearby spot. However, this picture cannot be equated with the other examples since, in contrast to other cases of foreground reduction, its overall recession of planes into depth is quite weak. Another example is the view from *Jas de Bouffan* in the Metropolitan Museum of Art (V. 648, R. 566). A weakening of the foreground can be discerned in the two views of the "Petite Route du Tholonet" from the park entrance of Château Noir (V. 666, 663; R 900, 899), although to a far lesser degree than the pictures already mentioned. In the landscape from the environs of Gardanne (priv. coll., V. 436, R. 575) (figure 8.10), that characteristic is strongly pronounced, and this will be described in greater detail below. In the *View of Mont Ste-Victoire* in the Stedelijk Museum, Amsterdam (V. 456, R. 608), the section in the foreground of the field's summarily vaulted large surfaces is considerably reduced. The drawing with the chestnut avenue of *Jas de Bouffan* (V. 1495) shows the pronounced horizontal extension of the field of vision.

The peculiarity of the foreground reduction, once it has been recognized in clear examples like these, can be found frequently in Cézanne's landscapes, in varying degrees. The reduction of the foreground emerges as a characteristic feature of Cézanne's formation of space, which, unlike the narrow field of vision in the overall section, is not associated with the distant-space type of painting. Sometimes its perspectival effect is supported by a characteristic fading away of the spatial and surface accents toward the lower edge of the picture. For example, in the earlier mentioned picture in the National Gallery, London (V. 787, R. 880), in which the reduced size of the foreground boulder was already noted, this boulder's value relative to the rocks in the middle ground also recedes. The main accent of the painting is concen-

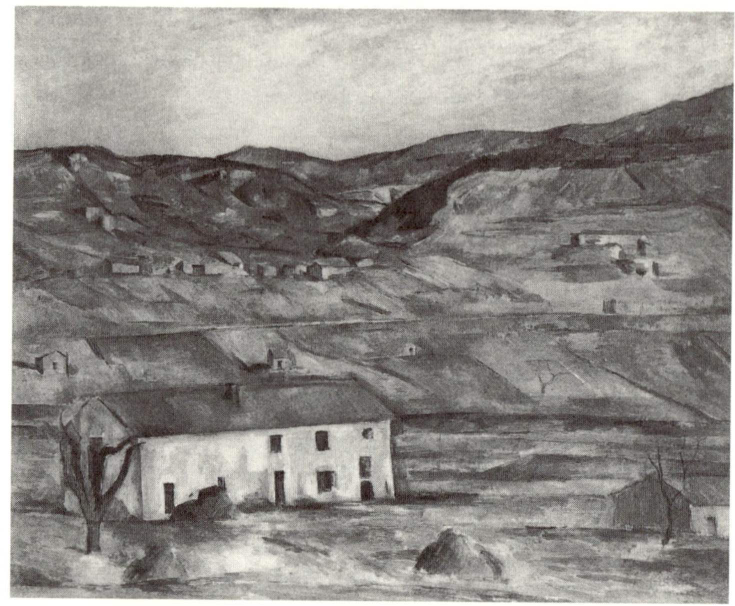

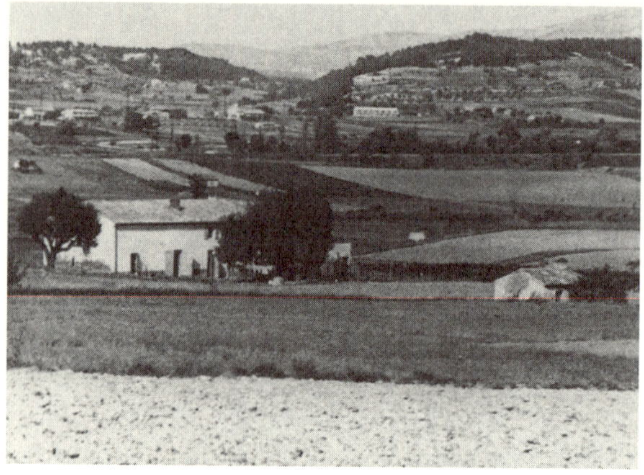

Figure 8.10. Paul Cézanne, *Landscape near Gardanne* from John Rewald, *Cézanne: A Biography* (New York: H.N. Abrams, 1986).
Figure 8.11 (below). Photo by John Rewald from Rewald, *Cézanne: A Biography* (New York: H.N. Abrams, 1986).

trated in this middle ground (insofar as one can speak of such a thing in Cézanne's representational mode). Two paintings that show related sections of the same rock motif near Château Noir indicate how little the perspectival values of space determine the distribution of emphasis. In the painting in the Musée d'Orsay, Paris (V. 786, R. 909) (figure 8.12), the large boulder on the right is strongly emphasized, not so much as a block that creates space but more as a firm link to the structure of lines and patches that make up the rocky shapes in the middle ground. In a watercolor in a private collection, on the other hand, the boulder is hardly indicated at all (V. 1060, R. 436). In one of the watercolor views of Mont Ste-Victoire from the Lauves (V. 1033, R. 593), an olive tree, the single foreground object, is only faintly suggested.

Every once in a while, the formation of the landscape's foreground also relates to that other expressive form — or at least the possibility — of the reduction of contrast: the view from above. A comparison of the two views of Mont Ste-Victoire as seen from the edge of the Bellevue forest (Phillips Collection, Washington, D.C., V. 455, R. 598, and Courtauld Institute Galleries, London, V. 454, R. 599) (figures 8.13 and 8.14) can reveal the nature of this relationship.

Common to both variants of the panorama, alongside the related form of the section viewed from a distance, is the foreground framed by the trunks and branches of two pine trees at the edge of the forest.[11] A fundamental distinction, however, is that in the painting in Washington, D.C., the hilly slope dropping from the forest edge to the valley is included with its trees and bushes as foreground space, whereas this slope is missing from the other picture. This difference in the form of the spatial section seems to be related to a further difference between the two landscapes in the representation of space: the middle-ground terrain in the first picture is shown as rising up more than in the sec-

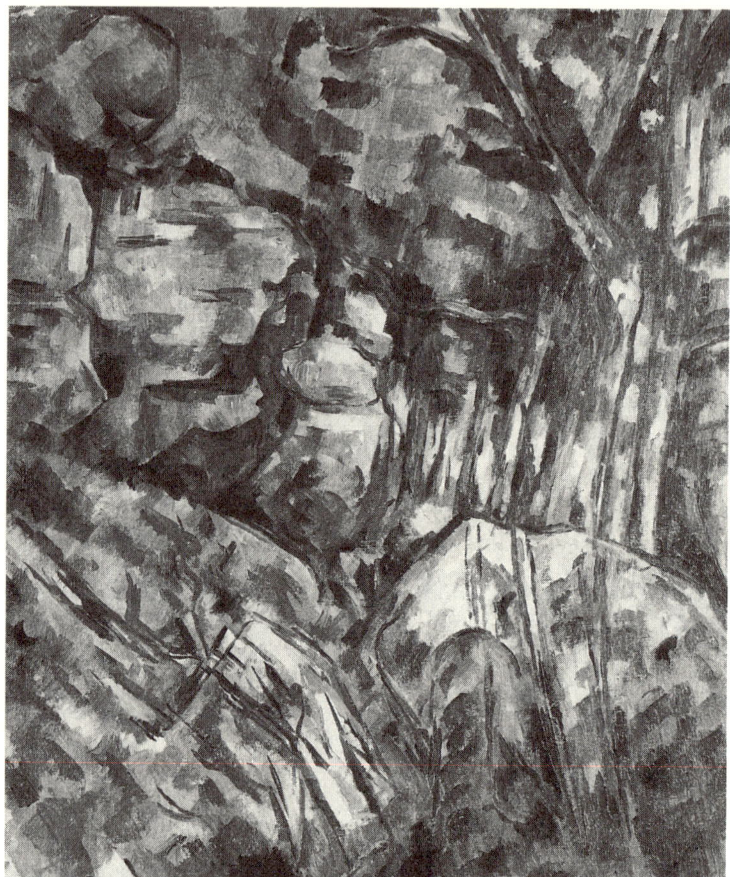

Figure 8.12 (above). Paul Cézanne, *Rocks near the Caves above Château Noir*, Musée d'Orsay, Paris.
Figure 8.13 (opposite page, top). Paul Cézanne, *Mont Ste-Victoire with Large Pine*, Phillips Collection, Washington, D.C.
Figure 8.14 (opposite page, bottom). Paul Cézanne, *Mont Ste-Victoire with Large Pine*, Courtauld Gallery, London.

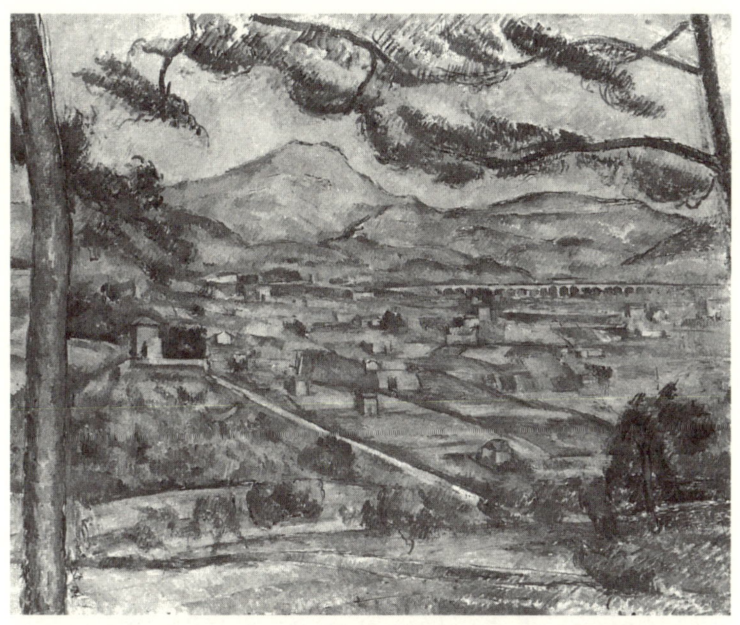

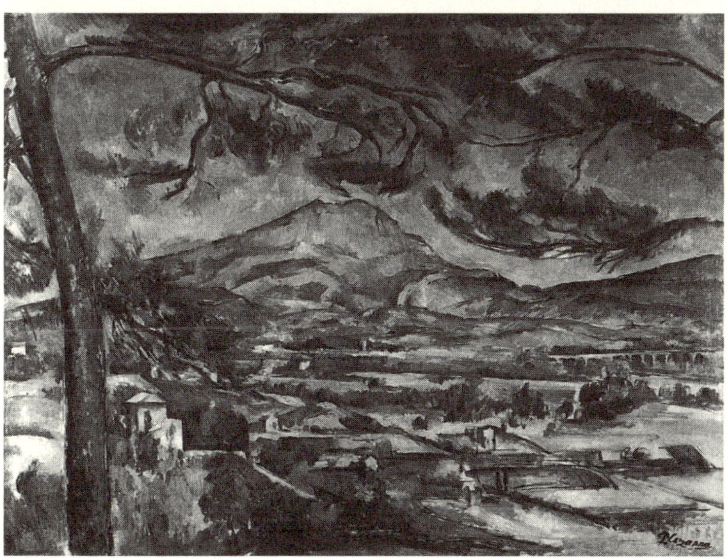

403

ond picture. Since a fundamental difference in the viewpoint of the two scenes is out of the question, the representation of the terrain in one of the two cases must correspond to the natural view more than in the other. In fact, in the London variant, the internal structure of the broad terrain, up to the mountain, agrees with the natural appearance. (This is reproduced well in the photograph of the motif by Rewald.) In the other case, it is very noticeably elevated. In the latter picture, the foreground terrain is included in the space of the picture, in the former, it is not. Based on everything discussed thus far, it seems that the reason for this lies in that striving for a reduction of contrast discussed above. A foreground scene would stand in strong contrast, both physically and spatially, to the expanding depth of the valley's hollow, which stretches over a large distance. However, this kind of foreground scenery *is* employed (one could say it is permitted) where the middle ground and background space are depicted as rising up. (A third variant of this motif, the watercolor in the Collection Paul Cézanne Jr. [V. 914, R. 241], shows nothing new in comparison with the two oil paintings; in its formation of the section and of space, it corresponds to the version in Washington, D.C., with the difference that the tree trunk at right in the watercolor, as in the London picture, is not visible.)

This kind of approach to the problem of foreground formation only seemingly contradicts the earlier observation that Cézanne did not avoid conspicuous foreground objects and, indeed, even seems to have had a preference for them. This fact is a general one, subject only to the limitation imposed by the feature of foreground weakening. What that comparison of the two panoramas with Mont Ste-Victoire shows, however, applies to the special case of the landscape in distant space. Here the inclusion of pronounced foreground scenery in the pictorial section seems tied to certain conditions within the overall form of space. A certain layering of the heights in the middle ground and background, with the aim of reducing the contrast, can be recognized as just such a condition. In this case, Cézanne apparently decided simply on the use of a wide foreground coulisse, and that sinking away of the foreground in the section does not occur (which can also be noticed, for example, in the London landscape of Mont Ste-Victoire in figure 8.14).

The building up of height can be founded in the natural view itself just as well as in an alteration deviating from natural perspective, as in the picture in Washington, D.C. This happens, for example, in the *View of Gardanne* in the Brooklyn Museum of Art (V. 431, R. 571), in which the stacked-up complex of houses in the town and mass of hills beyond terminate toward the bottom with the trees and the sloping hill on the near side.

The *View of the Bay of Marseilles* in the Philadelphia Museum of Art (V. 411, R. 515) (figure 8.15) represents another case. Here again it is the distant landscape that "permits" the large forms of the foreground to appear. The reason for this must actually lie in the fact that the views of the bay of L'Estaque that can still be identified also appear "normal" in the lower section of the painting. No foreground reduction can be discerned, assuming one notices the foreground at all.[12] These scenes are almost all seen from the slopes of the mountain range rising from the shore, which offers a fairly high view onto the settlements and the bay.

Today the spatial formation of these motifs may still be compared with their appearance in nature. We can add yet another example of an apparently elevated high point of view, of the sort produced by a diminishment of the perspectival reduction in size. This occurs in representations of a broadly extended horizontal expanse of terrain. In Cézanne's rendering, these kinds of expanses appear as ascending pieces of land, as if they have been folded up, if only to a small degree. Thus, in the painting of

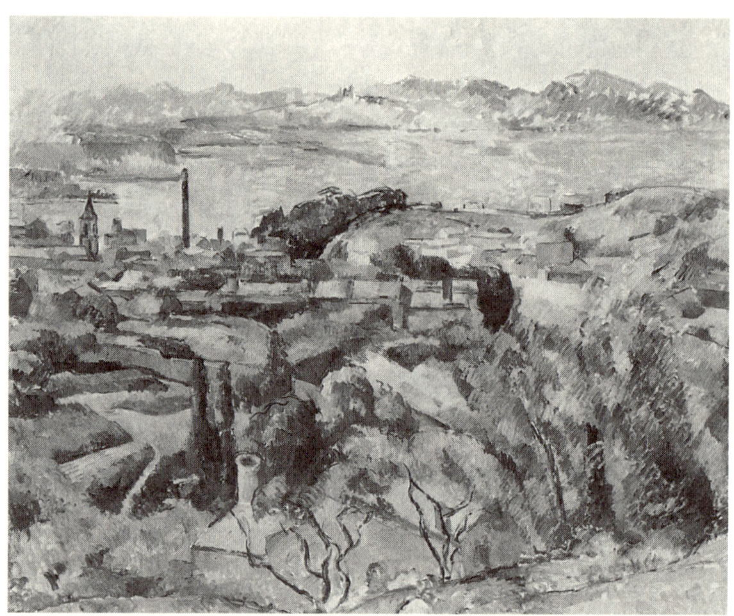

Figure 8.15. Paul Cézanne, *View of the Bay of Marseilles with the Village of St. Henri,* Philadelphia Museum of Art (The Mr. and Mrs. Carroll S. Tyson, Jr. Collection).

the hilly country at Gardanne (figure 8.10), the two houses in the foreground and the base of the mountain range in the background are represented not — corresponding to the natural appearance of the motif (compare the photograph in figure 8.11) — as a gently rising surface stretching with an even slope of the terrain to the beginning of the hills.[13] Rather, the area of land in the foreground looks like a horizontal plane (in reality, its surface falls gently away to the houses and beyond), and directly behind the larger building on the left, the ground seems to rise quite steeply. This elevation of the terrain, in comparison to the level plain (or almost level plain), is visible in Cézanne's painting not only in the nearer strip of land all the way up to the road passing horizontally through the middle of the pictorial section but also in the area beyond the road up to the series of houses in the left background. In both cases, it is recognizable above all in the slant of the perspectival lines that separate the individual fields. Thus, one does not have the impression that one is looking at the valley from a slightly elevated point of view, from a low rise, corresponding to the standpoint in nature. Nor is there an exaggeration of the top view. Rather, one sees an ascending expanse of land enclosed by a range of hills as if from a normal point of view, that is, from a level point obtained from a flat strip of land fairly close to the houses. Perspectival alterations produce a landscape that has a slightly different terrain formation from that of the section in nature.

From all this, it is clear that the impression of an elevated terrain structure, of spaces that are built up one behind the other, in short, of that which in Cézanne's landscapes is generally meant by "unfolding" or "opening up of the surfaces toward the plane," is based only in small part on the peculiarities of linear perspective. If this impression nevertheless exists, and is occasionally emphasized in studies of his work,[14] then it is precisely its special character that must be emphasized, one that hardly ever consists in *measurable* deviations from correct perspective, for example, in the simple impression of opening up in medieval representations of space.[15]

At this point, a distinction is necessary, one that needed to be considered in all the observations made up until now: the distinction between the impression of a particular, fundamental feature that comes from knowledge and comparative examination of the *entire oeuvre* (of a large number of pictures) and the impression produced by the (at least relatively) independent effect of the *single work*. An intense but unclear impression of a single landscape's perspectival appearance, which is not further comprehensible except in negative form (something seems "wrong" with the perspective), can be corroborated and clarified through the examination of a larger number of works. The vague impression in a single picture of an unusual perspectival formation, which resists conceptual clarification no matter how detailed the analysis, can in this way be broadened to an understanding of certain specific methods of formation in order to ascertain what this reduction of the natural appearance means in the perspective of this picture. If anywhere the comparison of a larger totality of works can assist the direct examination of an individual work, then it is in this case of the perspectival formation of space in Cézanne's depiction of the landscape. For it is typical of the perspectival structure of Cézanne's landscape paintings that, in a very concealed manner, deviations from natural linear perspective may only be discerned occasionally, as demonstrated above. If a large number of deviations, in varying degrees, from the laws of linear perspective are taken as a basis, then sometimes these deviations can be more clearly recognized behind, as it were, the "layers" of the specific treatment of surface and the forming of volumes.

To the deviations from natural perspective already mentioned should be added, finally, the forced frontality of buildings or other flat-surfaced, enclosed shapes, that is, of a vertically rotated "folding into surfaces."

Here, too, cases that clearly deviate from correct linear perspective can rarely be detected. An example of this kind was already mentioned earlier with the *Basin at Jas de Bouffan* (figure 8.6), in which the edge of the basin appears to have been reworked into an elongated plane parallel to the picture surface. In the same picture, the figure of the dolphin standing perpendicular to the edge of the basin has obviously been rotated into the profile view. Another example is the *House on the Hill at Jas de Bouffan* (V. 470, R. 688), the two walls of which, with regard to the overall spatial situation, are brought too close to the frontal view. In a case like this, the spatial impression produced by the formation of the building is not captured by an exact linear perspective; what is certain is only the reduction of investigation of the convergence of perspectival lines, which in such cases produces precisely the effect of forced frontality. After all, this tendency cannot be discerned in pictures like the views of Gardanne in the Barnes Foundation (V. 430, R. 569) and the Brooklyn Museum of Art (V. 431, R. 571), where the motif would readily allow for alterations tending toward pervasive frontality.

It has already been remarked that the frontality of the houses stressed in some views of l'Estaque does not imply a *forced* frontal position.

Finally, the use of a foreground strip isolated horizontally near the middle ground should be mentioned. We have already had to refer repeatedly to these cases as examples of an altered direction of perspectival lines, of a "delayed movement of flight lines," for instance, in the foreground formation of the landscape in figure 8.3, or in *Railway Cutting* (figure 8.1). In some landscapes (V. 1531, 1070; R. 832, 426) and to a lesser extent in the forest landscape (V. 788, R. 908), the occasionally conspicuous poverty of detail and unnatural bareness give these foreground strips so much the appearance of necessity that one can speak of them generally as stock compositional formulas that have only the loosest connection with the objective form of the natural model.

*　　*　　*

In looking back and summing up, we need to discuss what all of these reflections have been leading to: what possible significance can scientific perspective have in this kind of pictorial space?

The extent to which the characteristics of Cézanne's landscape perspective can be explained by formal intentions and the extent to which they exist only apart from these intentions or even in spite of them — this relationship of perspectival form to Cézanne's art as a whole reveals the position of his painterly perspective within the historical development of painting. The following recapitulation will consider these questions: what in this mode of forming perspectival space is only a persistent conventional form and is therefore of secondary importance within the artistic formation, and what follows with direct necessity from formal laws? These questions will also be considered with regard to the significance of this perspectival space within the history of painting, which will be set forth in the second part of the present work.

Cézanne's pictorial perspective is most obviously in accord with the total phenomenon of his art in its position vis-à-vis natural perspective's capacity for emotional emphasis and associative enrichment. In nature, the sight of a curved hill crossed by strips of fields instinctively arouses a feeling of curiosity as to what it looks like behind the hill. Every bend in the road arouses a similar feeling of suspense. If one of Cézanne's many bends in the road or any other path leading into spatial depth (for example, V. 666, R. 900 and figure 8.8) is compared with any impressionist version of this kind of motif, for example, Sisley, *The Street*, Louvre, Paris, or Liebermann, *Dune Path*, private collection, then it becomes clear to what extent Cézanne diminishes the motif's atmospheric content — the arousal of curiosity, the temptation to follow the path, and similar sensations that, apart from painting, only poetic representation is capable of expressing — and to what extent impressionism accommodates this atmospheric content, even if impressionism does not intuitively emphasize it and is fundamentally not at all narrative. To the eyes of today's beholder, whose seeing has been fundamentally affected by impressionism, an avenue represented spatially in Cézanne's way (figure 8.8), without any of the seemingly natural spatial tensions in the succession of trees, seems stranger and one may even say more artistic than when the faintest gradations of light are exploited for spatial effects in the same theme, as in chalk drawings by Liebermann, for example. It seems that nowhere else in painting does one find such a radical "stripping of the meaning" of such effects in paths and avenues as in Cézanne's painting.[16]

In addition to perspectival sensations of this type, which essentially have their origin in feelings of movement, there are sensations whose emotional content is based in the experience of perspectival contrasts, in the charm of small, distant parts of the landscape that become visible by looking through the foreground and middle-ground planes.[17] The innumerable forms and nuances of these emotional experiences of perspective are so closely bound up with the *optical* facts of perspective that it takes more artistic reshuffling to suppress them in the picture than to express them. This may be demonstrated by comparing the way impressionist landscape painting deals with the inclusion of emotional and atmospheric values associated with certain effects of distance. Impressionist renderings do not detract from the emotional contents of a remote edge of forest, a valley view, a throng of people on a distant stretch of road, and similar things. Although this emotional content is not sought out or *expressly* depicted, as it is, for example, in the art of van Gogh, all paths leading to it are kept open for the empathic contemplation of the picture's viewer. This is the general attitude of impressionism within which there are, of course, degrees of intensity. Sometimes it is the formation of optical phenomena even in such subjects that draws more attention to itself, as is the case, for the most part, in the paintings of the French impressionists, while in many German impressionist works, the hidden content of emotion and meaning is more clearly perceptible. But even among the French, it is never completely concealed. Take, for example, landscapes by Sisley or, as a typical case, Monet's *Steep Coast* in the Kunsthaus, Zurich, with its strip of beach lying far below and its tiny figures. And in German impressionist landscapes, since they are after all impressionist, the detour by way of the picturesque and atmospheric effects of such distant motifs is always maintained. As a characteristic example of this, a work like Carl Schuch's *Landscape near Purkersdorf* in the collection of K. Haberstock can be cited, especially the distant edge of forest at the picture's right border.[18]

If this is compared with a pictorial detail like the distant scene of Marseilles with the church of Notre-Dame-de-la-Garde in Cézanne's views of the bay of Marseilles (in the version in the Musée d'Orsay, Paris, [V. 428, R. 390], for example, figure 8.16), it becomes clear how completely this style of representation is excluded from the depiction of this subject, which might have provided an opportunity to form various differentiated moods — in the hazy appearance of the distant, large city and the single building on the hill. The presence of a city cannot even be detected, and the vague quality in the representation of the cathedral is not an uncertainty that has the charm of mystery.

Or we can compare the sunlit houses in the background of

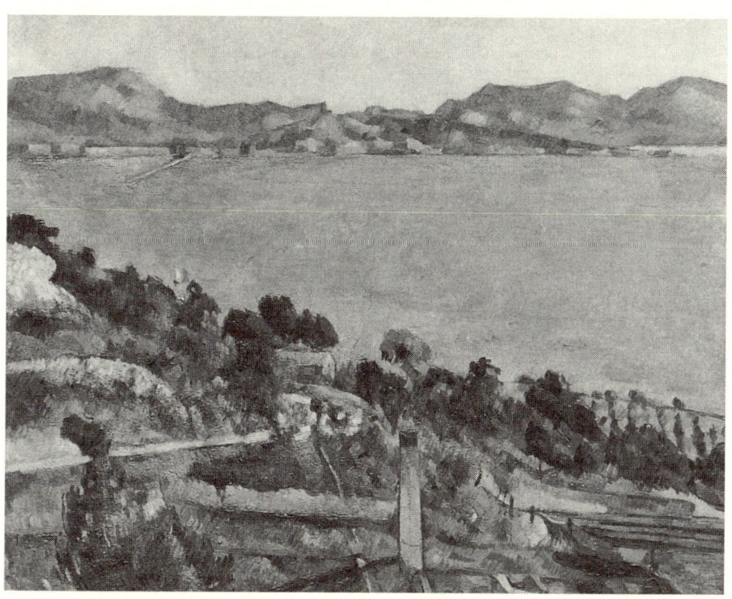

Figure 8.16. Paul Cézanne, *The Bay of Marseilles Seen from L'Estaque,* Musée d'Orsay, Paris.

Sisley's picture of an avenue in the Louvre, for example, with a similar motif in Cézanne's *House of the Hanged Man* (V. 133, R. 202) in order to see how the process of revoking atmosphere is already brought into play during Cézanne's "impressionist" period.

Another decisive component of this contrast between the way the impressionist conception treats such subjects and how Cézanne treats them is the stronger charm of *things* in the impressionist rendering. However, in addition to Cézanne's renunciation of the charm of things, over and above this reduction of the form of individual objects to physically and spatially elemental formations, the atmospheric value that would still be possible in the elemental effects of distance is also restricted to an extreme. This is how it must be in a pictorial space that no longer signifies an actual space accessible to empathy.

This is a significant step beyond impressionism ,which, admittedly, did not aim at the atmospheric content of those small distant details by a directly illustrative method either, as is the case, for example, in van Gogh's representational mode or in the pre-impressionist painting of the nineteenth century.

In view of all the other characteristics of his art, it is only natural that the emotional values of perspective are suppressed to extremes in Cézanne's representational mode. In the disenchanted world of his paintings, there was no room for them.[19] Wherever else romanticism in the broadest sense may appear in the final form of his art — in the tendency toward freer compositional invention, in thematics, in various heroicized and monumentalized forms — it is completely excluded from the expressive realm of formation of pictorial space.

If we are correctly to evaluate this complete elimination of everything romantic from the elementals of forming space, then the general reality content of this art should not be overlooked as a basis for examination. The problem of natural perspective in

Cézanne is touched by exactly this question of the reality content of the optical — more deeply than it is touched by the ineffectiveness of perspective in the sphere of emotional experience (an ineffectiveness that is only an aspect of the emotional value of the total spatial effect).

Up to this point, this content has been looked at again and again with regard to the motif's appearance, and the often surprising extent of this phenomenon has been emphasized. Then some of the main pictorial elements were shown, which we called formal counterforces because of their relation to the tendency toward faithful reproduction and retention of the landscape's basic optical schema. How much they are actually *counterforces* is obvious, particularly with regard to natural linear perspective. All of the described formal laws of the bond between surfaces and space, of the structure of contours and color application, with their consequences for the appearance of objects and space, are in an extreme way designed fundamentally to upset perspective in the conventional sense. Even more than that, they make it possible for perspective to appear superfluous. Earlier, the comparison with the natural view of the motif generated the question of why Cézanne deviates from a perspectival schema that is retained in the general features. Now the reverse question arises: why do the laws of perspective still have any value at all alongside those formal laws of the pictorial organism?

When examined according to abstract, formalist principles, a work by Cézanne appears to be a pictorial structure of modulated patches of color, infiltrated by a system of condensing color that often crystallizes into a configuration of linear structural veins, without this configuration ever becoming an independent, heterogeneous element. And this structure is frequently stabilized by an orthogonally or similarly constructed network of pictorial surfaces and masses.

Even if they were to remain in the service of the imitation of objects, would it not seem that these abstract forms, and especially the new pictorial space formed with them and bound to the surface, were especially suited for the creation of an art detached from nature and abstract in its overall appearance, an art for which compliance with the laws of perspective would only interfere with its own autonomous laws?

In reality, apart from a very few exceptions, Cézanne did not give in to the impulse toward abstraction that is necessarily connected with the elements of his form. His art appears to be one of the purest and most significant examples of a constantly antagonistic combining of abstract, ideal form and the natural data of reality, a combining that is carried out from inner necessity. Admittedly, that is a general formula which says nothing about the exceptional quality of the individual case. It becomes particularly clear, however, in a single feature like the artistic attitude toward scientific perspective, which is one of the basic conditions of natural appearance. By analyzing linear perspective, the conflict and the necessity of the two antagonistic forces' mutual dependence becomes evident.

It must be recognized that it is above all the formal laws that determine one of the essential principles of perspective throughout Cézanne's paintings: this pictorial perspective is of such a kind that everything that could detract from the homogeneity of the material and spatial totality in favor of individual objects has been removed. This explains the phenomenon of the *weakening of perspectival emphasis*, insofar as it occurs in the contours. The bond between space and surfaces also plays a crucial role. It is difficult to reconcile this bond with a strong, linear pull into depth. This is how the features associated with the *reduction of contrast* came about. In this way, like the pull into depth of perspectival lines, the pull into depth caused by relations in volumetric size is diminished through the decrease of perspectival distinctions in size, the "debilitation" of *repoussoir* elements, and the other measures of foreground reduction. Finally, the characteristics associated with the small angle of vision function similarly: the relative narrowness of the field of vision reduces the possibility of significant perspectival tensions in size.

An even more comprehensive cause appears to be also involved in all of these transformations. In Cézanne's representational mode, in which "molecular forces" rather than individual objects are the real building blocks of the picture's structure, the *small* components exercise an influence on the *large* elements of the pictorial structure (the partial masses of matter and space that occupy the various planes of the picture space). Those constructive elements, as they manifest themselves in individual patches of color, are in their essence comparatively undifferentiated; it is precisely through their relative similarity that they produce the homogeneity of the picture's appearance. In the fundamentally related impressionist representational mode, this form leaves the structure of pictorial space largely unaffected. In Cézanne's manner of projection, the formation of color patches is again brought closer to the individual forms of objects, even if only superficially and quite unevenly. However, all the characteristics of the formation of the contour and the perspectival structure militate against the possibility of this leading to a stronger emergence of individual objects.

The effect of the painterly microstructure on the overall compositional form is such an essential feature of Cézanne's art, and one of such great significance in the historical development of painting, that it must be emphasized now before its other effects are mentioned. We already discussed this effect when we considered the question of compositional interventions in the formation of the landscapes' space. In that discussion, only the doubtful, uncertain position of composition in the artist's oeuvre was emphasized, a position that was revealed by the juxtaposition of a conspicuous, occasionally even obtrusive compositional structure, on the one hand, and the deliberate avoidance of compositional structure altogether, on the other hand. Evaluations of Cézanne's art that are influenced by post-impressionist art generally view the simplified, overall compositional structure of the picture as something new when compared with impressionism. At best, they find in the impressionism contemporary with Cézanne a composition hidden behind a tangle of brushstrokes and existing in spite of this tangle. And they argue that this composition, always at work in the picture, is now unveiled by Cézanne and endowed with new monumentality. But these assessments overlook how little Cézanne's composition has of the strength of older, pre-impressionist kinds of composition and how much the strength of his painting lies in other elements that are not at all consistent with composition in the customary sense. It is overlooked that in Cézanne's art — and this is the central point — composition absolutely does not exist in the sense that the term has for all preceding art. Even a scientifically oriented examination of Cézanne's art is inclined to leave this out of consideration. In this case, the analytical habit again stands in the way of understanding. The concept of composition has two meanings. In the first meaning, composition exists in every picture because there is always a distribution of defined masses, surface, and spatial relations of size, in short, all the relations that result from the division of the pictorial rectangle. Alongside this kind of composition, which exists everywhere as an analytical category, there is the other meaning of composition, which consists of a distinctive, consciously artistic element of form that belongs to the content of the picture. Composition of this second kind has a restricted scope of significance. Of course, it is not limited to composition in the academic sense; yet it seems that it is tied to one of two preconditions: there must be a minimum of effective strength in either the *line* or the *modeling* in order to have composition in this second sense. Cézanne's painterly way of representing lacks this minimum of strength in both the line and the plastic modeling.

Of course, many fundamentally dissimilar kinds of composition have been distinguished, innumerable degrees of compositional strength have been established, and the lack of overall compositional form has also been emphasized, as, for example, in the case of impressionism. But this example demonstrates how inadequate customary descriptions are of composition's role. These descriptions are not capable of grasping the peculiar status of composition in Cézanne's art. Confronted with this case, analytical habit, as we already have said, leads to superficiality. Because Cézanne's art, when compared to impressionism, displays a more conspicuous, outward composition, one infers an inner and absolute strength to these compositional forms. But it is much more an (unconscious) conclusion than a sensation that produces this opinion. In the entirety of the pictorial phenomenon, the intensity of the effect of overall compositional forms is only superficially stronger in Cézanne's work than in most impressionist paintings; in reality, it is much weaker. The concealed strength of the composition in many impressionist works is justly emphasized, and the possibility of composition unquestionably existed in even the most broken-up structure of brushstrokes. The impressionist form of projection never threatened that minimum of stability in contours or volumes that is necessary for composition in the second sense; it was only superficially concealed. In comparison with this kind of hidden monumentality, or "secret composition," in Cézanne's case we could speak of a *secret lack of composition*, concealed behind an outwardly monumental form. The devaluating force of the painterly microstructure has its effect precisely in the stark, clear, almost crude compositional units of Cézanne, in their simplified contours and volumes. However much this overall composition may be superficially related to the old kind of composition, in its essence it is not related much at all. It is so unlike the old composition that a radical break must be seen between impressionism and Cézanne: between composition as an element of form, as understood in that second, narrower sense mentioned before, and composition in Cézanne's painting. Through various means of devaluation, Cézanne's composition is deprived so much of independence that it can be called an illusory composition when compared with all preceding forms (just as there is an only apparent accenting of forms and colors in his art). Since we have already looked at some of its characteristics and will discuss these matters further, a description of the characteristic weakness of composition in Cézanne's form can here be omitted.[20] Only its connection with Cézanne's specific pictorial space and the interdependence of these two characteristics will be emphasized, because the peculiarity of the role of perspective is also connected with this. Someone who sees the presence of a "genuine" composition in impressionist works might think that the occasional, complete impressionistic decomposition of linearity and plasticity argues against the stated assumption that a minimum effect of linearity or plasticity is the prerequisite for compositional strength. But in fact, the impressionist form of painting hardly ever truly destroys lines, and it is never really directed against the illusion of plasticity. These are always present in the illusionism of a space represented in reality, an illusionism that impressionism never abandons. If this illusionistic space does not have surface decoration and line as compositional elements, there is always the possibility of a firmly held, overall compositional form. Any possibility of pictorial composition is grounded in decorative surface pattern, on the one hand, and an illusionistic space of some kind, on the other. Cézanne's pictorial form, with its relations between space and the picture plane, remains far from each of these two paths; therefore, there is neither the effective strength of the overall composition nor that of perspective. It seems that linear perspective in its formal mode could not be undermined to such an extent if an analogous process did not apply to the composition of the picture.

If perspective transformed in this way *could* exist, such that it would satisfy Cézanne's formal tendencies with its relatively small deviations from the natural schema, then only one question remains: why did it *have* to exist?

The retention of the perspectival schema in Cézanne's art does not seem to have had its roots in the *peculiarities of pure form*; these only work *against* the perspectival value of the appearance or leave it unaffected. In principle, nothing in the linear perspectival structure of a section from nature accommodates the formal purposes in Cézanne's painterly representation.

Thus even the framework of the picture's linear perspectival structure was only adapted to Cézanne's formation of pictorial space, his schema of structural veins, through the reevaluation of line. When compared with the effects of natural perspective, this reevaluation meant a draining of force and even a loss of spatial clarity.

In the end, the most important reason for Cézanne's retention of the framework of linear perspective is that it was obligatory simply as an elemental condition for the appearance of natural space. Of course, this spatially significant structure of lines also supported a pictorial structure founded in its truest essence on color sensations, and it counteracted the danger of uncertainty and disintegration, the danger of the chaotic, which threatens this method of formation. (The chaotic resonates in the overall impression of Cézanne's represented world because it necessarily belongs to the "form of becoming" given in his representational mode, and so the danger also existed that something negative could develop from this element of the pictorial concept: the chaotic as lack of artistic coherence.) But other systems of linear and spatial strengthening that are not true to nature could also perform this service since, as we saw, they too are partially at work in the picture's structure.

In addition to the general challenge of holding on to the basic optical and spatial schema of the landscape, another very essential and comprehensive characteristic of Cézanne's art is extremely important for the problem of perspective.

Bound up with all of the characteristics of Cézanne's comprehension of matter and space is a *suppression of the subjective* that, in its manner and degree, is unprecedented in the history of Western painting. The elimination of the creating subject has been expounded so often as a fundamental feature of Cézanne's art that, for the moment, only its connection with perspective will be briefly emphasized.[21]

The greatest possible restriction of subjective participation is also clear in a typical feature of Cézanne's perspectival form: the preference for a normal or reduced opening onto the visual field. Through an excessively widened angle of vision, for example, in the art of van Gogh, though the perspectival appearance may itself be neutral, an intensified form develops that makes one especially conscious of the creative personality's forming activity and appears to be a crucial means for van Gogh's subjective animism. Conversely, the view with a smaller opening of the visual field works as a means of suppressing the beholder's awareness of the presence of a creating and reorganizing subject.[22] Only in this sense can one speak of Cézanne's representation of space as objectivist. A more comprehensive use of this term and of its opposite, subjectivist, does not at all seem useful; they can only be applied in a clear way to excessive forms of perspective, like those of van Gogh, and to understatements of perspective, like those of Cézanne. It would be mistaken simply to consider scientific perspective itself as a subjectivist principle and everything that is directed against it in Cézanne's painting, all the processes of weakening and reduction, as the expression of an objectivist principle in the representation of space.[23] This is because the act of choosing a small opening for the angle of vision — which can be described as directed against the subject even though sometimes it also alters the objective situation of the landscape — is relatively insignificant next to the fact that the summary retention of natural linear perspective was a necessary condition for Cézanne's subject-denying form of vision, as it appears in the entirety of his art. From whatever point of view the role of perspective in Cézanne's artistic consciousness is considered, it is completely clear that it did not emerge as the inevitable by-product of a strict system of color-patch projection. Rather, this perspective was part of objective reality and, like reality as a whole, the foundation of form as well as, to a certain extent, the occasion for a perpetual struggle to achieve harmony between reality and the aims of the formal forces.

In this attitude, Cézanne always found his most significant artistic strength; but wherever he departed from it, as in the figural compositions where he faced the task of copying the direct model in nature, there was, for all the greatness of these creations, a loss in aesthetic intensity. If we take, on the one hand, the landscapes, still lifes, and portraits that originated in front of nature and, on the other hand, freely composed figural painting, a comparative evaluation of Cézanne's complete works must arrive at this assessment, that is, as long as the role of abstraction is not overestimated on account of its significance for the art of the following period.[24] (However, it seems unwarranted to create a hierarchy of value within the genres of still life, landscape, and portraiture. Though all of his works have the basic character of still life — the material depiction of the landscapes lacks organic vividness and the portraits lack psychology — this is not enough to put the still life as a genre at the head of his works. If we consider the common traits among those works that originated as direct reproductions of nature, it does not even seem correct to say that the still life is the genre best suited to his formal peculiarities. This is only comparatively true, considering that Cézanne's form of representation eliminates many of the still life's natural effects as well, especially the charm of the material.)

Within Cézanne's painting, some of the essential significance of scientific perspective, both linear and aerial, has been lost, even if the laws of scientific perspective are rarely broken in an obvious way. The *life* of perspective has faded away. Perspective in the old sense is dead, and in an epoch when its natural manifestations were used as an artistic means of expression more than ever before in the history of painting. This occurs in Degas's spatial compositions, for example, and even in the art of Toulouse-Lautrec, in which the representation of the human face works as an expressive vehicle of emotions.[25]

What remains is a schema. But this character of schematic simplification of perspective in Cézanne's painting is so closely linked to the fundamental content of his representational mode that it cannot be thought of as merely a schema. The schema is not simply destined to serve as a foil for the real, central element of form, namely, the coloristic phenomenon. Rather, all the forms of reduction and simplification of objective reality are determined by a mode of seeing directed at the elemental spatial and objective form of the landscape. These devices make it possible for the artist to translate this way of seeing into pictorial form without resorting to the abstract invention of form.

This also answers the question we asked earlier: to what extent was Cézanne's approach to pictorial perspective the mere prolongation of a formal convention? There is *nothing* conventional in the way all of its representational and formal values cohere. One can only speak casually, for the purposes of characterization, of the retention of a perspectival schema.

NOTES

1. The word "section" has been chosen to translate Novotny's use of the term *Ausschnitt*. This is not a typical art historical term, and it seems that Novotny is purposefully coining a phrase. "Section" carries the connotations inherent within *Ausschnitt* of cutting away. "Pictorial section" refers to a view in nature that has been selected and cut away from a whole to serve as the motif for the painting. In other contexts, "section" can indicate a specific portion of a painting, defined in spatial or representational terms — TRANS.

2. The abbreviation "V." refers to the catalog by Lionello Venturi, *Paul Cézanne: Son art, son oeuvre* (Paris: Rosenberg, 1936) "R." refers to the catalogs by John Rewald, *The Paintings of Paul Cézanne* (New York: Abrams, 1996) and *Paul Cézanne: The Watercolors* (Boston: Little, Brown, 1983). Novotny's references have been updated to indicate the current locations of the works — TRANS.

3. Compare what Roger Fry has said about the formation of these ellipses in *Cézanne: A Study of His Development* (London: Leonard and Virginia Woolf at the Hogarth Press, 1927), p. 48; and also Albert Gleizes, *Peinture et perspective descriptive; conference faite à Paris le 22 mars 1927, à la Fondation Carnegie* (Sablons: Moly-Sabata, 1927), pp. 6ff.

4. The character of the contour formation in Cézanne's art has been most clearly described by Fry, esp. p. 49ff.; see also Fritz Novotny, "Paul Cézanne," *Belvedere* 8 (1929), p. 444ff. See below p. 72ff.

5. The views of Gardanne (V. 430–32; R. 569, 571, 570), the landscape of L'Estaque in the Musée d'Orsay (foreground) (figure 8.16), and the panoramas of Mont Ste-Victoire (figures 8.13 and 8.14) are examples of this manner.

6. In the introduction to his critical catalog (p. 33), Venturi briefly mentions the absence of perspectival effects in Cézanne's representational mode and sees the single exception in the landscape of Louveciennes painted after a work by Pissarro in 1872 (V. 153, R. 184). Here the effect of perspective is said to be used in an impressionist manner, and so it is, because the painting has a direct impressionist model. Such an exceptional position, however, is not appropriate for this picture; in other works from Cézanne's "impressionist" period (which lasted for about five years, from 1872 to 1877), there is also a very similar way of

handling perspective. Particularly during this phase, perspectival effects that are more like those of the impressionists as well as their antithesis appear simultaneously in a way that is far more complicated than Venturi's argument would suggest.

7. This does not mean that we have to reject altogether the interpretation of this phenomenon as an avoidance of the low point of view. That interpretation might be rejected, for example, on the grounds that it assumes an encounter between the artist and an objective perspectival fact and that it fails to shift the explanation entirely into a realm of aesthetic creation removed from any comparison with nature. These two things do not contradict each other; rather, in both we can identify a similar tendency.

8. A counterexample to Cézanne's way of representing the space of the avenue is Théodore Rousseau's *Chestnut Avenue in Soullier Castle*, which fundamentally corresponds to the spatial appearance of the motif as it exists in nature. In Prosper Dorbec's essay "Le Voyage de Théodore Rousseau en Vendée: Charles Le Roux," a photograph of the avenue in the painting is provided at the end (*Gazette des Beaux Arts*, 5.17 [1928], pp. 38–39).

9. In order to show this clearly, the Dutch landscape painting of the seventeenth century may be mentioned as a counterexample. In this painting, those two functions of foreground scenery possess complete equality and produce the characteristic unity that Eugène Fromentin defined in the short formula: "All Dutch painting is concave" (*The Masters of Past Time* [London: Phaidon, 1948], p. 103).

10. Johnson's photograph of the subject [E. L. Johnson, "Cézanne's Country," *The Arts* (1930)] captures the middle ground with reasonable accuracy, but the form of the mountain is clearly inserted later into the photograph.

11. The picture in Washington, D.C. (figure 8.13) has a slightly larger section and is painted from a spot at the edge of the forest a little to the right of the London picture's position (figure 8.14).

12. In the view of L'Estaque, we find the uncommon instance in Cézanne's landscapes of a conspicuously large, dominating foreground object: the roof section of a house, seen in a somewhat oblique view from the gabled side. (The motif is easily identified but at present cannot be photographed.) Venturi is mis-

taken when, in an analysis of *Bay of Marseilles seen from L'Estaque* in the Metropolitan Museum of Art in New York (V. 429, R. 625), he says that Cézanne has chosen a high point of view onto the bay in order to allow the size of the water surface to have an effect ("Cézanne," *L'Arte* [1935], pp. 386–87, figure 15). The height of this point of view would not be possible in reality. The view of the Gulf of Marseilles by Emile Loubon that is used for the argument (Venturi's figure 1) is not suitable for the comparison, since it shows the panorama taken in from a position much farther inland. The high point of view represented in these pictures actually ensues from the mountain range rising directly over L'Estaque, from which Cézanne painted most of his views of the bay. Because of the spatial situation, one cannot speak of a foreground plane that has been left out, even when standing right in front of the Metropolitan Museum's painting (Venturi, p. 386). In still another isolated case, in the late picture of Mont Ste-Victoire already mentioned (V. 665, R. 902), Venturi detects a reduction of the landscape's foreground (p. 408). But here, where the reduction of foreground actually makes itself felt, he explains it as an effort to give the size of the mountain a powerful effect; he does not mention the fundamental significance of this phenomenon for the formation of space and its connection with the structure of the picture. In fact, Venturi denies that an examination of spatial formation using the natural model as a comparison could have any value at all (p. 409). But then what he calls for in place of such a comparative examination, "Non c'è che da lasciarsi andare a seguire il modo di sentire di Cézanne, per intendere il suo dramma e la sua grandezza," insofar as it cannot be dismissed as a vague, meaningless remark, leads precisely to a more thorough examination of the formation of the space of the landscape in Cézanne's art.

13. The photograph taken with a telephoto lens reproduces the actual impression of space fairly accurately. The part of the photograph reproduced here corresponds to the "neutral" field of vision. It reveals that the painting's foreground fades away strongly (as mentioned already for this example) and shows the decrease in distance that is connected with this sectional reduction. On the other hand, the slope of the middle-ground terrain is quite different in the photograph than in the painting, but comparing the painting with the terrain

as it appears in nature reveals that the difference is not so pronounced. The painting does not diverge significantly from the actual form of the terrain. The edges of the gables of the larger building are positioned parallel to the borders of the fields beyond, and so, like these, they are steeply sloped. Also, the contours of the mountain are elevated a little too much, which accords with a field of vision that has been narrowed a little horizontally.

14. For example, in Alfred Neumeyer, "Zur Raumpsychologie der 'Neue Sachlichkeit,'" *Zeitschrift für bildende Kunst* 61 (1927–28), p. 71.

15. Of all the motifs that have been compared with their models from nature, only the previously mentioned watercolor with the mountain range of Pilon du Roi shows a terrain structure that has been excessively elevated (V. 909, R. 246).

16. Whereas impressionist street views usually represent the convex swelling of the road surface, Cézanne's do not. This too demonstrates how Cézanne's representation reduces the atmospheric content of space, since renouncing that objective detail also means giving up the atmospheric charm of perspective.

17. On how distance is experienced when contemplating a landscape, see H. Marcus, "Distance in the Landscape," *Zeitschrift für Ästhetik und allgemeine Kunstwissenschaft* 11 (1916). For the small view of distant space as an expressive motif, see Fritz Novotny, "Van Gogh's teekeningen van het 'Straatje te Saintes-Maries,'" *Maandblad voor beeldende Kunsten* (1936), p. 376ff.

18. Reproduced in Heinrich Schwarz, *Künstlerdokumente zu den Werken der Galerie des 19. Jahrhunderts* (Vienna: Schroll, 1928), figure 76.

19. Here another example should be mentioned to demonstrate that Cézanne does not avoid spatial situations in which those feelings of tension would naturally occur. In the *Landscapes with Mont Ste-Victoire* in the Metropolitan Museum of Art in New York and in a private collection (V. 452, 453; R. 511, 512), with their foreground scenery of a group of pine trees, deep view of the valley's open land, and road winding vertically into the picture's space, the natural effects of space are made to serve Cézanne's artistic purposes, especially the optical and emotional value of contrast reduction.

20. This devalued composition is one of the characteristics of Cézanne's painting most difficult to convey with a descriptive explanation. For some viewers, the existence of a superficially vivid and succinct composition signifies an absolutely strong composition, for instance, in *Card Players* or *Boy in the Red Vest* (V. 681, R. 658). To these viewers it should be replied that just because something exists in a work of art does not mean that it exists artistically as well. They will say: but there *is* a completely obvious composition there! Whereupon it would be objected: if it is viewed detached and for itself, then it can legitimately be asserted that there is indeed rich material for an analytical assessment of the composition. But composition is *not* present if composition is defined as a dominating element of form, the effect of which is aided by other elements of form.

Admittedly, this should not be considered a strict rule since, after all, representational techniques differ to a great degree in Cézanne's paintings, and it is precisely these differences that have an influence on the effective strength of the composition. There are elements of "genuine" composition with Cézanne also, but these consist especially of those cases in which the law of the large form complies with that of the microstructure, for example, when orthogonals appear in the pictorial structure. (Of course, here the monumental compositions of the early period, like that of the *Still Life with the Black Clock* [V. 69, R. 136], are not being considered since the characteristic of the devalued composition belongs only to Cézanne's mature art.)

21. See my attempt at representing its form of expression, which extends from the negation of everything affective to the specific characteristic of the picture as a formal object, in Fritz Novotny, "Das Problem des Menschen Cézanne im Verhältnis zu Seiner Kunst," *Zeitschrift für Ästhetik und allgemeine Kunstwissenschaft* 26 (1932), p. 291ff.

22. Since a correspondence between van Gogh's and Cézanne's formation of space and objects has been pointed out again recently, namely by Walter Ueberwasser in his study *Le Jardin de Daubigny: das letzte Hauptwerk van Goghs* (Basel, Cratander, 1936), it must here be objected, against this parallel, that it is precisely the formation of pictorial perspective that represents the deepest

contrast between them. In the chapter "Form and Perspective in van Gogh," if Ueberwasser means that the "fundamental forms" of circles, rectangles, ovals, and so on that are significant for van Gogh's pictorial composition correspond "to similar occurrences in Cézanne's art" (p. 53), then he emphasizes a relationship that amounts merely to the fact that the elementary, constructive forms in both masters' art have a new value. The artists' perspectival conceptions of these constructive forms, however, differ strongly. Nothing is capable of demonstrating this deep contrast more clearly than the way in which the perspectival ellipse is represented by both painters. In contrast to the weakened perspectival form of Cézanne's ellipse stands the intensified ellipse by van Gogh. Van Gogh's spatial ellipses are often distorted obliquely into depth, for instance, in the two examples shown in Ueberwasser of the basket with apples (figure 26) and of the pond (figure 28), and also the fountain in the reed pen drawing from Saint Rémy, J.B. de la Faille, *The Works of Vincent van Gogh* (New York: Reynal, 1970) (no. 1531).

23. On the problem of the applicability of the concepts objective and subjective to perspectival representation, see Erwin Panofsky's fundamental discussion in "Perspektive als 'Symbolische Form,'" *Vorträge der Bibliothek Warburg* (1924–25), p. 290; translated as *Perspective as Symbolic Form,* trans. Christopher S. Wood (New York: Zone Books, 1991), pp. 71–72.

24. As substitutes for the direct view, the pictorial models that Cézanne used for figural representations were generally too weak to counteract the pull toward summarizing, compositionally limited abstractions.

The pictures painted with the use of photographs seem to occupy a special position here. Bernard and Georges Rivière have argued that Cézanne occasionally decided on this method. According to Rivière, the portrait of Chocquet is supposed to have been painted after a photograph (V. 532, R. 460; compare Venturi's note on the picture). However, three cases of this kind can be proven with certainty. In an early self-portrait (V. 18, R. 72), the features, posture, and conduct of light so strongly resemble those in the photograph of the artist from the year 1861 (reproduced in Leo Larguier, *Le Dimanche avec Paul Cézanne* [Paris: L'Edition, 1925], next to p. 13) that a connection between the painting and the photograph is beyond doubt. (I have Leo Marschuetz and Dr. Rewald to thank for the reference to this correspondence; see also Venturi's comment on the portrait.) More instructive than this early work, which is atypical, is the second instance: the *Self-Portrait* in a private collection (V. 1519, R. 587). It is painted from a photograph from the year 1872. Here the representation of the face and clothing is also characterized by a sharp contrast in the rendering of light, which has its origin in the black-and-white form of the photograph. One would be inclined to explain the clumsy foreshortening of the crossed leg in this way as well, but it is improbable that there are copies of the same photograph that show the legs of the sitter. These have presumably been added in the painting, and the odd foreshortening and fashioning of the hands can be explained by the fact that this part of the picture was painted without a model.

As far as the distortions occurring in it are concerned, this picture occupies a strange and revealing intermediate position. At first glance, it is like the portraits painted after reality and makes it possible to recognize by contrast those forms that were developed in response to painted or drawn models with their arbitrary features. Generally, this reveals the difference between Cézanne's relationship to the real object and space and to a reality that is already transformed into a picture. To a certain degree, the photograph can still be treated like the formal material of reality. On the other hand, even the photograph could not entirely replace three-dimensional reality as model for the painter. This can be seen in the small displacements, instances of clumsiness, and distortions (for instance, in the odd, flatly pressed right half of the face) that, just like those sharp contrasts in the distribution of light, differ from the alterations of proportion and reorganizations that occur in portraits painted after nature.

Cézanne's peculiar reaction to the photographic model can be further clarified if Degas, for whom the photograph has the value of an image of reality, is compared as a counterexample. This can be seen, for example, in the portrait of Princess Metternich painted after a photograph (reproduced in John Rewald, "Un Portrait de la princesse Metternich par Edgar Degas," *L'Amour de l'Art* 18 (March 1937). The third known case of Cézanne's use of a photograph occurs with the drawing in the Musée d'Orsay of Pissarro (V. 1235). A group portrait from Pontoise from the year 1877 (reproduced in John Rewald, *Cézanne et Zola*

[Paris: Sedrowski, 1936], figure 32) serves as model. In this drawing, however, the reorganizations that characterize the former painting do not occur.

25. By exploiting the effects of real space for psychological content, Toulouse-Lautrec's art indeed represents an evolutionary high point and end point for the numerous associations between the depiction of human beings and the effect of space. For example, in the portrait of Baron Delaporte (reproduced in Gustave Coquiot, *Toulouse-Lautrec* [Berlin, n.d.], plate 29), the entire surrounding space, the space lying outside the pictorial section, as external appearance as well as stage for an event, is incorporated into the pictorial content by the eyes and the half smile of the portrayed subject. All of this is supported by the structure of curves opening to the left in the seated figure. Analogous, superficially related examples of this no doubt exist in the portrayal of human beings from preceding times, but scarcely anywhere do they have the same intensity. An older, speculative and mathematical approach to the indirect expansion of space is represented, for example, by the depiction of mirrors from Van Eyck's Arnolfini portrait to Velazquez' *Las Meninas* and on to Manet's *Bar in the Folies Bergère* and Toulouse-Lautrec himself. A more recent approach based on physiognomy and psychology leads to the forms of the late nineteenth century. These latter forms — and here Toulouse-Lautrec's pictorial spaces with their abundance of associations stand at the fore, even before Degas or Vuillard — are still built on the impressionist conception of space. (Even in a portrait like Rembrandt's *Nicolaes Bruyningh* in Kassel, which can serve as an example of the second approach, spatial expansion through the representation of the face is created by an outward gaze that essentially establishes the relation between two centers, the portrayed and a person who is not visible.)

Translated by Kimberly Smith.

Part Four

Contemporary Responses

Walter Benjamin, "Rigorous Study of Art: On the First Volume of Kunstwissenschaftliche Forschungen" (1931/1933)

Walter Benjamin (1892–1940) was born in Berlin, studied philosophy and literature, and eventually settled in Berlin, working as a literary critic and translator. His Habilitationsschrift "Der Ursprung des deutschen Trauerspiels," which might have led to a university career, was rejected by the University of Frankfurt in 1925. Benjamin left Germany in 1933 and settled in Paris. He committed suicide in flight from the Gestapo.

Benjamin took an interest in Alois Riegl already as a student and in 1929 wrote that "in the last four decades no art-historical book has had such a substantive and methodologically fruitful effect" as Late Roman Art Industry. *Benjamin's admiration for Riegl governed his generally approbatory reading of the first volume of Hans Sedlmayr and Otto Pächt's* Kunstwissenschaftliche Forschungen. *He was impressed by the adventurous essays by Pächt and Carl Linfert but seems to have overestimated the materialist and "philological" aspects of the structure-analytical method.*

Benjamin's first version of the review was rejected by the editors of Frankfurter Zeitung. *A revised version was published in 1933, several months after he had left Germany for good. This translation combines the two redactions: the text is the more polemical first version; passages deleted for the published version are given in pointed brackets; passages added for the published version are given in footnotes.*

(Source: Walter Benjamin, "Rigorous Study of Art: On the First Volume of Kunstwissenschaftliche Forschungen," *trans. Thomas Y. Levin, October 47 [1988], pp. 84–90. ©1988 October Magazine Ltd. and the Massachusetts Institute of Technology. Interpolation of two versions of "Strenge Kunstwissenschaft. Zum ersten Bande der Kunstwissenschaftliche Forschungen," first version 1931, second version published in Literaturblatt der Frankfurter Zeitung, July 30, 1933 [vol. 66, no. 31]; both*

*reprinted in Walter Benjamin, Gesammelte Schriften, ed. Hella Tiedemann-Bartels
[Frankfurt: Suhrkamp, 1972], vol. 3, pp. 363–74.)*

Rigorous Study of Art: On the First Volume of *Kunstwissenschaftliche Forschungen* (1931/1933)[1]

Walter Benjamin

In the foreword to his 1898 study *Classic Art: An Introduction to the Italian Renaissance,* Heinrich Wölfflin made a gesture that cast aside the history of art as it was then understood by Richard Muther.[2] "Contemporary public interest," he declared,

> seems nowadays to want to turn toward more specifically artistic questions. One no longer expects an art historical book to give mere biographical anecdotes or a description of the circumstances of the time; rather one wants to learn something about those things that constitute the value and the essence of a work of art.... The natural thing would be for every art historical monograph to contain some aesthetics as well.

A bit further on one reads: "In order to be more certain of attaining this goal, the first, historical, section has been furnished with a second, systematic, section as a counterpart."[3] This arrangement is all the more indicative because it reveals not only the aims but also the limits of an endeavor that was so epoch making in its time. And, in fact, Wölfflin did not succeed in his attempt to use formal analysis (which he placed at the center of his method) to remedy the bleak condition in which his discipline found itself at the end of the nineteenth century.[4] He identified the dualism of a flat, universalizing history of the art of "all cultures and times," on the one hand, and an academic aesthetic, on the other, without, however, being able to overcome it entirely.

Only from the perspective of the current situation does it become evident to what extent the understanding of art history as universal history — under whose aegis eclecticism had free play — fettered authentic research. And this is not only true for the study of art. In a programmatic explanation, the literary historian Walter Muschg writes:

> It is fair to say that the most essential work being done at present is almost exclusively oriented toward the monograph. To a great extent, today's generation no longer believes in the significance of an all-encompassing presentation. Instead it is grappling with figures that it sees marked primarily by gaps during that era of universal histories.[5]

Indeed, the "turn away from an uncritical realism in the contemplation of history and the shriveling up of macroscopic constructions" are the most important hallmarks of the new research.[6] Hans Sedlmayr's programmatic article, "Toward a Rigorous Study of Art," the opening piece in the recently published yearbook *Kunstwissenschaftliche Forschungen* (Research essays in the study of art), is entirely in accordance with this position:

> The currently evolving phase in the study of art will have to emphasize, in a heretofore unknown manner, the *investigation of individual works*. <Nothing is more important at the present stage than an improved knowledge of the individual work of art, and it is in just

this task, above all, that the current study of art manifests its incompetence.> ... Once the individual work of art is perceived as a still unmastered task specific to the study of art, it appears powerfully new and close. Formerly a mere means to knowledge, a trace of something else that was to be disclosed through it, the work of art now appears as a self-contained *small world* of its own, particular sort.[7]

In accordance with these introductory remarks, the three essays that follow are thus rigorously monographic studies.[8] G. A. Andreades presents Hagia Sophia as a synthesis between orient and occident; Otto Pächt develops the historical task posed by Michael Pacher; and Carl Linfert explores the foundations of the architectural drawing.[9] What these studies share is a convincing love for — and a no less convincing mastery of — their subject. The three authors have nothing in common with the type of art historian "who was really convinced that works of art should not be investigated but rather only 'experienced,' but who proceeded to investigate anyway — only badly."[10] Furthermore, these authors know that headway can be made only if one considers contemplation of one's own activity — a new awareness — not as a constraint but as an impetus to rigorous study. This is particularly so because such study is not concerned with objects of pleasure, with formal problems, with giving form to experience, or with any other clichés inherited from a belletristic consideration of art. Rather, this sort of studious work considers the formal incorporation of the given world by the artist

not a selection but rather always an advance into a field of knowledge that did not yet "exist" prior to the moment of this formal conquest.... This approach only becomes possible through a frame of mind that recognizes that the realm of perception itself changes over time and in accordance with shifts in cultural and intellectual direction. Such a frame of mind, however, in no way presumes objects that are always present in an unvarying manner such that their formal makeup is merely determined by a changing "stylistic drive" within perceptual surroundings that remain constant.

For "we should never be interested in 'problems of form' as such, as if a form ever arose out of formal problems alone or, to put it in other words, as if a form ever came into existence for the sake of the stimulus it would produce."

Also characteristic of this manner of approaching art is the "esteem for the insignificant" (which the brothers Grimm practiced in their incomparable expression of the spirit of true philology).[11] But what animates this esteem if not the willingness to push research forward to the point where even the "insignificant" — no, precisely the insignificant — becomes significant? The bedrock that these researchers come up against is the concrete bedrock of past historical existence. The insignificance with which they are concerned is neither the nuance of new stimuli nor the characteristic trait, which was formerly employed to identify column forms much the way Linné[12] taxonomized plants. Instead it is the inconspicuous <or also the offensive aspect (the two together are not a contradiction)> that survives in <true> works and that constitutes the point where the content reaches the breaking point for an authentic researcher. <One need only read a study such as the one on the Sistine Madonna published years ago by Hubert Grimme (who does not belong to this group) in order to observe how much such an inquiry, based on the most inconspicuous data of an object, can wrest from even the most worn-out things.>[13] And thus, because of the <focus on materiality>[14] in such work, the precursor of this new type of art scholar is not Wölfflin but Riegl. Pächt's investigation of Pacher "is a new attempt at that grand form of presentation exemplified in Riegl's masterly command of the transition from the individual object to its cultural and intellectual function <as can be seen especially in his study 'The Dutch Group Portrait.'"[15] One could just as well refer to Riegl's *Late Roman Art Industry*,[16] particularly since this work>[17] demonstrates in exemplary fashion the fact that sober and simultaneously undaunted research never misses the vital concerns of its time. The person who reads Riegl's major work today, recalling that it was written at almost the same time as the work by Wölfflin cited in the opening paragraph, will recognize retrospectively how forces are already stirring subterraneously in *Late Roman Art Industry* that will surface a decade later in expressionism. Thus one can assume that sooner or later contemporaneity will catch up with the studies by Pächt and Linfert as well.

<There are some methodological reservations, however, regarding the advisability of the move that Sedlmayr attempts in his introductory essay, juxtaposing the rigorous study of art as a "secondary" field of study against a primary (namely positivist) study of art. The kind of research undertaken in this volume is so dependent on auxiliary fields of study — painting technique and painting media, the history of motifs, iconography — that it can be confusing to constitute these as a somehow separate "first study of art." Sedlmayr's essay also demonstrates how difficult it is for a particular course of research (such as the one represented here) to establish purely methodological definitions without reference to any concrete examples whatsoever. This is difficult, but is it necessary? Is it appropriate to place this new aspiration (*Wollen*) so assiduously under the patronage of phenomenology and Gestalt theory? It could easily be that in the process one loses nearly as much as one gains. Admittedly, the references to "levels of meaning" in the works, to their "physiognomic character," to their "sense of orientation" can be useful in the polemic against posi-

tivist art chatter and even in the polemic against formalist analysis. But they are of little help to the self-definition of the new type
of research.>[18] This type of study stands to gain <more>[19] from
the insight that the more crucial the works are, the more inconspicuously and intimately their meaning content is tied to their
material content.[20] It is concerned with the correlation that gives
rise to reciprocal illumination between, on the one hand, the historical process and radical change and, on the other hand, the
accidental, external, and even strange aspects of the work of
art. For if the most meaningful works prove to be precisely those
whose life is most deeply embedded in their material contents —
one thinks of Giehlow's interpretation of Dürer's *Melencolia*[21] —
then over the course of their historical duration these material
contents present themselves to the researcher all the more clearly
the more they have disappeared from the world.

It would be difficult to find a better clarification of the implications of this train of thought than Linfert's study located at the
end of the volume. As the text explains, its very subject matter,
the architectural drawing, "is a marginal case."[22] But it is precisely
in the investigation of the marginal case that the material contents reveal their key position most decisively. If one examines
the abundant number of plates accompanying Linfert's study, one
discovers names in the captions that are unfamiliar to the layman
and, to some extent, to the professional as well. As regards the
images themselves, one cannot say that they *re*-produce architecture. They *produce* it in the first place, a production that less often
benefits the reality of architectural planning than it does dreams.
One sees, to take a few examples, P. E. Babel's heraldic, ostentatious portals, the fairy-tale castles that Jacques Delajoue has con-
jured into a shell, Juste-Aurèle Meissonnier's knickknack architecture, Etienne-Louis Boullée's conception of a library that
looks like a train station, and Filippo Juvara's ideal views (*prospet-*

tiva ideale) that look like glances into the warehouse of a building dealer: a completely new and untouched world of images, which Baudelaire would have ranked higher than all painting. <In Linfert's work, however, the images are submitted to a descriptive technique that succeeds in establishing the most revealing facts in this unexplored marginal realm. There is, as is commonly known, a manner of representing buildings using purely painterly means. The architectural drawing is sharply distinguished from images of this sort and is found to have the closest affinity to nonrepresentational work, that is, the supposedly authentically architectonic presentations of buildings in topographic designs, prospects, and *vedute*. Since in these, too, certain "errors" have survived up through the late eighteenth century despite all the progress in naturalism, Linfert takes this to be a peculiar imaginary world of architecture, which is markedly different from that of the painters. There are various indications that confirm the specificity of this world, the most important one being that such architecture is not primarily "seen" but rather is imagined as an objective entity and is experienced by those who approach or even enter it as a surrounding space sui generis, that is, without the distancing effect of the frame of the pictorial space. Thus, what is crucial in the consideration of architecture is not seeing but the apprehension of structures. The objective effect of the buildings on the imaginative being of the viewer is more important than their "being seen." In short, the most essential characteristic of the architectural drawing is that "it does not take a pictorial detour."

So much for the formal aspects.> In Linfert's analyses, however, formal questions are very closely tied to historical circumstances. His investigation deals with "a period during which the architectural drawing began to lose its principal and decisive expression."[23] But how transparent this "process of decay" becomes here! How the architectural prospects open up in order to take into their core allegories, stage designs, and monuments! And each of these forms in turn points to unrecognized aspects that appear to the researcher Linfert in their full concreteness: Renaissance hieroglyphics, Piranesi's visionary fantasies of ruins, the temples of the Illuminati, such as we know them from *The Magic Flute*.[24] Here it becomes evident that the hallmark of the new type of researcher is not the eye for the "all-encompassing whole" nor the eye for the "comprehensive context" <(which mediocrity has claimed for itself) but rather the capacity to be at home in marginal domains. The men whose work is contained in this yearbook represent the most rigorous of this new type of researcher. They are the hope of their field of study.>[25]

NOTES

1. A translation, interpolating both the first (unpublished) and the second (final) version of "Strenge Kunstwissenschaft. Zum ersten Bande der *Kunstwissenschaftlichen Forschungen,*" which appeared, under Benjamin's pseudonym, Detlef Holz, on July 30, 1933, in the literature section of *Frankfurter Zeitung* 66.31; both reprinted in Walter Benjamin, *Gesammelte Schriften* (Frankfurt: Suhrkamp, 1982), vol. 3, pp. 363–74. All notes are by the translator.

2. Richard Muther (1860–1909), an art historian and critic often cited as paradigmatic of the old school of nineteenth-century art history; his work was a mixture of religiosity, sentimentality, and eroticism.

3. Heinrich Wölfflin, *Die klassische Kunst. Eine Einführung in die italienische Renaissance* (Munich: Bruckmann, 1899), pp. vii–viii; trans. from the 8th ed. by Linda and Peter Murray as *Classic Art: An Introduction to the Italian Renaissance* (London and New York: Phaidon, 1952), pp. xi–xii (translation modified).

4. In the second version (hereafter referred to as V2), this sentence reads (changes in italics): "In fact, Wölfflin did not *entirely* succeed in his attempt to use formal analysis (which he placed at the center of his method) to remedy the *depressing* condition in which his discipline found itself at the end of the nineteenth century and *which Dvořák would later identify so precisely in his obituary of Riegl.*" See Max Dvořák, "Alois Riegl," *Mittheilungen der K.K. Zentralkommission für Denkmalpflege* 4, no. 3 (1905). pp. 225–76; reprinted in Max Dvořák, *Gesammelte Aufsätze zur Kunstgeschichte* (Munich: Piper, 1929), pp. 279–98.

5. Walter Muschg, "Das Dichterportrait in der Literaturgeschichte," in Emil Ermatinger (ed.), *Philosophie der Literaturwissenschaft* (Berlin: Junker und Dünnhaupt, 1930), p. 311. Compare also Benjamin's citation of the same passage in his essay "Literaturgeschichte und Literaturwissenschaft," *Gesammelte Schriften*, vol, 3, pp. 289–90.

6. *Ibid.*, p. 314.

7. Hans Sedlmayr, "Zu einer strengen Kunstwissenschaft," in Otto Pächt (ed.), *Kunstwissenschaftliche Forschungen* (Berlin: Frankfurter Verlags-Anstalt, 1931), vol. 1, pp. 19–20.

8. In V2, this sentence reads: "Consistent with these remarks, the principal components of the new yearbook are three rigorously monographic studies."

9. G. A. Andreades, "Die Sophienkathedrale von Konstantinopel," in *Kunstwissenschaftliche Forschungen*, pp. 33–94; Otto Pächt, "Die historische Aufgabe Michael Pachers," in *ibid.*, pp. 95–132; Carl Linfert, "Die Grundlagen der Architekturzeichnungen (mit einem Versuch über französiche Architekturzeichnungen des 18. Jahrhunderts)," in *ibid.*, pp. 133–246.

10. Hans Sedlmayr, "Toward a Rigorous Study of Art," p. 174.

11. Although Benjamin repeatedly attributes this formulation to the brothers Grimm [see also Walter Benjamin, *Briefe,* ed. Gershom Scholem and Theodor Adorno (Frankfurt: Suhrkamp, 1966), p. 794], it does not appear as such in their writings. Instead, as Roland Kany explains in his recent study *Mnemosyne als Programm* (Tübingen: Niemeyer, 1988), pp. 234–35, Benjamin's definition of philology as the "esteem for the insignificant" has a somewhat different genealogy. The expression first occurs in a letter to Goethe in which Sulpiz Boisserée describes a review of the Grimms' *Altdeutsche Wälder* by A. W. Schlegel. According to Boisserée's account, Schlegel "praises what is to be praised but ridicules with Grimm-like sarcasm the trivial and inconsequential production of meaning and wordplay, all their esteem for the insignificant." See Sulpiz Boisserée, *Briefwechsel mit Goethe* (Stuttgart: Cotta, 1862), vol. 2, p. 72. As Kany notes, following the publication in 1862 of Boisserée's correspondence with Goethe, the phrase is first taken up — albeit stripped of its initially pejorative thrust and enshrined as the paradigmatic expression of Grimmian philology — by Wilhelm Scherer in his biography *Jacob Grimm. Zwei Artikel der Preussischen Jahrbücher* (Berlin: Reimer, 1865), pp. 79f. Indeed, in the second edition of the Grimm biography (1885), Scherer makes a point of his discovery: "Their esteem for the insignificant! What a beautiful phrase this is that Boisserée came up with" (p. 149). The irony resides in the fact that Benjamin employs this very expression as a polemical counterposition to the "positivist concept of philology of the Scherer school" (Benjamin, *Gesammelte Schriften*, vol. 3, p. 289).

12. Carl von Linné, also known as Carolus Linnaeus (1707–1778), a Swedish naturalist considered the founder of modern systematic botany, having devel-

oped the system of binomial scientific nomenclature, according to which each living being is classified according to its genus and its species.

13. Hubert Grimme, "Das Rätsel der Sixtinischen Madonna," *Zeitschrift für bildende Kunst*, no. 57 (1922), pp. 41–49.

14. In V2, this is replaced by "underpinnings in the philosophy of history."

15. Alois Riegl, "Das holländische Gruppenporträt," *Jahrbuch der Kunsthistorischen Sammlungen des allerhöchsten Kaiserhauses* 23, nos. 3–4 (1902), pp. 71–278: reprinted, edited, and with a preface by Karl M. Swoboda (Vienna: Oesterreichische Staatsdruckerei, 1931). Pages 7–25 of this later edition translated by Stephen Kayser as "Geertgen tot Sint Jans' 'The Legend of the Relics of St. John the Baptist,'" in W. Eugene Kleinbauer (ed.), *Modern Perspectives in Western Art History: An Anthology of Twentieth-Century Writings on the Visual Arts* (New York; Holt, Rinehart and Winston, 1971), pp. 124–38.

16. Alois Riegl, *Die spätrömische Kunst-Industrie nach den Funden in Österreich-Ungarn* (Vienna: K.K. Hof- und Staatsdruckerei, 1901); 2nd ed. *Spätrömische Kunstindustrie* (Vienna: Österreichische Staatsdruckerei, 1927); annotated English translation by Rolf Winkes as *Late Roman Art Industry* (Rome: Bretschneider, 1985).

17. In V2, this sentence begins: "It is precisely Riegl who."

18. In V2, the preceding paragraph was replaced by the following: "Furthermore, in a short essay 'Art History and Universal History' ["Kunstgeschichte und Universalgeschichte," in Alois Riegl, *Gesammelte Aufsätze*, ed. Karl M. Swoboda (Vienna and Augsburg: Filser, 1928), pp. 3–9], which was published in 1898, Riegl also differentiates the methodology of the older practice based on universal history from a new approach to the study of art for which he himself paved the way. The latter consists of a penetrating interpretation of the individual work that, without in any way betraying its principles, uncovers laws and problems of the development of art as a whole."

19. In V2: "everything."

20. Benjamin's employment here of the conceptual pair "material content" and "meaning or significative content" recalls a similar formulation in the introduction to his essay on Goethe's *Wahlverwandschaften* written nearly ten years

earlier. In the latter context, the terms are employed to elucidate the even more fundamental conceptual distinction between commentary (*Kommentar*) whose object is the Sachgehalt, and critique (*Kritik*), whose object is the *Bedeutungsgehalt* or the *Wahrheitsgehalt*. See Walter Benjamin, "Goethes Wahlverwandschaften," *Gesammelte Schriften*, vol.1 pp. 125–26.

21. Karl Giehlow, "Dürers Stich, 'Melencolia I' und der maximilianische Humanistenkreis," in *Mitteilungen der Gesellschaft für vervielfältigende Kunst*, supplement to *Die Graphischen Künste* (1903).

22. Linfert, "Architekturzeichnung," p. 153. In V2, the following paragraph was inserted at this point: "Already in *Late Roman Art Industry*, the marginal case — and indeed goldsmithery, which considers itself applied art, is just that — proved to be the point of departure for the most significant overcoming of conventional universal history with its so-called high points and periods of decline. When all is said and done, Wölfflin also adopted the same strategy by being the first to understand the baroque in a positive light, a period in which even Burckhardt could see only evidence of decline. And what is more, Dvořák's research on mannerism [Max Dvořák, "Über Greco und den Manierismus" (1920), in *Kunstgeschichte als Geistesgeschichte. Studien zur abendländischen Kunstentwicklung* (Munich: Piper, 1928), pp. 259–76; translated as "On El Greco and Mannerism" in Max Dvořák, *The History of Art as the History of Ideas*, trans. John Hardy (London: Routledge and Kegan Paul, 1984), pp. 97–108; compare also the translation by John Coolidge in *Magazine of Art*, no. 46 (January 1953), pp. 14–23] demonstrated what historical insights can be gleaned from a spiritualist distortion of the now empty schemata of the pure classical period. All this was overlooked by a rigidly periodic universal history."

23. Linfert, "Architekturzeichnung," p. 231.

24. Benjamin is probably referring to Karl Friedrich Schinkel's epoch-making stage sets for *The Magic Flute* in 1816, whose neoclassical exoticism became a model for many subsequent stagings. Benjamin might even have seen a performance of *The Magic Flute* with these Schinkel sets, since they were still being used by the Berlin State Opera as late as 1937.

25. In V2, the concluding lines read: "with which the sedate mediocrity of

the founding period used to be completely engrossed. Rather, the most rigorous challenge to the new spirit of research is the ability to feel at home in marginal domains. It is this ability that guarantees the collaborators of the new yearbook their place in the movement that — ranging from Konrad Burdach's work in German studies to the investigations of the history of religion being done at the Warburg Library — is filling the margins of the study of history with new life."

Translated by Thomas Y. Levin.

Meyer Schapiro, "The New Viennese School" (1936)

Meyer Schapiro (1904–1996), one of the most brilliant figures of American intellectual life in this century, was born in Lithuania but grew up in New York City. He studied at Columbia University and submitted a dissertation on the sculptures of Moissac in 1929. Schapiro was equally innovative in two fields, medieval and modern art. He was open to Marxist and Freudian theory before almost anyone else in the discipline.

Schapiro corresponded with Otto Pächt from 1934. He was acutely aware of the ideological turmoil within the academy in Germany and wary of any scholarship that invoked racist or nationalist constants. Schapiro's 1936 review of the second number of Hans Sedlmayr and Pächt's Kunstwissenschaftliche Forschungen *reflects the customary, skeptical Anglo-American response to the New Vienna School that for a long time obfuscated the reception of Alois Riegl. Schapiro actually admired Riegl greatly and was impressed by the work of Pächt and Fritz Novotny. In his review, reprinted here, he summarizes the arguments of all the essays in the volume and pointedly addresses the program of* Strukturanalyse *expounded in earlier writings by Sedlmayr.*

(Source: Art Bulletin *18 [1936], pp. 258–66.)*

Chapter Ten

The New Viennese School (1936)

Meyer Schapiro

The *Kunstwissenschaftliche Forschungen* is perhaps the most ad
vanced organ of European academic writing on art history today.
It is published by a group of very cultivated and sensitive young
art historians — mainly Viennese, but including several Germans
and Russians — who follow in the tradition of Riegl, and are concerned with the structure of individual works of art and the principles underlying styles and their development. Although some of
this group (especially Alpatoff and Kaufmann) are also interested
in the content of art and the specific historical conditions under
which new forms arise, their attention has been given mainly to
the study of forms as an independent science. The references to
meanings and to the causes of historical change are usually marginal or are highly formalistic and abstract. The strength of the
group lies in the intensity and intelligence with which they examine formal arrangements and invent new terms for describing
them. They draw on contemporary writings in philosophy and
psychology and welcome suggestions from neighboring fields in
the effort to build up a "science of art." Drs. Sedlmayr and Pächt,
above all, have found in Gestalt psychology formulations and tendencies congenial to their own views on the nature of art; they
have also excerpted from the logical positivists and related writers

on the philosophy of science (Lewin, Carnap, Reichenbach) various observations on method.

Precisely because their writings are often programmatic, being presented as examples of new approaches to art or as corrections of inadequate current methods, it is necessary to summarize the general notions underlying their work, especially for American students who have been fairly indifferent to theoretical problems. Unfortunately, their views have nowhere been published in a carefully reasoned and systematic form but have appeared in programmatic essays or reviews or in parenthetical dicta in the course of monographic writing. It is therefore difficult to describe their theory as more than a tendency, still fluid and changing; the essays in this volume are hardly uniform in character, and whatever directions and theoretical assumptions are revealed in them have perhaps already been modified or abandoned by some of the writers.

Dr. Sedlmayr has been somewhat more explicit than the others. He has published two articles on the theory and method of the history of art: "The Quintessence of Riegl's Teachings" (the introduction to Riegl's *Gesammelte Aufsätze*, Vienna, 1929), and a programmatic essay, "Toward a Rigorous Study of Art." The latter heads the first volume of *Kunstwissenschaftliche Forschungen* and may be taken as an introduction to the program of the group or, at least, of the editors. Here Dr. Sedlmayr distinguishes a first and a second science of art, the first, simply gathering and ordering the material according to outward signs and evidences, like documents, inscriptions, conventions of shape, and those symptomatic elements that for some scholars constitute "style"; the second — his own — concerning itself more with "understanding," with the underlying structure of forms and the pervading principles according to which the work of art becomes an organized expressive whole. The second is considered the higher science but admittedly presupposes and utilizes the first; for without the ordered materials and assured data of the first, the second cannot operate successfully. On the other hand, the second, through its insight into forms, may even throw light on unsolved problems of classification.

The logic of the methods of the second science is unfortunately not presented in the article; but constant reference is made to Gestalt psychology as a scientific basis for explaining the organized character of shapes, colors, and spaces in works of art. Following this psychological theory of how perception is organized, the investigator of the work of art or style of art looks for an underlying pattern or configuration or ordered mode of seeing that constitutes the basic principle of the work or style. From this he deduces not only the character of the parts but many nonformal aspects of the work, even its content and its history; for a given mode of seeing, in virtue of its peculiar nature, can admit only certain embodying objects and has limited possibilities of development. To discover this basic pattern or principle, the student must possess first of all the "correct" attitude to the work; he must approach it as an organized whole before he can acquire insight into the necessity of its structure and formal relations. The insight is then verified by analysis, which confirms in the formal connections of numerous details of the work the discovered principle of the whole.

The distinction made between the merely descriptive and classifying nature of the first science and the higher "understanding" of the second is not so much a distinction between the values of observation and theory, such as agitates some physicists and philosophers of science, but corresponds rather to the distinction made by many German writers between the natural sciences, which "describe" or classify atomistically the inorganic and lower organic worlds, and their own sciences of the spirits (*Geisteswissenschaften*), which claim to penetrate and "understand" totalities like art, spirit, human life, and culture. The great works of the latter depend on depth of insight, of the first, on ingenuity and exactness.

Such a distinction, often directed against the plebeian manipulation and matter-of-fact, materialistic spirit of the best in natural science, puts a premium on wishful intuitiveness and vague, intangible profundity in the sciences that concern man. The natural sciences, no less than the sciences of history and culture, require insight, and the latter, no less than the natural sciences, require accuracy and the utmost respect for fact. Actually, there is little difference, so far as scientific method is concerned, between the best works of the so-called first and second sciences of art. They both depend on relevant hypotheses, precise observation, logical analysis, and various devices of verification.

The sense of a fundamental difference in scientific status arises from two aspects of the work of the second "scientist of art." In the first place, he is concerned with shapes or qualities that are not immediately apparent and that are rarely described in a definite manner. In the second place, the qualities that interest him are often involved with judgments of value and with modern artistic interests that have developed only recently and in opposition to older interests and are limited to small groups of people who are never required to present their preferences or insights in an explicit and universally accessible form. We value insight into the "form" of a work more than we value knowledge of its date or author. To acquire the latter, it is often unnecessary to study the character of a painting as a work of art. But it is overlooked that the validity of either knowledge is established in the same way and that in both we deal not with absolute wholes but with isolated aspects of the work of art, from defined points of view.

The change in viewpoint hardly constitutes a new science of art. The break with past methods is more apparent than real. The difference lies in the type of problem and in the interests of the investigator, the Viennese group showing a special predilection for questions of formal arrangement. If in this respect, they are more advanced, let us say, more subtle, than their predecessors, in other respects they resemble those much deplored scholars who devote themselves largely to problems of attribution or the discovery of the subject or provenance or historical antecedents of pictures. Like the latter they are interested mainly in individual objects, isolated from the conditions of their creation; or, if they deal with a style or group of works, the larger field is again considered in itself, without respect to causes of its unity, diversity, or development. The hypotheses with which they approach historical problems can hardly be considered an advance on those employed by the ordinary run of art historians. The works of the "second science" are relatively poor in positive historical conclusions and rich in ingenious but unverified insights and in vague assertions.

A single instance will show how ill founded is the hierarchical pretension of the second science of art. In his article on the system of Justinian, Dr. Sedlmayr tries to discover what elements or qualities distinguish medieval from classic systems of architecture, a question that has been asked by many historians of the lower class and that in itself constitutes no real novelty. One of the three essential qualities or elements he finds is incommensurability and imperceptibility of proportions. In this he repeats the common idea, already well established in the nineteenth century, of the contrast of the mathematical order and clarity of the classic building with the irregularity and unclarity of the medieval. But there is a difference between the approaches of Dr. Sedlmayr and the archaeologists of the first school to this problem: the latter would verify their point by referring to actual measurements or would engage in a detailed and critical discussion concerning the trustworthiness of existing measurements of buildings that stand in ruin or have been affected by numerous contingencies. Dr. Sedlmayr, on the other hand, presents his generalization in an aphoristic manner and leaves it to others to do the measuring and verification. His procedure is all the more contrary to ordinary scientific practice, since it is well known that a difference of opinion exists among archaeologists concerning the nature of medieval proportions; any discussion that pretends to treat of proportions as an essential aspect of architecture must make clear in what sense the concept is applied. Dr. Sedlmayr refers to proportions as *schaubar* and *unschaubar*, although it is evident that proportions are not grasped by the eye; we do not *see* the proportions of a Doric column or a Greek interior, in contrast to an imperceptible Romanesque proportioning. What he means perhaps is that the shape of a Greek building or element is fully visible, or that its proportions can be inferred through a module, unlike the medieval churches in which many parts are ill defined or overlapping and no single unit can be used as a means of judging the scale. But even such interpretation is far from the rigor that Dr. Sedlmayr has indicated as one of the distinguishing goals of his second science of art.

Yet it is precisely his avowed desire to give to the special "understanding" of art the exactness of the natural sciences that distinguishes him from the ordinary exponents of the "sciences of the spirit." He is interested more in the artistic object, less in the state of mind or worldview of its creator, and constantly cites scientists and logicians of empirical tendency.

I do not know whether all the contributors to *Kunstwissenschaftliche Forschungen* would subscribe to the programmatic statements of Dr. Sedlmayr or if their articles are considered by the leader as valid examples of the "right" tendencies and methods. It must be said that however sensitive, intelligent, and searching are some of the articles in the first two volumes of the series, they depart far from scientific rigor. Anyone who has investigated with real scruple a problem of art history knows how difficult it often is to establish even a simple fact beyond question and how difficult it is to make a rigorous explanation. To criticize the articles from the viewpoint of an ideal rigorous science — that is, a science scrupulous with regard to fact, probability, and implication — would be an act of malice and would blind us perhaps to important approximations arrived at in reasoning, groping, and guessing, and embedded in half-truths and errors. The articles, in general, are sketchy, clever, unsystematic, and full of original aperçus and untested "belletristic" characterizations. No group of psychologists or physicists would venture to announce articles of such looseness as a contribution toward a more rigorous science of psychology or physics.

In several of the articles we meet with spiritualistic conceptions and with allusions to qualities or causes that we have no means of verifying. The authors often tend to isolate forms from the historical conditions of their development, to propel them by mythical, racial-psychological constants, or to give them an independent, self-evolving career. Entities like race, spirit, will, and idea are substituted in an animistic manner for a real analysis of historical factors. Professor Kaschnitz von Weinberg tells us that the feeling for mass among the Egyptians must be due to a racial inclination because this quality appeared so suddenly, without signs of a gradual development. And Dr. Sedlmayr explains to us that the system of Justinian, being "rational," could not last more than thirty years, whereas the succeeding Byzantine system, being irrational, was capable of a life of six centuries. This is palmistry or numerology, not science.

Although the subject of Dr. Sedlmayr's article is the system of Justinian, we have no inkling why it is of Justinian, what it has to do with this emperor, beyond the coincidence of time and place.

All that the author admits is that the conditions (unspecified) of the reign of Justinian were favorable to the immanent emergence of this system; but what these conditions were, how they were favorable, we are not told; at any rate, the system is attributed to Justinian not because the emperor or his particular society exerted a positive influence but rather because the immanent destiny of the idea of a certain system of architecture was favored — or, at least, not blocked — by the tasks set for architects by Justinian. The relation of the tasks to the system and its development is nowhere discussed. This neglect of concrete relationships is masked by the brilliant variety of aspects, largely formal, treated briefly by the author. The appearance of comprehensiveness conceals the lack of historical seriousness in such writings. We reproach the authors not for neglecting the social, economic, political, and ideological factors in art but rather for offering us as historical explanations a mysterious racial and animistic language in the name of a higher science of art.

The new Viennese group wishes to be concrete in analysis of works of art as individual, objective, formal structures; but in turning to history, they lose sight of the structure of the historical object, namely, the particular human society, and deal with absolute general categories that seem to produce history by their own internal logic. The new Viennese school has, in fact, no historical objects. They tend to explain art as an independent variable, the product of an active spirit, or a *Kunstwollen*, which has an immanent goal and which may even determine the conditions congenial to the kind of art this *Kunstwollen* is destined to produce. The school lacks an adequate conception of history to direct their historical interpretations in the sense of that scientific rigor that they require in the analysis of forms. They prefer, in short, teleological deductions to an empirical study of historical conditions and factors.

It cannot be argued that their real aim is to create a science of art rather than a history of art; for while this distinction expresses, perhaps, the inclination of some of the writers, no article in this volume is strictly a work of *Kunstwissenschaft*, i.e., dealing systematically with supposedly inherent, general, historically unconditioned aspects of art. A problem of history is often at the center of the formal analysis and interpretation, and the writers usually cannot refrain from ambitious historical conclusions.

It must be pointed out further that the limitations of the school are not confined to the historical aspect of art. Their attitude to the work of art as a historical object corresponds to their formalistic approach. Just as the abstract *Kunstwollen* creates its own history, so the "structure" or "principle" of the work as a whole seems to create its own parts. Dr. Sedlmayr apologizes for the remnants of positivist, naturalistic thought in Riegl and begs us to read "part-whole relation" when Riegl says "cause." The nature of the individual work is grasped more and more as something strictly internal in its origin, that is, dependent on a logical working out of structural principles and forming finally a kind of self-regulating aesthetic machine in which there is very little that cannot be deduced from the autonomous whole or center. The multiplicity of conditions that enter into the formation of a work of art is reduced to the action of a "principle" and the discovered structure or principle is sometimes substituted for the work itself.

The doctrinaires of the school have not investigated their own method of approach or inquired into its relation to contemporary values in art and social life. They assume that it is a purely "scientific" approach without presuppositions or sets of values that operate in the choice of objects and aspects and in the application of a method. When we observe the broad abstractions and unverifiable subtleties, the straining to create insights, the conceits of formal observation that often crop up in such writings, we are reminded of the practices of contemporary art and art criticism, in which the inventive sensibility creates its own formalized objects, delights in its own "laws," and enjoys its absolutely private fantasy, justifying this activity as an experimental system of artistic deduction or as an intuitive perception of essences and wholes.

Despite (or, perhaps, because of) the abundance of references to contemporary philosophy (and other fields) in the writings of the theoretical leaders of this group, they lack a consistent theoretical foundation. It is significant that Dr. Sedlmayr turns to idealistic philosophers and sociologists (Scheler, Vierkandt) when he discusses history and society, although he continually appeals to methodologically materialistic and empirical writers (Reichenbach, Lewin, Carnap) to document his ideas of rigorous scientific method. The inconsistency is apparent enough but has not been sufficiently felt by Dr. Sedlmayr. His admission in 1929 that the further development of Riegl's methods depends on the recognition of their weaknesses should be taken more seriously. Unfortunately he has not made clear just what these weaknesses are.

Despite these defects, American students have much to learn from this new and already influential school of German historians of art. We lack their taste for theoretical discussion, their concern with the formulation of adequate concepts even in the seemingly empirical work of pure description, their constant search for new formal aspects of art, and their readiness to absorb the findings of contemporary scientific philosophy and psychology. It is notorious how little American writing on art history has been touched by the progressive work of our psychologists, philosophers, and ethnologists.

I have summarized in detail the articles in this volume in the hope that students who do not read German will be enabled to form some idea of the character of formalistic art history in Germany and Austria today.

1. The first essay, "Remarks on the Structure of Egyptian Sculpture," by Professor G. Kaschnitz von Weinberg, is vaster in scope and more systematic in intention than the title indicates. It is an effort to deduce the underlying principles of Egyptian art and to distinguish Old Oriental art from European as a whole. The author's conclusion that Egyptian sculpture is the conservation of organic life through inorganic forms, the effort to achieve an absolute stability and immobilization, a quality of timeless, incorruptible being, is familiar enough since Hegel and had been felt by the poets before it was formulated by the scientists of art. But Kaschnitz von Weinberg's conclusion differs in several respects from the common poetic characterization, apart from the more systematic formal analysis and the effort to distinguish precisely between early and later Egyptian art: first, in that he formulates the nature of Egyptian art as having grandiose, quasi-metaphysical properties, which are presented as prior to and above the works themselves; second, in that he holds these properties are willed by the Egyptians and are inherent in some aboriginal psychological predisposition of the people of the ancient Orient (cf. on this point the article by Andrae in the recent Dörpfeld Festschrift); third, in that he concludes the structure and qualities described are altogether independent of Egyptian culture as a whole, and even of the mode of representation: he sees the content merely as a material poured into a preexistent ideal mold. It would be hard to discuss these views critically in the author's broad and often intrusive terminology. To say that Egyptian art is "petrified form, not formed material," or to speak of the "timeless endlessness" of Egyptian space, or to comprehend all European art since the Neolithic period under the categories of ornament, activism, and incorporeality, whereby the expressionism of the twentieth century and Neolithic art become identified psychologically, all this stimulates our fantasy and sug-

gests possible distinctions, but it carries us far from the objects, to the irreducible particularity of which the second *Kunstwissenschaft* is dedicated. It is a typical practice of expressionistic art criticism and cultural history.

2. The article of Dr. Sedlmayr on "The System of Justinian"—a chapter from a projected book on architectonic systems—analyzes the buildings of Justinian as the first medieval system and Hagia Sophia as the most crucial structure in history, summarizing the whole past of architecture and pointing to the medieval future and even beyond.

The characteristics of the system of Justinian are: (1) the embracing or overlapping (*übergreifende*) form—a large arch that spans two or more subordinate arches, (2) the embracing or overlapping baldachin, (3) incommensurable proportions. Not all medieval architecture has these three elements, but all architecture that has these is medieval. Late classical art knew the baldachin vault, but a baldachin resting on a wall or on supports distinct from the dome or vault, whereas in medieval art the baldachin is primary and homogeneous, continuous with its supports, and embraces, or grows into, the wall as well. It is the distinct skeleton of the walls, which constitute a filler. Given the embracing baldachin, which is the spatial application of the simpler principle of the embracing arch, Dr. Sedlmayr deduces a whole series of characteristics of medieval architecture, including the numerous vertical bays of Romanesque and Gothic, their fugitive proportions, their diaphanous structure, their technical complexity and calculation. In the single idea of the embracing baldachin is latent the whole variety of types of the period of Justinian, and in the latter is contained the variety of subsequent forms. This unfolding of immanent possibilities could be realized only where the material problem or task was favorable to the logical implication; that conditions were indeed favorable was due to a peculiarity of medieval thought, which was itself dualistic in a manner analogous to the formal dualism of the embracing baldachin.

If in this highly deductive and compact article few of the broad assertions are supported by historical evidence, the author has promised subsequent articles to provide fuller proof (see *Byzantinische Zeitschrift*, 1935).

The following difficulties may be observed in his theories. The concept of system is not sufficiently clear; it is only vaguely distinguished from formal structure. Proportions and various stylistic qualities are included in the discussion of the system, but the exteriors of buildings, the structure of the galleries, are neglected, though integral elements of the system. The system of Justinian is called the first medieval system because of the embracing forms; yet it must be admitted that there are whole groups of medieval buildings — Carolingian and Romanesque — that lack this principle. Nonetheless, in discussing the architecture of the fifth and sixth centuries in Syria and Asia Minor, which reminds many scholars, including Dr. Sedlmayr, of Romanesque architecture, he states that it is unmedieval because it lacks the embracing form. Thus in delimiting a style, the "principle" or system becomes an atomistic concept, as in nineteenth-century archaeology, which distinguished Romanesque and Gothic architecture by the round and pointed arches. I do not doubt that a scholar proceeding from a study of Romanesque and Gothic art might arrive at other definitions of the medieval, which would exclude the buildings of Justinian as unmedieval. At any rate, Dr. Sedlmayr's broad definition entails a theory of the Byzantine origin of Western medieval architecture, a theory that is very doubtful and that will probably shatter on the difficulties of establishing a genetic continuity of Byzantine and Romanesque building.

Thus we cannot deduce from his conception the embracing vertical shafts (comprising two or more stories of superposed arches), which are crucial for the development of Romanesque and Gothic architecture. Dr. Sedlmayr assumes that the numerous stories and the verticality of the Western medieval systems follow directly from the baldachin principle, but I believe this assumption is neither historically nor logically plausible. If, in the history of the system of Justinian, the form of the dome seems to precede the form of the wall, in the medieval systems, the reverse is true: the vertical shafts are prior to the vaults. In the first, the wall was skeletonized after the dome had long been employed; in the second, the skeletal wall form preceded the application of the vault. This difference in process of development corresponds in turn to the difference between the opposed centralized and basilical loci of the two developments. The superposed stories and long naves of medieval churches are presupposed in the traditional basilical type, which is essentially foreign to the system of Justinian. The vertical shaft, embracing two stories, on the other hand, can be cited in Persian and Mesopotamian architecture (Ctesiphon, Hatra) and in the Spanish-Roman aqueducts (Merida), as well as in later northern wood building. It may, however, be an independent invention of the early Romanesque architects. Significant for the distinction between this embracing shaft and the embracing arch form is the fact that in many medieval churches where both the embracing shaft and arch are used (Caen, Mont St.-Michel, Laon, St.-Remi, Reims) the horizontal moldings run across the supports of the embracing arches but not across the free vertical shafts. The verticality, in other words, is determined here not so much by the supposedly Byzantine element as by the non-Byzantine and possibly native shaft. If S. Vitale shows a tendency toward accented vertical bays, we cannot infer therefore that Gothic verticality is inherent in the system of Justinian, any more than we can say that Romanesque verticality or squatness is inherent in classical architecture because of the elongated or dwarf columns that appear in certain late classical buildings. The particular character of Gothic verticality is a matter not only of the proportions of individual bays or wall units but also of the relations of these to the various axes of the building, relations that are irreducible to the early Byzantine baldachin.

Dr. Sedlmayr concludes from his study of the historical stages of the baldachin in late Roman architecture that the system of Justinian is essentially a development in Roman architecture, in opposition to those who have stressed an East-Hellenistic or Oriental origin of early Byzantine building. He admits, however, the importance of an Eastern contribution in mass, space, and decoration; but unfortunately he does not attempt to evaluate it or define it precisely and therefore remains unconvincing, somewhat unclear, despite his emphatic assertion of a Roman origin. The dependence of the solutions of Justinian's architects on the pendentive and squinch, which are hardly Roman inventions, also weakens the strength of his conclusions. Similarly his description of Armenian architecture as a merely provincial style is inadequate. Our knowledge of the architecture of the fifth century is still so slight that we hesitate to consider an element first documented in the earlier sixth century as necessarily an innovation of that period. Already in the first part of the fifth century there appears in Italian churches the great apse embracing an open arcade, as in the apsidal and niche spaces of Hagia Sophia and S. Vitale; and in the Orthodox Baptistery of Ravenna a great arch embraces three arches on the inner walls. Dr. Sedlmayr eliminates it as irrelevant by the argument that the great arch does not really belong to the columns but rests on a projecting console, as in some Roman buildings. The principle however is there; in none of the Roman examples does such an arch embrace three smaller arches.

There is one important consequence of the embracing arch for proportionality that has been overlooked by Dr. Sedlmayr, although it reveals the interplay of two of his (otherwise unconnected) principles. In the arch embracing two or more arches, the large arch and the smaller encompassed arches often spring from a common support or from adjacent members of the same height. Therefore a given unit of height may be associated with two or more distinct spans. This bivalence of units is a common medieval trait; but it is already foreshadowed in late classical art, where adjacent arches of different span spring from one level or surmount bays of uniform height.

The problem of proportion emerges again in Dr. Sedlmayr's discussion of the technique of the system of Justinian. He recognizes the importance of the technique of construction for the interpretation of the building, though he treats technique more as the form of technical thinking than as the total means and method of construction. After Choisy, he sees that in Hagia Sophia *tout est calcul* and judges that in this respect system and technique are one. But we are led to ask: Are they formally analogous, or are they simply related as end and means? Since the building was admired in its own time as a scientific accomplishment, are we to believe that the aesthetic structure has qualities of scientific-intellectual order? How can system and technique be analogous if the system shows no spirit of calculation, but the very opposite, in its incommensurable proportions?

These difficulties are perhaps resolved in the unintelligible section on the *Denkweise* of the building and its analogy with the religious-philosophical conceptions of the Middle Ages.

In spite of these shortcomings, the article is extraordinarily stimulating because of the problems raised, the numerous insights, and the comprehensive scope. It should inspire fresh investigations of early medieval architecture.

3. Professor Swoboda's "Toward the Analysis of the Floren-

tine Baptistery" applies the method of Andreades's article on Hagia Sophia (I) to a smaller monument but derives its categories independently. First, the author reconstructs the original appearance of the exterior, which has been modified by later accretions. This original form is skillfully presented in a retouched photograph. By analysis of the fine variations and irregularities, the qualities of surface and mass, the divisions and subdivisions, Professor Swoboda reveals the great complexity of the building as a design. He defines its Romanesque character in terms of the compact, composite structure of wall masses and the distinction of a light outer and heavy inner layer within this wall. He tries also to isolate a specifically Florentine quality, which is verified in other monuments of the region. Florentine are: (1) the classical orders of the outer layer, replacing the outer wall layer yet maintaining the layer character, (2) the banded decoration that attenuates the plastic contrasts through its own surface ornament and linear effects, (3) the sketchy, suggestive, tenuous, and untectonic nonfunctional character of the imposed classical elements, (4) the contrast of these attenuations and linear and ornamental elements with the overt drastic assertion of the masses of the building in the corners and cornices. Professor Swoboda observes also the precocious artistic autonomy of the architecture with respect to cult. The design is independent of immediate practical conditions, whether religious or constructive. He does not tell us, however, what it *does* depend on.

The article includes also some historical observations, which are inseparable from the preceding analysis. Professor Swoboda shows the relation of the building to early Byzantine and Roman interiors, as well as to contemporary Romanesque works, and finally deduces a dating in the first half of the twelfth century.

4. The essay of late Maria Hirsch, "The Figure-Alphabet of the Master ES," is unfortunately a posthumous and incomplete

work. Her sensitive observations make us regret all the more the fragmentary character of this essay. It was published from her notes by the editors and is not entirely homogenous. The merit of this paper lies in the formulation of the aesthetic principles of Gothic script; on this basis, the author proceeds to analyze the alphabet in question, one of the most typical and expressive works of the mid-fifteenth century. She studies with an admirable precision the relations of the ornament to the structure of the letters and arrives at a valuable characterization of the artist's manner, his linear fantasy, and his mode of composition. She says very happily of his figure style that it is *zugleich maximal verklammert und maximal zerstückt*. The essay is one of the first of its kind and opens a large field in medieval researches, for it pertains not only to the ornament of medieval initials but to all works in which animals and figures have been applied to, or fitted to, an already determined form, like a trumeau or the head of a sword, or to any terminal object. In one point the study of the adaptation seems to me to fall into mechanical and inadequate analogies — in the assimilation of the movements of the constituent figures to the normal ductus of the script. I could not verify the analysis made at this point; the directions of the figures in the K are opposed in fact to the normal script ductus; and one could infer from the nature of the style of ES that he would not practice such an assimilation. I feel also that the distinction of the two modes of alphabetic figuration, by conformation to the letter as a frame and by approximation to the letter as a framework, while valid as possible modes, which can, in fact, be verified elsewhere, is not valid here and is invoked by exaggeration of minor differences and by liquid subtleties.

5. The article by Dr. Otto Pächt, "Design Principles of Fifteenth-Century Northern Painting," deals with the relations of spatial composition to surface pattern in Dutch, Flemish, and

French painting of this period and with the distinction of national constants in these three arts on the basis of differences in such relations. He observes correctly that the formal development of Western painting cannot be grasped through studies of space or perspective alone, that for aesthetic experience the pattern formed by the projection of the spatial elements on the pictorial surface is an essential component. Two modes of organization may therefore be distinguished within a painting of this period— one in depth, a second in surface. It is to the surface form, however, that Dr. Pächt gives the greater importance, even to the point of deriving the space composition from the mode of surface patterning. The peculiarities of perspective in Flemish art prior to the mid-fifteenth century he explains by the character of the surface design, by the will to obtain continuous, dense patterning, with analogies of neighboring elements. The depth composition becomes a sort of reversed projection of the surface into the picture. "The capacity of the pictorial space depends on the projective capacity of the pictorial surface." This is a "law" of all pictorial fantasy in the Netherlands. The silhouettes of units are close together or overlap, and one may serve as the background of the other. Hence the equality of the human figure and his surroundings and the homogeneous character of the visible world. The decorative unity is independent of schemata or clear order but is determined by balance and continuity of forms. Flemish art is therefore elastic and adaptable to the most varied problems of representation. These qualities are for the most part typical of early Dutch and French painting too, but with several differences.

In Dutch painting there is no *horror vacui*, no close connection of adjacent contours, but a separation or isolation of objects and a tendency toward broad empty ground or decorative intervals. Dutch art discovers the value of free space, of emptiness, and of breadth and bareness of surface. When Flemish compositions are copied by a Dutchman, they are widened, and the units separated. Dutch art therefore has plain, unarticulated silhouettes, without striking correspondences of adjacent elements — an isolating verticalism, distinct from the Gothic in that it is not the vertical that is accented or isolated but the continuous free space between and behind the figures that is developed as an aesthetic factor. The substitute for the internal pictorial unity, destroyed by the isolating method, is the connecting gesture. New types of figures are created in Dutch art, speakers who function only as guides and whose gestures are addressed to the spectator. Dutch art therefore has a unity involving the spectator, a *geheimes Mitwissentum*, the whole evoking a purely passive remote contemplation, which in turn reflects an unconnected juxtaposition of unrelated single objects.

In France, there is a third type of surface order. Surface and depth are built up according to a preexistent geometrical schema, a system of diagonals that organizes both space and surface into a regular and clear network. This schema is not directly felt as prior or imposed, because the world that is rendered is also subject to it, because the topography, the buildings, the people are all cast in shapes congruent with such regular and clear schematism. Hence the orderly cultivated world of French art, the lack of variety, the inexpressiveness. A preconceived form is prescribed, no matter what the subject. The slight variability of the a priori fixed pictorial pattern makes it impossible in many cases to realize the individual illustrative suggestions of the subject in more than a superficial way. The schemata have only slight adaptability and are relatively little subject to changes in period style. The characteristic lozenge form of composition is found in the Limburg brothers, Fouquet, and Callot. It is concrete and clear, a projecting skeleton. In French art, originality is a variation on a given theme, not the invention of a new theme. Hence the inaccessibility to foreign influence except in a minor way, but the greater susceptibility to Italian art, which provides regular forms.

I have taken pains to present the main ideas of Dr. Pächt as fully as a review permits because of the rarity of thinking and observation like his in the English and American writing on the arts he deals with and our real need of formal analysis and fresh historical generalization.

His conclusions are to a certain degree read back into fifteenth-century art from descriptions of French and Dutch art of later periods — this is especially evident in his conception of Dutch art, where he leans heavily on Riegl's characterizations of the painting of the sixteenth and seventeenth centuries, and to that degree one may question the adequacy of his analysis of fifteenth-century art. It is for the special students of these arts to judge whether Dr. Pächt's observations have the generality he attributes to them. A layman, attentive to his method and reasoning, will observe within his subtle, but sometimes obscure, analyses an excessive tendency to centralize the aspect that interests him and to interpret it as the determining factor of the whole. The obvious interaction of the formative elements is neglected, as if the mode of perspective and the spatial design had no influence on the surface pattern, as if the manner of drawing, the particular expressive values, and the content were mainly by-products or neutral factors subject to an a priori surface form. Instead of studying the interrelation, functioning, and historical development of the essential aspects of fifteenth-century painting, Dr. Pächt tries to *deduce* them all from a single aspect that is presented as the principle of the whole. The agreement of the perspective form and spatial representation with a particular surface pattern seems to imply for him their origin in that surface pattern or their purpose in the maintenance of just such a surface pattern. There are indeed such subordinations of aspects in art, but if formulated in a one-sided

way, as is done by some German writers, we could never understand why there should be space or perspective at all. Such formalism leads to the common error, associated with the practices
and theory of modern art, of assuming a one-sided relationship
between formal pattern and representation, the latter existing
only to effect a certain kind of pattern, itself prior to or superior
to the representation.

The historical portions of Dr. Pächt's article also suffer from
the dogma of autonomous principles. His conception of the principles of fifteenth-century art as constants, persisting to the present day, is historically formalistic and abstract in that the life and
duration of these principles are thoroughly self-determined, independent of concrete conditions inside, or tangent to, the arts.
Thus he makes the reception of foreign influences by French art
and the historical mobility of the latter depend on its schematic
surface form, a view that is historically inept. It corresponds to
the Hegelian notion that whatever befalls a being arises from its
own inner nature — as in Chesterton's story of the man whose
nature it was to be shot at constantly and whose enemies were
therefore exempt from any responsibility.

It is not clear, further, what Dr. Pächt means by his formal
"constants." This concept, borrowed from the natural sciences,
where it has a precise and controllable meaning, is applied here in
a triple sense: first, as a specific quality that persists in a given art
during an indeterminate period of time *while other qualities are
changing*; second, as the formal principle of an art, the *Gestaltungs-
prinzip* itself; third, as the goal or ideal that the art is approaching.
He assumes not merely that a given quality persists but that this
quality is a central principle, since it is from the constant that he
derives numerous other aspects of the art, including even its history. To establish the first sense of his "constant" it would be necessary to indicate the historical and spatial limits in which the

constant is observable, since it is predicated of historical, changing objects, like styles of art. This Dr. Pächt does not attempt to do, beyond attributing the constant to such indefinite entities as French art, Dutch art, and Flemish art; he therefore leaves the reader with the vaguest idea of the constancy of his principle and the extent of the field to which it applies. Further, since Dr. Pächt holds to a Gestalt theory of art, according to which the formal structure of a work or a style is an organized whole with interdependent and interacting parts, determined by a principle of the whole, we are led to ask how a constant is possible in a historically developing art; how there can be a rigorous structural unity in a style, if the style manifestly changes while a certain principle within it, often a central principle from which Dr. Pächt tries to deduce almost everything else, remains the same. And if the constant itself changes, exactly what is meant by the "constant"? If the constant has a history, how can one pretend to establish a constant without indicating its historical limits?

Considered empirically, Dr. Pächt's method of establishing his constants is open to obvious criticism. His example of the Dutch constant is found in the work of Bouts, a painter who worked mainly in the Flemish region (and whose *Epiphany*, to me, is much nearer to the Flemish "constant" than to the Dutch as described by Dr. Pächt); his example of the French constant is the work of a Dutchman, Paul of Limburg. In fact, he verifies the constancy of the French constant by reference to the works of Poussin, a Norman who worked mainly in Italy, and of Callot, an Italianate artist from Lorraine. In his comparisons of artists of different countries, he takes little if any account of differences of generation or period to establish the constancy of national oppositions; thus he contrasts Rembrandt and Rubens, the Master of Flémalle and Bouts.

6. The article by Michael Alpatoff on the self-portrait of

Poussin differs from Dr. Pächt's precisely in its recognition of the variety, interaction, and even possible mutual independence of the qualities and aspects of a work of art. This difference is due partly to the difference in subject, Alpatoff being concerned with a unique painting of which he recognizes the complexity and ultimate irreducibility, whereas Dr. Pächt wishes to discover the principles common to a class of objects and to whole traditions of art.

The self-portrait is unique in Poussin's entire production, first, as a portrait, second, as a work dealing directly with the artist. Hence the great interest of a thorough investigation of this painting of which the special character seems to have escaped the attention of previous writers on Poussin. It is, paradoxically, a self-portrait commanded by a patron. The artist is thrown back into self-contemplation, contrary to his usual practice and interest, by the will of another person. He shows himself in the middle of the picture, a realistically portrayed face of strong will and clear gaze, but surrounded by a bare wall, by picture frames and a fragment of a painting with the bust of a classical woman in profile, that is, by the professional environment of an artist rather than by the common world of society or nature. This private world exhibits an insistent geometricality of form, rectangular shapes, sharply defined objects, which are related to the rectangularities of the artist's figure and are dominated by it.

Alpatoff has hardly exhausted the interest of this work, but he has revealed in his short study its extraordinary complexity and its density of meanings and qualities. His study is not so much thorough as searching. It is attentive to numerous aspects and exhibits a highly developed critical sensibility, if not a systematic philosophy of art. He examines in turn the principles of formal organization in the regular divisions of the field, in the constellation of bodies, in the geometrization and framing of the parts; then the principles of the representation considered psychologically and in terms of content, the significance of the facial expression and the glance, their relation to the inert, geometrical world around them; then the interrelations, cooperative coincidence, and simple juxtaposition of these principles, the social and individual factors in the qualities of the portrait, its historical position; and, finally, the character of our impression or contemplation, the mode of reception this portrait seems to entail in the spectator. All this is done experimentally, with insight and finesse, and with a frank admission of the limitations of these approaches and the necessary incompleteness of analysis.

Several criticisms may be made of Alpatoff's interpretation. He speaks of the symmetrical relation of the female head at the left with the artist's hand at the right, but this relation is not sufficiently explored. It is a real symmetry only with respect to an imaginary diagonal axis that twists the pattern of the picture frames. Alpatoff neglects also the possible meaning of the juxtaposition of the artist's ringed hand with an idealized female profile head, though he discusses at length the possible meanings of the head itself. The jewel of the ring, dark on light, is the counterpart of the woman's eye and strengthens the assumption of a meaningful relationship of the opposed head and hand. He overlooks also the relation of the horizontal frames to the eyes of Poussin; the picture frames and the lines of the door seem to issue from the eyes, like a cross, and confer on them the force of a generating center. Because of material difficulties, Alpatoff could not see the original painting again and had to omit all discussion of color. The interpretation depends largely on the photograph reproduced in the article. In this photograph, the light and shade of the original are considerably weakened. The author therefore overlooks in his analysis the strong shadow on the lower right part of the painting. The light and shade as a whole are relatively neglected, though important in the structure of the work.

In his investigation of the interrelation and accord of principles, he admits that certain principles simply exist side by side,
without discoverable interaction or accord, but he overlooks a
conflict that he has himself unwittingly described. In one place he
characterizes the work as a mirror portrait, as distinguished from
those self-portraits in which the artist presents himself as seen by
a spectator; but elsewhere he observes that the eye level of the
portrait is in the center of the field, that is, at Poussin's chin. This
discrepancy appears a second time in Alpatoff's description of the
head, first, as seen from below, later, as thrown back.

In discussing the plurality of meanings as one of the principles
of the work (apropos of the woman at the left, who may be a
muse, a sculptured bust, or a figure on the represented canvas), he
refers to symbolist poetry and medieval theological interpretations as examples of such plurality. But here he seems to confuse:
(1) the possible plurality in our interpretations, (2) the possible
plurality of Poussin's allusion, (3) the modern uncertainty or
unclarity about an originally definite and single meaning, and
(4) the original uncertainty of the form of an object arising from
ambiguities or insufficiencies in representation. Furthermore,
Alpatoff does not make it clear whether he is describing in this
plurality a quality present in many of Poussin's pictures or a novel
quality arising in this special, unique, and uncharacteristic situation of self-portraiture. He evidently identifies this plurality
of meaning with unclarity, for he contrasts the character of the
meaning with the un-baroque clarity of the forms of the painting
as a whole. This negative reference to the baroque is inadequate,
since the concept of clarity is relative to the field or part delimited. Thus Alpatoff discovers real or latent squares in various objects, but, as he says, no object in the picture is square as a whole,
but only by segmentation, only as an incomplete or intercepted
form. The unclarity or, better, the uncertainty of the meaning of

the bust of the woman arises precisely from this concealment of the greater part of the field to which she belongs.

Alpatoff indicates interesting analogies of the portrait to contemporary literary portraiture, to the psychology of the time (Stoicism, the tragic heroes of Corneille), and to Cartesian philosophy (geometrically formed world and a central thinking point). The sociological paragraphs are rather sketchy and slight, concrete social factors being neglected and the author attending mainly to Poussin's consciousness of the autonomy of the artist and his national French loyalties. It is to be hoped that analysis of this aspect will be carried further. In the common view of Poussin as an intellectual artist, the specific content of his intellectuality, its original value and function in the concrete experience and society of his time, is a substantial aspect disregarded or reduced to a system of analogies between various fields of culture.

7. It is the great merit of Dr. Emil Kaufmann, in his excellent article "The City of the Architect Ledoux," to have resuscitated Claude Nicolas Ledoux, a remarkable architect of the eighteenth century who wished literally to found a new architecture. His work fell within the period of the neoclassic movement, but in him we perceive more clearly, through Dr. Kaufmann's study, the modern tendencies and aspirations of the architecture of his period. Although Ledoux was hostile to the French Revolution, his designs and his writing express more powerfully than those of any other architect of his time the moralistic, practical conceptions of the insurgent French bourgeoisie. Even in the formal aspects of his art it has been possible for Dr. Kaufmann to find analogies to the structure of the new bourgeois society. Ledoux himself was consciously engaged in a struggle with the accredited architecture of the past and conceived of his own style as revolutionary, as the beginning of a new art, adapted to a new philosophy of life. The very title of his book, *L'Architecture considérée sous*

le rapport de l'art, des moeurs et de la législation, which is a tendentious projection of his aims, declamatory, heroic, theatrical, points to the architectural propagandists of our time. Ledoux is, in a sense, the David of the French architecture of his age; he might have constructed the setting of the *Horatii* or the box and bathtub of *Marat*.

The article by Dr. Kaufmann deals with the city plan designed by Ledoux in 1776 for the saltworks of the king. Besides the purely practical buildings — industrial and domestic — Ledoux imagined a series of Utopian structures, houses of peace, culture, fraternity, and godless religion, and even an *oikema* for the purgation of sexual passions, which suggests that literary psychiatry of the twentieth century. For Ledoux, the industrial and domestic buildings, though unornamented and severe, are as important architecturally as the buildings of religion and royal power. The central building of the city plan is significantly the Bourse.

In presenting and analyzing this plan (which should be studied further in relation to utopias and the visionary cities of literature), Dr. Kaufmann attempts to formulate the general character of Ledoux's art and, incidentally, of all architecture since the end of the eighteenth century (this part is developed further in his more recent book, *Von Ledoux bis Le Corbusier, Ursprung und Entwicklung der autonomen Architektur*, 1934). He finds the essential contribution of Ledoux in his discovery of an autonomous principle of architecture as opposed to the heteronomous nature of preceding building. By this, Dr. Kaufmann means that in contrast to Renaissance and baroque architects, who conceived of a building in terms of imposed sculpturesque, plastic, or pictorial qualities of mass and relief or in terms of a symbolism expressing authority and hierarchical relations, the architecture of Ledoux and of modern times derives its aesthetic from the internal demands of construction and use and is independent of any foreign, imposed artistic conception. A second distinction between the baroque and modern styles, evident in Ledoux, is that in baroque art the elements fuse or coalesce in terms of a higher unity differentiated according to picturesque, plastic, or hierarchical conceptions, whereas in later art the elements become independent entities combined inorganically in such a way as to maintain the clear singleness and completeness of the units. The first system Dr. Kaufmann calls the *Barock Verband*, the second he calls the "block or pavilion system." The contrast corresponds roughly to the Wölfflinian opposition of the baroque singleness (*Einheit*) and the classical or neoclassic plurality (*Vielheit*). It is interesting that the Viennese city planner Camillo Sitte over forty years ago had called attention to the block character and the unorganized, additive design of modern building groups.

Whereas Wölfflin and others have treated this opposition as an automatic development or reaction, Kaufmann has attempted to explain the artistic changes by specific social changes. The *Barock Verband* pertains to a feudal and absolutistic social structure in which the classes are mutually interdependent and each has a necessary, but differing, place in a transcending scheme, whereas the block or pavilion form reflects the character of bourgeois society, which thinks of itself as composed of isolated, equally free individuals, each seeking his own life and subject to no transcending force that does not emanate from the will of these individuals. The latter correlation is with bourgeois ideology, not with the actual class structure and conditions of bourgeois society, and depends more on quotations from Ledoux than on a study of social and economic history.

Although Dr. Kaufmann tries to establish a direct relation between the forms of society and architectural forms — an effort unique in the work of the group that publishes *Kunstwissenschaftliche Forschungen* — he minimizes the strength of his argument by qualifying the correlation as simply a product of ideas, with little regard to the interplay of social forces and conditions. And to avoid the onus of materialism, he stops to point out that prior to the use of concrete, Ledoux already employs the prismatic support, thus showing that new forms are not determined by materials — a "refutation of all materialistic art history." This is certainly a misleading bit of reasoning, first, since the prismatic form might be determined by material conditions other than the use of concrete and, second, since a materialistic view of art history is not necessarily a theory of materials but of the concrete historical determination of forms as against a purely immanent, automatic, logical, or animistic determination.

The unexpected modernity of Ledoux — who, though born in 1736, could speak of hygiene, economy, and use as the real bases of building, could formulate an aesthetic of pure geometrical masses without ornament, and could insist on the equal nobility of all construction, whether royal, religious, or industrial — has blinded Dr. Kaufmann somewhat to the specifically eighteenth-century character of Ledoux's art and has led him to an under-critical description of the style, wherein Ledoux appears to be little less than a contemporary of Le Corbusier and his work, which still has on it the stamp of the Renaissance, appears to be at a pole opposite everything the eighteenth century had produced. Ledoux is for the author the founder of modern architecture and the specific individual source of the art of men like Gilly and Schinkel in Germany. It is evident from even a cursory observation of the engravings in Dr. Kaufmann's article and book and the older monographs that the designs of Ledoux are still tied to a formal symmetry and regularity that are the very opposite of modern design and relate more to the traditional styles of the eighteenth century. Also of his time is the accented massiveness of the architectural units. In these respects, we cannot think of

Ledoux as a forerunner of Le Corbusier, although his work may have had a deep influence on the architecture of the nineteenth century.

In his programmatic views on a new style, Ledoux makes little, if any, reference, as is to be expected, to a change in technique, to new materials or modes of construction, but only to a new style arising from simplicity, clarity, sobriety, and such. In these respects, he is part of a wider movement of his time and continues the theories of writers like the Jesuit Laugier, who in the early 1750s wished to strip all ornament from buildings and to limit columns to purely tectonic applications. But the Jesuit father believed that a new style could arise only from a revision of the forms of moldings, whereas Ledoux, standing in a closer relation to the progressive elements of his time, anticipated a new style based on a new morality or new social conditions. In his conception of the universality of architecture as a practical, yet noble, art embracing all human construction, and in his effort to provide for all possible needs in building — including the ethical, the cultural, and the erotic — and to express in the physiognomy of the individual dwelling the occupation of the owner — the facade of the hooper's house being designed in concentric rings — he displays an encyclopedist temper. Nearer than Laugier to Ledoux, and probably independent of him, proceeding from related bourgeois values and interests, were the numerous English architects of the late eighteenth and early nineteenth centuries who published designs for rural buildings. Some of the projects in Gandy's treatise on farmhouses, published in 1805, the year after the appearance of Ledoux's book, are much closer in outward aspect to twentieth-century architecture than anything in the albums of Ledoux.

Dr. Kaufmann has not yet located Ledoux clearly within his own time. We do not grasp from his analyses how Ledoux relates to the parallel tendencies in the architecture of the latter part of the eighteenth and the early nineteenth century. We have the impression of a purely individual innovation that arises from the conditions of the time and yet remains unique and prophetic. Similarly, the relation of Ledoux to the architecture he seems to anticipate is somewhat obscured by the failure to state the characteristically eighteenth-century qualities of Ledoux. One of the important aspects of recent architecture, foreign to Ledoux, is the informality and picturesqueness of design, even in apparently regular and unornamented constructions. These qualities were highly developed in the historicizing architectures of the nineteenth century, but especially in the medieval revivals, which influenced so deeply many of the progressive architects of the second half of the nineteenth century. These architects asserted the values of an "autonomous" architecture in Dr. Kaufmann's sense; yet they arrived at such values not from the tradition of Ledoux but from the needs of contemporary society and their experience of medieval architecture.

It must be said in conclusion that although Dr. Kaufmann's description of the loose, synthetic composition and of the block form of Ledoux's designs is excellently made, the categories like "autonomous" and "heteronomous" are inadequate to represent the characters and differences of Renaissance and modern art and may confuse the student of art history. Is it correct to describe the sculptural qualities of baroque architecture as a heteronomous imposition from without? The concept of the sculptural in architecture is used metaphorically to designate an extreme plasticity, but this plastic quality in the buildings is sufficiently different from sculpture in character, in context, in effect, for us to admit its distinctively architectural nature. It is a plastic quality that could exist only in a construction; it is thoroughly dependent on the scale, materials, spaces, and purposes of a building. And in the same way, to assert that the architecture of modern times is "autonomous" is to overlook the degree to which the designs of the architect are affected by pictorialism, by the modes of seeing and drawing developed in modern, and especially abstract, painting. If a mode of life and various interests of the society of Le Corbusier suggest luxurious smooth surfaces, terraced roofs, and bare walls, must we call this an autonomy of architecture in contrast to the symbolic and directly expressive decoration engendered by the society of the baroque period and correlative with the values and mode of life of the owners of baroque palaces? Terms like "autonomous" and "heteronomous" presuppose that there is such a thing as an inherent nature of architecture or of building, a pure Platonic nature, apart from the individual, concrete, historical examples of architecture. When the architect subscribes to this nature, he is supposedly an autonomous architect; when he seems to draw on other arts, his art is heteronomous. The conception of an autonomous architecture is therefore related to that idea of a "pure art" that arises constantly among artists who wish to justify the theoretical or seeming autonomy or absolute independence of their activity as artists. They know only the "laws of art" and submit to no others. In the name of a similar purity, an architectural aesthete might deduce an art that conceals or suppresses the tectonic, constructive elements as nonartistic and that constructs independently of these factors its own effects of mass and space and light. It is as an "autonomous" architecture that Geoffrey Scott defended the baroque.